Mobilising the Audience

Mark Balnaves is Associate Professor of Public Relations and Journalism at Edith Cowan University in Perth.

Tom O'Regan is Professor in the School of Film, Media and Cultural Studies at Griffith University, where he is also the Director of the Australian Key Centre for Cultural and Media Policy.

Jason Sternberg is a Lecturer in Media Communication and a researcher with the Creative Industries Research and Applications Centre in the Creative Industries Faculty at Queensland University of Technology.

UQP Cultural and Media Policy Series

Series Editor
Stuart Cunningham

for the Australian Key Centre for Cultural and Media Policy

This series is designed to build a foundation of research and scholarship in policy-related cultural and media studies in an Australian context.

Also published in this series:

Stuart Cunningham and John Sinclair (eds), *Floating Lives: The Media and Asian Diasporas*
Lisanne Gibson, *The Uses of Art: Constructing Australian Identities*
Ruth Rentschler, *The Entrepreneurial Arts Leader: Cultural Policy, Change and Reinvention*
Deborah Stevenson, *Art and Organisation: Making Australian Cultural Policy*

Mobilising the Audience

edited by
Mark Balnaves,
Tom O'Regan and
Jason Sternberg

University of Queensland Press

First published 2002 by University of Queensland Press
Box 6042, St Lucia, Queensland 4067 Australia in association
with the Australian Key Centre for Cultural and Media Policy,
Griffith University, Nathan, Queensland, 4111.

Series Editor: Stuart Cunningham
Publications Manager: Susan Jarvis
Desktop Publishing: Bev Jeppesen and Susan Jarvis

Cover image: "The Potato Eater" by Garry Anderson, painted in 1994.
Oil on board 90 cm x 120 cm. From the collection of Murdoch University,
Western Australia.

Cataloguing in Publication Data
National Library of Australia

ISBN 0 7022 3205 X

Contents

Contributors

Mark Balnaves is Associate Professor of Public Relations and Journalism at Edith Cowan University in Perth. He has recently published the *Penguin Atlas of Media and Information* and *An Introduction to Quantitative Research Methods: An Investigative Approach*, with Sage. He has also published on issues in social equity and telecommunications, social psychology theory and the impact of new media.

John Banks is Community Relations Manager for Auran, a Brisbane-based games company. He is completing a PhD at the University of Queensland on gaming and gamers.

Stephen Cox is a Research Adviser with the Faculty of Business, Queensland University of Technology. He has a background in social psychology and his field of expertise is in multivariate statistical analysis.

Stuart Cunningham is Professor and Director of the Creative Industries Research and Applications Centre (CIRAC), Queensland University of Technology. He is co-editor (with John Sinclair) of *Floating Lives: The Media and Asian Diasporas* (UQP, 2000 and Rowan & Littlefield, 2001). Previous publications include (with John Sinclair and Elizabeth Jacka) *New Patterns in Global Television: Peripheral Vision* (Oxford University Press, 1996) and (with Graeme Turner) standard Australian media textbooks *The Australian TV Book* (Allen & Unwin, 2000) and *Media and Communications in Australia* (3rd edn, Allen & Unwin, 2001).

Patricia Gillard is Managing Director of User Insite Pty Ltd, a company formed in 1997 to apply new audience and user research in museum and online contexts. She has held senior research, management and advisory positions in universities, museums and the broadcasting industry, most notably Head of Communication Studies at RMIT University, Melbourne; Board Member, Museum Victoria, Member, Broadband Services Expert Group and Head of Research and Development for the Australian Broadcasting Corporation. She is author of *The Lively Audience* and *Girls and Television*, both published in 1986. During 2001; Patricia was a Fulbright Fellow, conducting user research in the Web Program of the National Museum of American History, Smithsonian Institution, Washington.

Kerry Green is an Associate Professor at the University of Canberra's School of Professional Communication. He specialises in newspaper audience research, computer-assisted journalism, multimedia journalism, and news media organisation and management. He has a background in the print media, with a PhD in journalism from the University of Queensland, and has been a journalist since 1967. He was editor of *The Queensland Times*, and deputy editor of *The Cairns Post* and the Brisbane *Telegraph*. He is president of the national Journalism Education Association.

Chris Lawe Davies is Director of Studies in the Faculty of Social and Behavioural Sciences, University of Queensland. He teaches and researches in Media Studies and Journalism. His research areas include multicultural broadcasting, media industry structure and regulation, news analysis and indigenous popular culture. He is series editor of *The Media and Indigenous Australians* project — curriculum materials for reporting Indigenous cultures.

Michael Meadows is Associate Professor of Journalism at Griffith University, Brisbane. He worked as a print and broadcast journalist for ten years before moving into journalism education in the late 1980s. Since then, his research interests have focused on journalism practices in the representation of Indigenous affairs and Indigenous media production in Australia and Canada. His first book, *Voices in the Wilderness*, dealt with images of Aboriginal people in the Australian media and was published in 2001. A second book,

Songlines to Satellites, co-authored by Helen Molnar and published early in 2002, centred on Indigenous communication in Australia, the South Pacific and Canada.

Tom O'Regan is Professor in the School of Film, Media and Cultural Studies at Griffith University, where he is also the Director of the Australian Key Centre for Cultural and Media Policy. He is the founding editor of *Continuum: The Australian Journal of Media and Culture*. His main publications include *Australian Television Culture* (1993) and *Australian National Cinema* (1996).

John Penhallurick is Associate Professor of Communication at the University of Canberra. He received his PhD from Columbia University in 1981, was Deputy Head of the Centre for Communication Studies, later the Communication, Media and Tourism Division, and from 1994–97 was Head of the School of Communication, Media & Tourism. His research interests lie particularly in the fields of Human Information Processing, Persuasion and the analysis of demographics. He is an acknowledged authority on multidimensional scaling and demographics. Recent publications include chapters on the role of affect in decision-making, role stress in communication and the role of gender in corporate communication.

Jason Sternberg is a Lecturer in Media Communication and a researcher with the Creative Industries Research and Applications Centre in the Creative Industries Faculty at Queensland University of Technology.

Acknowledgments

The editors wish to thank the Australian Key Centre for Cultural and Media Policy (CMP) for its support in developing this book. The book initially began as a pilot project on the Australian television audience, undertaken by Mark Balnaves and Tom O'Regan and funded by the CMP in 1999. The project acquired its current, more expansive form through an "Audiences Research Workshop" organised by Tom O'Regan and Jason Sternberg in September 1999. This workshop was designed to bring together research on cultural and media audiences. Six of the chapters in this collection were generated from this initial workshop, as well as suggestions for other contributors drawn from the CMP's national research network.

The book has benefited greatly from the intellectual milieu of and supportive environment provided by the CMP as a national research centre. The initial pilot project was generated through a grant to Murdoch University in Perth. The workshop was organised by researchers at Griffith University and the Queensland University of Technology (QUT). Contributors were drawn from the CMP's national research network. The suggestion for a book on the theme came from series editor Stuart Cunningham.

We owe special thanks to the University of Queensland Press for their forbearance and continuing commitment to a project that took longer to realise than either we or they anticipated. Thank you senior editor Sue Abbey, publisher Carol Davidson and managing director Laurie Muller for your support. We would also like to thank Sue Jarvis of the CMP for her endeavours to keep us on "track" and for her expert and timely editing and formatting of the manuscript. Thanks also to our respective institutions — the School of Film, Media and Cultural Studies, Griffith University, which houses the CMP (O'Regan); the Faculty of Creative Industries, QUT (Sternberg); and variously the School of Media, Communication and

Culture, Murdoch University and Faculty of Social and Behavioural Sciences, University of Queensland (Balnaves).

Tom O'Regan and Mark Balnaves wish to thank Rita Shanahan and Michele Balnaves for their good humour and support. For her help with the index, thanks also to Mary Claire Balnaves. Jason Sternberg wishes to thank his parents, Margaret and Neville, for never losing faith, and Belinda Jennings for an email that started a great adventure.

Introduction

Mark Balnaves and Tom O'Regan

This is a book about mobilising audiences — what James Ettema and D. Charles Whitney (1994, p. 5) usefully call "audiencemaking". Its central concern is how diverse communicators — TV stations, museums, gaming companies and arts agencies — "mobilise their audiences" through their use of audience research. The focus is therefore upon how audiences are enlisted, projected and in some cases brought into being by the actions of particular corporate, government and other actors. This is audience research designed to develop audiences for particular purposes — to quit smoking, to promote the value of the arts, for online services, to arrest newspaper readership declines and so on.

The conception of audience worked with here is necessarily an "institutional" one, inasmuch as the audience research examined here is integral to various management modalities. With its fourteen case studies, the book is designed to demonstrate some of the scope, diverse purposes and varied character of this "institutional" audience research. It asks and answers several questions. How has audience research become implicated in and an integral part of larger processes of decision-making? How are audiences enlisted? How do they (and the audience research on them) become integral to the systems of evaluation and accountability of diverse actors? In short, how are audiences "governed"?

There is a growing need on the part of a variety of people inside and outside the media and arts industries to become "audience minded". This is not just a management issue for upper levels of organisations; it is also an issue for various practitioners, from journalists to exhibition curators to theatre producers. They share a common need to better understand their audiences, readers, users, visitors, voters and clients. They face the common challenge of developing a working facility with the techniques, scope and limits of audience research. They are increasingly required to develop strategy and implement changes based on audience evaluation. Bearing in mind this steadily growing institutional requirement, this book provides a series of case study snapshots to illuminate the available methods and techniques of research likely to be encountered and the ways this research can be used in decision-making processes. In documenting actual cases where these techniques and methodologies are being used, we aim to provide an informed understanding of the nature, character and opportunities available from utilising audience research.

This book fills three very large gaps. While there are numerous titles on audience research, these are usually either general discussions on the changing nature and character of the audience for a medium like broadcasting, or contributions to the development of audience theory and modelling. Such studies leave out of consideration the increasingly diverse (in terms of method and actors) practice of audience research covered in this book. Second, existing studies generally omit a significant shaper of audience research in the ways audience research is informed by and located within a larger cycle of decision-making — a central theme and innovation of this book. Third, there is a dearth of literature covering instances of empirical audience research. Our aim is to showcase the uses of audience research by various actors, identify the different kinds of audience research practice currently being undertaken, and draw out the implications of audience research processes of the wider strategic and policy processes within which such research is situated.

Within audience studies, "industry" or "structural" research is often derided as one-dimensional and instrumental, and is seen as not having the audience's best interests in mind. On the evidence provided in this book, these research undertakings are inventive, multi-dimensional, challenging, publicly minded and often collaborative undertakings between researchers and their subjects.

The book is structured around audience research projects mostly commissioned by a variety of actors. The first chapter, Mark Balnaves and Tom O'Regan's "Governing the Audience", takes a social communication campaign — the Quit smoking campaign — to indicate broader cycles of governance within which audience research is implicated. Here health ministers and ministries commissioned research as a part of the wider "government of health" within which "communication strategies" play an increasingly important part.

In Chapter 2, "The Ratings in Transition: The Politics and Technologies of Counting", Balnaves and O'Regan consider how television stations, advertising agencies and their audiences negotiate the form and character of audience measurement technologies and methodologies to capture the broadcast day. By focusing on the ratings service provider, the authors emphasise the public "service" character of syndicated research and explore the nature of the consensus required among those who pay for and use the ratings by attending to controversies over different ratings systems.

In Chapter 3, "Small Worlds: Research on Children and the Media in Australia", Patricia Gillard considers how research on the child audience has undergone constant change and innovation over an extended period. Her analysis shows how diverse educators, regulators and broadcasters have instigated — singly and collectively — research on the child audience, and how the public discussion of audiences, shifts in government policy and changes in the media industries have both enabled and constrained that research.

Jason Sternberg takes up the issue of how audiences are "created" and subsequently used as the basis for public commentary and market development in Chapter 4, "'I didn't get it, but I liked the name': Generational Profiling through Generation X". Sternberg focuses on how a set of contingent circumstances led novelists and ad agencies to develop and promote the idea of "Generation X" as a generational profile distinct from "Baby Boomers". He charts the emergence and subsequent deployment of the term as a means of focusing public and marketing attention on the nature and character of supposed generational differences. "Generation X" is simultaneously an object of description and commentary and a project for market and product innovation.

Following this principally broadcast media focus, there are three chapters on arts and cultural audiences. In Chapter 5, "Arts Audiences: Becoming Audience-Minded", Tom O'Regan situates the diverse and multi-faceted audience development program of the Australia Council as part of a broader international response to changes in cultural policy and cultural consumption. Here the adoption of paradigms of mobilising the audience within the subsidised cultural sector has focused attention in two related but distinct areas: on the building of arts audiences; and on the building of broad public support for the arts. O'Regan sees the different Australia Council research projects reported in the chapter as part of broader processes in which the arts sector and arts audience are becoming increasingly regularised, normalised and thought of as differentiated along similar lines to the commercial cultural industries.

In Chapter 6, "Towards an Ecology of Cultural Attendance", Tom O'Regan and Stephen Cox are concerned with the emergence of ways of thinking about audiences as audiences for and consumers of several cultural, entertainment and leisure forms. In this case, knowing one's audience increasingly means knowing what else your audience does in its cultural and leisure pursuits. O'Regan and Cox posit an ecology of cultural attendance as a way of understanding the place of the different cultural venues for diverse populations within the broader ensemble of cultural forms.

In Chapter 7, "Museum Visitors as Audiences: Innovative Research for Online Museums", Patricia Gillard considers the ways in which the contemporary movement to build new museums and renew existing ones has generated a growing interest in the museum visitor and developing audience research services for museums. This new visitor research inescapably connects the new museology and new technology applied to the museum context (in the form of online and interactive components) as museums are now not only interested in the visitor in the museum space (usually a building) but also in the virtual visitor via the museum's internet site. Gillard identifies the central problem facing museums as one of understanding how "visitor experiences build on each other across the material and virtual sites".

John Banks takes up the theme of mobilising the audience in his study of the important relation between gamers and computer game companies in Chapter 8, "Gamers as Co-creators: The Virtual Audience — A Report from the Net-Face". Banks considers how gaming fans have become increasingly important in the very development and marketing of games software, to the extent that managing "community relations" is becoming an explicit feature of gaming company innovation and product development.

In Chapter 9, "Mobilising Readers: Newspapers, Copytasters and Readerships", Kerry Green evaluates the evidence for the takeup of reader and audience research in Australian newsrooms. The problem of declining newspaper circulation has led newspapers to increasingly carry out reader research. But this research has typically not gone much beyond senior figures in the newsroom. Green suggests that Australian newsrooms would benefit greatly from restructuring the flow of this market research within newspapers and other news organisations to include practising journalists, to help them better understand their readers.

Mark Balnaves outlines audience research undertaken for its predictive value in Chapter 10, "Finding an Audience for a New Service". Using the Telstra-commissioned "Gungahlin study", examining the factors affecting the likely uptake of new media in the home, and the Productivity Commission's 1999–2000 Broadcasting Inquiry which projected the likely failure of the government's high-definition digital television model, Balnaves shows how audience research can be used to question and subsequently reformulate strategies for the development of new media services.

In Chapter 11, "'Tell Me What You Want and I'll Give You What You Need': Perspectives on Indigenous Media Audience Research", Michael Meadows starts from the premise that both government agencies and the audience research industry know little about Indigenous people and how and why they use media and communication technologies. Such audience research is identified as critical to improving interaction among government agencies, service providers and Indigenous people to facilitate strategic planning at national and international levels. Meadows indicates the need for a holistic research approach utilising culturally appropriate methodologies rather than mapping existing commercially driven approaches over Indigenous communities.

For Stuart Cunningham in Chapter 12, "Theorising the Diasporic Audience", the central issue is the nature of the public spheres generated by the substantial use by ethnic minority communities in Australia of their own media — usually, but not exclusively, video. Building on previous studies which indicate how ethnic video functions for communities as a parallel TV service, Cunningham theorises the communicative space these videos operate in as a number of "sphericules" which raises important cultural and communication policy issues.

In Chapter 13, "After *South Park*", Chris Lawe Davies provides a detailed examination of the SBS-TV audience, showing how SBS conducts its audience research to simultaneously check on how it is meeting its charter obligations by appealing to a broad range of language and interest groups and to promote SBS as an advertising vehicle by building strong audience figures around a narrow band of program genres. In this context, SBS has been "patiently 'turning around' the expectations of the advertising industry to accept a high quality viewing environment, with smaller average audiences".

The final chapter, John Penhallurick's "Voter Communication", outlines how political parties are increasingly understanding their voters in both geodemographic terms and through cognitive mapping techniques. Geodemographics is based on the insight that like-minded people generally live in proximity to each other — for example, in suburbs or parts of suburbs — so it is possible to describe several identifiable population clusters. Cognitive mapping techniques in political campaigning are based on models of human information processing which assume that it is extremely difficult to convert voters, but it is possible to "shift voters a small distance in the desired direction". The focus, therefore, is on identifying the "persuadables" and tailoring communication strategies for that cohort.

Cover Image

Garry Anderson's painting on the cover of this book, "The Potato Eater", is a compelling representation of the audience. The "Potato Eater" of the painting's title is eating in front of the television and has one pea left on his plate. He appears to be giving the TV his undivided attention but he does not appear to be watching anything. He looks pasty and thin, he might be unhealthy, he has a sunken chest (is he undernourished?). His lack of a shirt might indicate informality, a working-class status, institutionalisation or impoverishment. Certainly the TV set is modest — it looks like a portable set. He is not one of TV's beautiful people. Perhaps he is one of its social problems. Or just maybe he is an ordinary viewer watching TV informally for relaxation. He is certainly looking intently at the screen and is involved with it in some way.

We are watching someone watching. We are measuring him, arraying him, inspecting him. To be an audience is to watch and be watched; and just as importantly to give consent to be watched. Just as this is a book about this audience relation, this painting is about the important audience relation so representative of our contemporary experience.

The painting also has a sense of it being a representation of a representation. This is enhanced by the presence of a vertical line on the TV screen — the sort you get either when the picture needs adjustment or when a TV camera is trained on a set. So, on closer inspection, we might not be able to see the image on screen because of the presence of another camera — a TV camera taking this picture of a viewer watching TV. That there might be others seeing this man seeing is a nice metaphor for the external window on to the audience provided by the various audience research represented in this book.

The painting's title — "Potato Eater" — and its use of colours connect this painting to Rembrandt's famous painting of a family group eating. The potato has become a pea. The group has become the single viewer. Viewing — being an audience — becomes our everyday condition, as apparently basic as other conditions like eating. Our surveillance, his intense engagement with the television and eating are intertwined.

The eponymous "Potato Eater" could be a representation of the passive "mass" audience. Like the TV zombies of lore, he does look intently at nothing. Perhaps the one pea on his plate suggests the impoverishment of the experience — promising much but delivering little. He could be an alienated individual cut off from the world and social intercourse and his viewing might not be helping him. Perhaps he is seeking and gaining comfort from a relation with TV, substituting technology for real experience.

Then again, he could equally well be the recalcitrant audience resisting TV's blandishments. He is watching under imperfect conditions. He is looking at a small (black and white?) screen. Perhaps he is one of those viewers more taken with the test pattern than with the programs. He may be sitting and attending closely but we really are not sure just what he is attending to. Is his intensity itself a kind of wandering off? If this is the case, he's not the passive viewer but the feral viewer — highly individualistic with his own ways of dealing and connecting with television (a Mr Bean, perhaps?). Certainly his TV is on a padded surface — a chair or couch of some kind — rather than the more normal supports for a TV set. Watching black and white TV, he might be the "problem viewer" resistant to taking up new technologies in the home. Perhaps he is an unwanted viewer in that he is not likely to be a consumer advertisers are interested in.

This uncertainty about him mirrors the considerable uncertainty and provisionality about audiences, visitors and users attending all kinds of cultural consumption and service delivery. Our uncertainties about him usefully point to the more general problem experienced by those who interact with audiences of whatever kind — audiences are individualistic. From an institutional perspective, they are "feral", protean, mobile (and immobile), resistant to the intended message, capable of doing too much, too little or not the right kind of thing with the service, the program, the art objects provided. Those who do audience research and those who rely on such audience research as the basis for making judgments, taking decisions and making plans routinely encounter such problems with contemporary viewers, listeners, visitors to museums and galleries, and gamers.

The painting is playing with us. Our eye is drawn along the subject's line of sight to the TV set only to find nothing on it to see — instead, our eye must travel straight back to our viewer. We don't see through him to the television — we see through the TV to him. The audience relation is the central feature of this image. Is that why this is such a confronting picture? The painting is the most controversial in the art collection at Murdoch University in Perth. Wherever it goes, the university receives complaints about it. No one wants it around. People don't like looking at him — they would rather look at the something he should be looking at but that's not provided. He gives rise to all sorts of unsettling questions. Why can't he sit further away from the TV set? Why can't we see what he's watching? And what are we doing complaining — why can't he do what he's doing? Isn't the privacy of one's own house, one's own TV chair, one's own TV viewing one's own and not anyone else's business? The painting throws back to us the complexity of the audience relation — something to be represented, surveilled, but at the same time a private experience.

The painting is a metaphor for the focus of our book. Our various contributors are attending to this viewing, consuming, attending, visiting and playing relation. At its heart is the figure of the audience. Rather than taking this shadowy, recalcitrant figure as disrupting the carefully laid-out strategies of the demand management system of advertising agencies, program producers and technological entrepreneurs, our book begins with the assumption that this audience relation is a foundational starting point for any industry audience research. The process of mobilising audiences — the subject of the chapters in this book — does not have perfect communication as its starting point, but rather its imperfections. The various organisations reliant on audiences — whether they be gaming organisations, museums or children's TV producers — face the same problem of identifying, attracting and keeping audiences. They do research on audiences not to discipline them, but to figure out ways of gaining their trust and attention. They often fail — they don't get any audience; they get only some of the target audience; they get an audience they don't want; they lose their audience. They do research to try to minimise the risks of audience, visitor and gamer ungovernability. They undertake audience research as part of their systems of accountability — to shareholders, to advertisers, to investors, to the public; consequently, audience research is part and parcel of contemporary evaluation.

CHAPTER 1

Governing Audiences

Mark Balnaves and Tom O'Regan

Introduction

Institutional audience research typically has been tied up with the politics of power and citizenship; competition for market share and competition for viewer attention; it has been a vehicle for adjusting campaigns and for adopting program formats. Knowledge about media audiences is integrally tied up with the strategies and plans of action of industry players, campaigners, professional bodies and interest groups who take up and apply this knowledge to prosecute their own agendas. There are many "wills to govern" media audiences through the application of research findings on the audience.

Using audience research examples from Britain, the United States and Australia, this chapter demonstrates how social marketing campaigns bring together government, commercial and public interest groups in a new system for decision-making on modern audiences. Government agencies now commission private media agencies to participate in the development and implementation of strategy for social marketing campaigns. The chapter will show that this is a recent phenomenon, and a change in the way governments deal with media and audiences and the implementation of public policy. It will also show that the resulting strategies and empirical audience research cross national boundaries and form part of a governance cycle of global media audiences.

"An Educator in the Broadest and Highest Sense of the Term"

Professor Elton Mayo was Chair of Psychology and Ethics at Queensland University when he gave the major address at the Second [Australian] Advertising Men's Conference in 1920. Mayo went on to become internationally famous in the area of industrial psychology for the Hawthorne Experiments of the 1930s and 1940s. Mayo's speech is extraordinary for the exemplary public role he assigns the "ad man":

> The ad expert is an educator in the broadest and highest sense of the term. His task is the persuasion of the people to be civilized ... You must think for the housewife and if you do that for her and if she finds you are doing it, you will have her confidence ... It is necessary to understand the fear complexes that are disturbing our social serenity. It is not the slightest use meeting Satanism or Bolshevism by organized rage or hate. Your only chance of dealing with these things is by research, by discovering first and foremost of the cause of this mental condition. (Mayo 1920, cited in Braverman 1974, pp. 144–45)

This positioning of the "ad man" as a promoter of public education, civility, philanthropy (an ethic of doing things for others) and a developer of social understanding on the important matters of the day is in marked contrast to later estimations. Thirty-nine years later, Peter Coleman (1959, pp. 677–78) was reporting a different but common perception (and self-perception) of the "ad man":

> a sort of mixture of con-man and artist manque, an unreliable, sentimental, cynical huckster with bags of sympathy for mankind when he was not contemptuous of it, a man who drank too much, lived on his nerves, grew ulcers, seemed to thrive on scandals which never affected his business, and who ended-up in the fundamental corruption of believing the rhetoric his trade taught him to think.

For Mayo, the advertising agency's role is almost the opposite. Its role is to "educate in the broadest and highest sense of the term". It is to identify the reasons for social disorder. It is to persuade in order to protect order. But Mayo goes further: "you must think for the housewife". While we can see Mayo as being paternalistic and condescending to women here, he is certainly not being derogatory.

Housewives were the major advertising market of the time. In this era the audience was typically conceptualised as a "she" and the most important business of advertising agencies was to collect data about women. More importantly, advertising agencies were seen to be entering into a particular kind of social contract with housewives. They were to be seen by the housewives themselves as doing research: "and if you do that for her and if she finds you are doing it, you will have her confidence".

Mayo anticipated the complex role advertising and marketing plays in contemporary society. Advertising and marketing are not simply part of a merchandising and management cycle, but are an essential part of a "governance" cycle. Research about audiences has to be seen to be legitimate and an accurate representation of the interests of the audiences concerned. Mayo believed that government of audiences involved a sense of co-creation. If that governance is seen to be manipulation, then it is no longer regarded as legitimate — it lacks "understanding" and it will fail.

"Satanism" and "Bolshevism" were not to be met by rage and hate. Scaremongering and unplanned campaigns against these were likely to be useless. Social evils of whatever kind needed to be countered by other means — means which sought out motivations and entered into the same relation with audiences and publics as Mayo prescribed for housewives. Government needs tools that do not appear to be using the public for manipulation — indeed, quite the contrary, says Mayo: in thinking *for* her, you must think *with* her. This implies consent, representation and representativeness, accountability and transparency — in short, "good government". The dual process of "co-creation" and "representation" has had an impact on the nature of media audiences, influencing lifestyle, demographics, uptake of media and expectations about media content.

In this chapter, we argue that this governance relationship, anticipated in a radical way by Mayo, has become increasingly more complex and global. Advertising, marketing and public relations have become part of strategic planning and implementation of public policy in English-speaking countries. Nowhere is this more evident than in their respective anti-smoking campaigns.

Social Cause Marketing in the Quit Campaign

The tender for the 1997–98 Quit campaign in Australia was unusual. The tobacco advisory group asked the eight ad agencies who pitched for the contract to "develop strategic, not creative, ideas". Marketing industry commentator and journalist Neil Shoebridge (1999, p. 67) covered the story:

> Eight ad agencies pitched for the lucrative assignment ($7 million was spent on the campaign between July 1997 and December last year [1998]). The advisory group asked the agencies to develop strategic, not creative, ideas. Seven agencies presented creative ideas; the one that stuck to the brief, Brown Melhuish Fishlock, won the business.

Brown Melhuish and Fishlock's "assignment" was to create a new strategy for Australia's stop-smoking Quit campaign. At first sight, there is nothing new in an advertising agency winning a campaign brief. This campaign, however, is a "category breaker" — an advertising agency term for campaigns that differ significantly from "standard" campaigns. Indeed, social cause or social concern marketing campaigns have for the past two decades been perceived as category breaking (Drumwright 1996). This is because advertising and public relations agencies have taken on strategy development roles, providing governments not only with advice on communication strategies but also on the nature of public policy itself and its implementation — how to define audiences and how to change their behaviour.

In 1996, the then Australian Minister for Health and Family Services, Dr Michael Wooldridge, set up a tobacco advisory group, drawn from federal and state health departments and anti-smoking groups, and chaired by David Hill, director of the Centre for Behavioural Research in Cancer at the Anti-Cancer Council of Victoria. Health Department research had found that the decline in the proportion of Australians who smoked had noticeably slowed. The tobacco advisory group decided on a cessation rather than a prevention strategy targeted at the 32 per cent of 18–39-year-olds who smoked. As Hill explained the decision to Neil Shoebridge (1999, p. 66):

> While the political risk–benefit ratio of a transparently teenager-directed campaign would be favorable for a Minister of Health, the risk-benefit ratio in terms of effectiveness among teenagers was likely to be very different. Worse than simply being ineffective, teen campaigns carry greater risk of backfiring. To his credit [the Minister] accepted the advice to target 18–39s.

The tobacco advisory group consulted research in Britain and the United States and exchanged information with fellow experts in those countries. The advisory group had identified health clients in the 18–39 age range as those at substantial risk from smoking-related illnesses and addiction. In this, it was taking a deliberate and well-researched departure from the predominant emphases of previous Australian Quit campaigns and similar campaigns in other cognate countries which targeted children and teen populations (see Lesch and Middendorf-Brand 1997). These younger age groups are inherently harder to reach in targeted campaigns of any kind; furthermore, they are either in the process of forming smoking habits or might smoke at some time in the future. While the teen group was still a key concern, smoking members of that group would be addressed indirectly in a campaign that was directly and obviously targeted at smokers in the next age group up — an age group to which the teen group might be expected to look to for behavioural models and values.

After deciding that it wanted to "change the behaviour" of the 19–39 age group, the advisory group then outsourced strategy to advertising and marketing agencies. "Every cigarette is doing you damage" — using high-fear appeals — was the result.

Unlike previous campaigns, which pushed the risks — giving smokers the chance to think they could beat the odds — "Every cigarette" focused on certainties: "That's where the slogan came from, as a way to focus on the damage that occurs with every cigarette, rather than clinical outcomes of smoking," one of the campaign designers said (Shoebridge 1999, p. 67). Evaluation of the "Every cigarette" campaign was undertaken by the Institute of Health and Welfare Research in order to "calculate the effects". That evaluation then fed back to the advisory groups. Help-lines, counselling, and various other campaign supplementation techniques were designed not only to provide assistance to smokers and non-smokers at a health level, but to gain feedback from "citizens" about the campaigns.

Like the Australian campaign, the British government anti-smoking campaign is titled Quit. In Australia, the United States and the United Kingdom, a range of medical and health groups are involved in anti-smoking education and other anti-smoking messages. Medical associations like the American Medical Association (AMA) have recently worked "hand-in-glove" with the US Surgeons General to regulate and oppose smoking (Lipman 1992; Bishop 1995; Lambert 1995; O'Neill 1997). Anti-smoking interest groups are described as being "at the helm" in identifying at-risk groups and promoting anti-smoking messages (Koeppel 1990; Massing 1996). Many of the anti-smoking groups are linked internationally. The major targets of the smoking companies — children and teenagers — are also the targets of the anti-smoking groups keen to "prevent" the smoking habit from taking root (Lesch and Middendorf-Brand 1997). The smoking habits of youth, and the proportions of youth who smoke, are almost identical in Australia, Britain and the United States. Anti-smoking groups, including the World Health Organisation, are involved in the education and management side of health care. Indeed, for Australia, Britain and the United States, it is a matter of "managing health care".

There is a point where these health-related organisations are not "management-minded", but "audience-minded" or "citizen-minded", and there is a significant difference between them. For example, *Adweek* reported Florida's then Governor Lawton Chiles as inviting advertising agencies to compete for $70 million in anti-smoking campaign funds. Only agencies with at least $40 million in billings, who had no ties to smoking companies and expertise in changing the behaviour of youth, were eligible — "creative work will not be expected" (Fitzgerald 1997). Dealing with audiences is different from dealing with clients of the health service. Florida wanted its youth to know they had a problem.

The joining of "public" and "private" that is evident in the Australian Quit campaign is explicit in announcements of the launch of anti-smoking campaigns in the United States. In 1998, the National Youth Anti-Drug Media Campaign was launched as follows:

> With $195 million appropriated by Congress for 1998 (about 1 per cent of the federal drug budget), this is the largest and most comprehensive anti-drug media campaign ever undertaken by the federal government. It will operate much like a commercial marketing campaign, managed by professional advertising agencies which will buy prime-time media exposure to reach key target audiences: children aged nine to 18, especially middle-school aged children, along with parents and other adult mentors ... The campaign will be constantly monitored and adjusted, with a formal evaluation conducted ... Media companies will be asked to match the government's ad buys with equivalent value public service donations. (USA National Youth Anti-Drug Media Campaign 1998)

Health organisations and anti-smoking lobby groups in Australia, Britain and the United States have already identified youth and young adults as a key risk group. The role of the advertising agencies is to develop a strategy that ensures that key risk groups are aware that they *are* a risk group and recognise that they need to "change their behaviour". It is not surprising, therefore, that phrases like "training the audience" have emerged in trade journals. Social marketing strategists now recommend training of audiences using various forms of supplementation. They also critique the legitimacy of organisations like Benetton and The Body Shop, which look like they merge "public" and "private" but in fact do not, recommending that they "leave politics to those who know what they're talking about" (Crain 1994, p. 22). These criticisms are of the legitimacy of Benetton and The Body Shop as both "interventionists" and as organisations that genuinely "represent" the audience.

Audiences also react as citizens when people try to influence them or when proposals for intervention are made. These reactions are recorded and monitored in modern democratic societies. For example, the Federal Drug Administration in the United States proposed a regulation which generally limits tobacco advertising in all existing media forms to a black-and-white, text-only format. Outdoor advertising is prohibited within 1000 feet (350 metres) of public playgrounds, elementary schools or secondary schools. Advertisements in publications read primarily by adults and advertisements placed in adult-only locations are exempt from any advertising restrictions. The reaction of "audiences" to pro and con campaigns to influence people is recorded by the Federal Drug Administration:

> The agency received more comments on the proposed rule — some 700,000 pieces of mail — than at any other time in the history of federal rule making. Both supporters and opponents organised campaigns to generate reactions to the proposed rule; the agency identified more than 500 different types of form letters. One massive campaign, which opposed the rule, generated over 300,000 pieces of mail — 42 per cent of all the mail received. Some 95,000 people, including more than 35,000 children, sent individual views. The children's comments were overwhelmingly supportive. The largest single comment, submitted by the cigarette industry, consisted of approximately 45,000 pages. (Director of White House Drug Control Policy 1998)

As a population, we are used to government health directives and campaigns. We are generally well disposed towards them, seeing them as life affirming and as optimising social well-being. It is through such interventions that the public understands the role it has to play in governance (and is trained into that role). Members of the public are not only trained to use the medium in particular ways to particular ends, but are also trained in the processes and logics of government, including its recursive/feedback loops (of which there is an expectation of a public presence).

The training of the audience in audienceship and citizenship is evident here in the participants who "know" themselves and their social behaviours (like smoking in certain ways); who will elect to self-govern and govern themself (e.g. seek solutions, follow recommendations). But the audience is also trained into social cause marketing messages as a way of "participating" in imagined publics and imagined communities. Smoking is projected to the public as both a social and an environmental concern — articulating the personal or individual horizon and the social (intergroup) and public horizon simultaneously. The smoker-citizen and the non-smoking citizen "know and approve" this campaign.

Social cause marketing campaigns like Quit, where strategy is outsourced and implemented by private companies, are relatively new and have become more sophisticated over the past two decades

(Drumwright 1996; Logan and Longon 1999). "Social concern" and "social cause" marketing originated in the 1970s (*American Demographics* 1996, p. 60). The most radical involvement of advertising and public relations agencies in public policy formation to date was, however, undertaken outside the social marketing remit. Funded by Kuwait, Hill and Knowlton undertook a multi-million dollar global "campaign" to gain US public support for the American government's military intervention in the Kuwait/Iraq War. The campaign organisers acknowledged the radical nature of the Kuwait assignment, and especially the role of Hill and Knowlton in effectively formulating and implementing aspects of foreign policy. American audiences did not see themselves initially as part of the Iraq and Kuwait conflict. The strategy was to signal to American audiences that they were in fact part of the conflict.

It is beyond the scope of this paper to explore in detail the ethics and disadvantages of this new development in modern democratic government. However, it is new and it is also now well established. Trade journals in the fields of advertising and public relations swap information about this development and identify opportunities. Organisations that have traditionally been conceived as "public-interest", such as charities, have also entered the debate about the advantages and disadvantages of this merging of "public" and "private" (*Charity Times,* 1999, p. 45), with some calling for "clear guidelines for such partnerships" (*National Post* 1995, p. 25). Kellogg's in India, for example, has repositioned itself as a "public interest" organisation by creating the "Partnership in Action" program with the Indian Dietetic Association (Rath 1999).

In ordinary language, these relationships are seen as a form of "government". Such developments satisfy aspects of "social conscience" and "governance" (*Grocer* 1995, p. 14). Models of political action recognise that public-interest groups can be a potent element in the generation of policy, but advertising and public relations agencies are not normally included in these models.

The processes involved in the Quit campaign are mirrored in the United States and Britain. The research evaluations from the different health agencies are shared between the countries. Similar audiences with similar behavioural characteristics are identified and acted upon.

On the basis of Australian experience, therefore, American agencies are quite happy to replicate a strategy of using high-fear appeal advertisements to scare US smokers into stopping smoking. It is not surprising that "systems theorists" have found that unravelling advertising and marketing problems involving public policies is extremely difficult (Lesch and Middendorf-Brand 1997).

Social cause marketing has the role of identifying audiences and intervening in their attitudes and behaviour to achieve governance objectives. This is seen as a "global" activity among English-speaking countries. This role is so extensive that it includes understanding the social forces that drive social change in English-speaking countries and removing barriers to a "global audience". But, as Ammitrati Puris Lintas (APL), one of the major research agencies, noted to advertising agencies, "traditional development of societies hinders global marketing". So behavioural change was required of both marketers and audiences (Walker 1998, p. 20).

"Marketing" and the Governance Cycle

Social cause marketing not only merges "public" and "private", but also shares a "common technology" of government of audiences — and, indeed, of power. Here we find combined in Ian Hunter's (1994, p. 46) terms the "application of knowledge and the exercise of power" which allows "new levels or departments of social existence" to come into being. These technologies are not "good" or "bad" as such. They are, rather, a means of "subjectification" as targeted populations — who are simultaneously audiences — can be expected, if the campaign is successful, to diffuse, multiply and facilitate the takeup of the behavioural norms and values being promoted. Not only will some groups be empowered to alter their risky behaviour (by quitting smoking), but all those reached by the campaign are encouraged to think of themselves and their actions in the light of the social campaign message. Consequently, smokers need to stop smoking and self-manage their own risk of morbidity and the threat their behaviours pose to others (through passive smoking); at the same time, the non-smoking community more broadly needs to act proactively to protect itself (as potential victims) against the threat posed by these behaviours.

We see the origins of this form of self-governance not only in the strategising that follows any use of audience research by management but also in the emergence of legitimate research processes that audiences believe identify them and their needs accurately. Mayo's call to the "ad man" to be an educator in the broadest and highest sense of the term has become a reality.

We are now in a position to specify the governance cycle within the context of the Quit campaign (Figure 1.1).

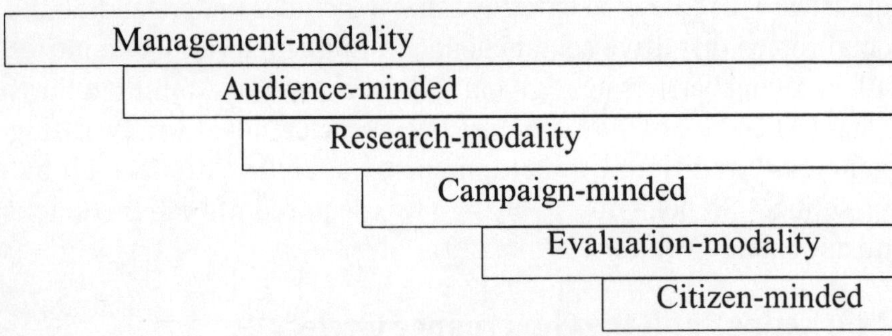

Figure 1.1: Governance Cycle

Modern governments and their bureaucracies are *managers* — they provide services or regulate services. Public-interest groups also service their constituencies. A "client-focus" becomes an "*audience-focus*" when targeted groups need to be told they are an audience and to be influenced as an audience. This trebling of public, client and audience in a social marketing campaign is part of the larger "trebling" of audiences and targets of (welcome) intervention: the citizen interested in community well-being; the client of welfare provision (in this case health); and the audience of media. In the Quit campaign, this trebling is manifest in the health bureaucracies and agencies involved in developing campaigns as part of their wider provision of services and it is evident in the construction of audiences for social campaign messages — in this case, anti-smoking messages.

Modern governments and other organisations turn to *research* to find out about their clients. They commission research which often requires specialisation (outsourcing) or coordination with other similar agencies who have already conducted research (often already completed in other English-speaking countries). In the case of anti-smoking regimes, research is often cited by health and public-interest groups as a prelude to campaigns, as justification for the campaigns themselves and their large expenditures.

Organisations become "*campaign-minded*" when they have decided to influence an audience. Such a stance is inevitable in a society "rationalised through publicity" (Ericson et al. 1987, p. 357). Everyone must become campaign or publicity minded if they want to influence audiences or change their behaviour. "Campaign-mindedness" is present in the very "reduction" of health actions to a series of "campaigns" — in this case, the long-running Quit campaign. The campaign is an apex and public face of the larger health industry enterprise geared to optimising the health of the population and reducing morbidity. Campaigns are expected to give rise to healthier individuals, less risky behaviours, lower health care and social costs, fewer days lost through sickness and ill-health and so on. Here the health professionals and health minister are publicity minded and diverse interest groups and lobbyists are enlisted in this action (the department, the states, the minister, the health professionals, the media).

The actual campaigns themselves require *evaluation* and calculation of effects. This is a part of accountability and transparency in decision-making. These evaluations occur before, during and after the physical appearance of the campaign.

The "citizen" is addressed in these campaigns in multiple ways. The smoker is both a governed and self-governing subject. The "people" are seeing their government spend monies on campaigns for citizen health — legitimately promoting the "happiness of the people" through these measures. The desired "change" is accomplished through a variety of intermediaries, of which the media campaign is only one. Citizens see their taxpayer dollars well spent. Here the audience is trained to accept particular categories (smoker, non-smoker, age groups and notions of generational styles associated with them) which are also statistical categories, and population categories become self-identifying categories for groups making up the "social" and communal order.

The governance cycle — the idea that audience behaviour can be regulated and controlled through media campaigns — is particularly effective in English-speaking countries where "co-creation" is well established and where the research technologies are transparent and accountable. In this sense, the government of media audiences is global. As R.A. Bauer's (1971) classic study shows, there is a difference between indoctrination of audiences and governing audiences. Many non-English speaking countries, like France and Germany, come close to having similar systems of "governance", but these countries often fall short at the "citizen" level because of weak feedback mechanisms for citizen contributions.

Integrating Audience Research

The increasing specialisation in the different players (into psychological research, market research, the advertising agencies, the government of the day) that we can see in operation for the Quit campaign places a premium on the integration of diverse sources of advice and materials. This specialisation, itself a kind of outsourcing, has involved the progressive hiving off of functions previously undertaken within the advertising firm. It has led to the concentration of expertise which becomes simultaneously more tailored and more generalised (and generalisable) across industry. In this sense, the contemporary trend to contract out a variety of services is not new at all, but part of an older and broader movement organising the relations among different parts of the services sector.

Modern audience research is, then, not simply "instrumental" — designed to evaluate *market* needs in order to service a client; it is also "representative" — designed to reflect *audience* needs. Audience research is an intervention into people's lives, finding out how they think and "thinking for them". Research organisations are intermediaries between government/firm/ad agency and consumer/audience/client. The process of legitimation required of "intermediaries" like the advertising agencies applies regardless of who is trying to persuade or inform audiences. Audiences themselves can become producers or providers of services — for example, citizens joining together to form anti-smoking lobby groups. Those groups, however, are subject to the same processes of legitimation as research organisations if they wish to make claims about how audiences think (and, more importantly, to make claims that they think *for* them).

The accountability of the research technologies developed to analyse media audiences is, in these circumstances, especially important. "Accountability" and "transparency" in decision-making through the development of public audience research technologies are now well established, even though this might not be well known. For example, CASIE (a joint project of the Association of National Advertisers, Inc. and the American Association of Advertising Agencies), with the support of the Advertising Research Foundation (ARF), is attempting to develop interactive audience measurement techniques that involve full disclosure of methodology and full accountability by third-party research organisations (as broadcast ratings research already requires).

But how do audiences come to *recognise* from the results of the research that they are members of an audience? This has historically been the role of "signalling". Fragmentation, factionalisation, regionalisation and decentralisation were, according to Joseph Turow (1997), the buzzwords of the 1980 meeting of the Association of National Advertisers in the United States. For Turow, the "image tribes" — the advertisers who construct images of our society for the media — recognised many years ago that there was no single audience, but many different demographics with different lifestyles. There are, in fact, thousands of possible combinations of demographics of audiences.

Since the 1980s, the professional media communicators have developed more complex ways of signalling to their audiences. Signalling is the way advertisers create media materials to indicate to certain types of people that they ought to be part of the audience. This is done by splitting audiences into different categories to establish appropriate emotional relationships and to establish an image of the advertisers and media as having the same values, activities and interests as the audience.

"Formats" and "brands" guide this approach. A format is the layout and general approach to content that a specific media group, such as television, takes to its material. Turow (1997, pp. 91–92) explains the relation between the format and the brand:

> It is the format that creates what people think of the "personality" of a network, magazine, newspaper. When a company touts the distinctive

identity of its format, that identity is known as a "brand". So, for example, CNN is a branded cable news format and *Ladies Home Journal* is a branded woman's magazine.

Complex strategies for signalling, such as "versioning", have evolved to create different campaigns for distinct audiences. Turow (1997, p. 109) takes the example of the ad campaign of the telecommunication company MCI, targeted at Generation X audiences. The company's executives were "worried that their broad-based campaign aimed at baby boomers might not be connecting with the cohort that followed them". They decided to create a special version of their general campaign for this target group. It consisted of "inexpensive series of ads" which ran on "GenX cable networks such as MTV and VHI". Turow (1997, p. 109) continues:

> To carry it out, the copywriter and art director of the project, GenXers themselves, chose three somewhat off-kilter incidents in the lives of young adults into which they expected people of their age cohort could project themselves or their friends: a couple getting married under water; a male Xer in a tattoo parlor; and a young man at a professional baseball game catching a foul ball with his popcorn cup. At the end of each vignette, a voiceover that reflected the age target asked, "So what have your friends done since you last spoke to them?"

Conclusion

This chapter is a contribution to the growing interest in cultural and media studies into how audience research relates to the management priorities of diverse institutional actors. James Ettema and D. Charles Whitney (1994, p. 4), following what they call the "money arrow" — the networks, ratings, advertising agency, program makers' nexus — describe this as a focus on how "communicators make audiences". Our focus, following the logics of social marketing campaigns, identifies a related but more nuanced process at work — one best captured by the concept of governing the audience. Conceiving "audience-making" relationships as "governing relations" can usefully contribute to emerging understandings of the "institutional" character of audiences. While acknowledging the "social engineering" — manipulation and control — aspects of audience management identified by Ang (1991, 1996), we also foreground the socially productive and ethical character of the self-governing populations constituted through this same audience management system. This nuanced model of audience management can better explain the kinds of directive audience research examined above.

Audience research, whether commercial or public, and the results of that research, are *prima facie* "negotiated". "Governance" is therefore a more correct description for the process of negotiation and mobilisation at work. Governance gives a sense of strategy, plan of action and an ethical relation of "management" with the "subjects" of the campaign — subjects who in the Quit campaign were simultaneously clients of health provision, citizens, publics and audiences. This implies a shift in our thinking captured by Mitchell Dean and Barry Hindess (1999, p. 6) in their discussion of contemporary problematics of liberal government. The processes involved here are not those of society "as an artefact of the intricate labours of multiple agencies of rule" — here the ad agencies, health departments, media networks and researchers — but "that of society as a network of spontaneous orders, as something to be known by specialised forms of theoretical knowledge".

Once a group makes a claim that it is "thinking for" the audience, then that group is subject to the rules of government of audiences. Who gets identified as an "audience" and how they are "signalled" are important, and not simply an "abstract" affair. Disenfranchised groups may well feel that they are either not "represented" as audiences and lobby for recognition through formal government mechanisms such as broadcasting authorities, or are not represented *accurately* as audiences (e.g. they are portrayed in racist ways). Much public advocacy work has gone into minoritarian public campaigns for a better deal which would see minority communities as part of the readership and viewership of sensitive programs — part of the "we" community rather than a "they" community (Hartley 1992a, p. 207).

At the beginning of this chapter, we quoted Mayo as implying the possibility of "breaking the contract" — of a failure by ad men to deliver on the contract with the audience, where the contract is the invitation to dialogue, to thinking for and thinking with the audience. The examples provided to this point show that this breaking of contract happens when:

- the methods for finding out about what the audience wants do not work or are inadequate (Mayo in 1920 advocated not only the collection of aggregated, survey data, but motivational data);
- the "intermediary" is not thinking for the audience but for someone else (leading to audiences being treated as "subjects" and not as "agents/citizens");
- the research is not transparent, demonstrable and visible;
- the audience does not have confidence in the client of the research (a breach of trust in the source, the service provider).

Cumberbatch and Howitt (1989), in a British review of media effects, concluded that market forces and market research inevitably mean "media cannot stray too far from audience interests and so will usually reflect the values, beliefs, concerns, etc. of a substantial body of the audience" (1989, p. 1). Outsourcing of audience research, rules of accountability for research and signalling are all part of the modern media scene. There is an established system of decision-making that affects those who want to make claims about audiences and those who want to influence audiences.

It is important to recognise in this context how national governments have become part of this system and how this system can now be called "global". When Bauer conducted a study of Soviet refugees in the 1950s, he found that Soviet methods of indoctrination were singularly unsuccessful. Bauer knew that virtually every Soviet citizen was regularly exposed to meetings at which some news was conveyed, along with the party line on various issues and general political agitation and indoctrination. The Soviet refugees were asked: "From what sources did you draw most of your information about what was happening?" Only 19 per cent specified the meetings, compared with 87 per cent citing newspapers, 50 per cent radio and 50 per cent word of mouth. "Gradually the obvious dawned on us," wrote Bauer (1971, pp. 338–39). "Our respondents were telling us where they learned what *they* wanted to know, not where they learned what the regime wanted them to know." The higher Bauer went up the social ladder of the Soviet refugees, the more likely those groups were to rely on word of mouth to better understand the official media. "Viewed from the vantage point of the regime's intention, the widespread dependence upon word of mouth was a failure in communication. From the point of view of the citizen and what he wanted, his own behaviour made eminent sense." (Bauer 1971, p. 339)

Bauer was aware that persuasion does not work when the "government of the audience" is not perceived by the citizens to be legitimate. This is consistent with Hannah Arendt's conception of power. Arendt (1986) argued that, from Voltaire to Dahl, the traditional conception of power has been force and violence. For Arendt, force and violence are instruments, or implements, of power and not power itself. The extreme form of power, on the basis of this view, is All against One and the extreme form of Violence is One against All. If one person wants to dominate a group, then violence is the most efficient way to achieve command-obedience but not power. Power always stands in need of numbers, says Arendt (1986, p. 64); violence always relies on implements:

> Power corresponds to the human ability not just to act but to act in concert. Power is never the property of an individual; it belongs to a group and remains in existence only so long as the group keeps together. When we say of somebody that he is "in power", we actually refer to his being empowered by a certain number of people to act in their name.

Advertising agencies do not employ force or violence to achieve their objectives — at least in modern democratic societies. The power they exercise is closer to the governmental relation Foucault argued for (see Dean and Hindess 1999). They are in the business of organising the "conduct of conduct". We need to attend to such ad and research agencies as one among a number of "various authorities and agencies, invoking particular forms of truth, and using definite resources, means and techniques" (Dean and Hindess 1999, pp. 2–3) which operate both inside and outside *the* government of the day.

Audience theories have tended to focus on issues of passive versus active audiences, media effects and ideology (Webster 1998) and reception and media use (Alasuutari 1999). Very rarely do audience theorists focus on the actual techniques used in decision-making and the impact of these techniques across a range of different corporate actors.[1] As we have seen in the Quit campaign, a significant number of corporate actors were mobilised, from the ministerial level through to the relevant federal and state departments of health, various research centres and agencies, professional associations, non-government organisations, ad agencies, media outlets, para-professional groups, health clients, citizens and audiences.

Indeed, the explanatory power of any theory about the audience often comes from taking one part of the cycle and using that part to represent and stand for the whole. There can be little doubt, for example, that audience research involves "surveillance" and "social control", but it is unlikely that those aspects can be reduced to the figure of a panopticon. The idea of surveillance misses the co-creation mechanisms and the "failing" character of the audience governance cycle — indeed, it misses the very thing which makes "surveillance" itself necessary. The concept of a "governance cycle" allows cultural and media studies analysts to examine each part of the cycle and to analyse the nature of the corporate actors and actions involved in decision-making.

Audience research in English-speaking countries is coordinated and shared and the processes of identification of audiences and signalling to audiences are very similar. It is not surprising, therefore, that — despite some cultural variation — many of the expectations and behaviours of audiences in English speaking countries are also similar. Edward Herman and Robert McChesney (1997) correctly identified an emerging global audience research industry — and our analysis of the Quit campaign confirms the increasingly international character of social marketing campaigns. But they also argue that this industry is an uncritical and unreflective part of management and capitalist processes which produces homogeneity of audiences as its result. Such an argument loses something of its explanatory force when the full cycle of governance is recognised and understood.

Note

1 For a useful discussion of the concept of corporate actors see Hindess (1988).

CHAPTER 2

The Ratings in Transition: The Politics and Technologies of Counting

Mark Balnaves and Tom O'Regan

> The public is an audience, but it is also a market. It could not be a market unless it had given its consent to be an audience, and it could not remain an audience … unless it had proved itself as a market. (Potter 1967, p. 54)

Introduction

This chapter focuses on the "ratings" — the broadcasting industry's audience measurement standard designed to document the audience size of competing media outlets. It is concerned first with identifying the contours of the rating system and their transformation over time as various technologies have been deployed to arrive at ratings results. And it is concerned with exploring the various controversies surrounding the ratings as the broadcasting industry's "common currency".

Particular attention will be paid to three controversies over different rating results. The first such controversy persisted from mid-1944 to 1974 as the media industry maintained two different ratings systems. One was based on diaries and the other on interviews, providing sometimes differing results. These two systems were consolidated into one in 1974 as the media industry moved to a single ratings currency based on the diary system and subject to external audit. The second controversy related to the transition from diaries to people meters from 1989–91 and the third to the aftermath of the winning of the lucrative metropolitan television ratings contract by AGB Italia in 2000 over the incumbent ACNielsen. For the first part of 2001, discrepancies between the two rating systems — AGB Italia's figures for OzTAM and ACNielsen's figures — made headlines and occasioned much anxiety and heated debate within the industry and outside over the "truth" of the ratings.

The "Ratings" as Currency

What are the ratings and how are they used? A form of audience measurement, ratings data at base provide a measure of how many homes or people are viewing a program, a set of programs, particular advertisements, a station, a network or even the medium itself. The ratings panel — the households reporting its viewing and listening — is expected to be representative of the population as a whole. Television ratings panels, for instance, take into account variables such as age, sex, postcode, size of household (family size), income (and therefore buying power), education, and number of television sets and VCRs in the home. These panels are designed to yield a variety of demographic information about viewing (demographics are descriptive classifications of individuals and households). The viewing and listening behaviours of particular demographics within defined geographical areas are a central concern.

Ratings measurement systems are at base concerned with measuring media exposure — who is being exposed at what time and, increasingly, for how long. They are therefore not — as the word "ratings" might imply — a subjective measure of program quality, an indication of undivided attention, or for that matter an indication of the intensity of the viewing experience.

Ratings systems organise viewing and listening information according to several measures.[1] The *ratings* are the percentage of all people or households in a population (a city, a nation, or a particular demographic) with a television or radio tuned to a specific channel. The formula is: Households/population = Rating. For example, if 600 households of a 3600-household sample watch the ABC, then approximately 16 per cent of households are tuned to the ABC. *Households using television* (HUT) is a measure of the set or sets in use at any given time of day. Obviously there are a greater number of households using television between 6.00 p.m. and 10.00 p.m. than outside this period, and the HUT measure picks this up. The *share* is the percentage of the total TV viewing (or radio listening) audience at any given time watching (or listening) to a particular program or station. It is a measure of the relationship between the sets tuned in to a specific program, compared with the total number of sets tuned to any television (or radio) in a specific area. Share is "a competitive evaluation, denoting how a given program is performing opposite others at the same time" (Brown 1971, p. 33). For example, if 500 households of the 3600-household sample are not watching television, then the ABC has approximately a 19 per cent audience share. Programs have an audience *profile* — that is, they have a particular demographic composition. Because broadcasters and advertisers have particular target markets in mind, *TARPs* — Target Audience Rating Points — are particularly important. They measure a specific demographic audience of a station at a specified point, or for a specified period, in time. For instance, 11 per cent of women aged 18+ might be watching the news on a particular station. The various media players are also interested in a program or ad's *reach*, which is a measure of the number or percentage of individuals or households exposed to a program or ad within a particular timeframe. A related measure is the *average frequency* of a program, advertising message or campaign. This is the average number of times people or households are exposed to the program, ad or campaign within a particular time period.

The ratings are used by broadcasters, advertising agencies and advertisers as a mutually agreed upon common standard for measuring the audience size of competing media outlets. These several players come together with ratings providers to develop an agreed upon audience measurement instrument to be used in their daily calculations and transactions. In his seminal article on the logic of ratings in the United States, Peter Miller (1994, p. 58) emphasises how ratings instruments are not only enabled and shaped by those who pay for and use the research, but also by the audiences who participate in ratings surveys. The survey participant's capacity, willingness and diligence to provide information cannot be taken for granted. With these diverse inputs, ratings systems are always the result of "complicated trade-offs" (Miller 1994, p. 63). They are not "perfect" so much as a negotiated settlement as to the scope of "imperfections" to be tolerated.

The fundamental design compromise of all ratings systems is that, because they need to encompass a variety of media offerings and be useful to a variety of clients, they impose a one size fits all approach which enables "apples" to be compared with "apples". Ratings research provides advertisers with "a standard way to judge alternative vehicles for their messages" (Miller 1994, p. 63); broadcasting sales with information relevant to a sales pitch to advertisers; and broadcasters with information on how well their programming is going against the competition and on who is watching. In these circumstances, ratings research provides a generalised rather than a specific and tailored view of a media product. Ratings research is therefore the exact opposite of the customised research approach which typically reports on a limited number of media offerings so as to examine them in more detail. Syndicated studies, by contrast, may "lose" information about specific audiences and programs precisely because they are standardised, but gain information through the breadth of their research undertaking.

Ratings research is a large-scale research undertaking. It is not only costly — the current Australian metropolitan cities TV ratings contract alone is worth $90 million over seven years — but also challenging to implement. Take, for instance, the costs and logistics associated with distributing and collecting diaries in regional television and radio markets, something which made for less frequent surveying of these audiences over several decades. Both costs and logistics ensure that ratings research is syndicated in the sense that its cost is principally borne by the various media players — usually the media outlets in the first instance. These outlets have an interest in coming together despite the often intense competition among them — they have "something important in common — the same market to sell" (Barnathan 1964, p. 172). To this end, it makes sense for them to support the provision of regular, comparable "longitudinal information about audiences that can be used to sell advertising space and time" (Miller 1994, p. 63). Both the television and radio companies have a common interest in ensuring that the ratings data are taken up by advertisers and media sales people. The scale of the costs involved also mean that there tends to be no more than one or two competing syndicated ratings research companies operating in one area at any one time. To ensure the credibility of the ratings system among the several groups who rely on it, the organisation providing the syndicated research must be (structurally) separate from both media businesses and advertisers. Ratings providers must function and be seen to function as independent brokers.[2]

What syndicated audience measurement companies like ACNielsen and AGB Italia seek to establish is an "official truth" — a social convention for the description of audiences for a number of media products which can be offered for sale to a number of clients. As Miller (1994, p. 66) notes, a ratings convention arises when all parties have a common interest in the coordination rule, none has a conflicting interest and none will deviate lest the coordination is lost. This "consensual" aspect of ratings is not imposed so much as "won". As Miller (1994, p. 67) puts it:

> A service's case for becoming a convention is heightened to the extent that it can claim to capture all of those viewing, reading, or listening — every audience member for every program or articles, at all times. This criterion is particularly important to media clients who will pay the most toward the service's existence. The service's bid to offer the official reality will also benefit from a demonstration that its method detects only real viewing, reading, or listening and not false or misleading impressions. This criterion is particularly important to advertisers on whom the media clients rely for income.

The ratings convention works if media outlets and advertisers see the ratings services as providing useful information about viewers and if a measurement approach can be settled on which is "an acceptable compromise between the partially conflicting goals of these two client groups" (Miller 1994, p. 67). Persuading the full range of media players from the competing media companies through to advertisers that a particular technology for collecting and analysing audience data is suitable is no small achievement. As the ratings provide the basis for expensive transactions among media players, ratings agencies need to continually "prove themselves". This is particularly the case when new systems or new players win ratings services contracts — as happened when AGB Italia secured the metropolitan TV ratings contract for 2001 onwards. In this case, elaborate procedures of testing and validating were put into place.

Media and cultural studies writing, as well as much public discussion of the ratings, focuses on their conventional and constructed character. John Hartley (1992b, p. 105) describes the audience for ratings research as one of those "invisible fictions" which are "produced institutionally in order for various institutions to take charge of the mechanisms of their own survival". Ratings are here grasped in their role as a common currency, lubricating the transactions of the various industry players, and for the ways in which they underwrite conceptions of the audience as a commodity (Streeter 1996, pp. 275–308). While the productivity of the ratings convention in organising relations among diverse industry actors is foregrounded in works like those of Hartley, these approaches rest much of their criticism of ratings on its constructed, conventional character. The constraints and relationships necessary to shape the "reality" of the media audience as it is known through commercial audience measurement are therefore criticised as distortions. For Eileen Meehan (1990, p. 118), measurement techniques are transformed from "scientific measures" to "business" and "corporate" practices. This viewpoint centres those who use the currency to such an extent that the ratings convention as a currency is almost unrelated to the technology of collection and analysis.

One consequence is that not enough attention has been paid either to the services themselves or to those involved in carrying out ratings research and development. To do this, we need to shift our attention from an emphasis on the *commercial interests* of those who use the ratings as part of their publicity and marketing campaigns to those with a *service interest* in the provision of "disinterested" and standardised research services, of use to an industry marked by competing interests and priorities.

This services perspective emphasises the ratings as a technology of "evaluation" that is part of and subject to wider accountabilities — of broadcasters to advertisers and audiences; of ratings agencies to broadcasters, ad agencies, advertisers and audiences; and of program-makers to broadcasters and their clients. In providing such a service, ratings bodies bear comparison with other research providers constructed on "disinterested" public-interest grounds, such as the Australian Bureau of Statistics. Indeed, in Canada, ratings service companies are treated as equivalents of governmental statistical bureaux and are required to provide governmental agencies with rating services free of charge!

Don Neely (2000), who joined the ratings agency Andersons in 1959, gets at this "public-service" character of ratings in his recall of George Anderson's approach to doing regional television ratings sweeps in the 1960s. Anderson sometimes made a loss to ensure the correct result — his commitment to providing a public service could take precedence over making money:

> When we were measuring a country television station, we would over-provide, for the reason George [Anderson] said "it's their livelihood. Forget the agencies, it's the station that's got to live or die by these numbers, and I want them to be right." Now the fact that we've quoted a price and are providing a service which was more expensive than we quoted was quite irrelevant to George. As long as he was right. And that's why the company was never really financially flush.

Ratings systems are notoriously blunt research instruments. They provide, in Miller's (1994, p. 68) words, "a superficial, but generally reliable and comprehensive measurement of the entire broadcast day". Customised research — especially tailored research, which is usually commissioned by a media client to focus on its own audience — is required to provide more extensive information about the audience (see Miller 1994, p. 60). The tradeoff between syndicated and customised studies is in the amount of information each provides about a program, a service and an audience: the former provides breadth, while the latter offers depth.

The Emergence of the Ratings

In those countries which established commercial broadcasting media early, such as Australia, the United States and Canada, audience measurement grew out of the customised research undertakings of advertising agencies and stations. This trajectory from customised to syndicated research suggests that collective understandings need to be in place in a broadcast market to support the consensus necessary for ratings services to develop. Such services — the convention of standardised measurement — cannot be imposed. Rather, the need for them has to grow out of the experience, requirements, understandings and interests of the various media players. This requires a sufficiently developed, competitive and differentiated media market to be in place to require competitors to become collaborators for the purpose of supporting an independent media broking service as a means of developing what they have in common — the same media market.

Consequently, the idea of an independent industry-wide audience measurement service took some time to emerge in Australia and elsewhere. Most of the several elements we are used to seeing as differentiated and often carried out by different companies — audience research, audience development, marketing and advertising — were initially carried out by advertising agencies themselves and in some cases by the radio stations. Because audience measurement began as customised research by advertising agencies and radio stations, such research was often partial and limited by the interests of the commissioning agent. Nonetheless, customised audience research was the currency and advertising agencies were well placed to function as "brokers" and coordinators of a fragmented radio marketplace. In these circumstances, customised research was, according to Miller (1994, p. 63), "*the* only way for advertisers to learn about the audiences for media outlets".

In these circumstances, the advertising agency and the individual station faced a credibility problem with advertisers and media outlets because each had a vested interest in the research. Advertising agencies had a potential conflict of interest as media buyers and planners, while radio stations had a vested interest in promoting research favourable to themselves — indeed, radio research was part of the radio station's promotional campaign before advertisers. These custom studies inevitably "created a cacaphony of incomparable audience claims" (Miller 1994, p. 63).

A different approach was needed — one that could arbitrate competing claims and be accepted by all as a fair and representative measure. For this to happen, the several interests involved — competing media outlets, advertisers and advertising agencies — had to come together to help construct and accept a standard measure. Syndicated audience research was born out of this necessity to construct "a common template for assessing the audience" so as to permit the orderly development of an advertising and media market. Writing about the US experience, Miller (1994, p. 63) argues that advertisers sought a tradeoff in survey design, which meant that more outlets would be measured in less detail "but with the same level of detail".

In Australia, such ratings-like services were initially provided by the large United States-based advertising company J. Walter Thompson (JWT). As a big advertising agency, JWT was interested in servicing an array of large advertising clients and so had in interest in the audience for several competing radio outlets. Its move to develop a "standard" for the Australian radio industry unsurprisingly seems to have come from its own pragmatic response to advertiser needs. In the early 1930s, JWT started to train a team of interviewers in Sydney for survey work. In 1934, radio was gaining a sizeable audience but was still a developing advertising medium. The circulations of all Australia's newspapers and magazines were known, but all one could say of radio was that, courtesy of Post-Master General figures, each city had a certain percentage of homes with licensed sets (from the 1930s to the early 1970s, radio and TV sets were subject to an annual licence fee). American radio audience research at the time was also based on telephone calls, but in the 1930s only 15 per cent of Australian homes had telephones. In July 1934, JWT did its first study in Australia on the listening habits of the "top economic classes". It made 1546 calls in all; of these, 303 homes either did not answer the call or refused to participate. Full-time research staff at that time included the poet Judith Wright. This was the beginning of the development of syndicated research in Australia.

The approach carried some inherent problems. JWT was not "a disinterested party". As an advertising agency, it represented advertisers with an interest in survey results. Bill McNair, a researcher with JWT, established the McNair Survey on 10 July 1944 in a move designed to dissociate "ratings" control from JWT and create an "independent" service. This structural independence was designed to ensure that competing advertising agencies and their clients had confidence that the JWT group was not being given an unfair advantage through its ownership of the "ratings standard".

Around a month earlier, on 9 June 1944, George Anderson registered the Anderson Analysis of Broadcasting as a competing, but also independent, survey research company. In contrast to McNair's ad agency background, George Anderson had been a "radio man" at 2GB and elsewhere. With the establishment of both companies within a month of each other, Australia's first syndicated ratings controversy began. Not surprisingly, the personnel for these two ratings services came from the two arenas with an interest in "disinterested" research — advertising agencies and radio broadcasters.

The First Ratings Controversy: McNair versus Andersons

McNair's survey used personal interviews — an aided recall methodology which asked people to recall their listening. The Anderson Survey started using personal interviews but in 1946 moved to a modified diary method, used by Columbia Broadcasting System (CBS) at the time. This diary system is much the same as that used today to measure Australian radio audiences. Both radio surveys provided the same basic demographics, including age, economic class and listening times. As Don Neely (2000) recalled, these systems were not only different but "were getting slightly different results", which "caused some consternation in the marketplace".

Given the current fashion for single audited ratings services, it might seem surprising that advertisers and radio stations (and then, after 1956, TV stations) supported two rival syndicated systems. There were several reasons for this. Competition between two competing systems in the absence of any agreed upon auditing standard was an effective method for ensuring the independence of the data. The early use of ratings was also, for the most part, a check on performance of individual stations and their programs — much like an internal audit on performance — as well as a currency for trade. Indeed, there was no expectation that audience ratings *should* be made public on a routine basis — that would come later. As a consequence, discrepancies were a largely intra-mural matter for the broadcasting industry and were not available or open to public controversy and dispute. Early ratings surveys were also not conducted on as regular a basis as today. Diary and personal interview data were necessarily limited in scope and in the frequency of their collection. In the absence of computational power, the possibilities for massaging the data were also limited. Homes were the basic unit for television ratings and very broad demographics for radio ratings. Consequently, in the early ratings period, the "window" to the audience was narrow and the "window" on to the data even narrower.

The various users of the ratings had to deal with these inbuilt limitations. Agencies and stations could only ask so much of the data. Ratings research could only collect and analyse so much data from the audience. Ratings sweeps became the norm and opportunistic broadcasters programmed special events to coincide with these sweeps. Station managers and advertisers wanted certainty that the audience was there and both methods provided it. The motivation for "independence of the data" was driven by the need for accurate data that did not bias any one commercial player over another. In the absence of any agreed auditing standards, and in circumstances where comparisons of both systems revealed minor discrepancies, maintaining two providers ensured that one could act as a check on the other. In addition, stations that scored higher in one system were loathe to accept a system that would score them lower in another. This stalemate was to last for nearly four decades and survived McNair's adoption of the diary method in the mid-1960s for the television ratings. Rival ratings systems were similarly maintained in the US market in this period. Jacob Evans (1954, pp. 18–24) cites four principal ratings services in operation in the 1950s that "the radio salesman [sic]" needed to "understand the major characteristics of".

For Don Neely, the history of the two-ratings system can best be understood as a tradeoff among the various actors. McNair, as a JWT man, started with the implied support of the national advertising agencies. By contrast, Anderson — a radio man at a time when "local" stations characterised the commercial broadcasting mix —

needed advertiser credibility and a national platform. As a consequence, he enlisted the support of the Advertisers Association, formed a board of governors "to get some sort of status" and worked on his broadcasting connections — both individual stations and the main radio networks. But Anderson's radio background — he had been a station manager of 2GB and sales manager for the extensive Macquarie Network — did advantage him in dealing with radio stations in competitive marketplaces like Sydney, where he initially concentrated his attention.

Given that the diary system eventually "won out" over the aided recall method, it would be tempting to see the latter method as anachronistic. But Gwen Nelson, in an interview with one of the researchers in 2000, suggests that it was ideally suited to the ratings needs of the time. The social structure made it much easier to represent the audience. As she points out, "the household was a household, it was a family". Family members "weren't scattered here, there and everywhere". And there "was one radio set and the family sat around and listened to the radio". The "housewife was always, or mostly at home" so there were no problems with people being "out". In these circumstances, it was possible to get a "very reasonable cross section of all the groups and all social structures". This made personal interviews an ideal medium for eliciting viewing information and identifying the dynamics of family listening and later viewing.

Unlike today, when telephone interviews are used in a variety of market research contexts including the establishment surveys for the panels, telephones were not used at all. This was partly because levels of phone ownership were not high enough to warrant the use of the telephone, but it was also because "it was so impersonal that your interview had to get the confidence of the person you were interviewing, and make them feel that they were really contributing to something". This sense that audience members were co-creating the ratings with their audiences was an important part of the "contract" between McNair and its audiences.

The personal interview had another important function that Gwen Nelson hinted at here. It placed the researcher close to the audience and provided stations and advertisers with significant informal contextual information besides the pre-listed recall data which may have contributed to the longevity of this system. This aspect of audience measurement did not so much disappear as find a home in the careers of McNair graduates such as Hugh Mackay, supplying audience and generational profiles based on focus group and other interviewing techniques.

Gwen Nelson also suggested that both ratings services had an important educative function to play in turning around the perception of advertisers:

> The advertiser thought it was ridiculous, nobody would sit around and listen to a voice. They'll read the advertisement when they see it in print, in the newspaper, and they'll believe it, but they won't take any notice of an odd voice talking to them over the radio.

Nelson reflected that it would no longer be possible to work as she once had. It would be "an impossibility to do house to house interviews; you wouldn't find the people at home". Furthermore, these larger demographic changes made personal interviews — the McNair methodology — unsustainable in a large-scale ratings environment. While the diary method also posed logistical problems, these were not as great as those involved in interviewing. With television becoming the dominant broadcasting medium during the 1960s, and radio consequently beginning to fragment and become increasingly important outside the home, increased pressure was brought to bear upon the ratings system. Just as importantly, the public was being educated about the media and media businesses. The ratings were starting to become a public matter — and the discrepancies between the two providers were becoming more visible as a consequence.

For Don Neely, the immediate impetus for bringing the two ratings providers together in the early 1970s came from the Federation of Australian Radio Broadcasters (FARB). By contrast, Ian Muir recalls merger discussions being initiated by the ratings providers in response to narrow profit margins. FARB was not only concerned with the "differing results", but also with the costs of supporting two research companies. It set up a research committee "comprising three of the managers of the day from different network backgrounds". One of them was sent on a study trip to the United States to "try [to] find out what was the best methodology". Involving the Americans made sense. They had a history of grappling with several competing syndicated systems. They had also earlier established a Broadcast Rating Council to audit rating services and impose minimum standards (Barnathan 1964, p. 172) and had recently moved to evaluate competing ratings research systems and methodologies through the All-Radio Methodology Study (ARMS). Of particular relevance to the Australians was the study's finding that "the most reliable form of radio audience measurement was the personally placed and personally collected, pre-listed diary".

FARB called for tender for the supply of radio audience surveys, with the rationalisation of McNair and Anderson a key motive. Part of the tender was the requirement for an independent auditor to check the surveys. As a consequence of FARB's activities, McNair and Anderson merged in 1973 to become McNair-Anderson Associates. In that same year, the commercial television stations undertook to use the McNair-Anderson surveys exclusively for two years.

There was now significant consensus for the diary method as the best method to handle developments in radio and emerging reporting needs in television. Ian McNair, who worked for his father, conceded the benefits of thc diary method:

> When we merged we decided we would continue using the diary method. The main single reason that persuaded me and my colleagues about that, even though that wasn't the McNair method up till then … was that being seven days, from the same respondent, we're able to work out reach frequencies much better than we could with the single day samples. You got data over a whole week from a diary, that really persuaded us to continue on with that method for both radio and television.

Competition had been used as a method for ensuring independence of the data; independent auditing now took its place. There was now sufficient confidence in an independent auditing function and experience in audience research methodologies for the different actors — broadcasters, agencies and advertisers — to agree on standard methodologies.

An important but neglected feature of both this turn to the diary method and the determination to find a methodological resolution to competing systems and promotion of a single syndicated service was the revolution in the radio broadcasting environment which occurred in the late 1960s and early 1970s. It overturned the circumstances and times of radio consumption. Radio stations had to deal with radical changes in the sizes of their audiences, the technologies of delivery and program formats.

For Des Foster (2000), who was involved in FARB at the time and a manager of 2GB, the extent of the changes in radio after the takeoff of TV as a mass medium in Australia in the 1960s called for a fundamental reassessment of the way business was being done. Not only did the radio audience shift from night-time to daytime, but the night-time audience fell away dramatically under television's onslaught. Radio moved, in Foster's words, from being "a monstrous console in the living room, listened to by the whole family" to a situation where "television became the big console in the living room". Radio moved from being a medium for "groups" to being a medium for "individuals". It moved as much outside as inside the home, with the burgeoning development of car radios and portable transistor radios over the 1960s and through the 1970s. Transistorisation, for Foster, "gave us very very quickly the capability to transform the medium from a group medium, a medium for a family, into a medium for a person, one person". The rapid transition of radio into a "portable, personal medium" — that you could have "in your car", "take to the beach", have in your bedroom, "do what you like with" — ensured that one-radio households effectively came to an end. With it, family listening also ended: "now junior's got his own radio, and sis has got her radio and they could all be doing their homework in their different rooms, listening to different programs". The medium was transforming itself, with the major emphasis shifting to music formats. According to Des Foster:

> Suddenly the 12–18 year old group became a very identifiable segment — 12–18, whatever you like. But I mean all these age demographics became very, very relevant and it was possible to tailor programs for them. And instead of thinking in mass terms, mass audience, it was no longer quite so important to be number one in the ratings if you could be number one in 10–17. You had some very very exciting times there in the '70s and '80s, with stations emerging and blossoming. 2SM came up and dominated the scene for many years.

Ratings services were under pressure to find ways of representing this fragmentation. The panels needed to be larger to capture this increasing diversity. In particular, radio's mobility presented radical problems for ratings collection agencies. In these circumstances, diaries embodied an acceptable but always limiting "tradeoff" — they could capture radio's mobility better than competing systems could.

In the United States, these same factors caused radio ratings measurement to move from household-based audimeters to the diary method. With radio's greater mobility, the more sedentary "meter" measurement simply had to be replaced by the personal diary (Miller 1994, p. 69)![3]

This radio experience is an important precursor to the developing fragmentation of TV with the emergence of two and three or more television households, increased viewing options including those outside the home, and competition for the use of the monitor from video games and VCRs.

From Diaries to People Meters and Databases

In 1980, McNair-Anderson was partially acquired by the United Kingdom-based AGB ratings research group. One reason the Australian side was happy with this acquisition was that AGB was investing heavily in developing ratings technologies such as meter and other related technologies — the sums involved in developing ratings technologies had virtually become outside the scope of an Australian company. AGB McNair lost the metropolitan television station ratings tender to Nielsen for start-up in 1991 (Muir 1992, p. 141). Both AGB McNair and Nielsen tenders were for people meters — "an electronic push-button way of recording the presence of individual viewers, with periodic prompts and the meter itself automatically recording which channel is on at the time" (Barwise and Ehrenberg 1988, p. 176). At this point, the long-standing use of diaries for this purpose in major metropolitan television markets ceased. When Robert Maxwell died in 1992,[4] AGB worldwide went into crisis, resulting in a management buyout. ACNielsen subsequently bought out the Australian interests in 1994 and became the main provider of Australian radio and television ratings — a dominant position it held until AGB Italia won the metropolitan television stations contract in 1999 for start-up in 2001.

With people meter technology now in place to record information on which member/members of the household were watching at any one time, the mixed diary and meter system was no longer necessary in Australia. People meters, which sit on top of the television set, transmit viewing data directly via telephone lines to the ratings agency's computers. They record and store information on time, whether the TV set is on or off, the channel tuned to and the persons viewing for each household.

The trial (1989–90) and subsequent implementation (1991) of people meters in metropolitan television markets occasioned much public discussion. With the people meter trial occurring alongside the diary method over several months, differences between the two systems became evident. People meters showed more television viewing; they also picked up more viewing in non-peak times (as much as 20 per cent more) and the same amount of peak viewing. The difference in non-peak viewing can be explained by people meters being better than diaries at picking up single-person viewing. Single viewers tended to under-report their viewing under the diary method. For Mark Neely (2001), who worked at AGB McNair at the time, this under-reporting was widely known within ratings agencies prior to the introduction of the people meter. Single viewers often under-reported for both privacy reasons (not wanting other members of the household to know) and because they were less likely to remember to fill in the diary when unaccompanied. The ratings for the ABC improved — this was partly due to the greater reporting of viewing of the ABC by single viewers and to the people meters registering ABC viewing that was wrongly registered in diaries as being for another commercial station. By registering continuous viewing, people meters picked up more audience movement within programs. They showed a more random selection of programming on the part of viewers because they were measuring what viewers actually *did*, as opposed to what they *recalled* doing.

People meters were seen to have a number of advantages over the diary method. They partly removed people from the equation by their continuous recording of viewing direct from the television set. They required less of their household respondents, as people were no longer required to maintain diaries (the problem of diary-keeper's fatigue, truthfulness and stamina seemed to have been circumvented). Instead, they were now required to push buttons when they came into and went out of their television viewing (this seemed an easier and less intrusive method). For Miller (1994, p. 68), the people meter permits the "assessment of all televised offerings that can be received by the sets; it does not tire no matter how long the sets are on; and it counts reception time continuously".

This last aspect of the people meter was particularly important, as it permitted a more detailed analysis of viewing patterns within programs, including advertising breaks and measured "television surfing" — the movement of audiences from one station to another. Because the people meter apparently removed human fallibility from the equation, in that it did not require audiences to recall their viewing (only requiring them to push buttons when they began and ended their TV viewing), it seemed to promise a more accurate picture of audience behaviours. Later these aspects of the system gave rise to considerations of "button fatigue" and concerns that the system was measuring television sets being on when no one was watching — "uncovered viewing" (both considerations led to refinements of methodology).

According to Mark Neely (2000), unrealistic expectations for accuracy and levels of information were held out for the people meter by TV stations and advertising agencies in the early 1990s. These simply could not be met within the limitations of the technology. This was partly the result of the Australian market having had limited experience with meter-based systems — unlike the United States, where from the early 1950s meters were in place. Different Australian actors had to "discover" the people meter's limitations for themselves.

For all the importance given to the turn to people meters, the most significant "revolution" in ratings after 1970 was not the replacement of diaries by people meters but the quiet revolution associated with the coupling of ratings with computational power. In this context, people meters and computers permitted greater detail and a wider range of operations, better interrogation of data and additional manipulations of ratings data in analysis routines. Computer-related programs started to become a feature of syndicated audience measurement from the early 1970s in Australia. In this period, the computers were all mainframes requiring specialist programmers within ratings agencies to run them. Over the 1970s, a number of different types of services were explored or set up, including combined media-monitor products. McNair, in 1970, had as its single source Prime Prospect Profiles. AGB also provided marketing information for products and services from a single-source data collection from 1971 called Consumer Market Profiles. AGB McNair installed the first online ratings data delivery service to all the main advertising agencies in 1981. AGB Australia introduced the world's first electronic diary consumer panel in 1986. The computer concept provided for use of in-home, online portable computer terminals recording purchases of all bar-coded products to map grocery buying. The people meters were established in 1990 with a 2400-strong Sydney, Melbourne, Brisbane, Adelaide and Perth panel replacing the 1200-strong Sydney and Melbourne panel. People meters permitted the ratings results to move towards becoming an overnight service, as results from people meters from the previous day were "uploaded" to the ratings agency's computers via the telephone line for processing overnight. (This "overnight" phenomenon had initially emerged as a premium ratings service in the United States in the early 1970s for large markets such as New York and Los Angeles (Brown 1971, p. 35) — now it was becoming a feature of the basic service in Australia.) Large-scale and immediate data collection also brought a greater demand for publication of ratings results, unknown in the early history of ratings. Viewers today can look in a magazine and see the current program and station ratings.

The advent of people meters coincided with the PC revolution, which not only distributed to the individual desktop computational power that was previously the preserve of mainframes, but also encouraged the development of software programs designed to carry out data analysis routines which were previously the preserve of programmers. This combination ensured that a greater range and variety of data massaging of ratings results was able to become routinely available and delivered to the burgeoning workstations of advertisers, television and radio personnel and the like.

While the range and variety of uses of ratings data did not immediately change, these operations were definitively moving from the back rooms of ratings agencies to the front rooms of media businesses, advertisers, agencies, media planners and media buyers. What had been a more incidental, *ad hoc* and expensive research undertaking on the part of ratings agencies for selected clients requiring a programmer with advanced programming skills now became a more frequent, routine query on the part of dispersed users of ratings with a database available on their desktops and with data delivered through software programs which had routinised the work of programmers. The ratings book was being replaced by the ratings database.

ACNielsen's *Media Advisor* was integral to its provision of ratings services over the 1990s. This personal computer software package was designed to run under Microsoft Windows and allowed the user to examine audience trends over time. The database program used statistics such as ratings (TARPs), share, reach, frequency, hours and minutes viewed, audience profile and the number of people watching as its base. It contained a variety of software modules designed to cover all aspects of analysis and planning for programmers, media business sales departments, schedulers, advertising agencies and advertisers (ACNielsen 2001a).

To begin with, *Media Advisor* included modules for dealing with smaller periods of time (quarter-hour periods), with larger day-parts, and for tracking the performance of a program over time. Over the decade, additional features were added: tools to enable the user to analyse a television advertising campaign after the fact, to display the ratings according to a person's viewing patterns, to analyse audience "loyalty" for programs and stations, and to build media schedules "based on TARP or budget objectives". Software was also developed to better handle reports generated by *Media Advisor*; packages included modules for "viewing and formatting" and "managing" reports. The official ratings provider from 2001 for metropolitan television markets, OzTAM, provides a similar facility to *Media Advisor* with its AGB *WorkStation*. It has a similar audience database that promises "individual-by-individual, minute-by-minute data delivered overnight, 365 days of the year" (OzTAM 2001b).

The development of this ratings software and the databases ensured that the ratings became available to a larger variety of ratings clients who now had access to a greater variety of pathways into the ratings data which had previously been the preserve of the agencies and their largest clients. Advertising agencies and media companies alike were now conducting their own analysis of the ratings data.

With this move to a ratings database came a corresponding increase in the complexity of data collection and analysis and in the complexity of intermediate decisions on the audience and its relative value to advertisers and to stations. Media planners emerged as intermediaries in the buying and selling of advertising, based on the ratings and consumer profiles research. Other intermediaries emerged who were capable of interpreting ratings data and linking ratings data either to other datasets or to customised qualitative and quantitative survey instruments.

The "window" to the data was clearly changing to response to new circumstances, including advertiser needs. In the 1930s, soap manufacturers were the largest advertisers and their judgments were based on a simple categorisation of the audience as housewives. By 2000, there were thousands of advertisers with judgments based on hundreds of different classifications of audience composition. There is no doubt that the need to know about what audiences and consumers do has increased in its complexity, and computers have provided one means of drilling down to provide this information.

Slowly and imperceptibly, a paradigm shift occurred in ratings research with the move from the ratings book to the online-, disk- and CD-based ratings database. At one level, not much had changed: the databases provided the same basic information as the ratings books did, and people meters were still the basis for this information. But the presentation of the information had changed from being pre-structured to cover the most common analyses of the data in a book-based delivery system to a more open-ended resource capable of offering diverse users a variety of manipulations of constantly updated data based on their individual needs.

With the ratings book, the end users had very limited means of handling, responding to and interpreting data — they were inevitably constrained by the costs of data manipulation. With the ratings database, it was now the users who were doing the manipulations. The ratings agencies were now concerned to facilitate their users in their use of, and facility with, the software/database, to ensure that the analytical tools met client needs and to develop tools to allow additional queries to be made using the software. "Knowing their audience" was now the business of ratings agency clients in a new way: the program-makers, the schedulers, the space sellers and buyers, the media campaign managers/creators, etc. were now "constructing several pictures" themselves from these databases. If the ratings have always had an "end user" focus, this embodiment as a ratings database placed a special onus on the users of the data to manipulate, extract, evaluate and generally make meaningful the ratings information.

The ratings database also placed a different onus on the ratings agencies. They now needed to provide users with a sophisticated understanding of the nature and character of the audience and of the database. Ratings agencies were having to cooperate with their clients, not only to facilitate the generation of information but also to illustrate, train or otherwise inform an increasingly larger range of clients in how to use the system and carefully explain its limits. Because the focus was now on the client generating meaningful data from the system, ratings providers had a significant and ongoing information management and software training problems. Products like *Media Advisor* required the employment of people who could use the software in sophisticated ways, who knew the limitations of the database and had developed appropriate research techniques.

Like any software or database, there were significant risks for users and providers alike. Clients were being presented with a mountain of information and a variety of pathways through this information. And this carried a risk in that too much information could potentially complicate rather than simplify the decision-making of users. Another risk was that the end users might have an imperfect understanding of the meaning of ratings and ratings methodologies — leading to poor decisions on media placements, media vehicles, presentation to clients and so on. Consequently, training needs increasingly occupied personnel in ratings agencies who were looking for ways to disseminate information and to develop capacity for handling media database product on the part of those already in or likely to go into advertising agency and media positions. For clients to use the ratings efficiently and effectively, they needed to understand both the potential and limits of the data. With the increasing range of manipulations able to be done, the tolerances and uncertainties in the ratings instrument were becoming more visible and less a specialised understanding.

With only a narrow bandwidth of uses of data collected in the old system, end users and the public had been habituated into seeing the ratings through a "tablet" book metaphor. But, as for any database system, you have to know which questions to ask and why. The proliferation of user choice requires more sophisticated understandings on the part of users than were needed before.

With the move to PC-based information ratings, services around the world discovered that new clients were emerging for these services. As the principal costs for ratings measurement are "first copy" costs — the costs associated with the measurement process and producing the database — once the database is set up, the service can be sold to additional clients at minimal expense. These new clients placed additional training pressures on ratings providers.

The rapidly developing PC market also made it possible for additional services to be developed which sought to develop more comprehensive understandings of audiences in relation to different media, and not just in relation to different outlets within a particular medium. From one side, organisations such as Roy Morgan developed *Roy Morgan Single Source* based on a large interview sample (50 000) with questions related to "lifestyle and attitudes, media consumption habits (including TV, radio, newspapers, magazines, cinema, catalogues, pay-TV and the internet), brand and product usage, purchase intentions, retail visitations, service provider preferences, financial information and even recreation and leisure activities". From the other side, ratings providers like ACNielsen started to bring together their range of previously separate software/ database products.

ACNielsen's *Panorama* is one such "syndicated multi-media marketing database that integrates consumer demographics, product usage and media consumption" (ACNielsen 2001b). Here the aim is to add value by fusing together its various products. In mid-2001, *Panorama* was drawing on ACNielsen's TV and radio ratings data, its readership surveys and specifically designed product and service usage questionnaires, with plans to "incorporate consumer goods purchasing information from the ACNielsen Homescan consumer panel". This fusion product promised media planners and sellers the capacity to "go beyond demographics when analysing media consumption patterns". It was sold as enabling media strategists to "conduct detailed analyses of viewers by demographics, print and television media, and product usage"; brand managers to "define target markets and profile consumers by demographics, lifestyle habits, product usage and media consumption"; and media salespersons to "learn about your target's buyergraphics and doergraphics" and "profile programme audiences against category and major brand users to demonstrate to advertisers the niche audience efficiencies of lower rating off peak programmes".

The trend within ratings over the 1990s and into the 2000s was in two identifiably different directions. First there was the consolidation of various medium specific ratings services into larger integrated "all of media" ratings services. These recognised audiences as audiences for a variety of media products, as consumers of a range of goods and as possessing certain values and attitudes. The second trend was towards the ever more fine-grained drilling down within a particular medium so that a more complete "window" on audiences for that medium, for that program and for that advertising could be provided.

Sometimes these two trends are brought together. Current trials in Europe and the United States with "wrist watch" and "pager" technologies suggest that this method promises both greater breadth and depth of ratings results. As these technologies are designed to automatically collect "a person's exposure to encoded radio, TV and cable programming no matter when and where it occurs", they should permit a greater appreciation of media exposure across several media, as well as within a particular medium. In doing so, these technologies promise to eliminate the "need for people to constantly track their listening or viewing behaviour" by writing something down in a diary or pushing a button to indicate their viewing (Arbitron 2001). People are expected to carry such watches and meters for around fifteen hours per day (but will they always comply?). Additionally, both devices permit the rationalisation of the collection of ratings information across several media forms by offering a "one stop shop".

The "everyday watch" that ACNielsen in Australia is committed to is a specially designed watch which picks up sounds from wherever that person goes; these sounds are matched with sounds in a database. The portable people meter developed by Arbitron in the United States is a similar product and is similarly worn by subjects over the course of the day. Both are convergence technologies, as they are designed to combine television, cable and radio audience measurement into a single system.

If widely adopted, such products are likely to cause a new round of system-wide readjustments. On the basis of its US and UK trials, Arbitron (2001) claimed there was a "higher average quarter-hour audiences for all the combined electronic media" — higher for broadcast TV and cable and equivalent for radio. TV and cable viewing were up because of higher reported viewing on the part of men and of people under the age of 35 and because of the system's capacity to track viewing outside the home.

Despite all these developments, ratings instruments are straining under the weight of increasing social and cultural differentiations and proliferating media outlets, which is making it harder to develop and maintain representative panels and to measure "small audiences". As Ken Sievers (2000), former managing director of Anderson Analysis and a consultant with SBS, points out:

> We have had a major revolution in media measurement in that we now have cable and satellite Pay services also [need] to be measured. Digital transmissions really complicate measurement of audiences by meters because until now the meter was placed on or near the TV set, and it picked up the frequency emitted by the tube. In this way, it was able to identify the station to which the set was tuned. Now, with digital, a number of channels can be run through the one frequency and so the whole measurement technology has had to change. There are presently

> 56 pay channels as well as a number of interactive style services which will be available. There will be issues to be resolved with VCR recording and there are a number of further new services on the drawing board which can be run through the digital system.

The trend towards more tailored ratings, customised at the individual level, as well as "micro-audiences" and the shift of audiences to diverse media, will no doubt have a similar effect on television to the one it has had on radio. These different considerations no doubt weighed heavily on the minds of the technical people and executives from the networks when they met to write the specifications for the tender and to evaluate the rival metropolitan television ratings tenders in late 1999.

ATR/OzTAM versus ACNielsen

The ratings debate of late 1999 and the first half of 2001 was both similar to and unlike previous debates. Like the first people meter contract, it was over a change of provider as the incumbent. ACNielsen lost the lucrative metropolitan television ratings contract to newcomer AGB Italia — Advanced Television Research (ATR) — which provided OzTAM with its data. Unlike previous controversies, which were between different research technologies and methodologies, the OzTAM/ACNielsen controversy was over different results using the same people meter technology. This similarity undoubtedly made the reported discrepancies both surprising and disturbing.

There were two parts to this debate. The first part occurred in late 1999 in the aftermath of the announcement of a change in ratings provider. It centred on the networks' motives for dumping the incumbent in favour of a comparatively unknown newcomer. The second part of the controversy occurred in the first half of 2001 as discrepancies between the two systems became evident, and set the stage for public dissension over just "whose" figures were accurate.

Any change in the provider of ratings conventions is bound to excite controversy. The incumbent enjoyed all the advantages of incumbency — it had both experience and reputation as a known agency and service providing reliable and comprehensive measurement for a variety of media outlets and related syndicated services. It had been providing the "convention" for several years and in its provision of several syndicated services was well placed to provide ratings services for converging media environments. Furthermore, this was an incumbent that not only traced its history back to the beginning of ratings research in Australia, but also carried the Nielsen name — a global name in ratings technology and the major supplier of ratings services within comparable English-language markets.

By contrast, the new provider had to establish its credibility with both prospective users — particularly those not involved in making the decision to select the new provider — and with the broader public. In this case, ATR was a "new player", unknown in the Australian market. Its reputation for ratings services was in Latin America and Europe. Rather than setting its credibility against that of the incumbent, ATR promoted its service as an innovation — a technically superior service. Additionally, it attempted to secure the services of credible figures drawn from within the Australian ratings industry in the period leading up to and immediately subsequent to being awarded the contract. After the award of the contract, Ian Muir, a prominent figure in audience measurement in Australia, became OzTAM's CEO. Muir had been involved in drawing up the specifications for the ratings tender, and had led the losing AGB McNair bid for the people meter contract a decade earlier. His presence was critical to the local standing of the new provider.) ATR also relocated to Australia for the critical start-up period at least one of its European experts (Wilmoth 2001).

Further complicating the credibility problem facing the new provider was the move on the part of the television networks for them — and not the ratings agency — to "own" the data. ATR is supervised by OzTAM, a company established and financed by the three commercial networks. While ATR does the work, OzTAM owns the results and sells them to subscribers. This structure raised important and legitimate concerns as to the potential for conflicts of interest in the provision of ratings data. While it is not uncommon for media outlets to "own the data" internationally, this was not the Australian practice. This move raised several concerns about just how independent, rigorous and believable the OzTAM data were likely to be. Just how much control over information was being demanded by those who paid for it and how much was relinquished by the ratings provider? These integrity concerns were a real issue for those users not involved in the decision to change ratings providers, such as advertisers and media buyers. They were also a major concern for network television's competitors, such as pay TV providers. In a local climate where free-to-air television networks are widely perceived both locally and internationally as having inhibited pay TV and other new kinds of television development, the ATR decision was inevitably going to be read as another move by the networks to protect their patch at the expense of others. Certainly pay TV providers had less reason to cooperate with OzTAM, the provider of only free-to-air ratings, than with ACNielsen, an independent company which provided ratings for several media services.

As Miller (1994, p. 66) notes, persuading the full range of media players that a particular technology for collecting and analysing data for their audiences provides "the basis for their costly transactions" and involves the research firms in "an elaborate ritual of testing and 'validating' the new measurement system". OzTAM/ATR had to "prove" itself, particularly in the cross-over period between the two systems. With the television networks initially claiming that their choice of ATR was based on its "superior technology", they undoubtedly expected the new system to provide very little in the way of surprises. It would be more a tweaking of the system to reveal greater levels of detail on exposure to programs and advertising, and to prepare for the circumstances of television environments as much as seven years hence. However, what they got in the initial set-up period of the ATR panels in early 2001 was something quite different.

In the first weeks of the new rating period of 2001, there were considerable differences between the OzTAM and ACNielsen results. In the week beginning 11 February, Jane Schulze (2001a) reported OzTAM figures for Melbourne as Nine: 30.5 per cent, Seven: 29.5 per cent and Ten: 19.3 per cent, while ACNielsen figures had Nine on 33.4 per cent, Seven on 26.7 per cent and Ten on 21.4 per cent. The OzTAM figures "stunned the industry", giving rise to concerns that the system might be "seriously flawed". Commenting in the *The Age*, Ross Warneke (2001a) explored the implications:

> Top-rating shows on Nine such as *Friends*, *E.R.* and even the 6.00 p.m. news and *A Current Affair* suddenly have lost up to a third of their viewers. Nine's most successful Australian drama, *Water Rats*, performed so badly last week that, under normal circumstances, its future would be in jeopardy. But these are not normal circumstances.

While the discrepancies between the old and new results narrowed over the year, as the OzTAM panel was "fine-tuned" and new program lineups became established, by May it was clear that the OzTAM ratings system had resulted in an improved outlook for Seven (Lawson 2001). Nine may have won seven of the twelve ratings weeks up to that point, but it was only "narrowly beating Seven with a 30.5 per cent share compared to Seven's 30 per cent" (2001). Seven had narrowed Nine's lead considerably. This encouraged projections by analysts such as Credit Suisse First Boston of increased earnings for Seven and diminishing earnings for Nine over coming years (Schulze 2001b). SBS's ratings also went up (SBS thought the larger sample and new panel better covered minority and special-interest groups); the ABC's ratings went down; and the results for the Ten Network were mixed, though they improved over the year.

At the same time, the ratings results were also indicating trends towards less overall television viewing. This was predicted to translate into pressure on advertising revenues as media buyers reassessed the value of free-to-air television. It also showed that audiences were moving into and out of programs in ways which considerably complicated understandings of program popularity. David Keig of Keig and Co had taken a snapshot of who was watching every minute to "track the way a viewer flicks from network to network" (Dale 2001). Based on Keig's analysis of the average prime-time program in March 2001, only "36 per cent of those who dipped ended up watching the whole show, while 51 per cent of the supposed audience watched less than a third" (Dale 2001). For Keig, "[m]ost programs now are like revolving doors, with people coming in and out all the time". These audience behaviours would need to be factored into media buying and advertising placement.

A damaging controversy ensued. The controversy was not initially centred on the difficult methodological issues surrounding the construction and implementation of ratings systems, particularly its panels. Quite the contrary — it began as a controversy with a far simpler narrative. This was a "war" among the commercial interests of the various parties: Nine supported the ACNielsen results because it conferred upon them an unambiguous number one spot; Seven and later Ten supported OzTAM as its figures gave them their best chance in years to whittle away Nine's lead. There were allegations of "greed" on the part of those reluctant to accept the "umpire's verdict" — with Nine being seen as reneging on its own earlier ringing endorsement for the new official convention holder, OzTAM. Indeed, the Nine Network's chief executive office, David Leckie, was widely reported as having pushed the hardest for the AGB Italia bid. (In a curious way, this helped the "standing" of the OzTAM system among non-television station users of the system, as it indicated the "independence" of the system in that it could provide bad news for those who paid for it.)

The consensus underpinning the ratings system seemed to be falling apart. As none of the vested interests involved could settle the matter in their favour, queries about both systems intensified. Was there some circumstance polluting what ought to have be an objective, empirical project of determining the ratings? There was a crisis in confidence in the system. Journalists reported warnings from media buyers that their clients were "holding back from buying TV advertising" as the controversy continued (Schulze 2001a). With advertiser media buying decisions starting to be affected, a growing consensus from advertising agencies, media planners and media buyers was that the damaging controversy needed speedy resolution. Intermediaries drawn from advertising, such as the Media Federation (representing "most media specialist agencies"), emerged seeking to "broker a truce between warring factions". From their point of view, the issue would not be resolved by maintaining two parallel ratings systems — that would only "continue to show that they were different". The central issue for the Media Federation was, in its president Peter Cornelius's words, "why they are different" (Schulze 2001a). Because of the *prima facie* similarity between the two systems, the methodology — how ratings panels and data collection techniques are constructed — became the issue around which the conflict could be resolved. Was one of the panels flawed? Was it ACNielsen's panel or OzTAM's? Or both? Or neither?

With such a damaging "stand off" in place, undermining the credibility of the convention, and with two panels causing consternation in circumstances where advertisers had become accustomed to one agreed standard, an independent audit became necessary. Professor Peter Danaher, a New Zealand expert on sampling, was brought in to "adjudicate" the dispute — that is, to explain the differences between them. Central to his brief was the assessment of the representativeness of the two panels. In making his assessment, census data on the makeup and character of the Australian population would be central. While the report is confidential, the absence of commentary would seem to indicate that Danaher's report contained few surprises. It is almost as if his appointment as auditor brought the controversy to an end.

When Danaher reported his results, the differences between the OzTAM and ACNielsen results were narrowing; there was a growing consensus that the differences between them had been exaggerated, that there were not serious enough flaws in the OzTAM panels to warrant revisiting the ratings contract. Indeed, by June 2001, Ross Warneke (2001b) was reporting in *The Age* that the OzTAM figures "were now regarded as reliable"; a single ratings currency was needed to bring the system back into some equilibrium — so all had to "live with it" despite some having continuing misgivings. Danaher's report seemed to confirm these estimations of the reliability of OzTAM. Because perceptions matter — the perceived accuracy and credibility of the data from the ratings are important, just as they have been important from the moment researchers like Andersons and McNair opened shop in the 1940s — the auditor's report was there to publicly restore "faith" in the system.

As Julius Barnathan (1964, p. 72) noted in the context of public discussion of ratings in an earlier period in the United States, discrepancies between ratings systems are not issues to do with the rigging or fixing of ratings by broadcasters, but turn on the "operational flaws in the techniques used by each rating service". Typically, these flaws are "known to the sophisticated researcher but unknown to the layman". The problem the lay person encounters in these public controversies is the uncertainty of the ratings — the fact that they are "estimates" not "hardfact yardsticks" (Barnathan 1964, p. 173).

While the discrepancies between the two systems may be unsurprising to an insider, and may well be within acceptable bounds, to an outsider these same discrepancies point to flaws which undermine confidence in the ratings and therefore the decisions flowing from these.

All concerned had been educated in the "the problem" facing contemporary ratings technologies. Panels, by their nature, are "samples". They are liable to error, as the media players know. OzTAM's website (2001b) foregrounds the fact that, "like any survey, a sample will never be as accurate as surveying the entire population", so "results obtained can and do fluctuate". Anyone running an analysis using OzTAM's data will therefore need to "always consider the size of the sample from which you are drawing your results". Samples are part of the tradeoff for ratings research — no two samples are going to be exactly the same. It is difficult even with larger panels to be representative in a fragmenting media environment increasingly characterised by niche audiences and a culturally diverse society. It is therefore likely that both the OzTAM and ACNielsen figures are right.

The concerns that the OzTAM and ACNielsen debate has generated about the representativeness of panels, their size and therefore the accuracy of modern audience ratings techniques will not disappear. The increasing individualisation and sheer quantity of data create greater uncertainty and will put pressure on panel size. The problem existing panels pose for broadcasters such as SBS, according to Ken Sievers (2000), is that the current sample sizes have been "relatively efficient in measuring the mass audiences of the commercial stations who achieve quite high levels of ratings" but present difficulties when dealing with smaller, niche audiences.

OzTAM and ACNielsen were competing in the tender to become the "official" reality for audience measurement, but when their results conflicted the debate was not resolved among the players themselves but played out in the public domain, with the protagonists being the owners and users of the ratings. The issue of "truth" was not simply methodology, but the very process of coordination and agreement among the different players who defined and agreed on the social convention. Public trust is also a part of the agreement. The OzTAM and ACNielsen debate brought in all the media players because they all have a stake in how ratings, as currency, are defined and accepted.

Conclusion

Syndicated audience research such as that involving ratings is necessarily contentious. Some of this contention is structural because the reporting of syndicated research in ratings comparisons can never drill down to the levels of specificity required by the various players. Standardisation produces tension. In this sense, the ratings will always "fail" to satisfy the need for a more detailed picture of the audience. By definition, ratings systems only know the audience in certain capacities. The various interested industry parties — broadcasters, program producers, advertisers, regulators, media planners, ad agencies — need to supplement ratings with customised research.

The "problem with the ratings" is not so much a problem with methodology and sampling, as is commonly claimed, but with the ways various players perceive the ratings system and its limits. In circumstances where the ratings are seen as delivering "the perfect" picture of the audience, the structural imperfections of syndicated research — arrived at as they are by negotiations among several parties and interests — are ignored. Customised research is necessarily able to give a more in-depth picture of audience behaviours. It is not constrained by syndicated research's need to establish aggregate measures and agreement among dispersed stakeholders.

Research firms who supply customised research routinely comment on the imperfections and blunt character of ratings research, pointing to the need for alternative (additional) knowledge and research on audiences. In much the same way, public and academic commentary on the ratings system routinely draws attention to the conventional, constructed character of the ratings; their closure to social differentiation; their hegemonic construction as arbiters of program value and decision-making within the industry in comparison, for example, to the fickleness and changeability of audiences themselves (Ang 1996, pp. 171–94).

These several constructions of the ratings co-persist, alternatively overly inflating and diminishing the value and purpose of the ratings. This public "sound and fury" over the ratings can sometimes obscure the often precise understanding of the limits — and therefore value

— of the ratings on the part of the various actors and the complementary character of customised and syndicated research.

It is important to acknowledge the "public" character of ratings research as syndicated research. This aspect of ratings research is sometimes ignored when the ratings are considered as industry-imposed orderings of diverse audience behaviours and pleasures. From the perspective of the ratings provider, the ratings system is at base an auditing, and therefore accountability, measure. Those involved in delivering ratings systems understand themselves to be providing a public service. They necessarily operate "above" the interested stakeholders, who nonetheless support this auditing service and make it possible.

All the ratings people we interviewed for this research had a keen understanding of this public-service character and a keen appreciation of the obligations it entailed. Indeed, one of the most important distinctions between customised and rating research is that customised research is generally privately owned, is not subject to the transparent developmental processes and agreements necessary to be secured for syndicated research, and is therefore not as available to the same public monitoring and auditing as ratings research. In this context, the ratings providers' sense of their own public duty and service in providing the ratings is grounded in an auditing function — not a surveillance and disciplining function.

Private research companies run the service, the data are "owned" by either the companies concerned or a consortium of media businesses, and the "cost" of getting access to the ratings is prohibitive for wide public disclosure. But over the last 60 years, the public character of ratings research has become more, not less, evident. As we noted, ratings began as an internal audit amongst radio stations in a market; now the same ratings are "public", with the routine publication of headline ratings information and potentially public information for increasingly diverse media and non-media actors as ratings companies exploit what economists call the "public good" character of ratings research.

With the move towards ratings databases and the interlinking of several databases, the function and character of syndicated and customised research alike are changing. It is becoming increasingly common for syndicated research instruments such as ratings databases to form one basis for customised research activities which draw on other databases and qualitative research methodologies. In this way, "ratings research" databases are becoming an integral part of customised research. Ken Snfspublicity@bigpond.comievers' work at SBS provides one instance of this tailoring. Here the ratings instrument is one available resource for various kinds of customised research. The fire-walls between customised and ratings research are coming down as ratings agencies, responding to this demand, are providing diverse pathways through ratings data for increasingly diverse users. The "service" character of the ratings instrument is being extended in ways analogous to the "data mining" undertaken by private corporations on Australian Bureau of Statistics census data. Does this distract from the "core" task of providing independent, reliable and benchmarked data? Probably not, as any compromising of independence and of the ratings standard-setting function would diminish the market value of the research base for diverse users. But it certainly does mean that the ratings instrument is becoming less embodied in a "separate" system with quasi-firewalls between it and customised research activities and becoming more a function capable of being rigorously separated out from other uses of the datasets. In theory, this function could be carried out by a diverse range of actors.

The industry audience measurement process has come full cycle. As we noted, audience measurement started as a customised research program within advertising agencies. The gap between syndicated research and customised research has narrowed as "syndicated" research becomes an integral part of processes of customised research.

The relationship of media information to the users of that information is a complex one. Our brief survey of the ratings system gives us some guide to the key issues and trends. First there is the ongoing requirement, from the broadcasting and advertising industry, for the independence of the data collection and analysis which extends to ownership — advertising agencies and station managers as interested parties should not own ratings research companies — and the ongoing need for an independent auditor to check the data collection methods to ensure that they are transparent and not biased in any way. Second, it is in the interest of all parties to protect the integrity or "honest broker" status of the syndicated research so as to deliver "disinterested" research. Third, there is an obvious trend towards an increase in the frequency with which ratings are collected, an accompanying expansion of sample size and the emergence of more finely grained analytical tools to track audience movement within programs. Fourth, there has been a shift from "homes" to "individuals" as the unit for ratings data collection, owing to the increased number of radio and television sets in households. Fifth, the ratings system is becoming progressively merged with other data sets, whether these are ratings for different media or consumer profiles. In the former case, this is a response to convergence and the need to think across several media forms. In the latter case, it is becoming an integral part of the customised research industry. And finally, the increasing fragmentation of the media system and distribution platforms (VCR, cable, video on demand, etc.), together with dispersal of television viewing inside and outside the home, is presenting considerable difficulties for ratings technology to capture.

Acknowledgment

We would like to thank Liz Ferrier and Jason Sternberg for their assistance in preparing this chapter. This research was made possible by a grant from the Australian Key Centre for Cultural and Media Policy.

Notes

1 For a useful and publicly available description of basic ratings terminology see the OzTAM website: www.oztam.com.au (OzTam 2001a).

2 This need for structural separation is one of the reasons why ratings companies intent on expansion can either expand into other related syndicated research activities domestically or expand offshore into syndicated research, either by takeover or winning syndicated research contracts.

3 In 1970, US television was using a combination of meter (1200 meters) and diary (2200 diaries): the meter indicated when, on what station and for how long television sets were turned on, while the diaries provided an indication of who within these households was watching (Brown 1971, pp. 32–33).

4 Robert Maxwell became the principal shareholder in AGB Research in the late 1980s following the company's unsuccessful attempt to enter the US market.

CHAPTER 3

Small Worlds: Research on Children and the Media in Australia

Patricia Gillard

Introduction

The last 20 years of research on children, television and new media in Australia has turned on its head what was once common wisdom. This chapter explores two trajectories of that research. One story is about change and innovation in knowledge about children as media audiences. The other story is about public discussion of audiences and the shifts in government policy and in the media industries which limit that debate.

Anxiety about the Child Audience

The introduction of television in the 1950s and 1960s did not initially raise alarms about children as an audience. "Family" viewing was promoted as the incentive to purchase a TV set, and programming reflected the expectation that most viewing would be in family groups. Concerns about the economic viability of television meant that the needs of separate audiences were not considered at this early stage (Keys 1999, p. 15).

By the late 1970s, there was much more anxiety about television and children. An American journalist stands out as promoting the idea that television was bad for children unless it was strictly controlled by parents. The title of Marie Winn's (1977) book, *The Plug-in Drug*, seemed to be an indictment of television. It was no such thing, however. She blamed parents for "drugging" their children with too much TV and said that those who were actively promoting quality programming were merely trying to develop a superior drug. Her book was based on anecdote, not research. In ways that were to become familiar in most journalistic writing, she worked on the guilt of mothers (the word "parent" fooled no one) about their children watching TV at all.

Winn was the most articulate of a tradition of middle class "experts" who looked at the industry ratings and focused on presumed "neglect" by parents whose children watched TV for long hours. These were the "heavy viewers" who became the focus of so much research concern and social commentary. Later research showed that "heavy viewers" were more likely to come from poorer families, and viewing for long periods was accompanied by a wide range of activities (Palmer 1986b; Gillard 1994).

Research conducted in Australia led by Kevin Tindall (Tindall et al. 1975) mirrored the horror story genre, but focused on the TV rather than on parents. At Sydney Teachers' College, he published *Television: 20th Century Cyclops*, based on surveys of the amount and type of viewing undertaken by children. The research inside the covers is very useful for giving a summary of children's viewing at the time. It did not entirely support his picture of TV as a kind of monster, keeping children mesmerised and making them "bad" if they viewed the wrong programs, or viewed TV for too long. Tindall was reflecting a set of assumptions within American "effects" tradition of media research: that children were passive receivers of TV messages.

Most research from this time portrayed children alone with the TV and "captured" by it (Tindall et al. 1975; Dunn 1977; Cullingford 1984). This interpretation came directly from the authors' assumptions and methods. Surveys of children — or more often their parents — would quantify hours watched and categorise types of programs. Measures of "aggressive" behaviour or of school tests would then be correlated and an argument made about television's impact. There was very little notice taken of the viewing environment or children's own interactions and experiences. For this reason, we now have little information about the ways in which children were engaging with programming, or its role in the family, during the 1970s. It may be that changes in program content or scheduling were affecting children and families in alarming ways. However, surveys of viewing hours and correlations with behaviour defined as "aggressive" are too far removed from the viewing environment to give a reliable, retrospective picture of what was happening at that time.

Policy Changes and Network Funding of Research

In Australia, concerns about television and children were articulated by a number of groups, including the South Australian Council for Children's Film and Television, now Young Media Australia. Patricia Edgar, the author of *Children and Screen Violence* (1977), was one of a group of prominent activists who worked to develop regulations for children's television, which resulted in the Children's Television Standards in 1984. The Children's Program Committee had been established in 1979 as part of a process of deciding on the quality of "C" (Children's classified) programs, a quota of TV shows made especially for the child audience and scheduled on commercial channels at set times such as 4.00 to 5.00 p.m. The Children's Program Committee comprised seven members — three industry and four public members. Its task was to advise the Australian Broadcasting Tribunal on classification of "C" programs. Its principal virtue was its creation of a process whereby researchers, community members and TV producers cooperated to support quality children's television. I was a member of the Children's Program Committee from 1988 until 1992.

During the 1980s, links were also made between television networks and universities, resulting in research about children as an audience that was relevant to program makers. Grant Noble (1975) had begun this work early, conducting innovative research about children's social uses of television programs; however, with generous funding from the networks, he was able to do larger field studies over two years or more. HSV7 in Melbourne supported a program of research led by Mary Nixon at Monash University (see Nixon 1981), Penny Spence at TCN9 gained network funding for a program, *TV: The Child's View*, which I conducted with Henry Mayer at Sydney University (see Palmer 1986a, 1986b), while TVW7 in Perth funded research at Murdoch University led by Bob Hodge (see Hodge and Tripp 1986). All of these focused on children's own understandings of program content, rather than adult judgments and measures of amounts of viewing. Even the covers of 1980s research publications reflected a shift in thinking about children as an audience, focusing as they did on both their activity within the TV space and their engagement with programs (see Hodge and Tripp 1986; Palmer 1986b; Nixon 1981).

Research which incorporated children's experience of viewing confirmed what child development professionals had been saying: the child audience was more than a single group. For their part, producers found studies based on new concepts of interaction with TV content to be salient to their creative work.

Both a number of international studies and Australian research confirmed that children's tastes at younger ages for cartoons and comedy were very consistent. Older girls, aged eleven to fourteen years, by contrast had more realistic tastes, enjoying personal dramas set in everyday contexts, especially Australian ones. Boys of the same age still loved the adventure of goodies and baddies in cartoon and action stories, though they wanted the baddies to win sometimes. Research which spoke to children rather than their parents, and described their viewing in detail, identified definite tastes and showed with certainty that there was no such thing as "the child audience". Instead, there were distinctive groups within the age group. Gender and age were strongly associated with changes in tastes, interests and understanding.

The Shift to Descriptive Studies and Children's Experience

In Australia, the funding provided by TV networks made it possible, for the first time, to design larger scale and longer running studies. However, there was a profound mistrust within the academic community of those who accepted network money. It was assumed that such monies would compromise the research and reduce it to the kind of "administrative" audience research criticised by Todd Gitlin for serving industry interests rather than providing the audience with knowledge about itself (Nightingale 1996, p. 4). The funding was certainly given on the tacit understanding that research would be relevant to children's television programming. However, it was researchers, not the networks, who led the new developments in theory and method.

The networks primarily saw this funding as gaining them "brownie points" in their public licence renewal hearings. I was called as an "expert witness" for Channel Nine in its 1984 licence renewal hearing. The network's main anxiety was that I produce the report in time for the hearings! With the Nine Network seemingly not interested in the detail of the research, I had a very free hand in all aspects of the research itself, including the fieldwork, analysis and reporting. Ian Fairweather of Network Ten was more engaged. Over the next few years, he used researchers in small teams to develop pilot programs and then tested these to gauge children's understanding and interest.

When researchers began to use observation in natural surroundings, or interviews which were flexible enough to follow unexpected findings from children's own reports, they started to build a detailed picture of the patterns in children's lives around the TV set. I started to use observation methods in 1982, researching individual children in 23 homes for nine hours each. It was almost a shock to see how active and interactive the children were. Their viewing was very sociable, involving friends, dogs and cats and even fish, and it was immediately clear that the supposed "zombie" trance was rarely seen — and then only when children concentrated hard on favourite programs. More recent research on preschool viewers in New Zealand has described similar patterns (Lealand 1998). Research with infants shows they begin to make meanings from different television programs from eighteen months onwards (Cupitt et al. 1998).

The claim that children are an "active" rather than a "passive" audience does not mean they are wise and critical viewers, nor does it mean they are "unaffected" by TV. Children are canny in making the most of what is available to them, in their curiosity about the world and their desire for fun. The quality and creativity of the programs they view are crucial in determining what they can experience and respond to in the time spent viewing.

This observational research also revealed important features of the social context of children's viewing. It showed how their TV spaces were dominated by fathers who kept the remote control and chose the programs once they were home, how mothers in wealthier families structured children's leisure and kept turning the TV off whereas poorer families lived around the TV set and chose "family" programming. The TV was ignored if other tasks were important, or programs were dull. British researchers have coined the term "moral economy" to describe the constraints on children's viewing from economic and social aspects in and beyond their TV rooms (Morley 1986, p. 70). They see the relationships around the set as a microcosm of the "cultural power" exercised in wider society. We now understand that children actively negotiate family values and share their viewing experiences, most often with schoolmates. They shape an understanding of the world and themselves from whatever emotional and creative resources they have in their homes and schools.

Children's Changing Television Experience

Knowledge about children as media audiences is not directly perceived. Concepts and meanings are socially constructed and researchers, like anyone else, use available concepts to interpret children's behaviour around the TV set. If surveys are used to study audiences, interpretation of their behaviour is funnelled through the researcher's concepts and language from the study's inception. The researcher has more direct involvement with audience members in group discussions or observations in natural settings such as people's homes, but even here individuals actively construct what is spoken and seen, and researchers interpret and reconstruct those findings as if the behaviour is routine. In the observation research I conducted in the early 1980s, family members never appeared undressed in front of the TV, though a few grasped towels around their bodies as they came from the shower, and laughed that they did not usually cover themselves. Because the knowledge gained from research is constrained and produced by the assumptions and methods used, a discussion of children as media audiences must also be a discussion of the ways audiences are thought about, and the methods that are used to study them.

How, then, have children's uses for television changed over two decades? And how have television content and the changes in media forms altered what children watch? Because the research of the 1980s did include descriptions of viewing experiences rather than survey measures alone, comparisons can be made, although these are interpretations of broad patterns in a shifting environment.

The first difference, based on research by the Australian Broadcasting Authority (Sheldon et al. 1994; Sheldon and Loncar 1996) is that children are watching the news, rather than avoiding it as they seemed to ten years ago. There is still a high level of discomfort with the realistic violence and images of hungry children or mistreated animals, especially during meal times. However, news does seem to be part of most children's viewing routine.

The second major change is the greater interest and sophistication of 1990s and early 2000s audiences in attending closely to special effects, especially in horror films and those which construct violent scenes made possible by video players. Many children have learnt to make use of video replay, using videos or movies taped from TV. They even use freeze frame and constantly repeat segments to find out exactly how special effects are put together. Some are reassured when they spot how these effects are constructed. Video players were not available 20 years ago. As children have gained some control over TV images, they have become more fascinated with how special effects are produced and used in storytelling.

Sport is also far more dominant in the tastes and interests of older boys. Ten years ago, boys aged eleven years and over were closer to younger children in their tastes. This change may well reflect greater sports programming across the week and also the impact of such programming on pay TV. Boys aged thirteen to seventeen years are now amongst the "heaviest" viewers of TV according to ACNielsen (1999), whereas ten years ago girls watched for longer hours on average than did boys.

Looking carefully at children's understanding of the narrative and visual style of the *Kaboodle Cartoons*, Lee Burton (1993) suggests that children may have changed since the 1980s in their ability to understand TV itself. With children's greater knowledge of TV and film conventions, TV programs are able to demand that children draw on their social experience to a greater extent in order to enjoy the story. The research established that children's interpretations depended as much on their social experience as it did on their age and related developmental level. For example, with the cartoon *Molly*

Makes Music, children who had experienced separation were more sympathetic to the small girl named Molly, whose parents had separated. Children who had always lived with one parent were unsympathetic to Molly.

While these findings might seem common sense, this is not the way that children's relationships with TV have traditionally been studied. The recent findings are a result of applying cultural theories to the analysis of television programs. TV programs create a range of interpretations, and audience members draw on their own experience to place themselves in the story and to form their own conclusions.

Children's Uses of New Media

In the last twenty years, research practices have changed the kinds of questions asked and the answers obtained about new media. We are now more interested in how the family environment provides a context for children's uses; its rules and spaces and economic resources. We want to know where family members now watch TV, when and with whom? What is the relationship between computers, TV screens and other media? Who watches and plays with whom, who chooses, who decides, who pays? Do men still dominate the remote control and do women and children keep up their other activities while viewing? What personal media are carried outside the house, and what are brought in by friends and family? How do the program formats and characters which go across media and show themselves in toys and merchandising also inhabit family spaces and influence social values?

If survey statistics alone are used to give a picture of child audiences in this "moral economy", then the audience is becoming "fragmented". A 1997 press report claimed children were watching one hour a week less than in 1995, with Saturday and weekday mornings showing most attrition (Bye 1997, p. 16). The *numbers* are certainly breaking up, and possibly being distributed across a larger number of media forms and contents. One commercial survey estimated that 33 per cent of Australian children owned their own computer and 43 per cent had access to the internet (Bulbeck 1998).[1]

However, children have always moved between different activities, or undertaken them in parallel and in the company of others. Figures about the child audience are deceptive if they treat single media in isolation or assume children are a static presence in front of it.

A detailed picture of how children interact with new media has slowly been emerging. The largest study in Australia is the Australian Broadcasting Authority's own research, *Families and Electronic Entertainment* (Cupitt and Stockbridge 1996). Reflecting international trends, its subject is "the social world of the home and respondents' self-definitions of the meaning of electronic entertainment" (Sefton-Green 1998, p. 14). The research documents the rules and routines of families around new media, which are very consistent with rules about time and content originally applied to television (Gillard 1989). In general, they concluded that electronic entertainment had taken its place alongside traditional leisure, and the majority of parents were happy with the balance in their children's lives and activities. Australian families were adapting new media to their household values.

Kevin Durkin's (1995) review of studies of children's uses of computer games internationally gave similar reassurances about the family context. Computer games take up an average of 28 minutes a day (ACNielsen 1999), but computer games are not used "addictively". The picture of how children play computer games is reminiscent of the early days of TV. Durkin (1995, p. 3) reports that "social play with computer games is twice as high as social involvement in other media use" and "computer game play appears to have improved relations within some families".

Recent research on computer game playing in Australia has included the observational study of players at video arcades with some follow-up interviews. Group discussions were also held to explore issues from the point of view of players. The social and interactive nature of the game-playing environment, and playing with peers, was emphasised. The social nature of play was seen by players as mitigating the aggressive content of the games. Players also valued the control they exercised over the game, and the degree of autonomy they felt they exercised, compared with the viewing of film and TV (Durkin and Aisbett 1999).

The Emergence of the Internet in Children's Lives

In the absence of a large-scale Australian study, it is necessary to piece together a picture of children's actual uses of the internet at home. The Australian Bureau of Statistics (1998) tells us that in 1997 there were 1.7 million children aged five to seventeen years who frequently used a computer. This was half (51 per cent) of the children in their age group. The computer was used by approximately one-fifth of the children aged ten to seventeen years for internet-based activities, with internet use increasing slightly as children grew older. At five to nine years, 4 per cent of computer users were accessing the internet.

Within one study, *Young People, Gambling and the Internet* (ACOSS 1997), was a description of a group of heavy internet users, or "netheads" as they called themselves. This was a specially selected group, aged twelve to 21 years and mostly boys. Their time online was spent on Internet Relay Chat, participating in gossip about technical aspects of the net and sometimes "cybersex" discussions. However, there was little interest in pornography (ACOSS 1997, p. 47). What marked this group as different to others their age was their excellent understanding of electronic commerce and the possibilities for future online services

Two British studies give a view of new research approaches and the kinds of insight they may give us. One, described briefly on the project website, is exploring the domain of children's social networks online to investigate how the internet is "shaping their use of time, friendships and sense of community, local and global" (*Cyberkids* 1999). The second study was conducted on a broad scale, to map children's access to and use of screen-based media and its significance in their lives *(Young People, New Media* 1999). The detailed findings about uses of the internet at home and school may or may not find parallels in the lives of Australian children. The authors find inequalities in the access to new media consistently associated with age, gender and social class, and report that schools are one of the few institutions working against such a trend. Just as important is their use of a typology of "media styles" to describe the relationship between content interests and the forms of media that are preferred. Categories such as "screen entertainment fans", "low media users" and "specialist media users" all define groups of young people who are distinctive in their ways of mixing media within their daily lives (Livingstone and Bovill 1999).

The concept of "media styles" is an application of audience theory which may be important and necessary if the complexities of children's lives around a variety of media are to be described with any understanding. Rather than labelling children by age and gender labels, and then describing their media uses, new kinds of audience research will derive the audience concepts themselves from the particular setting, based on how the audience relationship is accomplished (Nightingale 1996, p. 146). Definitions of audience groups will arise from the interaction of particular media subjects with types or genres of media contents. The definitions are fluid, in terms both of audience members and of media types and contents. The need to understand audience reception of the internet and new media provides the exciting possibility that we might shift to research which has new audience theory as its conceptual base, rather than resorting to the demographic matrices that still underpin most industry as well as academic audience research. It is difficult to consistently apply theoretical notions of audience as relational concepts, rather than as imagined aggregates of human individuals. However, that is the challenge that researchers who wish to do innovative work will now be facing.

A recent Australian qualitative study has begun to address the lack of information about Australian children's internet use. A cooperative research project between the University of Western Sydney and the Australian Broadcasting Authority has used group discussions with 50 young people, aged ten to fifteen years, to explore their own ways of defining and dealing with "media harm" in relation to the internet (Australian Broadcasting Authority 2000). By actively seeking young people's own views about a subject which is used to justify regulation or even censorship, this study addresses one of the anomalies of research and regulation about children's media use, as expressed by David Buckingham et al. (1999, p. 75): "Perhaps the greatest paradox in this whole area is that children's needs have been defined and defended, although children themselves have largely been silenced." Research described earlier in the chapter has certainly incorporated children's perspectives about media experiences.

However, the study by the Australian Broadcasting Authority (2000) is the first study that sets out to understand their views of classification and regulation, and to test the adult notion of "media harms" through the day-to-day experience of young people.

The findings show that cultural patterns are being repeated with this new medium. Girls have to struggle for access to the internet at home against competition from fathers and brothers, and boys use sexual and aggressive content to express their male toughness. Content interests not only reflect those of film and television, but also the greater possibilities of the new information medium of the internet, with boys' interests focusing on sport and girls enjoying content dealing with horror and the occult. The negotiation of homework is another familiar theme.

Young people do have their own perspective on media harms, which demonstrates their knowledge of adult anxieties and "official" constraints, but also their negotiation of these. Apart from the possibility of being affected by violent or disturbing content (though "others" are usually seen to be more at risk), the major "media harm" young people describe is the punishment from parents or perhaps teachers when young people access material that is forbidden. The management of such situations, including for many the care that they do not breach the trust of parents, is a central concern in children's lives with the internet at home.

In Australia, we await a study which will build on these descriptive findings and describe young people's uses of the internet on a representative scale.

Children, Media and the Public Sphere

The sense that much has been achieved in research on children and media in Australia is moderated by the limited opportunities that now exist in the public sphere to discuss such research, or even to know about it. If the shift in research understanding about children's media engagement has been profound, this is not reflected in public discourse, most of which is still profoundly ignorant. Over the last 20 years, there has been a consistent refusal by commentators — especially politicians — to alter their frame of reference and accommodate a view of children as active negotiators of meaning and access in their own environments.

Parliamentary delegations and members of Senate Select Committees have even displayed a refusal to consider the views of experts they have called, because their evidence does not support intended political actions. In 1994, I gave evidence before a Senate Select Committee inquiring into R-rated material on pay TV. When it became clear that I did not support the banning of R-rated material, one senator became irate and accused me of a lack of concern: "It does not concern you that fourteen- to seventeen-year-olds could watch this material: we should just accept that as collateral damage in the situation?" I went on to reject his argument: "I am very concerned about children but I am also a concerned member of my society. Your black and white idea of harm and damage — which I do not agree with — would actually wipe out the evening news" (Senate Select Committee on Community Standards 1995, p. 562).

Politicians in Australia have adopted easy solutions to "protect" children by, for example, ruling a line across times in the television schedule at 9.00 p.m. or, in the case of pay TV, discriminating against it. These actions bolster the standing of politicians and possibly reassure individuals who are anxious about adult control in a time of social change. However, the actions are rarely based on knowledge of how children actually interpret and use the media concerned. They are likely to be ineffective or counterproductive in supporting children if they deny the knowledge that exists about children's day-to-day media engagements. The refusal to engage with research reveals the purpose to be political control rather than genuine concern.

Resistance to a public discourse about children as actors within their own media environments is not because individuals cannot understand the research, or because parents stubbornly prefer to feel guilty. My own frequent "appearances" on talkback radio between 1986 and 1996 provided a continuing opportunity to engage with audience members about new research. Mothers in particular have consistently been pleased and even relieved when discussion of research has provided new ways of understanding their children's media behaviour.

Recent public discussion about children and the internet seemed to promise a different approach, with amused references to children being more able to "surf the web" than their parents or teachers. However, warnings about active paedophile rings and aggressive pornographers on the internet have brought the familiar clichés back into public discourse, in time to justify the Broadcasting Services Amendment (Online Services) Bill 1999. This legislation set up a process for censoring internet content, administered by the Australian Broadcasting Authority, as well as resources for educating parents and others about ways of supervising children's internet uses.

Although the discussion of the legislation was low-key compared with the British "video nasties" campaign of 1983, the motive seems similar: to set up a new moralism which justifies direct intervention regarding media content and gives reserve powers to government (Barker 1984, p. 38). The difference with the internet is that direct censorship is likely to be completely ineffective.

Other trends have made it more difficult for research to be discussed publicly. Because of the time pressures, and the move to outsourcing, audience research which is conducted for government is more likely to be put out to tender, and supplied by private companies. The significance for the Australian community of the increasing privatisation of research merits a wider debate than this chapter allows. One decisive difference is that the research is not usually the researcher's when it is completed. Without permission, researchers cannot make public comment or take any action on the basis of their findings. The application of results to policy is in the hands of others.

Ironically, the media have also lost a rich source of content through this trend. Numerous short appearances on daytime television and radio talkback, which provided some opportunity to talk to audiences about themselves as audience members, have been replaced with official press releases. In the media as a whole, there are now far fewer opportunities for talking about audiences.

Research about children's engagement with program content is now very likely to be kept confidential. Extensive qualitative research is conducted by networks to test program concepts and to pilot new productions. The pay TV channels who target children or family audiences may be making a major contribution to audience research.

However, none of this research is public, so there is little discussion of how audiences are changing as the whole media environment is being transformed.

In 1992, after a well-orchestrated media campaign, the Children's Program Committee was disbanded, and the classification of programs and discussion of quality children's television became an internal administrative responsibility of Australian Broadcasting Authority staff. Looking back, the decision to disband the Children's Program Committee removed a valuable focus for public debate about children and television, and the opportunity for continuing cooperation between industry, researchers and interested members of the community. Although the Children's Program Committee was represented during the media campaign as being slow and obstructive in making decisions about programs, it had in fact been effective in building alliances with children's television producers within the networks and thereby forcing TV networks to resource children's programs more adequately. It was this success that was intolerable for the networks. Determining the priorities and budgets for children's television was "their business".

Research, publication and debate on children and their uses of media are continuing in Australia. The Australian Broadcasting Authority now has a strong tradition of research which is up to date in its findings and innovative in its methodologies. The recent research collaboration led by Virginia Nightingale at the University of Western Sydney to investigate media harms from young people's perspectives is an example (Australian Broadcasting Authority 2000). This research used the work of private research companies as well as recognised scholars. The Office of Film and Literature Classification has also commissioned new research and engaged in collaborations between industry and academe. Kevin Durkin and Kate Aisbett's (1999) study of computer games is the most recent. Both organisations have a fine record of publishing the results to encourage public comment, and of creating public forums to further such discussion. However, government agencies have limitations in the extent to which they can conduct a public education role. As organisations, they need to actively maintain the support of government, which funds them.

Creating public debate may threaten these fragile relationships if it leads to controversy.

Twenty years ago, the major concerns about TV and children were that the TV set damaged children's eyesight if they sat "too close"; "passive children" were absorbed by the TV; and "heavy viewers" were made aggressive by their long hours in front of the set. Research has provided a much richer understanding of children's engagement in the TV space, and their uses of program content. As new media have been developed, children's capacity for fun and their ability to negotiate several activities, narratives and relationships in parallel have made the "TV monster" story seem laughable. But in the public arena, where research should inform policy and creative enterprise, there are now silent spaces and gaps in public understanding. There are even horrifying echoes of the discourse about mute children needing strong adult control.

The success of the children's television industry in Australia, and the achievements of media research over the last 20 years, have been produced in the midst of public debate. Retreat into the small worlds of private companies, universities and organisations is a disappointing step away from such achievements. We need a continuing, active debate between producers, researchers and community members about changes in media use and their expression in the lives of children and families. A co-regulatory regime gives little impetus to innovative research or programming if the parties never meet each other publicly or challenge the values and practices of each other's work.

Note

1 No sample size for Australian children was given.

CHAPTER 4

"I Didn't Get it, but I Liked the Name":[1] Generational Profiling through Generation X

Jason Sternberg

Introduction: The A, B, C of Generation X

This chapter is perhaps exactly what the world doesn't need: more writing about Generation X. Through his 1991 novel, *Generation X: Tales for an Accelerated Culture*, Canadian author Douglas Coupland "created a monster" (France 1994, p. 11). In the years following the book's publication, it seemed as if the already bizarre and contradictory world of youth culture had been transformed forever because of Generation X. In a global cringe-fest of clichés, the world was characterised as having gone "berserk" (McCaughan 1994) over the term and its numerous spin-off labels such as slackers, twentysomethings and Baby Busters. It spawned more discussion about youth culture than "freckles on a red-head" (Ritchie 1995, p. 9). Coupland (1995, p. 72) himself labelled it "demographic pornography".

Used to describe groups ranging in age from about thirteen to 40, Generation X has its own heroes and voices — notably musicians such as the late Kurt Cobain from Nirvana and Pearl Jam's Eddie Vedder. It is characterised as having set the marketing world on fire, with a "mini-industry" (Ruddy 1994, p. 71) emerging to deal with it. It has been used to sell everything from clothes, to cars, to soft-drinks, Scotch whisky and telephone systems (Hicks 1996). It has inspired media products aimed at young people, including video games, magazines, sit-coms and even news programs. Almost every publication from *The Bulletin* (Tulich 1994) and *Reader's Digest* (McMahon 1996) to the Christian youth magazine *On Being* (Batt 1994; Deane 1994) has published a Generation X feature. Generation X has multiple discursivities — for Rushkoff (1994a, p. 3) it is "a culture, a demographic, an outlook, a style, an economy, a scene, a political ideology, an aesthetic, an age, a decade and a literature".

In 1995, Coupland declared Generation X dead (Coupland 1995). However, six years later the term still has currency with the growth of offshoot generational sub-groupings such as Baby Busters, Generation 2000, the MTV Generation and the Options Generation (Mackay 1995, 1997) and the establishment of new generations of young people such as the Nintendo Generation, the Net Generation (Tapscott 1999), Generation Y (*Sunday Mail* 1994, p. 29; Bagnall 1999), Generation Why? (Kellett 1994) and Generation Z (*Planet* 1994). Generation X and the idea of generation-based audience groups are firmly entrenched within popular discourse. In Jameson's (1984, 1991) terms, they are a "cultural dominant" — a seemingly commonsense way of discussing the cultural logic of late twentieth and early twenty-first century youth culture and media consumption. As Wice (1994, p. 280) notes, the rise of generational marketing has seen the emergence of "the first significant generation gap since the sixties ... in a flood of soft news features about 'Generation X', 'twentysomethings' and 'baby busters'. And in the media trade press young adults have emerged as the 'hot' target audience." For Rushkoff (in *Merchants of Cool* 2001), contemporary youth culture and youth marketing are synonymous. Members of the current generation of 32 million US teenagers — the largest in history — spend about $100 billion on themselves annually, with their parents spending half as much on them again (*Merchants of Cool* 2001). Companies employ a range of techniques to gain insight into the lives of young consumers and audiences, including surveys, focus groups, ethnographic methods and special correspondents or "cool hunters" — a former "cool kid" hired to find other "cool kids" and report back on the latest street trends. One employer of cool hunters, Look Look, makes its reports available on a subscription-only website for a $20 000 fee (*Merchants of Cool* 2001). As Rushkoff (in *Merchants of Cool* 2001) observes: "To win teens' loyalty marketers believe they have to speak their language the best. So, they study them carefully, as an anthropologist would an exotic native culture."

The public circulation of marketing terms like Generation X has played a major role in promoting the development of new forms of generational consciousness since the 1950s (Bennett et al. 1990/91, p. 136). The astonishing emergence of youth culture after World War II as a distinct, moneyed, seemingly homogenous subculture with its own set of rituals and practices prompted an almost instant response from consumer industries (Lewis 1992, p. 3). While sociologists and cultural historians talked of youth culture as a phenomenon, the advertising, recording, television and movie industries took aim at this new target market. Lewis (1992, p. 4) argues that:

> When we are talking about youth, we are talking about a fundamentally mediated culture, one that continues to re-present itself in terms of the products it buys, the art that defines it, and the art it defines as its own. This dialectic of cultural autonomy and media appropriation — the paradox of a media-made culture and a culture that makes media — resides at the heart of a by now half-century-old debate, one that has dominated the study of youth …

In order to study youth culture adequately, we must focus on the essential paradox that youth is both mass movement and mass market. Generation X fits into such a framework perfectly, as the media play a role both as one of the experiences that Generation X is linked with and as one of the perpetrators of the discourse.

There is confusion about Generation X. For example, a four-page lift-out feature in the 13 February 1994 edition of the *Sunday Mail* (Brisbane) began with the contention that "nobody knows what to make" of the group, but went on to declare: "They certainly don't want to be defined — 'Don't call us, we'll call you' is their catchcry to older generations." (Ruddy 1994, p. 71) Such claims strongly support Hall and Whannel's (1994, p. 70) claim that young adults do not want to be understood. Generation X's initial mysteriousness and problematic social presence became a strong framing device. The front cover of the July 1994 edition of *The Face* asked: "Generation X. Who is it? What is it? Does it really exist?" Similarly, another Generation X article asked: "Who are they, and what are they up to?" (Howe and Strauss 1994, p. 290)

Generation X is clearly not "an aggregate of previously existing and fully formed individuals" (Hartley 1999b, p. 21). It is not a "real" audience expressing a relationship to media products and power structures. Rather, it is a textual site created by those power structures that can be then "peopled" (Hartley 1999b, p. 21) at certain times to serve certain purposes. Generation X is, in Hartley's (1992b, p. 105) terms, an "invisible fiction": a construct "produced institutionally in order for various institutions to take charge of the mechanisms of their own survival". It enables the media to refer to young people in an homogenising and stereotypical fashion. But, as Baudrillard (1988, pp. 103, 69) contends, the universal face of youth is in fact only a product of the political economy of media institutions and no more represents young people than does exchange and commodity value, as the alleged characteristics of Generation X are manipulated and mapped on to various products and services (Baudrillard 1988, p. 64) to create demand for these. As Grossberg (1992, p. 191) succinctly puts it: "The category of youth has been appropriated by others who not only define it but struggle to essentialise it."

While understandings of youth culture such as Generation X may not be all that accurate, they shape understandings of young people. As Grossberg (1992, p. 183) observes, "the current generation of adolescents, baby boomers, parents and corporate media interests are fighting for control of its [youth's] meanings, investments and powers, fighting to articulate and thereby construct its experiences, identities, practices, discourses and social differences". Generation X is "real" and "material" precisely because it is "*real in its effects*" (Hall 1982, p. 83). Even if it is an invisible fiction, Generation X has undoubtedly had real consequences for how young people behave and see themselves. Ultimately, however, neither money nor the market can fully explain just how Generation X and other generational markers are used by the media and young people to signify aspects of youth culture (Hall et al. 1976, pp. 54–56).

In order to demonstrate the struggle between media industries and youth culture over Generation X, the remainder of this chapter is in four parts. The first part provides a history of Generation X, outlining its arrival within popular discourse and examining its incorporation within dominant discourse and the implications of this for our understandings of young people and youth culture. The following three parts examine the ways in which Generation X has been understood as an audience — as a postmodern audience, as a demographic and as a psychographic.

A Brief History of Generation X

Contrary to popular belief, Douglas Coupland neither "created" the term Generation X, nor was he the first person to use it. The term had its origins in social attitude research. In 1964, British writers Charles Hamblett and Jane Deverson compiled a book entitled *Generation X* (Hamblett and Deverson 1964) that recorded the views of a cross-section of England's young people and asked them about their attitudes and lifestyles (Miller 1995, p. 1). Generation X later became the name of a mid-1980s British faux-punk band led by Billy Idol. Coupland (1995, p. 72), however, claims he was inspired by the final chapter of Paul Fussell's humorous book on American social structure entitled *Class: A Guide Through the American Status System* (1984). It named an "X" category of people in its final chapter who "wanted to hop off the merry-go-round of status, money and social climbing that so often frames modern existence" (Coupland 1995, p. 72). For Coupland (1995, p. 72), these citizens of X "had much in common with my own socially disengaged characters: hence the title".

Coupland's *Generation X* is the simple story of three people in their late twenties and early thirties. All three know the "futility" of "yuppie, careerist" ladder-climbing (Wark 1993, p. 77) and have, in Coupland's words (1995, p. 72), "decided to pull back from society and move to the fringe of Palm Springs, California, where they worked at dreary jobs at the bottom of the food chain". As the book's back cover puts it, the protagonists "have been handed a society priced beyond their means". Having been "brought up with divorce, Watergate and Three Mile Island and scarred by the 80s fall-out of yuppies, recession, crack and Ronald Reagan", the characters "have nowhere to direct their anger, no one to assuage their fears and no culture to replace their anomie".

Generation X's tiny March 1991 printing had no publicity, and received almost no reviews. However, the first group to "discover"

Generation X after Coupland's use of it were market research and advertising companies. Generation X was really born on 19 October 1992, when Karen Ritchie, the "folksy fiftysomething" (Wice 1994, p. 281) director of media services at McCann-Erickson Detroit, borrowed the term from Coupland and used it in a speech on marketing to young people at the American Magazine Conference in Bermuda (Ritchie 1995, pp. 7, 21). In her speech, Ritchie warned that "there are 46 million adult consumers out there who are 18 to 29 years old. We are kidding ourselves if we believe that these people truly care about the crisis of turning 40, or coping with teen-age children or one more reunion of one more 1960s sitcom." Ritchie's speech turned Generation X into an audience *and* a set of consumers. It "spawned the mass scramble to hunt out, examine, define, make friends with and sell stuff to this strange new body of alien beings" (Hicks 1996, p. 72). As Bob Guccione Jr (in Ritchie 1995, p. 9), editor and publisher of *Spin* magazine, described it, "discovering and naming an audience of 46 million people" in the United States alone "is like all of a sudden noticing France". For Coupland (1995, p. 72), this was the start of problems with Generation X, as "trendmeisters" (advertising executives and journalists) "began isolating small elements of my characters' lives" and blowing them up to "represent an entire generation".

In the mass media's hands, Generation X quickly moved out of the marketing press, becoming "the phrase that launched a thousand magazine articles" (Bernstein 1994, p. 40). The 14 December 1992 edition of *Business Week* (Zinn et al. 1992) ran a Gen X cover story, extensively quoting Ritchie and other advertising executives, and the December 1992 editions of the *Atlantic Monthly* and the *New Republic* ran "duelling" Generation X cover stories (Guccione, 1995, p. ix).

In Australia, Generation X first appeared in market research reports. There was a brief reference to the novel in Clemenger Advertising's *20Twenty* study (Ricketson 1993). However, in late 1993, the Generation X market research "web" (Plomarit 1994, p. 4) reached Australia fully, courtesy of a local McCann-Erickson study. It did not take long after that for marketing companies and advertising agencies to "jump on the bandwagon" (Plomarit 1994, p. 4). Agencies such as Loud (Kellett 1994), DMB & B/Weekes Morris Osborn (*Courier-Mail* 1994) and others all produced their own Generation X-related marketing studies.

Generating X and Creating a Postmodern Audience

The change from using Generation X to describe fictional characters to using it to create an audience/cohort was achieved through the convergence of literature, marketing and journalism. As McCann Erickson's Dave McCaughan (1995) explains the process:

> The thing with the Generation 2000 — the Generation X — stuff was like our industry revolves around creating news for itself and this constant search for the new niche … because, how are you going to increase business, how do you increase in a major market like the USA and a mature market like Australia, how does the marketing industry increase business out of its clients? The only way it can really do that is to find new markets … You get a segment that is like nineteen to twenty year old Black guys who hate football, that's probably a million guys … So, shit there you go and we'll make up a fancy name for them.

McCaughan goes on to explain how Generation X happened for him:

> I got rung by a journalist to make a comment, had I read it, what did I think of it? And my comment was, I said it was bullshit, there's no such thing as Generation X, not in the terms of everyone in that generation is "blah". It gets printed and the next thing you know you get asked to speak at a conference because hey, you've got an opinion on this … oh yeah, I guess I do. So, that's when I decided we had to do something.

Indeed it could be said that Generation X has only ever really existed within media discourse.

Coupland (1995, p. 72) never intended Generation X to refer to a particular group of people, but rather to a way of looking at the world. It is, if you like, a kind of framing device:

> GenX is merely a kind of self-conscious irony, the ability to step back from direct experience and watch oneself experiencing life. The moment GenX began was the moment when the first buster "bracketed" his own experience, the minute someone stepped back and, in a wink-wink-say-no-more fashion, related the ironic distance he felt from his own existence. (Rushkoff 1994b, p. 10)

For Hebdige (1979, p. 80), youth culture "can never be completely 'raw'": it is always a complex mixture of the authentic and inauthentic. As a referent of the "scandalous category" of youth (Hartley 1983), Generation X certainly does transgress such simplistic binary oppositions and inevitably contains some radical potential. But Generation X was not "taken up" by the media from the world of youth culture. It was a media creation injected into the body of youth through the media. The term was taken from a novel and used by market researchers, advertising companies and journalists. Despite the trouble marketers, journalists and commentators went to in identifying it, in Hartley's (1992b) terms, Generation X is neither "real" nor external to its discursive construction. Generation X is not a subculture in the sense that the "Indigenous" audience or the "queer" audience might be, although it has certainly been attached to the grunge, rap and rave movements and most presentations on it are filled with statistics, vox pops and interviews with young people. Unlike a youth subculture, Generation X has no authentic or manifest existence. Bernstein (1994, p. 49), in what is perhaps an overstatement, claims that "no one has ever chosen to call themselves a slacker or a member of Generation X. It's a term used by a freelance journalist to get a quick positive response from a harried editor."

Generation X represents a shift in the media's relationship to youth culture because it is an audience concept that "makes sense only in relation to the economic formation that produced it" (Baudrillard 1988, p. 105). It is best thought of as a simulacrum, an example of the "hyperreal" which does not "merely replicate the logic of late capitalism" but "reinforces and intensifies it" (Jameson 1984, pp. 66, 85; 1991 pp. 18, 46). Such a trend not only confirms Grossberg's (1994, p. 183) argument that youth culture is becoming increasingly commodified and incorporated into hegemonic discourse through advertising, fashion and the media, but also suggests an increasing predetermination of such culture. It was a subculture that was created by the media in order to turn it into a media audience. The production of audiences has been abstracted beyond anything Marx could have imagined possible (Hebdige 1988, p. 165).

Generation X as Demographic

One of the hottest areas of public debate over Generation X was about what age ranges constituted it. Coupland originally used the label to refer to a group of young people born between 1961 and 1972, who at the time of his novel's publication were aged between nineteen and 30. This age range was also the one originally adopted by McCann-Erickson. Since then, it has been variously used to describe age groups ranging from thirteen to 40, eleven to 31 (Howe & Strauss 1993, p. 13) and thirteen to 24 (Strickland 1994, p. 26). It seems to have become a term to describe anyone younger than the Baby Boomers (McCaughan 1995), thereby lending itself to the creation of sub-demographics such as Atari and Nintendo wave Generation Xers (Howe & Strauss 1993, p. 13), Generation Y (*Sunday Mail* 1994, p. 29) and Z (*Planet* 1994).

The rather nebulous age groups making up Generation X, and the alternative demographic names coined for it, are clear signs of the difficulties involved in defining it. In trying to establish it as a demographic, the media actually exposed the tensions inherent in pinning down elements of youth culture. Fluctuations within generational cohorts make specifications of Generation X problematic. If this is a good example of the media's inability to police the categories which they themselves create, it is also an example of the fallacy Mannheim (1927, p. 278) pointed to of using the "law of the limited life-span of man" in order to "find a general law of historical development". While focusing on creating Generation X as a demographic was easy for the media, the difficulty remained in finding "the average period of time taken for the older generations to be superseded by the new in public life", and of finding "the natural starting-point … from which to reckon the new period" (Mannheim 1927, p. 278).

This slipperiness is what allows Generation X to still have currency nearly a decade after it entered public discourse. The age ranges associated with Generation X keep being shifted to accommodate a youthful definition, allowing the term to still refer to the age groups that were originally associated with the term as youth, even though the older members of that group are now approaching 40. Alternatively, labels such as Generation Y, Generation Z and the

Tweens (between children and teenagers) were developed to cater for younger age groups. How society refers to young people has undergone a significant change, in that the more nebulous demographic notion of the teenager and young adult has been replaced by generation-based psychographic cohorts.

Generation X as Psychographic

As the media recognised the limits of producing Generation X as a solely demographic label, its social and cultural features increasingly came into play. Generation X became a psychographic — a profile of values and lifestyles that could be used as the basis to distinguish between generations and as a measure against which to create new generations. For example, the teenage "Generation Why?" earned its title by being even more cynical than the Xers (Kellett 1994). Social definitions of generation entailed in psychographic profiles acknowledge and play on the complexity of youth culture. Such definitions allow for the fact that, while young people who experience the same historical situations may be said to be part of the same generation, groups within the same generation may "work up the material of their common experiences in different specific ways" (Mannheim 1927, p. 304), constituting different generation units. As we will see below, the media were able to constantly produce finer-grained permutations of Generation X based on lifestyle measures in order to serve their own ends.

This psychographic reproduction occurred through a very complex series of processes. At the most basic level, media and marketers rapidly developed a stereotypical portrait of Generation X. Moving quickly from the demographic-based notion of being the generation, "sandwiched between the baby boom of 1946–64 and the 'boomlet' of 1977 onwards" (Hicks 1996, p. 72), Generation Xers were apparently the "children of the recession", born into the 1970s economic crisis and maturing during the 1980s (Hicks 1996, p. 72). They were constructed as bored, frustrated, cynical, media literate, ethnically diverse, ironic, socially tolerant, but apathetic. They were seen as over-educated and under-employed, often remaining living at home with their parents for far longer than previous generations in order to preserve their limited finances (Hicks 1996, p. 73). They were also portrayed as pissed-off at the Boomers who grew up, found jobs and started families amidst the highest standards of living and levels of material wealth in the twentieth century "and then promptly sold out, leaving them with a plundered and fragile environment, mass unemployment, a fragmented social structure and the aftermath of the sexual (counter-) revolution" (Hicks 1996; Zinn et al. 1992; Howe and Strauss 1993; Liu 1994; Rushkoff 1994c; Ritchie 1995).

Constructing Generation X in this way influenced perceptions of their habits as consumers and media audiences. Ignored by the boomer-centric media, Generation Xers feel distanced from mainstream culture and bored by consumer-hype (Hicks 1996, p. 73). According to "Xperts" (Crawford and Perkins 1994, p. 36), this is the generation of "media babies" — media literate, media savvy and technologically adept. Indeed, this theme of mediatisation was central to Coupland's novel, which held that "people now feel empathy from others who grew up at the same time as they did *because they consumed the same media images*" (Wark 1993, pp. 76–77, my emphasis).

But immersion in the world of media is countered by a detachment from and an awareness of it, and a desire not to be "sucked in". For Wark (1993, p. 78), talking on behalf of Generation Xers:

> GenX are caught within the media portrayal of abundance and self-worth, available especially for you for only ten dollars down and easy monthly repayments. Yet we are also aware of the media as a manipulation. The alternative is to use our knowledge of how mass media culture works to carve a life and an identity for oneself.

Another central theme of Generation X speech was the emphasis on the "new generation gap" between Xers and their older demographic cousins, the Baby Boomers. Wark (1993, p. 74) suggests Generation X is a "generation of aliens who don't fit into the scheme that our parents and the older, post-war baby boomer generation expect from us". This was in some accounts not simply a widening of the generation gap, but a "polarisation of the generations" (Mitterauer 1992, p. 240). Generation Xers apparently watched the boomers being transformed "from hippies to yuppies to New Agers to landowners" (Rushkoff 1994a, p. 3). As Rushkoff (1994a, p. 5) proclaims:

> Gen Xers live in a world we feel is geared to people ten to thirty years older than ourselves. We watched as baby boomers went to college, got great jobs, crashed the economy, and left nothing but McJobs — low-wage menial employment or "temping" — for their vastly overqualified little brothers and sisters. We watched rock'n'roll take over the nation and then dry up like Mick Jagger before we got to college. We watched a generation drop acid and turn on, only to find an atmosphere of "just say no" and mandatory prison sentences by the time we were old enough to care for a buzz now and again. We watched the sexual revolution evolve into forced celibacy as the many excesses of the 1970s and 1980s rotted into the sexually transmitted diseases of our 1990s.

Defining Generation X against the Baby Boomers, and sometimes against even older generations (see, for example, Howe & Strauss 1993; McMahon 1996), allowed Generation X to be measured against the older generations' yardsticks. So Gen Xers don't spend as much as Boomers do (Zinn et al. 1992; Hulktrans 1994; Goldman 1994; Wice 1994), and they don't consume as much media (Landler 1992) or they consume more media, but of the wrong type — TV and not newspapers (Ruddy 1994). They also haven't had the same great life experiences. If the Boomers had Sputnik, the 1960s, free love, protesting, Vietnam, the Beatles and the Stones and man walking on the moon (Beachy 1994; Greenberg 1994; Ruddy 1994), what did Generation Xers have? From its first appearance in popular circulation, Generation X did not exist on its own terms, but was rather defined in terms of what it was not.

Generation X's clash with the Baby Boomers also scripted a "Boomer backlash". As the Boomers were transformed into "lifestyle entrepreneurs", Generation X became "the Whiny Generation" (Martin 1994). Almost as a natural by-product, we began to see "portrait of a generation" articles emerging for the Baby Boomers, constructing them as "the last innocents" (*Sunday Mail Magazine* 1996; see also Safe & Whittaker 1994). Equally predictable were the stories claiming that generational differences had been overstated. Boomers and Xers were actually similar in outlook: "*The Reader's Digest* survey shows that young people appreciate the enduring values that helped build this country. That has to be good for our future." (McMahon 1996, p. 25) But perhaps the ultimate permutation was to redefine Generation X as actually being better than the Boomers.

This was the generation that faced its future "with a mixture of bravado and fatalism" (Howe and Strauss 1994, p. 295). As the "repair" generation, it was going to correct the social, environmental and economic problems caused by the Boomers (Ruddy 1994). Generation Y, the current generation of teenagers and early twentysomethings, is constructed as being even more media savvy and cashed-up consumers than Generation X (Bagnall 1999; Maclean 1999). Largely the offspring of Baby Boomer parents, Generation Y has been used by the media to placate that older generation's collective angst about its children. A larger demographic than Generation X, Generation Y and its achievements will be "almost as important" (Zaldivar 1998) as the Boomer generation, who are doing a better job as parents compared with the parents of Generation X (Bagnall 2001).

The arrival of a new generation gap, and its construction primarily around issues of consumerism, market potential and *embourgeoisement* in the early to mid-1990s, revises the earlier and perhaps even more publicly staged original generation gap — that between the Baby Boomers and an older generation in the 1950s and 1960s. As young people, Boomers were constructed as the future of Western capitalism. They were also the archetypal youth generation and were themselves portrayed in market terms and against other generations, largely through the growth of mass communication industries (see Grossberg 1992; Hall et al. 1976; Mungham and Pearson 1976 for a comprehensive history of the Baby Boomers' discursive construction.)

If the Generation X lifestyle panic is essentially about hopes and fears for the future of capitalism, then what better way of combatting those fears than by saying the future of capitalism should be more like the past? More specifically, the panic surrounding Generation X may be seen to articulate hopes and fears about the future of the third stage of capitalism: the transition from a modern to a postmodern society. Indeed, Generation X has been referred to as "the nightmare of a postindustrial, postmodern age" (Rushkoff 1994a, p. 4). Simply, the Generation X phenomenon appears to be trying to reinvent the 1950s myth of youth affluence in the midst of a global recession that has been taking place since before the oldest members of the generation started school and its youngest members were born (Harvey 1989).

The themes of Coupland's novel influenced the inventory of characteristics that built up around the term "Generation X". The novel's appendix, containing data highlighting the attitudes and social positions of young Americans at the time, assisted this process. McCaughan (1995) refers to Generation X's traits being extended from those portrayed in the book as a process of "bibliosexuality". This is a process where you have "a societal base in which everything is justified by the existence of a book … You don't have to have read the book, you just have to know it exists." Manolis et al. (1997) tested the validity of Generation X's social attitudes by conducting a survey that used Coupland's novel as the basis for its questions. Hicks (1996, p. 73) argues that the initial stereotype of Generation X that was established was powerful, despite the fact that very few young people seemed to fit the criteria established. But this did not mean the term lost impact as a way of describing young people and youth culture.

Generation X acquired new characteristics as the term circulated throughout the marketing and media worlds. Attempts to define Generation X often used the scientific authority of statistical data (e.g. tables, graphs and charts), many of them from "official sources" (e.g. census), as a way of "objectively" proving their particular cases. These reports tended to mimic the style of the novel, with breakout definitions of important terms such as "grunge" and "slacker" and sidebar graphs and tables of social data (see, for example, Zinn et al. 1992; Deane 1994). Statistics worked to establish Generation X as both transparent to itself and to the subject being addressed by the text. In an attempt to cash in on the phenomenon, marketing studies mutated into volumes of popular sociology (see, for example, Howe and Strauss 1993; Mackay 1997), collections of writing by and about Generation Xers (Rushkoff 1994c; Liu 1994) and even a textbook on marketing to them (Ritchie 1995). To perpetuate continuing interest in Generation X, these studies and stories had to be sufficiently different, pointing out new features in the demographic to show clients and readers how "in touch" they were with young people. In the process, Generation X became redefined and re-segmented according to increasingly bizarre and paradoxical names (e.g. purple-haired people) and social measures — for example, from how they responded to survey questions such as "hard work is the key to getting ahead" and "unlimited opportunity is more important than ensuring equality of income" (McMahon 1996, pp. 21, 22) to studies of how many Xers owned small or compact trucks (Ritchie 1995, p. 143). Ultimately, this drive to segment and differentiate confirmed the claim that Generation X's main characteristics were its diversity and indefineability (Zinn et al. 1992; Ruddy 1994; Ritchie 1995).

The important point here is not whether the discourses used to construct Generation X are referentially adequate. Such a task is impossible, as one of the key features of Generation X as simulacra is the blurring of distinctions between truth and falsehood and reality and the imaginary (Baudrillard 1988, p. 168). Obviously, some of the characteristics used to construct Generation X would actually apply to young people and some would not. This is especially true when the demographic's primary characteristic is its diversity! What is important here is understanding that, regardless of whether they are correct or incorrect, the discourses which construct Generation X "are themselves part of the context in which youth is organised" (Grossberg 1992, p. 199). Because meaning here does not depend on "how things are" but on how things are signified, it follows that the same event (i.e. youth culture) can be signified in different ways under the same name (i.e. Generation X, Y or Z). Generation X is *homogenised* in the very face of diversity to produce a classless youth culture, where socio-economic, racial, geographical, gender and sexual differences seem to go "on holiday" (Mungham and Pearson 1976, p. 3).

Generation X's tactical and strategic power derives from the same source. Its semiotic excess made it difficult to contain while the same excess allowed the media to create a political economy of "imaginary universality" (Baudrillard 1988, p. 114). It was able to be constructed in such contradictory ways because its arbitrariness allowed it to defy comprehension. This, in Baudrillard's (1988, pp. 52–53) terms, is one of the great contradictions of consumer society: "The system is forced to produce more and more consumer individualism, which at the same time it is forced to repress more and more severely." Indeed, for Baudrillard (1988, p. 102), "the richest concrete development" of postmodern capitalism is its "qualitative and quantitative multiplication" of a sign's use value. Such a process relies on the exploitation of the signifier's strategic value and the signified's tactical value (Baudrillard 1988, p. 70). Because Generation X had such semiotic excess, advertisers, market researchers and journalists could — and *did* — create a *tabula rasa* on to which they wrote almost anything they wanted. As McCaughan (1995) puts it:

> Generation X: it's like a marketer's dream, it's a brand name[2] from the gods … It's just classic. If you had been a Coke, a Pepsi, any major manufacturer in the world would have died to have got a brand name as potent as that. It just brilliantly encapsulated the whole thing and at the same time it was a name that you could build into such a strong brand because it had such energy in its own right and you could attach all sorts of things to it and make it into something.

In making Generation X mean almost anything, the growth of the youth market no longer appeared to be an isolated phenomenon, but part of a generalised move towards affluence in which the traditional relations of capitalism are transcended by age-based relations of consumption (Murdock and McCron 1976, p. 17). Once again, the meaning of a term like Generation X did not depend on any external, empirical reality of youth culture, but rather on the classificatory systems involved, and the ways different elements were selected and combined to make different meanings (Hall 1982).

Some of the methods of classifying Generation X were crude. One strategy was to acknowledge Generation X's diversity, but homogenise it through jargon. For example, McCann's Australian Generation X report argues that it "is not a profile of the 'average' member of this demographic group. There is no average. Rather it is a review of *their most likely commonalities.*" (McCaughan, 1994, p. 2, emphasis added) Karen Ritchie (1995, p. 17), McCann's American originator of Generation X, used the concept of "peer personality" (borrowed from Strauss & Howe 1991) to reclaim Generation X's indefineability back into its definition:

> Peer personality consists of patterns of behaviour and beliefs that are dominant among a group of people born during the same period of time. Not everyone in a peer group will adhere to these patterns … but even

> those who march to a different drummer, will recognise the patterns as dominant. (Ritchie 1995, p. 17)

The concept of "peer personality" allowed Ritchie to take Generation X's indefineability and justify the construction of a definition out of it:

> I will plead guilty to stereotyping — *a certain amount of stereotyping is probably unavoidable* ... But each generation shares with its peers a common history, and living that history has in some way *defined* the world for us so that we mutually understand who we are and how we fit. (Ritchie, 1995, p. 17, emphasis added)

Social researcher Hugh Mackay (1997) dubbed young Australians the "Options Generation" despite the fact that the first of their "many ironies and contradictions" is that they are "the most dependent generation of young Australians in our history", staying in education longer, living with their parents longer, and moving on to unemployment benefits in large numbers (Mackay 1997, p. 141). However, Mackay (1997, p. 141) asserts that such a label is still valid because young Australians "rate 'independence' as one of their top priorities, and they report *feeling* highly independent".

It was fashionable to deny the existence of Generation X, prove its existence through market research, and then give it another name. Each new piece of market research or article that rejected the use of Generation X actually legitimated, if not the term, then at least the *use* of the term, perpetuating the category. For example, an ad for Cotton Inc claims: "There is no Generation X. There are no 'baby busters'. There is just you and the 40 million or so men and women who share common experiences, concerns and values." (Hicks 1996, p. 74) McCann-Erickson Australia claimed that, while the term might have worked in the United States, "there was no such thing as Generation X" in this country; it therefore chose to rename the demographic "Generation 2000". McCaughan's (1994, p. 1) report "saw that no demographic group can be definitively 'labelled'" and declared young people were "all just individuals". Nevertheless, it concluded by providing a seven-point plan for marketing to them. In similar fashion, the same survey found that if you ask 20 GenXers for their favourite song you would get 20 different answers but then went on to print a list of the bands and singers the group has the "best memories of" (McCaughan 1994, p. 5).

Here a search for knowledge about Generation X was clearly implicated in a broad strategy of power and control. As McRobbie (1994, p. 210) points out, such a strategy "requires surveillance of, and repeated looking at, the other and hence the frequency of his or her appearance in the relevant discourses of inquiry. And in seeing difference there is also the frisson of fascination". The institutional reproduction of Generation X through this continued surveillance maintains its presence as an "invisible fiction" — an audience category produced by media companies and mobilised to serve their needs, rather than those of the audience segment under examination. For Baudrillard (1988, p. 39), this is the logic of market research, "which pretends to uncover the underlying needs of the consumer and the real demand prevailing in the market, [but] exists only to generate a demand for further market opportunities".

By declaring Generation X to be — in Hicks's (1996, p. 3) words — the "target market that declares it is not anything of the sort", marketers declared it able to be courted with "anti-hype hype and anti-image images". Generation X, it seems, was "built on the paradoxical notion of identifying with anonymity" (Hicks 1996, p. 73). Hicks (1996, p. 73) quotes one ad agency executive as saying: "Generation X is going to try to keep staying under the radar … It's part of their identification. If they can be identified and marketed to, they've lost their identification." Such logic works powerfully against young people. If they claim they are not part of Generation X, reject any notion of an identity for their age group, and argue that their diversity cannot be reduced to a profile, these people become constructed as part of Generation X (and are thus able to be marketed to). Anyone who vigorously denies they are a Gen Xer probably *is* one (Hicks 1996, p. 73).

Generation X's diversity and origination from a work of fiction allowed it to be constructed as fiction. McCann's Dave McCaughan (1995) describes his Generation X research in the following way:

> Now at the end of the day, and I'll be blatantly honest, I could have pretty much written this thing before I got the guys involved and they did all the research. What I got out of that was confirmation and some nice quotes.

Indeed, McCaughan (1995) acknowledges that McCann used the Generation X phenomenon for the purpose of creating news for itself and that its market research played a vital role in generating this news:

> I could speak at every conference in the world about Generation 2000, but at the end of the day [what] if you say to me, "Can I have your notes?" or "Could I have a copy of wherever you got this stuff from?" And if I turn around and say, "Oh no, I just made it up off the top of my head. It's just my opinion." You'd sort of go "Oh okay ..." If I tell you I had done a report and I've had three people who've gone out and done lots of interviews and I've done lots of focus-groups and we've sat down and we did all these things blah, blah, blah, then you go, "This guy really puts a lot of work into it."

Elsewhere, Generation X was constructed as science fiction. Wark (1993, p. 74) wrote in an article for *Juice* magazine that "Aliens walk among us. Chances are, you're one of them." In this, he defined Gen X largely in fictional terms, a point which was not lost on one of his readers (Dean 1994, p. 7). Perhaps these are the "real-life" *X-Files*. It is certainly the true story of Generation X. Literature, marketing and journalism coalesced to turn a fictional category into real news and confirm Baudrillard's (1988, p. 84) claim that "the separation of the sign and the world" logically leads to "science fiction".

Generation X was at best "the next major demographic wave" (Tulich 1994, p. 23) and, at worst, "the downfall of the Western world" (Rushkoff 1994a, p. 4). As Boëthius (1995, p. 42) points out, this mix of commercial and ideological exploitation is common to moral panics involving young people. Even though many aspects of the Generation X phenomenon encompassed social issues, much of the discussion was about how these problems would prevent Generation X from becoming good consumers:

> My experience told me that people who were unacknowledged by advertisers and by the media did not somehow have the same advantages, the same visibility in our capitalist society ... If a group was ignored by the media, it was invisible in a larger sense to society as a whole. (Ritchie 1995, p. 6)

Indeed, in at least one article (Goldman 1994), the ability of the current generation of young people to enter the world of consumerism and therefore achieve social visibility became known as "The X Factor". In an example of the nexus between journalism and advertising, Brisbane's *Sunday Mail* reprinted in full a study by Sydney's Loud Advertising as the centrepiece in a four-page Generation X-related feature (Ruddy 1994). The paper even gave readers the chance to purchase a copy of the study! It seemed that, once the issues of diversity had been dealt with, the fiction of classless youth culture produced by Generation X could be re-articulated as an essentially middle-class phenomenon, where issues such as unemployment, political outlook, racism and sexuality were turned into consumer problems — or, at best, lifestyle issues. Even in the articles that did not focus on consumerism specifically, market researchers were quoted more often than social researchers and youth workers. Here many pundits adopted "the tone of social reformers", but their claims about Generation X's "invisibility" referred not to the lack of government services for young people, "but a paucity of twentysomething ad campaigns" (Wice 1994, p. 282). Youth increasingly came to be seen as consumer-citizens who appeared to have been granted new "rights" to be marketed to more vigorously than ever before, but were forced to retain their limited and tenuous rights in the polity (see Davis 1999 for a discussion of how young Australians are positioned within the public sphere).

Conclusion: Generation X as Discursive Sensibility

The idea and the words "Generation X" did not emerge spontaneously from youth culture. Nor did they initially come about from detailed marketing or sociological research identifying a particular cultural category. Rather, the genesis of Generation X may have been as crude as an agency person thinking it was a good idea at the time. Of central concern, however, is the way the idea of Generation X influenced media culture and society generally. Generation X is not a spontaneous expression of young people. It is an example of the marketing, media and economic system constructing the individual.

For "real" young people, the term was not important as something to identify with. In my own research[3] into young people's attitudes towards Generation X, conducted in 1995 at the height of the phenomenon, many respondents who were meant to belong to the group displayed ambivalence towards the term, but nevertheless incorporated many dominant Generation X discourses into their discussion. In keeping with the findings of similar research conducted by Williams et al. (1997, p. 271) in the United States, my respondents "were hesitant to align with the generational label or accept membership or commonality with a group they represented as too large and diverse to reduce to simplistic categorisation". At the same time, however, they used the term in a "discursive struggle to negotiate personal integrity" (Williams et al. 1997, p. 271). This type of tactical response to Generation X is seen in the following discussion between Melanie, Deanne and Alex, three 19-year-old TAFE Marketing students:

> *Melanie:* I don't understand it ... The nineties children don't really have a thing ... There's no real ... dress. Basically we wear whatever we want. There's no individual language like how these flower people ... spoke. There's no set dress. Not everybody's smoking drugs. We're just who we want to be. We're so much individuals that they don't know what to call us. X.
>
> *Deanne:* So is that what it means, that the nineties are like Generation X because ... like I really don't understand what they mean by it.
>
> *Alex:* I suppose we can be classed as the link between yesteryears and tomorrows. The kids who will be growing up next century, they'll be being brought up with all the computers and the Internet and the whole technical stuff and we're kind of half between that and half between our parent's lives of more or less a conservative ... I haven't really given any thought to Generation X.

It is possible to see many "Generation X discourses" — particularly those of media literacy — in young people's responses to the term. This use of "culturally available discursive resources to engage in an ongoing intergenerational debate" (Williams et al. 1997, p. 273) is exemplified in the following exchange between James, a 20-year-old Arts/Law student and Debra, a 19-year-old Commerce student:

James: I don't think Generation X defines us, I think we define Generation X.

Debra: That's a good advertising slogan. [Laughter] I don't think you say Generation X … has these characteristics. I think what Generation X is, is trying to look at us and … say, "What are these people on about?" I think probably most of the media is talking about us the other way. They say, "Generation X has these characteristics". That's what they think, but they don't seem to really look that closely.

In this way, Generation X and subsequent generational groupings such as Generation Y become incorporated into the "reflexive project of the self" (Giddens 1991) as "a site of discursive struggle" (Williams et al. 1997, p. 252) that young people have to negotiate as part of living in a world that sees fit to speak on behalf of them as audience segments. The terms become implicated in a dialectical struggle for agency in which young people's social identities are simultaneously realised in and constructed through talk, social action and media discourse. These "fluid, uncertain, and complex" (Williams et al. 1997 p. 257) identities involve young people both asserting individuality and heterogeneity and aligning with a communal definition of generation — or at least generational value systems. In this way, the Generation X phenomenon was part of the discursive reshaping of the concept of youth in the 1990s. As such, Generation X does not point to the discursive "end" of youth (Meyrowitz 1985; Postman 1983), nor even a change in its meaning. Rather, Generation X is a sensibility involved in the rearticulation of youth, "not only as a cultural category, but as a social and material body as well" (Grossberg 1994, p. 199). It is perhaps in this seemingly contradictory space between an artificial category created by the media and the increasingly fragmented "socially perceptible subjectivities" (McRobbie 1994, p. 180) of young people that the "real" Generation X exists.

Notes

1 Karen Ritchie, Director of Media Services at McCann-Erickson Detroit, describing her reaction to Douglas Coupland's novel *Generation X: Tales for an Accelerated Culture* (Ritchie 1995, p. 6).

2 McCaughan's reference to Generation X as a "brand name" is telling as it establishes the equivalence between commodities, signs and political economy that Baudrillard (1988) argues is at the heart of postmodern culture.

3 All focus group discussion excerpts are taken from research conducted as part of the author's PhD in progress, "Young Adults, Generation X and Television Current Affairs", Department of Journalism, University of Queensland. Ages of respondents are quoted as at the time of the research.

CHAPTER 5

Arts Audiences: Becoming Audience-minded

Tom O'Regan

Introduction

A concern for audiences has become pivotal to the industry development strategies and the political profile-building activities of arts policy-makers for much of the past decade (Valdes 2000; Costantoura 2000). Encouraging cultural organisations to become sensitive to and systematically oriented towards both their audience and their public standing is indicative of larger changes in the overall "government" of the cultural sector. Greater professionalisation, accountability and sectoral coordination (DiMaggio 2000; Craik 1996; O'Regan 1998) have been some of the responses to stagnant audiences, declining funding in real terms and problems with the standing of the arts on politicians' and broader public horizons.

An important vehicle for the carriage of arts audience-mindedness in Australia has been the Australia Council. As the federal government's principal arts funding and advisory body, the Australia Council exercises direct influence on the arts sector through its funding of various individuals and cultural organisations, and indirect influence through its broader policy development and public agenda-setting roles (Australia Council 2000, pp. 7, 10). From the mid-1990s, the Australia Council began to think strategically about its audience research and survey activities, connecting these to its role as an advocate for cultural activities and their broader public appreciation.

The Australia Council promoted an audience-mindedness through a comprehensive education and research commissioning program designed to assist artists and cultural organisations to think about and connect with their audiences and the general public. Its publication titles indicate the comprehensive and multifaceted character of this audience-mindedness: *Selling the Performing Arts: Identifying and Expanding Audiences for Music, Dance and Theatre* (Osborne et al. 1999), *Who's My Market? A Guide to Research on Audiences and Visitors in the Arts* (Close and Donovan 1998), *Older Australians and the Arts* (Australian Pensioners and Superannuants Federation 1995), *To Sell Art, Know Your Market* (Quadrant Research 1997), *Access All Areas: Guidelines for Marketing the Arts to People with Disabilities* (Wyatt-Spratt et al. 1997), *The World is Your Audience: Case Studies in Audience Development and Cultural Diversity* (Migliorini 1998) and *Australians and the Arts* (Costantoura 2000). Some of these titles relate to getting more "bums on seats", others to enhancing marketing capacity; some are concerned with access and equity issues, others with public and citizenship engagement. Alongside these broadly educative emphases, the Council and its various state counterparts required cultural organisations to demonstrate their commitment to audience development.

These several orientations register an important shift in the use of surveys and audience research by the Council and the sector more generally. Informal and anecdotal understandings of the arts audience — "gut feelings" — were being replaced by more formalised understandings. "Marketing" and "management" orientations were adopted as perspectives developed in commercial areas of the cultural industries were applied to the subsidised arts. Through audience and marketing primers, cultural organisations were encouraged to conceive their audiences as consumers of arts services. Through campaign-oriented research promoting the value of the arts on public horizons, these same organisations were encouraged to address the formation of public opinion and the broader public as citizens, taxpayers and potential advocates for and against the arts. Sometimes both these audience development strategies were attempted at once. In Migliorini's study, the aim was not only to develop audiences for the arts from amongst people of a non-English speaking background (NESB), but also to raise the standing of the arts in the eyes of those communities and to pursue a wider and more inclusive citizenship agenda.

The adoption of paradigms of mobilising the audience within the subsidised cultural sector has focused attention to cultural audiences and the research design appropriate to them in new and interesting ways. The chapter will firstly situate this turn to audience development in its policy and industry contexts. It will then examine two broad approaches to audience development: the building of arts audiences and the building of broad public support for the arts. As both approaches involve attitudinal research, some attention will be paid to evaluating the strengths and weakness of this audience research practice.

The Policy Contexts of Arts Audience Development

By the 1990s, Australian governments — state, federal and local — had identified the cultural sector more broadly as so many cultural industries (see Craik 1996). Reformulating various cultural sectors into so many connected cultural industries — the move from, say, a work of art to a cultural product — has entailed a shift in emphasis not only from the creator to the consumer/audience but also to "industry development". With cultural policy adopting aspects of industry development, new sector-wide priorities emerged (DOCA 1994). There was an attempt to build "capacity" by identifying and expanding the regional, national and international markets for these cultural industries. Positive assessments brought sustained governmental attention and interest in the cultural industries as a growth sector in terms of jobs and investment (see National Institute of Labour Studies 1994). Without these assessments, it is doubtful that the subsidised cultural sector would have been able to maintain its position on governmental horizons in an era of cost-cutting, corporate downsizing and microeconomic reform. With evidence of the use and takeup of broadly defined cultural services, governments could champion the "cultural industries" in ways they previously could not when culture was more readily identified with elite art (Craik 1996, pp. 183–84).

As part of the shift in focus from producer to audience, the Australia Council set up an Audience Development and Advocacy

Division in 1996. This division was instrumental in bringing marketing and management into a closer relationship with the arts sector. Marketing was no longer perceived simply as publicity for an existing cultural product, but was increasingly seen as a tool of management and planning to meet an organisation's artistic objectives. The presence or absence of marketing and management expertise in the sector came to be seen as critical factors in the success or failure of audience development. The Australia Council research published in 1997 reported that "almost 60 per cent of arts organisations don't have a marketing plan ... 70–80 per cent of arts organisations don't conduct audience or market research ... only a quarter of top management and half of marketing directors are very experienced in marketing; 72 per cent of arts organisations allocate no more than 10 per cent of their budget to marketing."

The closer alignment with management and marketing norms encouraged the adoption by cultural organisations of paradigms of strategic management — complete with mission statements, efficiency audits, marketing and business plans. This was accompanied by an emphasis on staff training, the development of expertise and the benchmarking of cultural administration. It brought with it greater attention to and expectations of accountability and transparency of cultural organisations, whether to funding agencies or to the community. This attention to developing a more businesslike approach on the part of cultural organisations is an international trend. Stanley Katz (1999) has pointed out how American Foundations like the Ford Foundation — a major patron of the arts in the United States from the early 1950s — wanted organisations "run efficiently" and "on business lines", rewarding organisations that did so and punishing those that did not. This insistence owed itself to a recognition that "arts organisations are businesses too, cultural businesses, not-for-profit businesses".

This focus on enhancing the "management, entrepreneurial and marketing capacities of artists and arts organisations" (Australia Council 2000, p. 9) has also entailed an orientation of both the cultural organisations and the broader cultural agencies towards a *services* perspective. Here the clients of these agencies are not so much the artists themselves as the arts consumer, audience, public and citizens who support that arts infrastructure. Consequently, there needs to be a focus on them and on being seen to meet their needs, demonstrate accountability to them, and involve them in decisions relating to cultural funding. This dovetails with a broader "democratic" orientation of purpose for the Australia Council when it stated that arts policy and support is for the people of Australia in the first instance.[1]

This services orientation encouraged the sector to think of its audiences and its publics in the same way as do the commercial cultural industries: as significantly internally differentiated and segmented. Arts administrators were encouraged to locate several arts audiences segmented in terms of cultural background, location, age, income, education, occupation and gender. So there was not one theatre audience, but several, depending not only on type of theatre but also variations within each type. Differentiating the arts audiences in this way becomes the means to develop effective promotion of both the value of arts and audience attendance at cultural venues and performances. Cultural organisations were bringing themselves into line with broader industrial practice within global consumer industries (see Peters 1987; DiMaggio 1996, p. 176), where "mass-market firms have shifted to product differentiation and the niche marketing of small-batch goods for discerning publics".

This made sense, as arts organisations internationally were operating in environments where tailored cultural services were the norm; where their "core" audiences were already being served in the majority of their cultural consumption through such strategies of differentiation; and where consumers used goods and services to "reflect distinctive self-fashioning personalities" (DiMaggio 1996, p. 176). Arts consumers are interested in and consume both high culture and popular culture forms — they are, by and large, "omnivores" (DiMaggio 1996, p. 163; Bennett et al. 1999). Arts organisations therefore need to understand the profiles — the various identities in aggregate terms — of their consumers and publics. The several strategies for arts promotion and management — strategic management, product differentiation, niche marketing, consumer research — are each pragmatic instruments for delineating and delivering arts services to these various population profiles. Cultural organisations are thus being encouraged to think and clarify their audience and their approach to marketing, and to see themselves as being in the business of audience and public-building.

Confronting the "New" Arts Audience: Selling the Performing Arts

The subsidised arts present particular difficulties for market research and audience development. The subsidised cultural sector is not like the broadcasting market. Even with the media fragmentation that is now becoming evident, broadcasters can still confidently speak of the broadcasting audience. There is a delimited range of program genres. Broadcasters work with established and agreed protocols for audience research and development. And there are few means of service delivery.

By contrast, the subsidised arts work with significant levels of internal differentiation and segmentation at multiple levels — in their various "markets", products, services, audiences and venues. The subsidised cultural sector is a producer of an array of quite distinct "products". There is diversity within each sector in, for example, the internal diversity of the performing arts — orchestras, chamber music, ballet, other dance, opera, theatre, jazz/blues, electronic music, musicals. There is diversity within each of these forms — for example, theatre can be broken down into comedy, drama, mime, circus, experimental theatre. There are also considerable differences between sectors — think of the difference between a gallery exhibition and a performance. In some cases, a product for an audience is produced; in others there may be neither a product nor an audience in any straightforward sense, as in community cultural development. These several characteristics of the sector — and therefore of its "audiences" — have made the development of audience-mindedness a particularly challenging, conceptually interesting and at times fraught task.

Selling the Performing Arts (Osborne et al. 1999) had to deal with just such a diversity of forms — music, dance, theatre and musicals, and performance genres within each type. The research grew out of a request to the Australia Council by performing arts organisations for more information on their audiences. It was also related to the difficulties these organisations faced in maintaining audience share in the context of new competitors such as (imported) and local blockbuster shows, and large arts festivals concentrating arts business in fewer outlets and in concentrated periods of time, as well as new competitors for audience attention in the broader consumer culture. Historically, the performing arts have faced particular difficulties in "modernising" themselves. Paul DiMaggio (1996, p. 176), writing in the American context, describes the generic problem with the performing arts:

> Performing-arts institutions, especially orchestras and opera companies, are a lot like traditional manufacturers. Their production technology entails getting everyone in the same place at the same time and doing the same things to them. Their marketing technology, until recently at least, requires them to sell full-season subscriptions to lots of people over and over again. The combination means less variety, less flexibility and more risk inherent in doing anything different or new.

Performing arts organisations do experience structural difficulties in dealing effectively with segmented audiences. In comparison, galleries and museums have inherently more flexibility, with their many galleries and rooms making them ideally suited to segmentation and giving their visitors control over their coming and going (see DiMaggio 1996, p. 176). Some performing arts sectors are making this transition to a cultural services orientation more easily and readily than others.

Where the arts become "more a set of resources, like many others, that are useful for establishing identities and linking oneself symbolically to a variety of groups and networks" (DiMaggio, 1996, pp. 166–67), new approaches are needed to think about the traditional arts and the audience for the arts. What is especially confronting for the performing arts in this regard is that an overhaul may be needed, not only of their campaign strategies but in what they perform, how they perform and where they perform. In short, creativity and innovation may be required across the board, including publicity, marketing, the artistic program, and the form and location of the performance.

While DiMaggio is writing in the American context, his findings have been substantially confirmed by Australian research. Presented as a contribution towards "developing new audiences, diversifying audiences and increasing attendances", the purpose of *Selling the Performing Arts* was to "enhance the sustainability and success of the performing arts sector" (Osborne et al. 1999, p. ix). It confirmed the significant segmentation of arts audiences and populations of American research, and formalised previously informal and anecdotal understandings of the differentiation within performing arts audiences with a view to developing effective promotion of cultural venues and performances. Osborne et al. argued that understandings of differentiated "arts audiences" and their varied attitudes to the value (including the emotional and spiritual value) of the arts needed to enter into the very design of the sector. There was little value in attempting to influence "mass" markets; the real value lay in thinking about particular audiences. The central message was that, in order to "successfully market any group or company, one must understand the composition and needs of its current and potential audiences, and creatively find means to strategically focus awareness and communication to those particular audiences, rather than using limited resources to try and reach broader and more difficult to influence 'mass' markets" (Osborne et al. 1999, p. 113).

The performing arts audience is segmented in a variety of ways. Osborne et al. (1999) begin by recognising the diversity of performing arts forms (dance, theatre, music, opera, musicals) and within these draw out a number of sub-categories (theatre is divided into humorous, drama, mime/circus and experimental). Through a survey, they developed a demographic profile of those who do and do not attend these various forms/genres and sub-categories. Their analysis then took into account frequency of attendance, area, sex, age, education, occupation, children, income, employment, whether members have learnt the "form" or not in school or elsewhere and whether they participate in a performing arts group. It then identified the characteristics of attenders based on this information. So we know, for example, that a classical ballet is attended more by older women.

Having established these behavioural baselines, the researchers then turned their attention to the "attitudinal" part of the survey. They established "general attitudinal differences" or "taste segments" with respect to art forms — which showed, for example, drama, contemporary theatre, modern dance and opera as "more likely to be intellectually involving" and comedy, classical music, jazz/blues, classical ballet and musicals as "simply relaxing" (Osborne et al.

1999, p. 11). Those "who enjoy contemporary forms" were found to "favour the challenging and unusual" and those who attend traditional art forms have intellectual motivators which include "educational, cultural and perceived sophistication and emotive motivators which include aspects of sensory pleasure, spiritual feeling and relaxing with the familiarity of the performance" (1999, p. x).

These attitudinal differences were then organised into several "attitudinal groupings", encapsulating "the differences in attitude which affect both frequency of attendance and choice of performance" (1999, p. x). These groups were then assigned names — "experientials", "conservatives", "big night outers", "uninvolved" and "the time and financially challenged" — which were then operationalised as a number of profiles, or "self-fashioning identities" in DiMaggio's terms. These profiles had predictive value for performing arts attendance, and gave performing arts organisations a set of ideal audience types to cater for in their marketing, publicity and programming.

"Experientials" like to "experience all sorts of performing arts, regard the arts as an important part of their life and like to support new groups" (Osborne et al. 1999, p. x). "Conservatives" self-identify as such and "they really prefer to see familiar rather than new or different work" (1999, p. 15). Members of the "big night out" group "really love the 'live' aspect of the performing arts, and the visual spectacle. They like familiar works and big hits, and tend to make a special occasion of their evening out." (1999, p. 16). The "uninvolved" groups "do not have commitment to the arts and do not see particular importance in experiencing these things, nor do they believe the performing arts offer any real advantage over the movies, even though they have attended in the past two years" (1999, p. 17) and "the financially/time challenged ... claim to be quite positive toward the performing arts, but they find the practicality of attendance difficult", with many not knowing what was available (1999, p. 18).

These profiles were then redistributed across the art forms, identifying the relative proportions of people from each category for each art form. So experientials "were the most likely group to have attended each of the performing arts", with the single exception of musicals — these are "omnivores". The "big night outers" and "conservatives" were fractionally more likely to go to musicals than the "experientials" (1999, p. 19) and so on. These different profiles provided performing arts companies with a feedback mechanism through which to consider the likely values and orientations of their audiences.

The report then goes on to identify a number of strategic implications of this research for arts organisations. First, it is not worth attempting to reach those who currently do not attend the performing arts and have indicated "no propensity or desire" to do so in the future. Too much effort and too many resources would be needed to shift attitudes in such groups, with little likelihood of effectiveness (1999, p. 85). There is some value in focusing on those who do not attend but indicate they would like to attend and those who have only been to between one and three performances in the past two years (1999, p. 85). Of more value, though, are the "current medium to heavy attenders", a group which accounts for 43 per cent of people. It is to this group that performing arts organisations should direct their attention. They should "focus on clearly understanding the needs of their current audiences, primarily to encourage loyalty, but also to increase attendance where possible via effective marketing and promotion to those who are likely to be persuaded to attend".

To assist in strategising, Osborne et al. divided the audience into a primary audience of medium to heavy attenders for each form (and each sub-category within each form) and a secondary audience of the light attenders and potential attenders. They recommended that organisations identify their primary and secondary target audiences and "their composition, needs and expectations" (1999, p. 90). The strategy was to ensure that "as many as possible of the primary and, if relevant, the secondary targets are made aware of the performance".

Any evaluation of *Selling the Performing Arts* turns on assessments of its handling and construction of this segmentation of audience and population. How adequate is this particular segmentation? How appropriate are these particular profiles? The move to become more audience-minded has proliferated understandings of and claims about the arts audience. There is a variability in the construction of the audience that comes from the diverse purposes for which the audience research is developed. Handling these several varieties of "audience" poses particular problems for administrators, policy people and activists alike, who are having to simultaneously accommodate the several guises of the audience and to develop fine-grained understandings of audience research methodology. All face the inherent danger of imposing a "one size fits all" approach as, for example, audience development strategies developed out of analysis of the major performing arts companies might be unwarrantedly generalised to apply to "visitor development" in the context of the art gallery and museum, the folk festival or the community cultural development program. Yet coordinating, sharing and translating the lessons and approaches developed in one subsidised cultural sector to another is not only necessary, but is an essential component of "cultural business".

Using "Opinion Polling" Strategically: *Australians and the Arts*

For many years, the Australia Council has run periodic surveys on Australians' attitudes to the arts (e.g. Tolhurst 1980; Australian Bureau of Statistics 1998). These surveys, taken in conjunction with the available statistical data on cultural attendances, employment and funding, have been used by arts advocates to press the political claims of the arts on government, parliamentary and public horizons. Such surveys have also featured in annual reports, pamphlets and various publications, and in promotional work of arts agencies and organisations at both federal and state levels.

Fundamental to both the generation and subsequent use of this research has been a desire to maintain, and if possible extend, the perceptions that politicians, social commentators and other opinion-makers have of the place and enduring significance of the arts by mobilising the favourable opinions of ordinary people. Maintaining the political support of prime ministers and other significant ministers for the arts has been an ongoing requirement since Prime Minister John Grey Gorton (1968–71) changed the place of the arts in the professional viewpoint of politicians. H.C. (Nuggett) Coombs (1981, p. 245) recalls that "Gorton's support was based on the belief that the arts were politically important; that support of them would earn him votes". While this high watermark of federal government arts support was continued into the Whitlam years, and was briefly reaffirmed as a signature of the Keating government in the early 1990s, grabbing the attention of politicians and convincing them of the electoral significance of Commonwealth, state and local governments continuing to support the arts has become more difficult, given the increasing competition for scarce public resources.

By the time the Australia Council commissioned Saatchi and Saatchi to undertake a research project on the value Australians place on the arts, it was clear that there were some problems with the existing ways in which arts advocates promoted the sector and dealt with politicians, opinion-makers and the broader public. This certainly informed the Australia Council's decision to rethink its relationship with the people of Australia in the full glare of the public gaze in a process which was to eventually become the *Australians and the Arts* report (Constantoura 2000). It also helps explain the Council's decision to deploy the marketing expertise of Saatchi and Saatchi as a leading multinational advertising and market research agency, to carry this research out and to subsequently develop a strategy for promoting the arts. The process of carrying out the research was designed from inception to be a "public event" involving, in a participatory way, "all Australians". The survey became a means of visibly bringing the Australia Council closer to the Australian public, whose political support would be essential to securing governmental support.

The Australia Council was not alone in fundamentally reappraising how the sector was "doing its political business", and the role that research using opinion polling and other cultural data could play. Such a reappraisal has been central to the rethinking of approaches to arts advocacy in the United States. Indeed, a seminal article by Paul DiMaggio and Becky Pettit (1999) on surveys of public attitudes towards the arts and their relation to "the Arts' political trials" contributed to Australia Council thinking in this area (the article was brought to my attention by Janice Besch, then of the Australia Council, in mid-1999).

While the Australia Council was not mired in the kind of controversies besetting its American counterpart, the National

Endowment for the Arts (NEA), it had nonetheless endured calls for its disbandment, for the reduction of its funding levels and regular criticism over the scope and character of the art works it supported. It had also seen the beginning of more targeted attacks on arts funding and practice from One Nation, a minor political party, and some interest in mounting arts attacks on the part of the Coalition parties.

DiMaggio and Pettit (1999, p. 32) wanted to understand the "ambivalent performance" of the arts on political horizons in such a way that, for instance, the Congress could vote to eliminate the NEA while the Senate could vote to increase its appropriation! The fundamental problem they identified was how to "square Congress's shoddy treatment of the NEA with arts advocates' assertions — backed by twenty years of polling data — that Americans love the arts". To do so, they analysed publicly available data on North Americans' participation in and attitudes towards the arts. Their analysis concluded that "neither arts advocates nor the NEA's opponents can claim a clear decision before the court of public opinion".

While it was true that Americans did "think very highly of the arts in general" and that huge majorities agreed that the "arts are vital to the good life", important to children's development and enhanced community life, there was considerably more ambivalence towards government arts programs. Support for some form of public spending on the arts was substantial but "shallow". Indeed, there was more support for local or state programs than federal ones and more support for libraries and museums than direct assistance to artists. (The relative non-contention of state and local government expansion of arts support, but significant vulnerabilities for federal support, seem mirrored in the Australian data, which reveal stagnant levels of federal arts funding since the 1970s but increasing state and local government funding over that period.)

For DiMaggio and Pettit (1999, p. 33) this shallow support made the NEA vulnerable to a "powerful, if small, coalition of Christian conservatives and Republican partisans committed to ending thirty years of federal support for the arts". The NEA's opponents may not have won "in the court of public opinion", but they were able to win "in the stadium of political strategy". The political problem facing arts advocates was how to handle "broad soft support" in the face of "narrow intense opposition". While the Australian arts advocates have not had to deal with intense opposition on this scale, they do have the same problem of handling "broad soft support". Equally applicable is the lesson drawn by DiMaggio and Pettit (1999, p. 35): "public opinion is uncertain, protean, up for grabs; that strategy matters; and that good information is necessary to develop good strategy". To face this challenge, arts advocates needed effective political strategising. Central to this would be a more effective use of survey research on their part.

DiMaggio and Pettit (1999, p. 35) identified a number of problems with the way the arts sector had traditionally approached research and polling data. The advocacy agendas of study sponsors had made surveys "less useful", as resources were "skewed towards data collection at the expense of data analysis". There had also been a "failure to monitor change by asking enough of the same questions on repeated surveys". At the level of survey construction, there were problems with "vague or leading questions ... [a] failure to establish what terms mean to respondents or how much respondents know or care about the arts". Additionally, the purposes of this research were flawed, as surveys were often "sponsored by arts advocates whose primary interest" lay in "'demonstrating' that the public is behind their cause", leaving out of the equation the improving of "public understanding by thoroughly probing survey results or by asking the same questions over time to monitor change". With advocacy purposes being paramount, arts research was actively "avoiding questions that would enable one to understand the ambivalence, multiple perspectives, and indifference that much of the public feels when (and if) they think about the arts". DiMaggio and Pettit (1999, p. 35) continue:

> Arts supporters have paid a high price for this naiveté. If one wants to shape public opinion, one has to understand it first. People in the opinion-making business would never settle for a survey designed merely to make their candidate or product look good. Instead, they recognize that the purpose of research is to inform the design of strategies of persuasions by understanding the views of the people they want to reach. Given the threats that the arts now face, advocates require information that will

> enable them to develop persuasive messages that can reinforce positive elements and deaccentuate negative components in the public's view of the arts, and guide efforts to target those messages most efficiently.

These findings are echoed in Costantoura's (2000, p. 29) report which, in reviewing previous Australian research, notes that it has often "been conducted relatively narrowly, most commonly among those who could be considered 'the converted'"; and that it has often been "directed more at demonstrating support for the arts than at understanding the motivating factors that prevent people from engaging more fully with the arts and determining how their attitudes might be changed".

For Costantoura, DiMaggio and Pettit, understanding public opinion is a precondition for acquiring the ability to influence it, and influencing public opinion requires a coherent research program based in part around surveys. As DiMaggio and Pettit (1999, p. 36) explain:

> Such survey techniques help us to see attitudes not simply as separate bits of data but as interlocking narratives — and thus enable us to understand the ambivalence, uncertainty, and complexity of the beliefs and opinions that drive people's political behaviour. The better that arts advocates understand these attitudes and opinions, the more prepared they will be to convert the public's vast reservoir of good will towards the arts into political support capable of influencing the arts' political environment.

Against this backdrop, Paul Costantoura (2000, pp. 15–17) and staff in the Australia Council embarked on a comprehensive research program designed to "bring about the long-term shift in attitudes and behaviour … to lead Australians to better appreciate, enjoy and engage with the arts". The research started from existing public definitions and attitudes. Participants were allowed to "devise, and reflect on, their own definitions of the arts"; "any possible expression of the arts" would be included to capture the diverse ways people perceived their experience of the arts; participants were encouraged "to describe the ways in the which the arts had value for them, both personally and in Australia today"; and were presented "with a suite of possible ways in which the arts currently does or possibly could have value, to see the extent to which these gained agreement among the general population". The research also sought to identify the organisations and individuals "who might be involved in a strategy to promote the value of the arts and what each person or organisation would do as part of the strategy".

The study sought to answer three questions: How do Australians view the arts now? How could they be influenced to have a more positive view of the arts in the future? What actions would the arts sector need to take to bring about any positive change? With a dual focus on establishing public attitudes and canvassing of the "arts sector for current ideas and activities", discussion groups were held across the country with a representative sample of people. An initial national survey of 1200 people was undertaken to clarify "early principles" and this was followed by a "major national survey of a further 1200 people" who were administered a 30-minute questionnaire exploring their attitudes and involvement in relation to the arts. Finally, there were "extensive consultations with people in the arts sector through a range of meetings and workshops covering more than 200 people representing almost every art form and approach to artistic practice".

The research showed that those who placed a high value on the arts were more likely to be female, possess tertiary qualifications, live in the inner city, be without children, be older and live in households with higher than average incomes. Respondents were also more likely to place a higher value on the arts if they were directly or indirectly involved, whether through friends or family. Conversely, the most "disaffected type of Australian" was likely to "be the Australian-born father and son, living in outer suburbs of capital cities or in rural and regional Australia, with a low level of education, a relatively low income, who received little encouragement from his Australian-born parents in relation to the arts when he was growing up, and who now feels that the arts are somewhat elitist activities that are simply irrelevant to his life or to his family" (Costantoura 2000, pp. 20, 21, 25).

Using cluster analysis to identify segments on the basis of their level of agreement or disagreement with different attitude statements, Costantoura (2000, pp. 26–27) identified a number of segments and sub-segments of those fifteen years and older to explain the differences in attitude with respect to the arts. The five segments included:

ARTS LOVERS (17%): Who are very positive about the arts and are in favour of change.

SATISFIED (21%): Who are generally quite positive about the arts and who do not see particular reasons for the arts to change.

INTERESTED (25%): Who are open to a positive experience of the arts but can see ways in which the arts could change to improve their attitudes towards them.

DISINCLINED (25%): Who are not particularly interested in the arts at present but can still see changes that would make them feel more positive about the arts.

DISENGAGED (11%): Who have little or no interest in the arts, give them a low value and are not interested in seeing them change in the future.

These major segments were then broken down into twelve sub-segments consisting of: the devotees (5 per cent), the highly involved (12 per cent), those who enjoy life (13 per cent), those who were established in their artistic tastes (9 per cent), those with an active interest (6 per cent), those with a lifestyle interest (12 per cent), those with a personal interest (7 per cent), those who were practically disinclined (6 per cent), those socially disinclined (10 per cent), those generally disinclined (9 per cent), those with other priorities (7 per cent) and those who were strongly disengaged (4 per cent) (2000, pp. 26–27). For Costantoura (2000, pp. 38, 37), these sub-segments constituted "attitudinal types that cross over demographics such as age, gender and other socio-economic factors".

While some overall strategies would be broadly effective in promoting the value of the arts, the arts sector would "need to focus on the perspectives of [these] individual segments and sub-segments to be truly effective". The research also confirmed that there were no simple measures available to "describe the complexity of the relationship Australians have with the arts" (Costantoura, 2000, p. 42). The segments were to provide the basis for targeted communications strategy development.

In formulating a strategy based on this research, Costantoura (2000, p. 16) worked within a set of unusual formal constraints. There were limited resources available to implement a strategy, and a national communications campaign was out of the question. There were insufficient funds for "funding generic arts-related advertising". In addition, the client — in this case, the Australia Council — was both conducting the study on the arts sector's behalf and envisaged itself as a catalyst for change, providing some coordination. Primary responsibility for delivering the strategy would need to lie with the arts sector itself. The "strategy" process therefore included "selling the strategy" to the sector itself, in order to then get it implemented by cultural organisations dispersed across the country and across art forms.

The resulting strategy recommended that the arts sector implement a series of objectives starting with an overall vision for promoting the value of the arts which was to "shape a vision for the future of Australia which sees the arts playing a role that Australians see is relevant and meaningful to their lives — personally and nationally — and distinctively Australian" (Costantoura 2000, p. 33). A series of objectives were developed relating to actions the sector could take to collectively contribute to promoting the value of the arts. First, there needed to be agreement within the sector to collectively "work towards promoting the value of the arts". Second, the informal networks making up the arts needed to be made more "tangible … to identify who can be involved in a strategy to promote the value of the arts". Third, the sector needed to collectively work to "raise best practice throughout the sector". Fourth, the Australia Council could make a difference by promoting the value of the arts to all Australians as an integral part of every one of its activities. And fifth, the arts needed to be made cordial — "more welcoming".

Parallelling these was a set of objectives aimed at the general public. Those involved in implementing the strategy needed to promote a broad range of creative activities to assist the public to broaden their definitions of the arts. They needed to promote "personal engagement with the arts" by encouraging Australians to explore the creative arts through both being "imaginative, creative and expressive themselves" and through enjoying "the imagination, creativity and expression of others". They needed to consider their task as assisting "Australians to find suitable entry points to the arts and be able to see the transition to elite achievement". The sector also needed to come to terms with "the strong imagery and branding that is currently associated with the term 'the arts'" and it needed to build collaborations "with business, government and other agencies, with a view to engaging the general public in the arts as part of their day-to-day lives".

The report and the lengthy processes of consultation and development indicate the extent to which the focus was on political strategising so that the "'brand image' of the arts is well-presented to the general population, to existing and potential consumers of the arts, to potential participants in the arts and to governments" (Costantoura 2000, p. 19). The report and its public processes were aimed at both the cultural organisations the Australia Council supports and the "public". These were directed at shaping the public opinion recognised by the political process. They were also about regularising and normalising the arts sector in relation to other sectors — the report and the public process emphasised the arts learning from the sporting and wine industries — as a way of increasing its standing. This too was part of strategy: to develop both research and a campaign which would be in a form that was recognisable not only to politicians, but also to other opinion-makers and shapers.

Australians and the Arts fits our cycle of media governance. It is research-minded in its attention to previous research on attitudes to the arts and attempts to move beyond these. It embraces a management modality in its use of audience research as a tool of management and planning. It is obviously audience-minded in its surveys, their design and the attention to audience segmentation. It is campaign-minded in that it attempts to not only formulate a campaign but to use the very doing of the research as a campaign device. It also entails an evaluation modality in its attempt to establish the contours of public perception, to identify variegated profiles of arts audiences as the research proceeds and to "road test" various proposal for change with respondents. It is publicity-minded in that the Australia Council paid particular attention to being seen to be conducting research into the arts and being seen to start from the position not of the cultural organisations or the agency (what the agency thinks is the case), but instead from the position of the public and what it thinks. It is also positioning itself on the side of public citizen-mindedness by being seen to attend to what the public wants rather than what the arts and cultural organisations think it wants.

Australians and the Arts was a remarkable attempt to intervene in and build political support for the arts. It entailed a strategy for reinventing and making relevant the subsidised arts funded by the Australia Council. It recognised, like the US research, that arts support is shallow and this could leave, as DiMaggio and Pettit (1999) put it, "legislators relatively unconstrained". It sought to make the arts a salient issue, to build the kind of political support that would maintain and extend governmental attention to the arts, and constrain legislators. To do so, it needed to publicly manage its relationship with voters; it needed to "go public". It had to invent a relation with the voter as citizen and therefore shareholder in public disbursement. It had to organise an evidently credible research program to deliver strategy for arts advocacy.

Such targeted research is necessarily limited research. It is research designed to transform public opinion and generate public, and therefore political, support for the arts. It "arms" cultural organisations with political and public attention-getting strategising tools. It addresses them as agencies which bear a responsibility to develop political and public support for the arts (to maintain the subsidisation of the sector in the face of competing governmental interests). It requires cultural practitioners to bear in mind two distinct "publics" — the political public which sustains the ongoing subsidisation of the sector, and the paying or visiting public (in the case of art galleries) which goes to see particular performances or exhibitions. The research might not be terribly useful in generating paying customers and visitors, as it is not designed to address the problems of the arts sector more generally. Rather, it is focused on the general problem of public support for an existing subsidised culture. The frustration that many in cultural organisations had with the whole process — namely, that it did not address their particular needs to develop their own cultural organisations and (reinvent) their audiences — points to the structural limitation of this research and advocacy enterprise: it might succeed in making people value the arts politically, but might not result in increased attendances and use.

Working from Attitudinal Research

At the centre of the analysis of both *Selling the Performing Arts* and *Australians and the Arts* are a series of audience profiles which are expected to orient future users and future uses of these reports by diverse actors. Profile-building is a common technique of market research and is extensively used by media planning agencies and in product development. Such profiles typically have a set of attributes — a kind of distinct personality — able to be summed up by a phrase. The use of such profiles is both extensive and now a common feature of our public discussion of, for example, the net generation (Tapscott 1999) and Hugh Mackay's (1997) description of today's young adults as the "options generation". There is a contemporary proliferation of these profiles, each of which has been developed for particular purposes but then acquires a life of its own and is put to work in other contexts — even becoming, as Generation X has, an identity category (see Chapter 4 in this volume).

Both reports are buying into what Joseph Turow (1997, p. 3) has usefully identified as "the new portraits of society that advertisers and media personnel invoke". These "involve the blending of income, generation, marital status, and gender into a soup of geographical and psychological profiles they call 'lifestyles'". Turow further notes how these new portraits of society are driven by logics of segmentation and differentiation — not only recognising difference, but accentuating societal differences for corporate strategy.

Their adoption by the Australia Council is part of a wider trend observable within commercial culture, government and political campaigning. Utilising them is therefore presenting information to government, opinion-makers and boards in forms which are recognisable and digestible to them. To some extent, these geo-demographic profile "cleavages" are supplanting the existing and more settled cultural stratification cleavages of gender, age, social class, geographical location, and ethnicity and race. It is not that these well-known stratifications are not important, but they lack individual explanatory power and efficacy and the means to organise a connection among them. Attitudinal research provides one way of organising the link among stratification data. It is a technique for handling and ordering segmentation. It is about knowing there is segmentation and knowing the attitudes of this segmentation.

Both reports use cluster analysis to place people into these categories — "to group together like-minded respondents" (Osborne et al. 1999, p. 12) to a series of questions designed to establish their attitudes. This approach to arts audiences is a generic application to the arts area of market segmentation techniques and strategies. Cluster analysis is the most common technique for market segmentation and is designed to reveal natural groupings within a body of data (psychographics, behaviour, product ratings, usage information and perceived needs and benefits). It does so by dividing (partitioning) data observations into homogeneous groups based on their proximity (closeness) to each other. As a technique for these Australia Council reports, it helps to "distinguish between segments purely on the basis of their level of agreement or disagreement with different attitude statements" (Costantoura 2000, p. 49). For *Selling the Performing Arts*, this involved 26 attitude statements which respondents who attended the performing arts in the last two years answered, while for *Australians and the Arts* there were more than 70 attitude statements involved.

Both reports then worked back from the clusters they derived from this attitudinal research to incorporate a variety of demographic data to better describe these groups. *Selling the Performing Arts* worked off population differentiations as to area (city/country), sex, age, education, occupation (white or blue collar), income, employment (working or non-working), children (none and less than eighteen years old). For its part, *Australians and the Arts* (Costantoura 2000, p. 215) connected these attitudinal clusters to four broad classifications: those of "age, gender" and "[lifestage and] children", "income and education", "location" and "national origin".

The result of this type of analysis is arguably a nuanced understanding of both the performing arts audience and Australian attitudes to the arts which is developed in a form suitable for intervention — whether to build audiences in or to generate greater appreciation of, support for and attendance at arts venues. The characteristic of both analyses is that several frames of analysis are used to fill out the clusters identified in the attitudinal analysis.

Like all market segmentation research, such research is basically saying that we need several frames of analysis to make sense of complex phenomena generated by demographic data. Cluster analysis is such a popular technique because it is a means of structuring and slicing through a "soup" of demographic information and parsing these into a series of digestible sentences. Indeed, the reliance on attitudinal questions — values and lifestyles questions — in this research is probably best understood as a practical response to the problem of regularising and stabilising a range of data through using attitudinal statements or questions to "ground the data".

Both research projects indicate significant variations in attendance and attitudes to the arts on the part of the broader population. Both produce a series of "segmentation maps" which produce novel "identities" which can become the basis for targeted marketing. Such research proliferates population profiles which can be used to shape a communications pitch. These profiles often contain words and phrases able to be directly used in publicity and marketing. What is produced is necessarily an artifice of the research, but it is one which is made "real" in the development of a marketing campaign to these categories of person.

With so much riding on the segmented profiles generated by cluster analysis, it is important to recognise the limitations of these audience research techniques. There are risks associated with this kind of research — risks associated with undertaking any attitudinal analysis and the risks of cluster analysis itself. Being based on attitudes rather than behaviours in the first instance makes the research highly dependent on the quality of the attitude questions or statements. Attitude items are intrinsically more arbitrary, more fungible and available to wider interpretation than is more "behaviour"-focused research. They are consequently more "creative" in their interpretation and sometimes described amongst market research practitioners as its "witchcraft" end.

Roger Wimmer and Joseph Dominick (1997, p. 451) summarise the widely recognised limitations of cluster as follows:

- Cluster analysis is "highly subjective", more "art" than science, because "it requires researchers to make a wide variety of subjective judgments regarding the procedures for conducting the study and the interpretation of the results".
- Because cluster analysis is so widely used by a variety of disciplines, "each discipline has interpreted what is and what is not required in conducting such a study". This generates a number of disciplinary "biases" such that "cluster analysis in one area of research may not be the same an in another area".
- The same data can generate different results depending on the clustering methods used, as Wimmer and Dominick note: "There are at least seven different methods of searching for clusters in a data set."
- Cluster analysis "imposes clusters on any data set" — thus risking "uncovering" clusters in data that are not actually there.

Great care clearly needs to be exercised in doing this research, as it is potentially riskier than other research which begins with observable behaviours. If you do not, for example, get your attitudes statements right, then the results of the cluster analysis will be skewed. It also emphasises the highly situational character of the research, the analytical and technical skill required of the researcher to process and interpret the results, and the risks attendant to using it for purposes for which it was not intended. The profiles generated are therefore highly situational and local — produced to achieve specific purposes.

The arts sector's increasing reliance on professional market research expertise is one means of reducing this risk by relying on the professionalism and professional credentials of those commissioned. But there is no guarantee that the problem the arts sector has always faced of tapping into qualified expertise (see Katz and DiMaggio 1998) will not continue to arise. The arts do not constitute a specialism within the larger and more professional market research organisations (there simply is not enough money in it). There is no guarantee that the "best minds" will work on lower priority arts clients unless these is some symbolic value in the association. The price arts organisations can offer for such professional services may lead these organisations to gravitate towards the lower end of the market research companies (unless the prestige of the association with the arts can be used to secure "subsidised" or *pro bono* services from leading market research companies). And there is a risk that a relatively naïve arts sector, inexperienced in the development of briefs and lacking understanding of market segmentation techniques and dynamics (including their limitations), might make serious mistakes in applying, interpreting and commissioning research.

The outsourcing of research by cultural agencies to market research companies is part of a wider trend within the sector. It is replicated, for instance, at a management level in Dr Helen Nugent's leave from Westpac to undertake a major review into the performing arts (DoCITA 1999), and the use of the big five accounting and management companies by various arts agencies for their policy analysis and development work. These moves are part of "regularising" the knowledge of the sector and ensuring that it is presented in a form digestible to, and connected with, that produced in other sectors. It is one of the means by which the sector is looking less like its own specialised *sui generis* sub-domain and is instead recognised for the connections it has with other areas of government and the cultural industries.

Conclusion

The encounter with marketing and management has posed particular difficulties for an arts sector with little experience and understanding of paradigms of market research and strategic management. Particularly confronting has been the assumption that "blow-in" researchers with a long list of corporate clients can provide better understandings of arts audiences than can the cultural organisations and cultural agencies who work daily with those same audiences. But such confrontations are not particular to the arts sector. Peter Drucker (1996, p. 106) contends that the "marketing realities" likely to be found in any good marketing analysis are in three overlapping areas: that "what the people in the business think they know about customer and market is likely to be wrong than right"; that the consumer "rarely buys what the business thinks it sells"; and that "the goods or services which the manufacturer sees as direct competitors rarely adequately define what and whom he [sic] is really competing with".

Marketing and market research directly challenge the value and significance of an organisation's own understandings of its audience — often a source of great pride. They introduce a layer of external expertise intervening in what many arts administrators see as their organic relations with their audience. They entail a perspective that the audience is never wrong, leading to research programs which start from "where people are at" rather than where the sector thinks "they should be". They give rise to new kinds of expertise needing to be accommodated by cultural organisations. Some claim it has shifted the power within cultural organisations, as market research and audience development initiatives challenge the primacy of creativity in the production process. Turning the arts into "just another business", and adopting the objectifying language of consumers, markets and the like, can be a profoundly alienating experience for artists and cultural workers, many of whom accept significantly lower salaries than they might receive in the private sector.

But both Australia Council research projects reported here are part of an inescapable process — the increasing regularisation, normalisation and differentiation of the arts audiences and the arts sector. Each in its own way situates the restricted and subsidised arts in relation to a broader continuum of cultural practices. Each provides more sustained and empirically grounded research on the arts audience and audiences for culture more generally. Each represents a different attempt to meet the challenge of a culturally diverse and segmented audiences for culture. By expanding the empirical knowledge base of arts audiences, each grounds policy analysis and program development in audience research.

Each points to a welcome pluralism in the specification and development of audiences as each ensconces at the heart of thinking about the arts and culture more generally the logics of segmentation and differentiation. The issue now is one of how this segmentation and differentiation will be handled in research analysis and policy development alike.

Note

1 For an organisation like the Australia Council, this shift from an artist-centred to a people of Australia-centred focus entails a major shift in policy focus and in self-understanding. It is also leading the different cultural organisations to increasingly resemble those in the film and multimedia area where attention to audiences was forced earlier. It is important to acknowledge, however, that previous incarnations of the Council's priorities understood that the welfare of artists was the same as the generalised welfare of Australians.

CHAPTER 6

Towards an Ecology of Cultural Attendance

Tom O'Regan and Stephen Cox

Introduction

Of late, a new "project" to connect diverse cultural forms has been emerging across the areas of audience research, cultural research more generally and policy-making. For audience research, this agenda means going beyond the audience for a particular medium or art form — or even cluster of art forms — to develop an overall ecology of audience participation and attendance across the variety of commercial and subsidised culture. For cultural research, this is an agenda to think beyond the horizon line of a particular cultural industry (like theatre or television) or cluster of such industries (the performing arts, the audio-visual sector), in order to apprehend the multifaceted relations among what has been variously called the "arts-related" (Guldberg 2000) or "cultural" industries (Throsby 2001).

For policy-making, this began as an agenda of coordinating and integrating these various industries into the many related "cultural industries" of the first national cultural policy, *Creative Nation* (DOCA 1994). More recently, there has been an attempt to turn the various capabilities of these industries into a larger and value-added capacity in the "creative industries". In a parallel fashion, cultural planning for "cultural and leisure precinct" developments over the part decade has routinely attempted to organise a diverse cultural and leisure field into complementary and synergistic relationships. In Brisbane, for example, this field comprises existing and new botanical gardens, (redeveloped) sporting arenas, new and existing galleries, museums, performing arts centres, swimming pools/beaches, restaurants and education facilities at South Bank, all of which need to be coordinated and developed into an integrated cultural and leisure precinct. Such planning is about helping "urban governments identify the cultural resources of a city or locality and to apply them in a strategic way to achieve key objectives in areas such as community development, place marketing or industrial development" (Ghilardi 2001, p. 119).

All of these areas — audience development, cultural research and policy development — are intimately connected. The development of a national cultural statistics framework by the Australian Bureau of Statistics (ABS) in the late 1980s was designed to help establish the cultural industries as a recognisable, tangible and measurable sector alongside other industrial sectors. This ABS research was used to demonstrate, among other things, that "cultural activity makes a significant contribution to the economy ... bigger (in the Australian case at least) than beer and footwear" (Throsby 2001, p. 111). Together with concurrent moves in the early 1990s to develop a coordinated national cultural policy, this statistical base encouraged members of the sector to recognise themselves as a part of a larger field, and to assess their own sector's standing in this field. It also assisted them in their collective lobbying of governments and politicians. For their part, governments and the broader public had a box within which to put several governmental initiatives ranging from support for artists and art forms to libraries, zoos, botanical gardens, museums, galleries, performance centres, film studios, the ABC and SBS.

Over time, this combination of national cultural policy frameworks and the routine collection of data for the cultural industries allowed diverse actors to scope the connection between these subsidised fields and the broader "commercial" cultural industries of advertising, design, craft, broadcasting and film. "Creative industries" policy-making organised on "industry development" principles looked to better coordinate and build something larger from the dispersed base of the "arts-related" industries (Creative Industries Taskforce 1998). Finally, this combination of policy-making, cultural statistics and trends within cultural research to embed cultural consumption in daily life and its diverse settings helped to generate a field of cultural research increasingly interested in ways in which populations intersected with various cultural forms and the ways in which these various industries could collectively be described in both economic and sociological terms (Throsby 2001; Bennett et al. 1999; Schroder 1999; Gray 1999).

The project of connecting the several guises of the audience also has its origins in commercial and industrial, as well as policy forecasting, priorities. The reality of an increasingly fragmented media landscape characterised by increased choice and differentiated consumption — audio-visual choices include broadcast television, varieties of pay TV, cinemas, specialty large-format cinemas, video rental and sell-though — makes it an industrial priority for audiences to be increasingly conceived as audiences for several media at any one time. Advertising agencies and their clients need to not only know about the flow of media usage through the day to develop effective campaign strategies, but they also need to know the particular patterns of overall media usage on the part of their desired demographics. Media planners are increasingly supplying a variety of clients from newspapers, broadcasters and advertisers through to policy agencies like the Productivity Commission with typologies of audiences developed from "whole of media" databases such as Roy Morgan's *Single Source*. By identifying groups sharing a similar pattern of media usage, media planners are able to provide behavioural profiles of media consumers for clients interested in understanding the "place" of particular media in an emerging ecology of media use. For the media industry managers who use these profiles, the audience becomes "a particular kind of consumer market with many subspecies" (McQuail 1997, p. 143).

In a similar way, cultural planners and managers of cultural precincts are increasingly concerned with how a particular kind of market for cultural attendance has emerged and the ways its sub-species — the audiences for the various cultural forms and venues for these — are evolving. Not only are the consumers of sporting, cultural and leisure services being thought of as existing on a continuum, but the synergies among them are being explored. Cultural planning in this context is about thinking "strategically about the application of the cultural resources of localities to a wide range of public authority responsibilities" (Ghilardi 2001, p. 118). These several audiences and activities go significantly beyond the sector-specific audience remit of the Australia Council discussed in the previous chapter.

What is instructive about this trend in audience research is its multidimensionality. Typically, several different behavioural variables are held together at any one time. BDA Marketing and Planning's research for the Productivity Commission's Broadcasting Regulation Inquiry identified nine "media types" (Productivity Commission 1999, p. 17). These ranged from those with low involvement in the media (20 per cent of the audience), those mainly young women who were focused on magazines and movies (6 per cent), those who were radio focused — the all-day radio audience (6 per cent) — the heavy viewers focused on commercial network television (12 per cent), the heavy readers focused on newspapers (19 per cent), those who use the media to fill time (15 per cent), the internet-focused (12.7 per cent), those into self-development, who use media to enhance knowledge and live life to the full (8 per cent) and the high-involvement people (1.5 per cent) who are "real media addicts". BDA Marketing and Planning (1999) further specified these nine profiles as having particular patterns: of overall media usage; of participation in other recreational activities; of income; of stage of life; of gender; of employment and occupational status; and of residential location. BDA Marketing and Planning was, in short, providing maps of cultural consumption, cartographies of cultural taste and doing it all based on behavioural rather than attitudinal data. Its audience typology was used by the Productivity Commission to forecast the likely failure of high-definition television to gain initial acceptance in the Australian marketplace.

This chapter provides a more arts-focused contribution to this new project of connecting diverse cultural forms in audience research. It starts from attendance at cultural venues. It begins by outlining the most comprehensive cultural research agenda yet undertaken from within cultural studies and cultural policy studies — the Australian Everyday Cultures project (AECP) as represented in Bennett et al.'s (1999) book *Accounting for Tastes*. After identifying some principal features of this project to "map the distribution of Australian cultural practices" (1999, p. 6), we will consider what the AECP datasets can tell us about how a broad range of cultural events relate to each other in a behavioural ecology of cultural attendance. We use a number of lenses — occupation, age, sex, residential location and education — to explore this ecology of cultural attendance. Within this analysis, we also investigate what light the data can shed on issues of cultural capital as a resource for identity construction.

Accounting for Tastes

Like their media planning counterparts, Bennett et al. (1999) examined a wide variety of cultural consumption, correlating this consumption with variables of class, gender, ethnicity, geography, education and age. Taking the dual sense of culture as creative production and way of life, they worked across the commercial and subsidised culture divides and reported a whole gamut of cultural activities, including body building, exercise, the keeping of pets, sport and tourism, crafts, reading, botanical gardens, zoos and theme parks. "Cultural tastes" were defined by everything that the authors could conceive as culture:

> including home-based leisure activities, fashion, the ownership of cars and electronic equipment, eating habits, friendships, holidays, outdoor activities, gambling, sport, reading, artistic pursuits, watching television, cinema-going, and the use of libraries, museums and art galleries (Bennett et al. 1999, p. 2).

In this way, cultural practices which demanded an audience were included alongside those which did not, one example being private cultural practices of collecting craft, CDs, records and books.

Like the ABS's National Centre for Culture and Recreation Statistics, Bennett et al. (1999, p. 2) worked within an encompassing definition of the cultural and leisure industries and developed a purposefully descriptive agenda of describing "the relationships between the patterns of participation in the different fields of cultural practice". The sampling frame for the AECP survey was based on the August 1994 Australian Electoral Roll. A total sample of 5000 non-institutionalised adults was obtained by firstly stratifying by state and territory and then applying systematic random sampling within these strata (1999, p. 270). Of 5000 questionnaires distributed, a total of 500 were returned undelivered. A further 450 were returned as refusals, with a total of 2756 useable returns, making a response rate of 61.9 per cent. The distribution of the resulting stratified sample closely matched that of the Australian Electoral Roll.

To operationalise the AECP class model, Bennett et al. collected information about their participants' current occupation to determine their employment status, as well as managerial or supervisory status: "On these initial filters we superimposed a measure of the occupation's skill level based on the either groups of the Australian Standard Classification of Occupations (ASCO) devised by the Australian Bureau of Statistics." (1999, p. 18) The resulting "class model" consisted of nine categories: never employed, employers, self-employed, managers, professionals, para-professionals, supervisors, sales and clerical workers, and manual workers. In a similar way, they organised their age cohorts into groupings of 18–25, 26–35, 36–45, 46–59 and 60+; their educational level cohorts into six groupings — primary, some secondary, completed secondary, vocational, part-tertiary and completed tertiary education — and their geographical cohorts into locations of inner city, suburban, small town, rural and semi-rural (acreage). Various cultural activities were then examined in relation to these settled groupings of demographic variables and used to generate novel research results.

Their social class research enabled them to draw a "schematic profile" of cultural consumption for the various classes. Professionals and manual workers emerged as having two diametrically opposed profiles of cultural participation. Professionals generally did more of everything than anyone else (see Bennett et al. 1999, p. 252). They holidayed more, ate out at restaurants more, participated in sport more (preferring tennis and swimming), owned more musical instruments and played them twice as much, owned more modems and more art of various kinds including books; they went more to art galleries, botanical gardens, public musical performances, public lectures, public libraries, orchestral concerts, chamber music concerts, ballet, movies, shows and expositions, film festivals and cultural festivals. They exhibited a greater preference for classical music and were most familiar with classical composers. They had the highest rates of preference for ABC Radio National and ABC Classic FM. They preferred the public broadcasters more. They did, however, do less than anyone else of some things — like smoking, watching sport and watching television. They had the lowest rate of viewing of commercial television and "of attendance at theme parks and night clubs" (Bennett et al. 1999, p. 252). Unsurprisingly, Bennett et al. declared professionals to have the most cultural capital of any group.

By contrast, manual workers did a lot less (see Bennett et al. 1999, p. 253). They had low rates of participation in sport — only employers played less sport.[1] They attended restaurants the least, and they exhibited the least preference for classical music, Radio National and Classic FM, public broadcasting and reading newspapers. They had the lowest overall rate of ownership of musical instruments and of many domestic technologies such as video cameras, computers, answering machines and modems. They owned less of every category of art objects and literature. They had very low attendance at art galleries, orchestral and chamber music concerts, ballet, musicals, opera, theatre, movies, special exhibitions and film festivals. They used computers for entertainment, not business or education. They did not like formal dinners, but appreciated barbecues. They had the highest rate of watching sport — whether at live venues or on television — they watched commercial television the most, they owned more guitars than anyone else, they had "the highest rates of attendance at theme parks, night clubs and pubs with bands and high rates at rock concerts". And they had the strongest preference for country and rock music. Unsurprisingly, they had the "least cultural capital".

The other social classes filled in the space between these extremes. In terms of cultural consumption, "the typical pattern is for managers to come second after professionals, followed by one of the employing classes, while sales and clerical workers usually have closest to the lowest rates of participation" alongside manual workers (Bennett et al. 1999, p. 234). Employers and the self-employed "have more in common culturally with the manual working class and with supervisors than they do with managers and professionals" (1999, p. 261). For their part, para-professionals were found to be ambivalent, "pulling at times towards professionals and at times towards the working classes" (1999, p. 252).

Cohort profiles for age, gender, ethnicity and geography were generated and these considerably complicated the class-based profiles. So, for example, they noted (1999, p. 236) that women are "considerably more likely than men to be involved across the range of activities comprising the realms of subsidised [classical music, ballet, theatre] and public culture [museums, galleries, libraries, gardens]; female participation in the former is 149% that of men, and 138% in the realm of public culture".

The patterns of public participation, attendance at cultural and sporting venues and styles of private ownership and consumption were all being considered on a continuum. Consequently, patterns of (subsidised) arts attendance were seen as part of a larger economy of participation and taste. When arts audiences are audiences for and participants in a gamut of cultural and social activities, the analytical priority becomes one of inserting culture back into "life".

To facilitate their consideration of this complex cultural field, and to help identify the relationships among several cultural forms, Bennett et al. used factor analysis[2] to group the cultural field into four distinct areas: a subsidised culture; a public culture; a private culture; and a public broadcasting culture. The *subsidised culture* consisted of those cultural activities which occurred outside the private home, but which were subsided to some extent by government funding. These consisted of public musical performances, public lectures, orchestral concerts, chamber music concerts, ballet, musicals, opera, theatre and cultural festivals. Most of these activities were a hybrid of user pays and government subsidies. The *public culture* consisted of cultural activities which occurred in public and relied primarily on government funding — like libraries, museums, art galleries, botanical gardens and special exhibits at museums or art galleries charging entry fees. The third set of practices, the *private culture*, consisted of practices that occurred within one's own home; these were primarily about the ownership of various cultural artefacts — 500+ books, signed limited edition prints, sculpture, CDs, art posters, art books, literary classics, musical instruments, and so on. The fourth area was the *public service broadcasting audience*. The ABC and SBS are reliant on public funding, but their reception takes place in the home.

These four areas of the cultural field were examined in relation to each other to determine the degrees to which they covered the social field. Unsurprisingly, on access and equity grounds, public broadcasting tended to score best and subsidised culture and private culture the worst. When we consider the emerging trend within cultural planning to group together and find synergies among diverse venues and kinds of activities, we can see that these planners are grouping together what Bennett et al. consider to be distinct arenas of cultural practice. Such planners are trying to bring into productive relation subsidised culture, public culture and — inasmuch as weekend arts and crafts markets, restaurants and central business district shopping precincts are also part of these equations — private culture. If Bennett et al.'s analysis is correct, such planners face considerable challenges to cohere such a dispersed cultural field.

Bennett et al. (1999, p. 260) insist on the basis of their research that there is no single cultural "hierarchy organising all regimes of value". Rather, the cultural field "is marked by a plurality of scales of value, in many of which age or gender or regional location, rather than social class, play a dominant role" (1999, p. 269). This confirms earlier research undertaken by DiMaggio (1987) in the United States. Both studies of taste and cultural participation reveal that professionals — those of high social status in DiMaggio's terms — do more of everything, not only consuming more elite and subsidised culture but also participating more in nearly every kind of cultural activity. It is undoubtedly the case that our artistic classification systems are "becoming more differentiated and less hierarchical" and our "classification weaker and less universal" (DiMaggio 1987, p. 452).

Bennett et al. (1999, p. 269) argue for the "weak" reproduction effects of cultural capital, claiming it plays a less exclusionary role than social capital in transmitting social advantage to the next generation. Instead, cultural capital is used by social classes, gender, age cohorts and subcultures as so much available material from which to fashion an identity. Furthermore, "it is not only in relation to high culture that the differential distribution of cultural capital serves to organise relations of distinction between those who possess the cultural skills in question and those who do not" (1999, p. 246). Subcultures also organise relations of "cultural inclusion and exclusion between those who can, and those who cannot, exhibit the kinds of *savoir faire* that membership of subculture requires" (1999, p. 246). In this context, the "officially sanctioned culture of art galleries and museums no longer enjoys universal or even widespread acceptance", and those who do not participate in these activities "do not experience this as a deprivation".

There is, in DiMaggio's (1987, p. 444) terms, no easy "isomorphism of taste and class". Professionals and managers do more of most cultural activities, and doing more of subsidised cultural activities is part of their wider public and cultural engagement. DiMaggio seeks to explain such findings by suggesting that those operating with "wide-ranging networks require broad repertoires of taste" (1987, p. 444). Their "role systems are highly complex", which suggests to DiMaggio (1987, p. 445) that "variation in tastes may occur more within persons, as they perform diverse roles, than between them". It seems that "high culture facilitates mobility", whereas "popular culture provides the stuff of everyday sociability" (DiMaggio 1987, p. 444). For DiMaggio, the audience for the traditional subsidised arts and public institutions like galleries and museums is neither exclusively sustained by these particular art forms nor likely to be engaged by art as a "sacred canopy". Instead, this audience enters into a variety of cultural experiences of which the subsidised arts are a part.

This sense of the very ordinariness of people's relations to the arts finds confirmation in the audience research conducted by the Australia Council and discussed in Chapter 5 (see Costantoura 2000, p. 325). Take the several prosaic motivators for classical music attendance and jazz/blues. Motivators for classical music were: "relaxing/helps unwind, overwhelms the senses, involving — follow the conductors (maestro), escape, sensory pleasure, spiritual feeling; uplifting, familiarity of music, cultural — a little elitist — for the more educated" (Osborne et al. 1999, p. 38); and for jazz/blues: "accessible, cheap, relaxing, involving, becomes part of one's life, become part of the scene, heavy attenders — pub scene, gutsy, real, emotive" (Osborne et al. 1999, p. 48). That cultural consumption is undertaken for a mix of relaxation, sensory stimulation and self-fashioning/ identity creation purposes suggests the existence of a continuum of cultural experience across the subsidised and commercial arts.

Bennett et al. (1999, pp. 247–48) conclude their wide-ranging inquiry by identifying four policy rationales for the role of government in the cultural field. The first, using the evidence of cultural dispersal and fragmentation as its guide, stresses the importance of "managing the relationships between the increasingly diverse ways of life that make up civil society". The second rationale, using the evidence of "the nexus between public culture and public education in enhancing and equalising the cultural life-chances of citizens", foregrounds education for policy attention. The third rationale relates to "the role of government in supporting new forms of public, and publicly educative, presence on the part of groups previously excluded from bourgeois definitions of the public". This implies a cultural policy specifically focused on Indigenous Australians, youth, regional Australians and people of a non-English speaking background. The fourth rationale is concerned with the continuing role of government in supporting public broadcasting as a component part of the broadcasting mix. For Bennett et al., the crucial policy concern is to "enhance the effective purchase of these grammars of publicness". Like their cultural research, this is an activism on several fronts aimed at bringing together and creating synergies among diverse governmental programs and rationales.

Towards an Ecology of Cultural Attendance

In contrast to the newer approach of examining synergies among diverse cultural practices, cultural audiences traditionally have been known by the number of people who have attended particular types of events or venues, with the audience segmented into a range of demographic categories such as age and gender. We used the AECP data to move beyond this traditional approach and examine the ecology of cultural attendance — that is, how does attendance at a range of cultural events coexist? Prior to doing so, however, we compare the AECP data to that collected by the ABS to ascertain the representativeness of the AECP data. The ABS data are clearly the most representative data used for the traditional approach to describe cultural participation in Australia. The ABS cultural attendance data are published in *Attendance at Selected Cultural Venues*, and have been collected and published three times (for 1991, 1995 and 1999). The data-collection methodology used by the ABS consisted of multi-stage sampling to collect data from a sample which was representative of the population of Australia aged fifteen years and older. In total, data were collected by interview from a sample of approximately 25 200 persons. About 80 per cent of the interviews were conducted over the telephone, with the remainder being face-to-face interviews. The ABS cross-tabulated the attendance figures with eight demographic variables, including age, sex, state, residential region (capital city or non-capital city), relationship in household (e.g. dependant, parent), birthplace (English-speaking or otherwise), employment status and educational attainment.

Participants were asked to indicate how many times in the previous twelve months they had attended each of twelve cultural venues or events. The venues and events included art galleries, museums, animal and marine parks, botanical gardens, libraries, popular music, classical music, theatre, dance, opera or musical, other performing arts and cinema. The ABS data provide information on attendance for each event, for each of the demographic categories listed. The comparable data from the AECP are provided in Figure 6.1. This figure provides a snapshot of cultural attendance across these several venues and outlines the extent of gender variation in overall attendance data.

Comparison with the data published by the ABS confirms much of the AECP data analysis.[3] Both data sets indicate that movies were the most frequently attended cultural event, with 67 per cent of ABS respondents indicating they had attended the cinema at least once in the previous year, and 64 per cent of AECP respondents indicating they attended the movies frequently or sometimes. As is known, the cinema is the mass cultural event of our society, and this is confirmed by these two data sets. The next most frequently attended event was shows, exhibitions or fairs, with 54 per cent of AECP participants indicating attendance. This event gains so many attendees partly due to the combination of several different types of events. The category might include many things, such as street festivals, particular events at cultural festivals and maybe some theatrical events. It is likely that this category combines some of the other events within the AECP list. The next most attended venues, as indicated by both data sets, were libraries and botanical gardens. Attendances at both were close to 40 per cent. These two venues are characterised by their free admission.

While the AECP indicates that theatre is the next most heavily attended event (33 per cent), the ABS puts the figure much lower, at 17 per cent. There is no clear indication as to why this discrepancy exists. Both data sets confirm attendance of approximately 25 per cent of the population at forms of popular music. This comparability is achieved despite markedly different questions being asked. The AECP questionnaire asked about attendance at three specific forms — live bands at pubs, rock concerts and night clubs — while the ABS asked about attendance at popular music venues. Despite this, the percentages are quite similar.

Classical music was attended by fewer people. The two data sets suggest that about 10 per cent attend, and the AECP data indicate that more of these come from orchestral concert attendance than chamber music attendance. Other subsidised art forms, such as ballet and opera, are attended by equally few or fewer people. Musicals were reported to be attended more by the AECP participants (26 per cent) than the ABS participants (13 per cent).

Other generally free venues include museums and art galleries, both attracting approximately the same proportion of the population (20 per cent according to the ABS and 25 per cent according to the AECP data). While free, these venues are of a more "restricted" nature than libraries and botanical gardens, and attract far fewer people. Interestingly, the proportion attending a special exhibit at a museum or gallery which requires payment is the same as those attending for free.

Both data sets confirm the importance of gender in cultural consumption. As Figure 6.1 shows, women generally attend cultural events more frequently than do men. Men only attend theme parks and live bands more than women, and in only one other event — attendance at rock concerts — is there an equivalent attendance. For all other events, women attend with greater frequency than do men. For some events — for example, ballet — female attendance is twice that for men.[4]

But frequency of attendance is a blunt instrument. While it allows us to specify overall frequencies of attendance at cultural venues, and can be used to show differences between men and women, those in capital cities and those outside, and so on, it can tell us no more

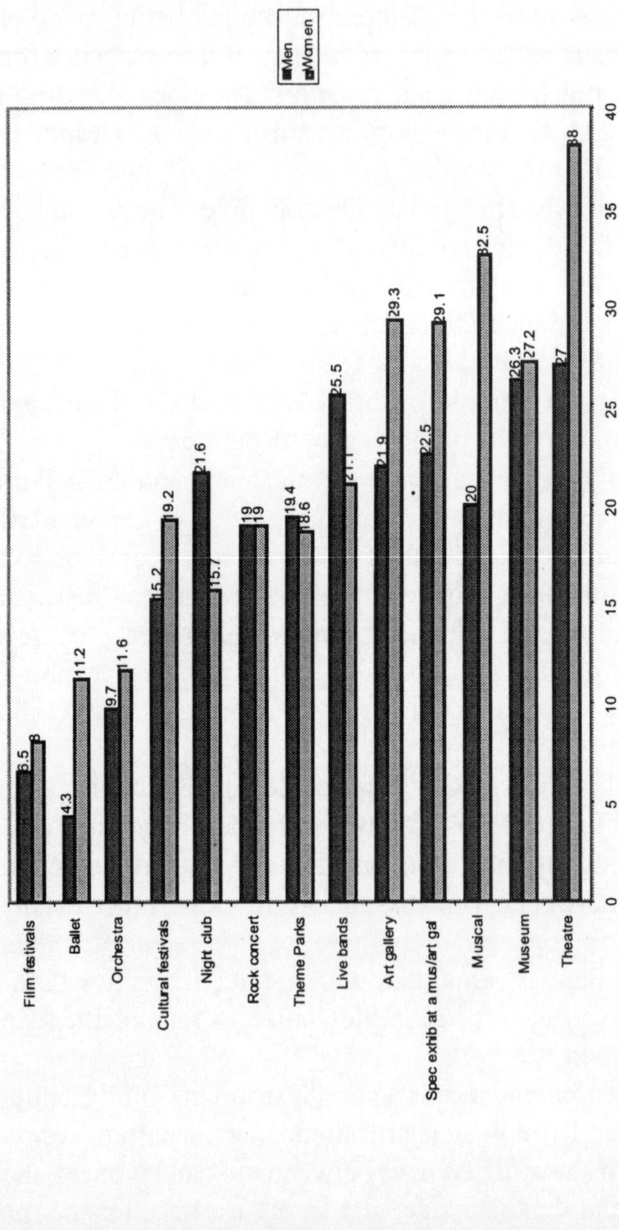

Figure 6.1: Attendance at Cultural Venues — Men and Women

than the average frequency of attendance at cultural venues of a given population. It does not, and cannot, address the problem that people on average across a population attend a cultural event with the same frequency but different people will be attending these different events. We need an instrument to locate these more subtle patterns of attendance across the population.

Our purpose in developing an ecology of cultural attendance using the AECP data is to move beyond description of the frequency of cultural event attendance. We are interested here in the patterns of that attendance — which events cluster (or do not cluster) with what other events? Which events are attended by the same people? How do cultural events "live together" in terms of their everyday performance? This investigation will be conducted in three stages. First, we look at how individual items of cultural event attendance relate to each other for the general population; and second, we examine the two occupational groupings known to be diametrically opposed — professionals and manual workers. We examine how attendances at particular arts events relate to and differ from each other. This will tell us about the audiences which attend cultural events. While it is obvious that attendance at movies and other mass cultural events differs from attendance at ballet and opera, other relationships are not so obvious. Where do film festivals or musicals fit into the scheme of event attendance? Is the ecology of attendance at these events more like a mass cultural ecology, or one of a more restricted nature? In the third stage of our investigation, we map age and gender, occupation and residential location in relation to cultural event attendance more generally to determine the ways in which these markers of socio-cultural differentiation result in similar and different patterns of cultural event attendance. As noted above, Bennett et al. (1999) provide a detailed sense of the distribution of cultural preferences among occupational groupings — how do these look if we just focus on cultural venues? How do inner-city dwellers differ from people who live in other locations? Are city dwellers similar or different from suburbanites? How close or apart from each other are the different age cohorts and, within these, the different gender cohorts?

Multidimensional scaling (MDS) permits us to conceive performance venues as ecological spaces. This statistical technique provides a way of examining how similar a set of "objects" are to each other. Objects used in a multidimensional scaling analysis can be almost anything. In the current study, they are the nineteen cultural events, and classifications of people based upon occupation, age, residential location and gender. To perform multidimensional scaling, data are required that allow a set of objects — in this case, the nineteen cultural events — to be viewed in terms of their similarity. A common way of getting such similarity data is to ask a sample of people to rate each object according to a number of characteristics. In the current study, the data represented the rating of each event in terms of how frequently it was attended by the participant. In terms of event attendance, this means that those events that are attended with similar frequency by the same people will tend to group together. If some events are attended by some people with a certain frequency and at a different frequency by other people, then these differences in the pattern of event attendance will be revealed.

Multidimensional scaling will therefore show how similar the frequencies of attendance at the events are to each other. It provides a spatialised picture of event attendance — a psychological or mental space — within which cultural events are distributed for populations. The closer two points are to each other, the more similar they are. It will also highlight "clusters" of events for which attendance patterns are similar. So if two events are attended with the same frequency on average across the whole sample, but are attended by completely different people within the sample, then in spatial terms, these two events will not be particularly close. For example, if attendances at, say, live bands and art galleries were similar in frequency (which they are, at 23 per cent and 26 per cent respectively), but these cultural events were attended by different people, then the two events would be far apart in the MDS solution. By the same token, if there are clusters of "event" attendance where the same people are likely to attend across the sample, then this will show up.

The results of the MDS analysis of the nineteen events are shown in Figure 6.2. This figure is a spatial representation of the distances between all activities. The larger the distances, the less similar activities. In the context of this particular analysis, the similarities concern patterns of frequency of attendance at events as previously

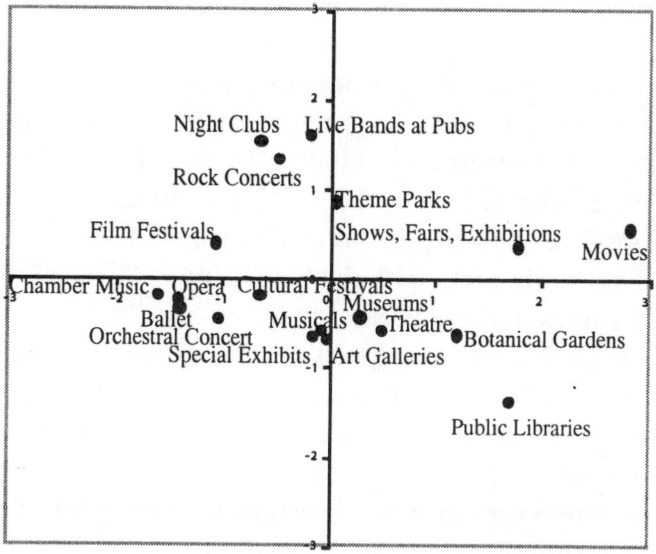

Figure 6.2: Events — Whole Sample MDS

discussed. On the left-hand side of Figure 6.2, and in the middle of it, we find a cluster of events (Cluster 1) which includes chamber music, opera, ballet and orchestral concerts — all of which are central items in Bennett et al.'s (1999) classification of subsidised culture. While attendance at these events is low for all demographic groups, attendance at them does form a cluster and attendance at one event indicates greater likelihood of attendance at other events within the cluster. This is the first ecological grouping present in the data.

A second cluster is found at the bottom of Figure 6.2 and consists of a set of other events which are attended more frequently (special exhibits at museums and galleries, art galleries, museums, musicals and theatre). Cluster 2, combining as it does elements of "subsidised" and "public culture" in Bennett et al.'s terms, is a more weakly established cluster than Cluster 1. This clustering indicates that theatre attendance differs significantly from the other performing arts, implying that it might be difficult to apply to theatre attendance the same assumptions that are applied to the other subsidised performing arts. The clustering of musicals and theatre, while in one sense predictable as both are forms of theatre, is surprising from another perspective. Over the last decade or so, Australia has witnessed the musical spectacular, optimised by the Andrew Lloyd Webber musicals. These have attracted large crowds and, traditionally, musicals have succeeded in drawing larger audiences than have "plays". The expected finding could be that musicals and theatre thus would have separated out more. But this was not the case.

Cluster 3 lies at the top of the plot. This cluster, which consists of night clubs, live bands at pubs and rock concerts, represents a popular culture/live music and night clubbing cluster. Cluster 3 events are attended with roughly the same frequency as Cluster 2 events (on balance, Cluster 2 events are attended more often than are Cluster 3 events), but they are clearly at some distance from each other, with little overlap of audience. Cluster 1 (the classical music-related performing arts) and Cluster 3 (popular music) events have the highest degree of symbiosis among their elements of any cluster.

These results indicate that there does indeed exist a classical music-related "high culture" arts audience. At the same time, many of those who attend these musical (and dance) forms attend a wide variety of other cultural forms, as discussed below. Closer examination of the attendance data indicated that, while about 85 per cent of those who attend Cluster 1 events also attend Cluster 2 events, only about 30 per cent of those who attend Cluster 2 events also attend Cluster 1 events. The audiences are overlapping, but maintain their distinction. Their overlapping but distinct character has a number of implications for our understanding of and strategising for these art forms. First, the bringing together of elements of the subsidised culture and public culture in Cluster 2 provides evidence of a connection across this putative divide. The proximity of theatre-going to museum and gallery attendance provides some grounds for the strategy of co-locating theatres, galleries and museums in contemporary cultural precincts. It also provides support for marketing strategies designed to leverage attendance for all three forms. However, the distinction between Cluster 1 and Cluster 2 audiences points to the limits of synergies between these two clusters. The classical music-related performance forms and attendance at museums and galleries seem to live in different cultural spaces, forming distinct sub-ecologies, and cannot be easily be treated as one. Cultural festivals share a partial symbiosis with Cluster 1 and

Cluster 2 events. The positioning of cultural festivals is understandable, as these festivals usually have elements from both Cluster 1 and Cluster 2, or are principally one or the other of these types. For example, there is a plethora of music festivals (e.g. Brisbane Biennial) and other more broadly based festivals (e.g. the River Festival of Brisbane) which include substantial musical elements. Further investigation of the data revealed that a sizeable minority (approximately 40 per cent) of those who attend the classical music-related events also attend popular music events. However, only about 15 per cent of those who attend popular music events also attend classical music events.

Theme parks and film festivals differ slightly from these other events. Obviously the expense of theme parks limits their audience, but while theme parks are closer to other events than are shows, exhibitions and fairs, and movies, this category still occurs in a significantly different space than the other mass events. The film festival audience, on these calculations, also appears to be a reasonably special audience with some limited connections with other subsidised cultural events. It shares a partial symbiosis with both Cluster 2 and Cluster 3 groupings.

On the far right of Figure 6.2 lie the most frequently attended events: movies, shows, fairs and exhibitions, libraries and botanical gardens. As such a large cross-section of the population goes to these events, they are outliers in the sense that attendance at them provides no level of prediction for attendance at other events. These are cultural venues which, because of their mass character, are largely undifferentiated within the AECP data. Of course, there are considerable differentiations of venue and movie type within the movies, just as attendance at shows, fairs and exhibitions is probably highly differentiated in terms of which types of shows, fairs and exhibitions are attended by various types of people. These differences, based upon the variety of events, are not captured by the AECP data. The same holds for botanical gardens and libraries, which are likely to have highly differentiated usage by families, senior citizens, young people and the unemployed. Significantly, those "cultural events" which are attended the most frequently and attended by the greatest cross-section of the population have little in common with each other, indicating that — although they are "mass events" — they have somewhat different "audiences".

While the pattern of event attendance illustrated in Figure 6.2 is not particularly surprising, it shows there are significant differentiations between events — even those with the same frequency of attendance. This suggests that populations at the most macro level tend to group particular events and venues together, and these groupings need to be respected in any analysis of and strategising for these cultural forms. Cultural organisations, policy-makers and cultural analysts alike need to view relations among events in ways that are consonant with how audiences view these events.

To alter the make-up of this ecology will not be easy, particularly for those sub-ecologies which are some distance from one another. While this ecology could be seen to have been the result of prior policy and associated infrastructure, this policy and its infrastructure have left a lasting legacy of cultural attendance patterns which will need to be worked from. As these patterns of attendance will not prove easy to shift, ambitions to transform them seem overly optimistic. These patterns of cultural attendance also help to explain why there might be particular sub-domains of policy-making — for example, in youth policy (which acknowledges distinct youth patterns of cultural attendance in popular music) and in classical music policy-making. The ecology presented here supports these two policy areas remaining quite distinct from one another, an issue taken up later in this chapter.

It also points to some of the challenges cultural precinct managements face in developing synergies among the several cultural venues (and therefore audiences) making up the precinct. Such precincts organise different audiences at different times for different venues. It is unlikely that the cultural events and facilities in such precincts will significantly build one another's audiences. Rather, other bases must be found for operationalising their contiguity in such spaces — such as the economies of scale that co-location provides for other things like access to public transport, car parking, security and other infrastructures. Arguments for co-location are not well supported from a purely cultural perspective, but they are more convincing from a cultural "industries" perspective which situates cultural activities within an industry and economic framework.

Figure 6.2 is a "whole of population" map representing the averaging across a population. This level of generality aggregates, rather than attempting to differentiate on the basis of particular populations. In aggregating cultural preferences, it necessarily treats the audience as largely homogenous. This begs the question of whether this same pattern of event attendance holds when we drill down below this level of generality to take into account particular distinct cohorts. Does the ecology shift around dramatically enough to compromise the validity of the "whole of sample" ecology indicated above when we consider two diametrically populations — professionals and manual workers? Do they share the same underlying "map" of cultural preferences? Are some of these linkages weaker? Are other linkages stronger for these different populations?

Professionals and Manual Workers

Figures 6.3 and 6.4 show the pattern of attendance for manual workers and professionals respectively. The same fundamental organisation of events into clusters and sub-ecologies that is evident for the whole-sample group can be seen to hold in a more attenuated form for both groups in this sample. The pattern of event attendance is, however, clearly different for these two groups — a difference not well captured by the whole-sample multidimensional scaling. Examination of the plot for manual workers (Figure 6.3) reveals that Clusters 1 and 2 from the whole-sample MDS collapse into one larger cluster, although the two original clusters are still distinguishable. In addition, both film festivals and cultural festivals collapse into this larger cluster. This pattern suggests that, for manual workers, all of these events — which incorporate all of the subsidised arts and some of the public cultural venues (specifically museums and art galleries) — are most likely viewed similarly. All of these venues and events are attended very infrequently by manual workers. The popular music events — Cluster 3 from the whole-population MDS — is still present at the top middle of Figure 6.3. As with the whole-sample MDS, movies, shows, fairs and exhibitions, theme parks, botanical gardens and public libraries are all relative isolates.

Professionals (see Figure 6.4) exhibit a much more nuanced pattern of event attendance: although the three clusters are still more or less intact, these account for only nine of the nineteen events. The remaining events are too scattered to be viewed as clusters, although the pattern is fairly understandable and familiar. For example, the bands in pubs category is still close to the other two popular music events (night clubs and rock concerts), but not close enough to be unproblematically included in the cluster. An equivalent positioning occurs with orchestral concerts, an event which easily clusters with the other restricted cultural arts events in the whole-sample MDS. For professionals, the orchestral concerts category has pulled some distance away from the other restricted arts events. The membership of Cluster 2 is somewhat different for professionals compared with the whole-sample MDS. For professionals, Cluster 2 consists of all the public culture venues with the exception of libraries. In contrast to the whole-sample MDS, the professionals' Cluster 2 includes no subsidised arts events. Interestingly, musicals and theatre are plotted quite separately for professionals, whereas for the whole-sample MDS, these two events clearly fell within the same cluster. Taken together, these results suggest that professionals attend many of these cultural events in a slightly different attendance pattern, while for manual workers most of these events can be described similarly: manual workers are more similar to each other than are professionals.

The implications of this analysis are that, for manual workers, there are two event audiences — one of which is a very infrequent audience — plus audiences for five other events. For professionals, however, it is much more problematic to describe "the audience". This last observation has deceptively important implications. It shows that the group (in occupational/social class terms) which attends cultural events the most does so in much more individuated ways than do other groups. It also shows that, as a group, professionals attend classical music-related events with the same relative infrequency as do other groups — they just attend slightly less infrequently. As omnivores, professionals do not only do more of most things, but they do so in ways which tend to differentiate events more than any other group: as a group, they tend to cluster events *less*. Multidimensional scaling reveals subtle differences within this cohort in their overall pattern of event attendance, as events generally draw away from each other more while the difference between mass

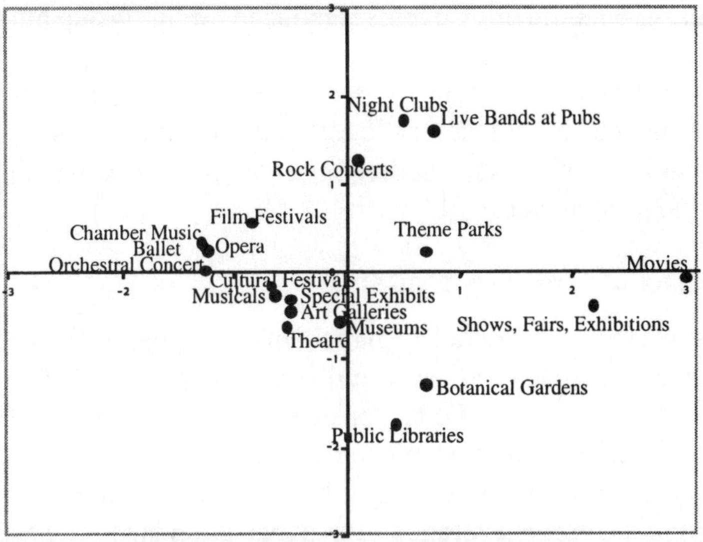

Figure 6.3: Manual Workers' Attendance

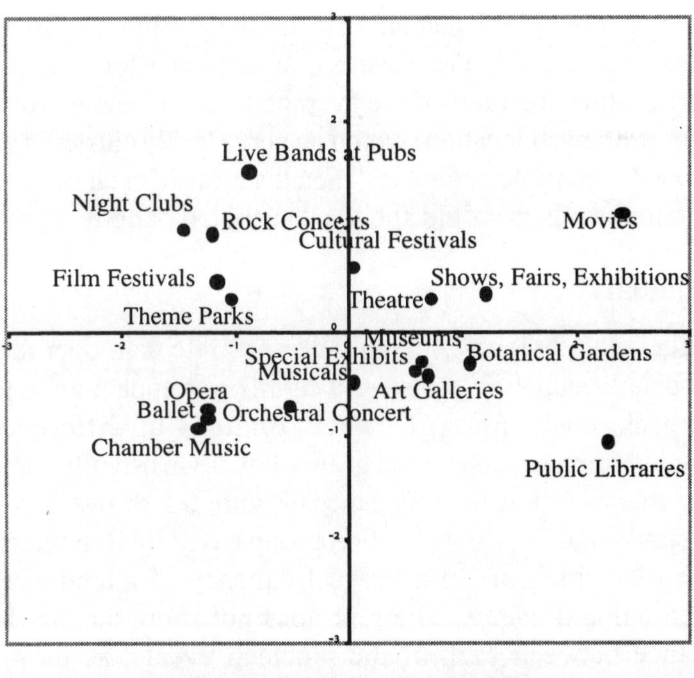

Figure 6.4: Professionals' Attendance

cultural events and other events is reduced for this group but remains distant.

This comparison of these two classes shows that the pattern of event attendance is different. Despite these differences, we do see the semblance of the same underlying ecology at work in both patterns of cultural attendance.

Patterns of Group Attendance

So far, we have considered the pattern of attendance at events seeking to locate an *ecology of events* in relation to each other. The reverse of this analysis would be to consider the same data, but from the standpoint of groups of people in relation to other groups — seeking *an ecology of group attendance*. To achieve this outcome requires developing "group averages" for event attendance. These group averages were arrived at by calculating the average frequency with which each group (occupation, age/gender group, residential location group) attended each event. Using the methods of multidimensional scaling, it is possible to test empirically the existence of multiple or singular audiences. If there were one audience for cultural event attendance, then the plots of the average for each occupation (or age group or residential location) would be very closely clustered together. If there were multiple audiences, then the plots of each occupation in relation to the others would show a distributed pattern.

Occupations

Bennett et al. (1999) convincingly demonstrate that, over the whole AECP data, occupation/class has a significant impact upon patterns of cultural consumption. Do their findings of differences and similarities among occupational groups hold as insistently for a subset of their study — cultural attendance? Figure 6.5 shows how similar (or dissimilar) the eight occupation groups used by Bennett et al. are to each other in terms of average frequency of attendance at the nineteen cultural events. The plot does not show the similarity in attendance between each of the nineteen events, as do previous figures, but how similar the eight occupation groups are to each other in terms of their average pattern of attendance of the nineteen events.

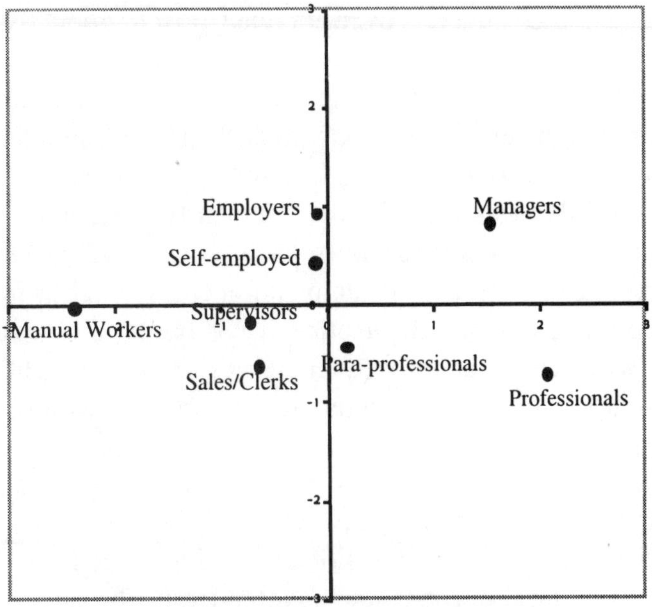

Figure 6.5: Occupation Event Attendance

Multidimensional scaling graphically supports Bennett et al.'s findings that occupation/class significantly impact upon cultural consumption. As with their larger range of cultural consumption, which included private culture and eating out, those occupational groups that are most similar in terms of cultural event attendance are employers and the self-employed; and supervisors, para-professionals and sales and clerical workers. It should be noted that supervisors are almost as close to the self-employed as they are to paraprofessionals. Managers, professionals and manual workers are all unique in their pattern of attendance. While the pattern of similarity is not particularly remarkable, the point is clear: the pattern of attendance is very different depending upon who the audience is.

When examining the pattern of data on attendance rates of the eight occupational groups, it is clear that managers and professionals (as Bennett et al. note) attended nearly all of the events and venues more frequently than most other occupational groups, and that manual workers attended nearly all events and venues less frequently than other groups. The exception to this pattern is attendance at the popular music events. Rock concerts were attended most frequenbtly by sales and clerical workers, but no occupational grouping is characterised by very low relative attendance at the events. All the other groups attended rock concerts at approximately the same frequency. Night clubs were also attended most frequently by sales and clerical workers, but also relatively highly frequently by manual workers and supervisors. Employers, the self-employed, professionals and managers exhibit a tendency to attend night clubs with less frequency than do other occupational groups. Live bands, however, were attended with almost equal frequency by five of the eight groups: professionals, para-professionals, supervisors, sales and clerical workers, and manual workers. Live bands were attended relatively less frequently by managers and employers, with the self-employed attending with a frequency somewhere in between.

While managers and proferssionals were both the most frequent attenders of cultural events and also attended the broadest range of activities, there are still substanial differences between the two groups. Professionals attended libraries, film festivals, and cultural festivals more frequently than did managers. The other occupational groups do not differ much in their attendance rates, but there does appear to be some overlapping in terms of the ecology of attendance of these groups, as discussed above.

Age and Gender

A consistent finding in ethnographically oriented studies of the television audience is the importance of gender to understanding processes of audienceship. Ann Gray (1999, p. 33) argues that "feminist work and that inspired by feminism has shifted the ground of exploration and inquiry in forcing gender and sexual politics on to the agenda" of audience studies. In a similar fashion, researchers such as Hugh Mackay (1993, 1997) have argued for the importance of generations — particular age cohorts — as significant units for thinking about social attitudes, values and cultural consumption. The former suggests the importance of gender in cultural consumption, while the latter indicates the importance of age cohorts. To what extent do gender and age inform patterns of cultural attendance? Figure 6.6 groups cultural attendance by age and gender, and confirms

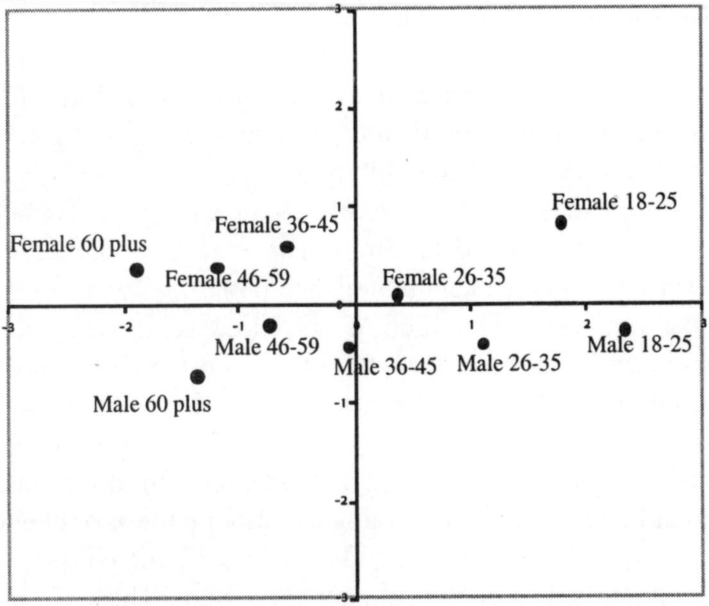

Figure 6.6: Age and Gender Event Attendance

the importance of both gender and age in organising the cultural field in this case into distinctive cultural attendance patterns.

In Figure 6.6,.the groups separate out along both age and gender lines, with age accounting for more of the separation than gender. Nonetheless, it is clear that there are significant differences between men and women in all age cohorts, suggesting the substantial "gendering" of cultural attendance. Young males appear to have a pattern of event attendance which is quite different from other age-by-gender groups. Young women are also somewhat different from other people, but not to the same degree as young men. This significant difference points to some of the difficulties attendant on developing a "youth policy". But it also confirms how much of an outlier the 18–25-year-old group is more generally. Males aged 18–25 are closer in cultural event attendance to females aged 18–25 than to anyone else; and females aged 18–25 are closer to females aged 26–35 than anyone else — although in both cases they are far apart. The data also shows that, on average, male and female 18–25-year-olds attend cultural events equivalently but do not necessarily attend the same cultural events. Investigation of the data revealed that 18–25-year-old women attended ten of the nineteen venues and events more frequently than did 18–25-year-old men, and that the majority of these differences occurred with Cluster 1 and Cluster 2 events, plus the other public culture venues (botanical gardens and libraries), shows, fairs and exhibitions, and cultural festivals.

If we were to take only age into account, a number of conclusions can be drawn from this data. From the age of 36, audiences become more similar in their event attendance patterns. Those aged 36–45 are most similar to those aged 46–59; likewise, those aged 60 plus are most similar to those aged 46–59. As is often commented upon, young people (18–25) do have a pattern of attendance markedly different from those of all other age groups. Those aged 26–35, while reasonably similar to those aged just older, are still different enough to demand being viewed as having a distinct pattern of attendance.

Those aged 46 and older attend the Cluster 1 and Cluster 2 events more frequently than do the younger age groups. These older groups also attend art galleries, museums (along with those aged 36–45) and botanical gardens more frequently than do the younger groups. Attendance at libraries exhibited a slightly different pattern, with these venues being attended with more frequency by those aged 36–45 and those aged 60 and older. Those aged 18–25 and 26–35 attended the three popular music events more frequently than older groups, and those aged up to 45 attended theme parks, shows, exhibits and fairs, and cultural festivals more frequently than the older groups. Two events, movies and film festivals, were attended most frequently by those aged 18–25. All age groups attended movies with a reasonable frequency, but the younger respondents indicated a very high attendance rate. And while the relative pattern of attendance at film festivals was similar to that for movies, with younger people attending much more frequently than older people, the overall attendance frequency was much lower for film festivals compared with movies.

Older age groups are closer to each other than younger groups are to each other. For most events, those aged 46–59 and 60 plus attended with approximately the same frequency. On some events, those aged 36–45 were more like the older groups (e.g. attendance at museums, and libraries, and to some degree chamber music concerts), but on other events they were more like the younger groups (opera, theme parks and shows, exhibits and fairs). Those aged 18–25 and 26–35 were similar for most events, but the youngest group almost invariably exhibited the more extreme high or low attendance rates. And, on some events, this youngest group differed from those aged 26–35 (film festivals, night clubs, live bands, movies and public music performances). It is for this reason that they pull away from the slightly older group.

This pattern suggests that, for many events — including most of the subsidised arts events and most free events (such as museums, galleries and botanical gardens) — those aged up to 35 can be viewed as one age group. For several other events (specifically those characterised by being in the popular culture idiom and listed above), the two age groups separate, with younger people attending more frequently. For these events, the two age groups can be viewed as being different species, the implication being there is a need for different policy agendas for the groups.

Residential Location

As noted above, Bennett et al. (1999) collected data on where respondents lived using a six-category system based upon geographical location, which included inner city, suburban, provincial city, small town, semi-rural (such as acreage) and rural. In Figure 6.7, the six geographical groups are represented in relation to each other in terms of their average attendance at cultural events. This pattern shows that, consistent with other research, those who live in the inner city and in rural areas differ markedly from those living in other geographic locations, as do those who live in provincial cities — though to a lesser extent. Second, and similar to our other analyses, there is an overlapping pattern of event attendance. The remaining three geo-demographic groups have a similar pattern of attendance, as indicated by their proximity on the diagram. Perhaps surprisingly, the attendance patterns of those living in suburban areas most closely match those who live in small towns and semi-rural areas. The capital city/non-capital city distinction usually employed in studies of cultural consumption may not be sensitive enough to capture this consumption accurately.

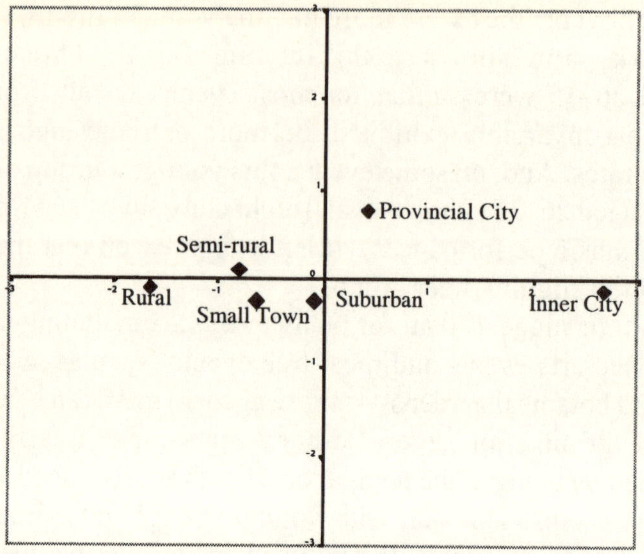

Figure 6.7: Geographical-based MDS

An examination of the attendance rates indicates that those who live in the inner city attended nearly all events and venues with more frequency than those residing in other locations. Inner-city dwellers attended all the Cluster 1 events except for ballet more frequently than any of the other groups. Those who live in provincial cities were also characterised by somewhat higher attendance at some venues and events, compared with those living in other areas — they reported relatively high attendance rates at all of the free cultural venues (art galleries, museums, including special exhibits at galleries or museums for which payment was required, botanical gardens and libraries) and also musicals, theatre and theme parks. This includes all the Cluster 2 events. For many events, those residing in rural areas attended with the least frequency. For one event only did rural residents attend a cultural event with relatively high frequency: shows, exhibits and fairs. Those living in semi-rural areas also attended these events with a higher relative frequency.

Those people living in the other areas (suburban areas and small towns) were characterised by exhibiting neither particularly high nor low frequency of attendance at any events. This pattern was also exhibited by those residing in semi-rural areas, although in a slightly weaker form. Overall, the pattern shows that those who live in the inner city are high attenders of most events and those who live in rural, and to some degree semi-rural, areas are low attenders. Small town and suburban residents are quite similar in their patterns, although — as highlighted — this is characterised by neither high nor low attendance rates.

This analysis confirms the importance Paul Costantoura (2000, p. 19) attaches to geography in *Australians and the Arts*. He observes, for example, that the "closer a person lives to the centre of a capital city, the more likely they are to have a more positive view of the arts". He goes on to interpret this finding as indicating that "people living closer to a city centre are more highly educated, have higher incomes, are closer to main city venues and are more likely to have some non-English speaking origin".

However, our analysis suggests that arts audiences cannot easily be categorised into distinct geographic regions. There is a degree of overlap between geographic areas which precludes easy classification. The capital city/non-capital city division often made when describing cultural attendance may not be the best division. Our data confirm that a better division is into three: inner city; rural; and other areas. It should be pointed out that this division can be made only after taking into consideration the differential availability of cultural events in different geographic areas across Australia. When conducting the current analyses, only those participants were included who indicated that a particular cultural event was available in their area. When examining whole-population data, there will be a skew toward lower attendance in rural areas due to lack of availability. But even when availability is taken into account, those residing in rural areas have a very different and much lower pattern of attendance compared with those residing in other geographical areas.

Connecting the Variables

What is the impact of these several demographic variables — sex, age, occupational grouping and place of residence — on attendance? What is the valence of various socio-cultural differentiations — class, gender , age, geography and education — for thinking about cultural attendance? As discussed in the previous section, the MDS plots revealed several clusters of events. Now we will take two of the more tightly clustered events — the classical music-related arts (Cluster 1) and the popular music cluster (Cluster 3) — and examine in more detail the demographic composition of their event attendance.

To perform the analysis, further data manipulation was required. It was necessary to develop indexes that represented attendance at the classical music-related arts and popular music events respectively. The scores for the items included in the clusters were averaged to form two scores for each participant. Examination of the distribution of these scores indicated that they were far from normally distributed, and were better broken into categorical variables according to whether or not the participants had ever attended one of the events. Results showed that approximately 35 per cent of participants had attended the subsidised arts events, and 56 per cent had attended the popular music events.

Due to the binary nature of attendance, the appropriate analysis for interrogating the relationships between demographics and attendance was logistic regression. As with any analytical technique, there are limitations on its use. For logistic regression, the major limiting factor is the number of levels or categories of predictors that can be used. As we were seeking the impact of several demographic variables on attendance, it was necessary to collapse some categories. To use the coding as employed in the AECP analyses would result in a very large number of categories. As all variables are crossed in logistic regression, it meant that a large number of empty cells would result, making the analysis unusable. The results from the MDS findings were used to assist this collapsing across categories. Occupational grouping was reduced from the eight categories included in the AECP project to four: employers and the self-employed; managers and professionals; middle workers; and manual workers. All five of the original categories of age used in the AECP were retained: 18–25, 26–35, 36–45, 46–59 and 60 plus. Place of residence was reduced from the original six categories to three categories: inner city; rural; and other areas (which included suburban, provincial cities and semi-rural/acreage areas).

Two logistic regression analyses were conducted to ascertain the impact that each demographic variable had on attendance and non-attendance at subsidised arts and popular music events. Each is discussed in turn.

Classical Music-related Events

Results indicated that attendance at these subsidised arts events was significantly predicted by occupational grouping, sex, age and residence. Specifically, a greater proportion of professionals/managers (58.9 per cent) reported attendance, and a lower proportion of manual workers (15.6 per cent) attended events than expected by chance. The proportion of middle-level workers (33.9 per cent) and employers and the self-employed (37.6 per cent) who attended subsidised arts events did not differ from the average proportion of the overall sample. A slightly but significantly greater proportion of women (37.6 per cent) attended these events than did men (32.4 per cent). Those respondents who were younger (18–35) (25.0 per cent and 26.8 per cent) attended subsidised events less, compared with those who were older (46 and older) (41.6 per cent and 40.3 per cent). The proportion of participants aged between 36 and 45 (37.3 per cent) who attended these events did not significantly differ from the average of the sample. Finally, a greater proportion of participants who lived in the inner city (50.0 per cent) and a lower proportion of participants who lived in rural areas (26.2 per cent) attended subsidised arts events than expected by chance. The proportion of respondents who attended subsidised arts events and who resided in other geographical locations did not differ from the overall sample (34.2 per cent attending).

To test the effect of education on these results, level of education was also included. Education was coded on a six-point scale representing increasing levels of education. The inclusion of education had no effect on the results for class, age or sex, but did have a marked effect on the results for place of residence. Place of residence was no longer significant after the inclusion of education. Examination of this result showed that education and place of residence covaried, with those living in the inner city having higher levels of education than those who lived in suburban and provincial cities and surrounding areas, who in turn had higher education levels than those participants who lived in rural areas. This suggests that the effect for residence is due to education. It is interesting that no such effect was found for occupational grouping, even though there was also a strong association between occupational grouping and education (professionals/managers were more highly educated than were middle workers, who were more educated than manual workers). This finding indicates that occupational grouping has an effect over and above that of education; while education is related to cultural attendance at restricted arts events, occupational grouping appears to further reinforce this relationship. If education alone had accounted for attendance, and occupational grouping had no further influence, than the arguments put forward by Bennett et al. and DiMaggio, which suggest cultural capital is material from which to fashion an identity, would be in doubt. The somewhat independent effects of education and occupational grouping support their explanation of cultural participation being an avenue for differential identity formation for different occupational groupings, at least as far as participation in the restricted arts is concerned.

Popular Music Attendance

Results indicated that only sex and age significantly predicted attendance at popular music events. Results showed that women (53.4 per cent) attended these events less than did men (58.8 per cent), and that younger people (specifically aged 18–35) (89.9 per cent and 69.2 per cent) attended them more than older people (36 and older) (43.2 per cent, 29.0 per cent and 22.8 per cent). The effect of education on accounting for this pattern was again tested: results indicated that education had no effect on these results. This result shows that the dominant demographic variable predicting attendance at popular music events is undoubtedly age. This effect runs through all other demographic variables: people who are younger attend popular music events more than do people who are older, irrespective of occupational grouping, gender or place of residence. While the relationship between demographic variables and attendance at subsidised events is complex, with all variables adding to the prediction, with popular music the pattern is relatively simple. What the simplicity of the relationship between popular music attendance and demographics suggests is that the breakdown of cultural elitism has occurred due to the 'cultural elite' taking up other cultural forms, not those who traditionally attended popular forms attending the subsidised events. This is the same point raised earlier and demonstrated by examining the overlap in attendance of the various clusters. In that earlier analysis, it was clearly shown that those who attend the restricted arts also attend other cultural forms to a greater or less extent: the reverse does not occur to the same extent.

Conclusion

Individual demographic items such as gender, occupation, residential location and age certainly provide evidence for the variety of standpoints which have become ensconced in the cultural studies, cultural policy, sociological and market research literature. Clearly gender, class, age, geography and occupation matter to cultural preferences and event attendance. Significantly more cultural options are routinely exercised by professionals and managers than any other group. The significant age cohort differences confirm the basis for generational differences and of thinking in terms of life cycles. They also highlight the singularity of 18–25-year-olds, both male and female, that forms the basis of youth policy-making. The gender profiles provide ample confirmation of feminist contentions of the importance of gender for audience research and policy action. The significant differences in cultural attendance between men and women of the same age cohort, and the generally higher cultural participation of women, indicate the important "gendering" of cultural attendance and cultural forms. The significant differences between age groups of the same gender also confirm the need to understand gender in relation to age. For their part, the residential location data tellingly illustrate the spatialisation of cultural and social capital as it relates to cultural attendance and cultural preferences. This confirms the move to prioritise where people live in understanding the shaping and exercise of cultural preferences that is the basis of geodemographic analytical techniques and targeted marketing.

Taken on its own, however, each demographic variable produces an inevitably partial picture of cultural attendance. With no variable sufficient on its own, cultural researchers, policy-makers and cultural organisations are inevitably faced with the need to entertain several demographic characteristics *at the same time* to understand cultural attendance and develop effective cultural policies for diverse cultural forms. Further complicating this picture is the fact that it is not only differentiations of the audience in terms of gender, age and residential location which need to be considered; events themselves need to be carefully differentiated from and connected to each other. Our exploration of the ecology of cultural attendance confirms that there is no "arts audience" — only a *number* of "arts audiences". Within each of the demographic cohorts, there are significant cultural taste biases. This provides some confirmation of the difficulties attending audience development for the subsidised and commercial arts. It also confirms the suggestion by Osborne et al. (1999) that there are "niche audiences" and that niche marketing approaches to audience development would be the most appropriate to use. This goes some way to explaining why techniques of market segmentation analysis — like cluster analysis, multidimensional scaling and logistic regression — are being used as a means to work across, and therefore combine, several coordinates to make sense of a dispersed cultural field. These results also help to explain why a dizzying variety of research is undertaken into the audience and a panoply of techniques applied to its study. The analysis of cultural objects requires the holding together of several (rather than just one or two) frameworks for doing the analysis.

In this chapter, we have been concerned first with the emergence of ways of thinking about audiences as audiences for and consumers of several cultural, entertainment and leisure forms, and second with how we might go about understanding the connections and disconnections among diverse audiences for and visitors to cultural venues. Emerging typologies of media users and ecologies of cultural attendance such as that suggested above are responses to research and policy agendas to integrate media and cultural services. Knowing one's audience increasingly means knowing what else your audience does in its cultural and leisure pursuits. Increasingly, cultural workers and practitioners are realising that their consideration of the direction, shape and character of their particular cultural form needs to take into account its place in a broader ensemble of cultural forms. At the same time, figuring out the several relations among audiences for cultural venues has become much more urgent, as state and city administrations around the world have adopted urban revitalisation programs aimed at reinventing their "downtowns". These programs connect previously distinct art forms, and strive to create synergies between the commercial and the public culture, and between leisure and the arts. In order to be successful, these revitalised cultural and leisure precincts — and the new cultural planning that supports them — will increasingly require robust audience research and methodologies capable of handling diverse audiences and events.

Notes

1 In only one sport, touch football, did manual workers score above the average for participation.

2 Factor analysis attempts to identify underlying variables, or factors, that explain the pattern of correlations among a set of observed variables.

3 The AECP results indicate a tendency to over-estimate the proportion of people attending compared with the ABS data. This is most likely attributable to the method of data collection. The AECP data asked respondents to indicate the relative frequency with which they attended each event, whereas the ABS asked respondents to indicate how many times they had attended each venue within the previous year.

4 These results illustrate a reasonable degree of comparability between the ABS and AECP data sets. We do not claim that the AECP data are based upon as representative a sample as the ABS data, but the consistency of the general pattern of attendance gives some assurance that further analysis is not without merit.

CHAPTER 7

Museum Visitors as Audiences: Innovative Research for Online Museums

Patricia Gillard

New Museums

When you hear about museums in Australia, or visit them, the word that recurs is "new". Over the past few years, major museums have been built and opened (for example, the Immigration Museum in Melbourne, the Melbourne Museum and the National Museum of Australia), or have been "renewed" (the Museum of South Australia). In parallel with this building of the material museums, there has been a rethinking of the significance of museums in the cultural life of localities, social groups and individuals. "New" museums are seeking a closer engagement with the intellectual and social life of the publics they serve. Indeed, continuing support from government depends on museums demonstrating their popularity with a broad range of visitors.

New Museology

"New museology" describes changes in thinking and professional practice which emphasise "the need for a shift of power inside the museum as well as outside it. Within the museum, the curator needs to learn how to share control with those responsible for interpretation and education" (Wright 1989, 135). New museology is shifting the definition of what constitutes a museum, and suggesting a closer engagement between the social and material histories they construct and the everyday lives of visitors. In many cases, increasing their understanding or knowledge is now stated in the mission of cultural institutions.

New Technology

There is another kind of newness which is represented as a transforming influence on museums. These are the new technologies which make possible online communication by museums to more distant publics, as well as visitors at the site. Websites, discussion lists and email feedback all make it possible for museums to engage in new ways with visitors and, by implication, with new kinds of visitor groups. Some have even claimed that, through new technology, museums are being "democratised" (Trotter 1998, p. 54). By offering a wider choice in the ways people engage with museum contents, the role of the visitor as an interpreter has become more visible. Contents which themselves encourage participation or interaction are seen as shedding some of the limitations of earlier forms of exhibition.

There is no doubt that the museum spaces and some of the technologies are new. However, it remains to be seen whether the exhibitions which are offered in the material museums or through their websites contribute knowledge and experience to visitors which have a different quality and value than previous interpretive work. Systematic research will reveal whether assumptions about the transformation of museums are perceived by visitors themselves and appreciated in the uses they make of their visits. While there is much discussion of the importance of visitors, and of visitor research, it is fair to say that, at present, museums are struggling to understand the visitor experience and how to make use of knowledge about publics in their management, curatorial and research work.

Unfortunately, it is more usual to find visitors used as a justification for enhancing the public relations budgets of museums (and the profile of directors) at the expense of research and exhibitions. When this happens, the communications and public programs areas risk being set in opposition to research and exhibition functions. In step with new forms of exhibition and communication, there needs to be a fostering of innovation in the design of visitor research and in the uses of research information across the entire work of the museum, not just its public communication.

Visitor research for museums begins from a very low base if it simply adapts the methods of advertising and marketing research or broadcasting measurement to understand visitor experience on site and online. These methods have sold audiences very short in conventional media, and have perpetuated myths about passive consumption. Television and radio ratings, for example, have concentrated on producing aggregate statistics so that advertisers will pay for what seem to be large numbers. Research which focuses on differences within audiences, and on their choices and interpretations about content, breaks up a seamless picture and makes it hard to demand top dollar for big numbers. In Australia, the numbers have actively hidden audience tastes, and made it impossible for public broadcasters or policy-makers to know much at all about the media engagements of Australians.

New Research

If cultural institutions are to understand their audiences, and build this knowledge into their continuing work, the research will need to be dramatically different to a ratings- or market-driven approach. It will need to highlight differences between audience members and relate these differences to the contents and services constructed in the museum. There has been an awareness of this need for some time. An introduction by Screven (1993) to visitor studies in *Museum International* concluded that a mix of research was needed, including descriptive, broad academic and small-scale localised studies. However, the research practices within museums do not yet reflect widespread adoption of new designs and methods which will be able to demonstrate the influence of new museology. Having shifted the focus of museum work to creating engagement by museum visitors, we must study visitors in action: how they construct meaning, experience and knowledge from their visit; what they do with it afterwards; and its significance in their lives.

The widespread use of the internet to provide information and exhibitions for museums makes the need for differentiated knowledge of audiences more urgent. Websites are able to simultaneously address very different audiences using databases of similar material, but the appropriate development of web content relies on an increasing sophistication in relating particular contents, services and online environments to the contexts and interests of particular visitor groups.

New research approaches are being developed by professionals, academics and businesses. However, at this stage, the traditions of visitor research used in museums are very different to the frameworks being employed as a basis for user research of museum internet sites. The picture is very fragmented. The most important feature of interpretation work for visitors may turn out to be the way online exhibitions, information, research and shopping are related to the on-site experience. If so, the practices of museum visitor research, variously named evaluation, market research, user research, visitor satisfaction and so on, will need to be applied across both real and virtual museum locations. The research designs will need to take both contexts into account and define audiences in more detailed and dynamic ways.

Audience research, as it has been developed within communications traditions, offers some promising conceptual and methodological approaches to the challenges facing museums. However, audience research as it has been theorised and practised brings its own limitations as well. This chapter presents an account of approaches to visitor research for online exhibitions, and outlines some of the major conceptual and practical challenges. This can only be a snapshot of a rapidly developing field. The individual studies will date, but the argument about what is needed for the task of understanding visitor experiences might provide a useful test for research to come.

Visitor Research in Museum Sites

In most publicly funded museums, there is increasing emphasis on visitor research for defining who visitors are and what they gain from their visit. Research companies and even management consultants are being employed to conduct satisfaction surveys, visitor evaluation studies and market research using conventional qualitative and quantitative methods. At the same time, there are moves to train museum workers in some of the basics of surveying and other forms of evaluation because they are unlikely to have the budgets to employ "experts".

Museums Australia, a professional association, has an Evaluation and Visitor Research Special Interest Group which has recently been very active in presenting basic training in research and evaluation to people employed in areas such as public programs and education within museums. A three-day conference held in 1998, "Visitors Centre Stage: Action for the Future", demonstrated a range of practical ways to study and measure museum visitors. There were case studies and working examples of the use of visitor information for a variety of purposes within museums and cultural institutions. The importance of communicating results of visitor research to the senior corporate and policy functions of the organisation, as well as the marketing and public outreach areas, was emphasised. Setting up internal databases to track visitation was particularly encouraged (see AMOL 1998).

As announced on the Museums Australia website, the Evaluation and Visitor Research Special Interest Group "recognises the role of the visitor as partner in the joint interpretation of culture; identifies evaluation and visitor research as a part of new museology practice; provides a professional forum for developments in theory and methodology, shares findings and develops standards" (see Museums Australia 2001). Presentations of visitor evaluation studies at major conferences are continuing — for example, at the Museums Australia Conference held in April 2001. These should soon be available online.

The area of visitor evaluation in museums is growing as a specialist study. There is an emphasis on research design that fits method to problem, and that is sensitive to particular contexts. However, the methods are those which have been in use for many years in social science, marketing or advertising. These include focus groups and interviews, observation and surveys. There is little innovation in the methods themselves, or in the thinking about audiences on which they are based.

After all the talk about "new" museums and the "empowerment" of visitors, it is disappointing to find that the visitor research that will be used to make judgments about the success of the innovations is so conventional in its definition and measurement of individual visitors. Visitor information is based on research traditions which are not well adapted to the dynamic, content-rich and interactive environments of museum sites (Gillard 1998).

For example, satisfaction surveys, which are currently the major form of visitor research at many cultural institutions, do little more than seek responses from museum visitors about a predetermined list of museum facilities, and usually on a numeric scale which may not reflect the ways those surveyed would describe their own experience. The outcome of satisfaction surveys is to give managements and marketers accurate percentage responses to their own questions. They rarely reflect the visitors' own perspectives of the visit — or indeed, visitors' ways of talking about it. Satisfaction surveys are particularly disappointing for the writers, curators and designers who work for cultural institutions. They do not give a "feel" for how visitors respond to the layered meanings and content in exhibitions.

Much of the visitor research that is currently conducted within museums is described as "evaluation" research — a description drawn from contexts such as education and program evaluation. Although there are approaches to evaluation which incorporate the perspectives of those who are researched, these are not widely practised. Museums have tended to use the more traditional forms of evaluation which set up criteria in advance and score responses from visitors in relation to predetermined issues. Like satisfaction surveys, such evaluations can rarely capture the novel reactions of visitors or explore interpretations of exhibitions in depth. They do not extend into the life contexts of visitors, but are usually limited to reactions on site on the day of the visit.

Evaluation using quantitative methods such as surveys also has very little capacity to identify the differences between visitors in the ways they relate to objects, spaces and other contents, except in predetermined categories such as age, sex and location. Evaluation is often undertaken when all the creative work has been finished. It is then taken to be an inherently judgmental activity, a kind of score card on the success of an interpretation activity by museum workers. The lack of fit between nuances of meaning and varied interpretations "designed in" to an exhibition and the simplistic information that is gained about visitor responses has meant that visitor research is rarely used to suggest future themes or creative treatments. Evaluation is more often kept at arm's length from the creative design and exhibition work within museums, and only used in public programs and marketing.

For visitor research to contribute to interpretation work, there needs to be some reflection of the specific contents and sites of the museum, and some possibility for visitors to express their experience in their own words. A recent review of museum marketing literature and research by Nobuko Kawashima (1998, p. 30) states: "What is missing is knowledge about the pattern of visitor encounters with an object or exhibition."

Visitor Research for Museum Websites

It is when the current methods for visitor research are applied to online activity that their limitations for understanding visitor experience are exposed. The dynamic environment of the web undermines the simplistic assumption that visitor uses and interpretations follow broad general patterns and can be known by seeking answers to a few simple questions. Instead, a far more complex "map" of possible forms of engagement across a museum website needs to be drawn as a basis for even beginning to question visitors about their online experience. Moreover, online visitors who are experienced with the Web often move very quickly and experimentally through sites, navigating by leaping from image to image and rarely reading complete sections of information. The Web environment gives a timely reminder that visitor interpretations are not easily predicted and summarised.

There are fewer studies of online visitors than of visitors on site, although in the past two years distinctive approaches to testing websites for their use by visitors have emerged. Most of these approaches come from an entirely different tradition to conventional evaluation and visitor research. They are drawn from systems testing and useability studies that have been developed in the laboratories of telecommunications and software companies. These, in turn, derive from psychological or engineering methods.

Currently, there are two distinctive approaches to testing the useability of websites. The first, often called *heuristic evaluation*, compares the functioning of the site with specific criteria and standards which are predetermined by authoritative experts in the field (see Heuristics for Web Communication 2000; Keevle 2000). The second, *user-focused evaluation*, seeks the cooperation of real users, selected according to relevant criteria, to conduct particular tasks with the website. The actual users test the site in ways that are structured in advance (Harms and Schweibenz 2001). Both of these approaches to useability assume that the focus of evaluation is in the site itself. Questions of whether it performs well are answered by interrogating the site, even if a "person-as-user" is often employed for this purpose.

Another source of information about online users is the web usage statistics often made available by internet service providers as part of their web hosting service. The sites of major cultural institutions are increasingly making these available within the site. The addition of "/statistics.asp" will sometimes take the user to their statistics page. Web statistics are likely to consist of numbers of "hits" to a website and for particular pages. Because "hits" measure the number of images opened on a page, not just the visit, a measure of visitor sessions is a closer approximation of users. However, these are usually calculated for periods of time, such as every 30 minutes, so that some of the actual visitors may be counted more than once. Visit statistics show the most popular pages and the country of origin through domain names or IP addresses, which may also be misleading (Bowen and Bowen 2000). Measures of average session length or the most popular "paths" around a site (the top three pages, for example) begin to give some information about patterns of use which can be related to the content in the site or compared with other websites. The statistics say nothing about the tastes, preferences and purposes of individuals or groups of online visitors.

The facility for visitors to send email responses to web administrators does give a form of feedback which some web administrators monitor closely. However, the emails are most likely to be comments on technical problems or questions about content. They do not give a systematic picture of the ways in which online content is being interpreted and used by a wide variety of visitors to websites.

Two recent evaluation studies, reported at the Museums and the Web conference in March 2001, showed the use of multiple methods — some of them descriptive — to understand visitor experience in new ways. At the British Museum, Fiona Marshall (2001) developed a series of research methods, including observation and interviews, at stages in the development of the COMPASS project, an online image database of over 3000 objects. COMPASS was designed to be used by children, family groups and those with little knowledge of the collections. Findings about the words used to search, and the use of plural rather than singular terms, were especially important in adapting the site to a non-expert audience.

The second study by Anthony Huberman (2001) was less structured. It followed an art exhibition in which email addresses for each artist had been provided as part of the captions on art works hung in the gallery. Emails for each artist were also provided on an exhibition website, and visitors were encouraged to respond to artists by email after their visit. When the exhibition was over, the researcher sought feedback from artists about the ways that visitors had communicated with them and the comments they made. The research did not attempt to produce summary statistics. However, it defined major visitor groups in terms of their engagement with the artist. One of the surprising findings was the use of email by collectors to purchase art directly from artists. There was also a significant group of individuals who expressed to artists the feelings inspired by their work. This was particularly appreciated by many artists.

An earlier study by Semper et al. (2000) used a combination of methods to evaluate the use of two online resource programs of The Exploratorium in San Francisco. The authors observed that:

> Although there is evidence that these resources are widely used by tens of thousands of users, there is little detailed understanding about who uses the resources and how they are being used. More generally, there is little understanding of the use of educational online materials. As the use of online learning resources for both formal and informal science learning continues to grow, it is important that producers of these materials and activities have a developing knowledge of their

audiences and modes of use, and of methodologies for evaluating their use and effectiveness.

New Visitor Research

For a new museology, we need new visitor research practices. A framework of concepts and values has been developed within British cultural studies which could inform new audience research, applied to museums. These main ideas will be outlined below, with illustrations from the few published studies, and the small-scale researches of my own students. I am also applying these ideas within my consultancy, User Insite. Because the details of commissioned research are usually confidential, they cannot be cited in detail here. However, some general comments will be made, based on research that has been developed across a number of projects.

Audience–Content Relationships

One of the major shifts in understanding occurring in new audience research is in the definition of audience as a dynamic relationship rather than groupings of human subjects. Virginia Nightingale (1994b, p. 40) warns that commonsense notions of audience are an artefact of the way we often study them: "A naïve and blissful trust in the survey and the interview blinds the novice to the fact that an audience is not a person (or a group of people) but a relation." Understood in this way, audiences are not social groupings existing "out there", waiting to be "targeted" by advertising or marketing campaigns, and choosing one kind of leisure "product" instead of another. Instead, audiences are understood as being forms of engagement created around contents. The relationships between audience members and contents are not accidental. The contents encountered or actively sought contribute to understanding, enjoyment and creativity in the lives of individuals and groups.

Put another way, cultural products or activities *create* audiences, as people engage with them. People may ignore contents or remain ignorant of them, but if they engage with cultural contents, patterns of audience groupings are created. Contents, media forms and sites engage particular groups in particular ways. For this reason, descriptions of audience groups should refer to this "audience-making" relationship, rather than using demographic labels such as age and sex, which describe the individual members of the audience groups. With this approach, emphasis is placed on the audience–content relationships. Research focuses on the forms of engagement between audience members and contents, and the ways audience-making is carried out.

The test of whether audience research is based on such an understanding is whether or not contents are described in relation to audience behaviour. There are potentially many ways to do this. The earliest examples of research which has attempted to describe relationships between audiences and contents point to some of the difficulties, and the rewards.

A website evaluation for the State Library of Victoria in 1997 conducted by User Insite and reported by Kurzeme and Herman (1999) is one example. The research design included analysis of contents as well as descriptions and measures of the responses of audience members. A sociocultural analysis of the site focused on the ways the State Library of Victoria represented itself and how it positioned its audiences by its contents, services, products and communications. This stage of research applied the methods of semiotic and discourse analysis to examine such aspects as the ways images and colour worked on the site, and the positioning of navigation devices and content lists. It was important to consider these aspects in combination, especially the ways images were presented and interpreted, because the site included a database of digitised images for the first time. Visitors could experience these contents in various sequences of their own choosing.

The analysis of the website revealed (amongst other things) a privileging of print-based forms of communication over more graphic styles. It showed an organisation wrestling with its traditional role, and trying to translate this into a new medium and convey it to new users.

Methods for researching audience members included interviews with librarians, who described some of the main ways people were using the collection of the traditional library. It was assumed that some of these user groups, such as people interested in family history, would be major users of the online image database. An online survey was also conducted to gain information from actual users of the site.

Results from the textual analysis were reported, alongside discussion of the kinds of material which users would be likely to be seeking, and the findings and comments from actual survey respondents. The findings from three different research approaches — sociocultural analysis, interviews and the survey — were not integrated into a single set of results. Instead, the information was presented from the different perspectives, and some conclusions and recommendations were drawn.

Two of the researchers, Cranny-Francis and Gillard (1990), had combined textual and empirical research previously in their discussion of television and teenage girls. Their work was presented in a parallel way because the theoretical approaches, and even the language of the ensuing discussion, were drawn from different research traditions. One of the ways to study both text and audience in combination is to include the work of two or more researchers who have different expertise. However, there needs to be some acceptance that the research design will not necessarily result in convergence to a single set of findings.

Presenting research in ways that open up possibilities, rather than reducing complex interpretations to a single set of information, will probably be a feature of new visitor research. This is likely to appeal to curators and writers who are seeking knowledge of the different kinds of audience–content relationships which are formed around their work. On the other hand, organisations which are seeking indices of success or failure, or single visitor measures, may not be so pleased with a multi-method approach and findings based on disparate methodologies.

Audiences as Cultural Groups

When researchers attend to audience–content relationships, it soon becomes clear that many of these relationships are stable over time and relate to broader social and cultural patterns. Audience members use cultural contents and the relationships they create to build shared assumptions and social practices.

Social groups built around consistent cultural practices have been called "interpretive communities" (see Lindlof 1988). Examples of interpretive communities are common. They range from the more visible and formalised "Friends of the Art Gallery" and fan clubs to more fleeting groupings around particular musical styles, cultural venues or TV program series such as *SeaChange*. Audience members can be part of a number of interpretive communities at the same time. As Tony Bennett (1995, p. 103) observes: "Contemporary societies with advanced media systems are shot through with diverse and co-existing interpretive communities." To define audiences as interpretive communities is to accept the shifting nature of audiences and to admit their complexity.

For work in museums, this understanding of audiences is useful for its emphasis on the relationship between social groups and cultural activities. It becomes important, from this perspective, to understand some of the social contexts and practices which might be a major aspect of those audience–content relationships played out online or at a museum site. Interpretive communities are not always evident, and information is unlikely to be requested about them. For museums, there are probably important interpretive communities that need to be made explicit. For example, child visitors to museums would be expected to engage very differently with contents in a museum when the context for their activity was their classmates than when they were visiting with an interested family member who talked through their own interests and provided an audience for their activity.

A small-scale student project at the Melbourne Museum in 1997 discovered that children engaged very differently with online content about dinosaurs — one part of a larger "Dinosaurs Alive!" exhibition — depending on who accompanied them. Based on observation, notes of conversation and a small number of interviews, the researcher established that children accompanied by a parent/adult or an older attentive sibling spent more time online. Other children spent less than a few minutes. The children with parents/siblings spent time showing the content to their audience, but also commenting on what they knew about how to move around the website. The behaviour was very consistent and suggested cultural patterns or expectations of "explaining" online contents to parents and other adults.

Answering the question of who it is that people consistently engage in particular kinds of activity *with* gives a clue to broader interpretive communities. The information could be very useful to those planning exhibitions which will attract new visitors. Some combinations of content/media/activity can be predicted to appeal to particular interpretive communities, and the link between them can be used to bring new groups into museums. Obvious examples are exhibitions with links to television programs such as *Star Trek*, but interpretive communities will also be linked to local activities and events, as well as symbolic objects and even features of the landscape.

Audiences as Narrative Practices

Recent writing from cultural studies about the fans of popular culture or about the users of websites has theorised audiences in terms of their active negotiation of texts. Readers and users seem to select consistent genres in their reading and viewing. With websites, the audience members themselves construct meaning from the website's offerings. It is their choices and the connections they make, rather than the website texts, which bring a narrative structure into being.

The many interpretations and understandings which are possible for visitors as part of their museum experience become more visible in the design and the evaluation of online exhibitions. The importance of researching what visitors are really doing foregrounds a desire which has been implicit in much audience research but never realised. Nightingale (1996, p. 107) expresses it like this: "But there is another text, just as important but infinitely elusive. It is the text which lives in the community of its users and which 'enters into life'. This is the text that I believe the cultural studies experiment tried to capture." At issue is the question of how visitors choose and shape their museum experience on site and online, and how they use it in the broader contexts of their everyday lives.

The idea of audiences as narrative practices places emphasis on the interpretive activity of audiences, especially their choosing of items to attend to, services to use and, if they are offered, ways to contribute their own statements or objects to the museum site. One of the major concerns in larger museums is with "wayfinding" and visitor movements through the site. Visitor interactions with the space and with contents must be understood in order to provide a visitor experience that works well for very different groups as they move around (Klein 1993, pp. 782–800). Once museums create exhibitions online, it is possible to construct multiple narratives or pathways through a number of information sites or web locations, or to construct particular configurations within CD-ROM or multimedia environments. It is evident that use of the internet can create a single pathway through material that may not be repeated by any others.

I have adopted the word "quester" as a way of emphasising the notion of a user as a purposeful navigator within a cultural domain. A quester takes their own pathway or creates their own narrative. Questers even have the potential to be producers as well, through creating online dialogue, networks or new products such as hypertext stories. Some museums are creating virtual spaces in which questers can cooperate to explore the site or create objects — for example, the Milan Science Museum, where visitors can operate Leonardo's machines together online (Barbieri and Paolini 2000).

Cultural institutions may need to think of visitors both as interpretive communities and as questers. They will need to build a picture of how their own cultural activity contributes to the lives of social and cultural groups, but also how it creates a series of idiosyncratic cultural journeys for single individuals.

The notion of audiences as being defined both as cultural groupings and as single questers is a challenge when it comes to designing fieldwork to study them. Conventional sociological research methods are designed to be applied to social groups. Psychological methods may focus on the responses of single individuals — for example, in useability studies which test uses of websites in laboratory settings. However, psychological studies are rarely focused on the process of meaning construction in relation to cultural contents.

I am now using the quester concept in visitor and online research. I usually begin by defining the main visitor groups and their likely content interests. From this outline, questers are described and drawn in detail. Contents and environments can then be designed for each of the questers, so that a range of activities on site and online will provide the kinds of audience–content relationships likely to be valued by each quester.

The evaluation of the State Library of Victoria's website, described earlier, defined a number of questers and made recommendations on improvements to the site which could be beneficial for each of them. In my experience, curators are well able to imagine questers for their site, because they have met many individuals who are committed and intensely engaged by their own specialist subject.

Future research may reveal that individual questers are part of an interpretive community which has remained "invisible" across different institutions. Recent research in a number of libraries and cultural institutions has consistently pointed to the emergence of family historians or genealogists as a very significant group of online users. While their own family interests are particular, and their uses of source material and web-based information trace a singular path, they share characteristics with many others. In some institutions they are called "genies". The existence of a nickname shows that their audience behaviour is not individual. They are no longer single questers, but are part of a larger interpretive community.

Audiences and Cultural Power

Audiences are usually unequal parties in their relationships with the museums and cultural institutions they visit. As Nightingale (1994b, p. 42) has observed, "audience relations always involve the exercise of power — someone always has the power to offer 'audience' and someone else must respond by accepting or rejecting that offer". The same can be said for the research relationship. Researchers, and the organisations they work for, usually call the shots when it comes to defining the kinds of questions they are interested in and the information they will use to answer them.

The unequal audience and research relationships call for care and creativity in designing research, so that what is produced is not merely the reflection of things the museum already knows, using methods the researcher has found to give few unhappy surprises.

Australian researchers (see, for example, Nightingale 1996, p. 116) have been critical of British studies which claimed to be "ethnographic" while neglecting the careful and systematic fieldwork which takes pains to incorporate the language and perspectives of those who are the focus of study. While the new definitions of audience have emerged from the tradition of cultural studies, this field does not have a strong empirical tradition which would translate core concepts into research procedures. Cultural studies provides a methodology for researching and theorising cultural material, and this sometimes extends to cultural sites which include people as audiences. However, the methods of cultural studies by themselves are inadequate for carrying out systematic social research which describes major findings and produces evidence for the conclusions of the research.

Indeed, the antagonism of some writers towards empirical research has discouraged experimentation in empirical fieldwork. Students should not be put off by the dismissal of "effects studies" that recurs almost as a ritual in many cultural studies texts. Simplistic critiques of US research have discouraged the kind of imaginative experimentation with eclectic research designs that might progress our understanding of audiences. Elizabeth Jacka (1994) has suggested that both critical and empirical approaches are needed to produce the kind of research information that is needed to understand relations between audiences and media content.

Visitor research for museums has a greater possibility to give some "cultural power" to visitors if it incorporates new information that comes from the perspective of audience members. However, it is difficult to find studies in a museum context which use such an approach.

One example from a small student project illustrates how different the visitor perspective can be. In the early 1990s, a touring exhibition of Egyptian artefacts, *Civilisations,* was shown at the Australian National Gallery, Canberra. A small-scale observation study of teenage school groups sought to document the ways students engaged with the objects and the spaces of the exhibition. One of the major activities observed was of students stepping over the prominent red line in front of exhibits when the security guard was not looking. For some of the students, the activity of testing the boundaries, and the reaction of alarms and officials, was more meaningful than engagement with the artefacts in the cases. No doubt the presence of peers provided a context in which these games were likely to be provoked.

Kelly (1999) reports three projects carried out in different museums which sought to understand whether visitors would like more access to collections, not just exhibitions, and how they might want to engage with the collections. In one of the examples, visitors were taken on a tour of two natural history collections at the Australian Museum, and participated in a free-ranging discussion afterwards about what they would like to do. The study revealed a lack of knowledge about the research and collections activity of museums. It also showed that visitors were interested in access to collections if they could be "in charge", deciding the kinds of areas they were interested in, and asking the questions of "experts" who were there to answer them.

The research used engagement with contents as part of the process of finding out visitors' responses, and as a result yielded rich and surprising information which could be used as a basis for design strategies and planning.

Making Visitors Visible in the Museum

Although it is possible to sketch the beginnings of a richer tradition of visitor research within museums and cultural institutions, a set of carefully related concepts, methods and designs which can be applied in particular contexts has not emerged fully. At this stage, there is a problem in finding ways of applying the conceptual understandings about audiences in systematic fieldwork that yields useful information to museum workers. This is especially true of research about online visitors to museum sites, who first have to be defined and made "visible" and then studied in new ways. The extra step of exploring the interrelationships of those who visit online and those who walk through the front door has not been attempted. When museums can understand how visitor experiences build on each other across the material and virtual sites, they will be able to create powerful strategies for exhibition design and for audience development.

The test of new visitor research is in the doing. The museum context offers an inspiring location for designing imaginative research. The process involves decisions about the kinds of information needed to fulfil the aims of the research that are appropriate and possible in that context. It is important to use a combination of methods which includes analysis of the material nature of the site or its contents. It is also necessary for new audience research to listen to the language and observe the meaning construction of participants.

In this approach, the researcher is not an outsider, but an interpreter. The research report is mediated by the language and concepts of the researcher as well as those who are researched (see Berg 1989). There may be resistance to this approach from those who are familiar with the claims of market research to provide objective, quantifiable results, equating this with accuracy and reliability. However, that kind of research commodity does not begin to deal with the complexity of audience relationships.

I have encouraged students to try new visitor research by doing it on a small scale and within small cultural sites such as flower festivals, cafes, video arcades and night clubs. Examples of how to define such a project, and how to write it up, are illustrated in Spradley and McCurdy's (1972) *The Cultural Experience: Ethnography in a Complex Society*. It has provided direction for a number of insightful small-scale studies. I would also encourage interested researchers to follow the debates and read the larger ethnographies in the *Journal of Contemporary Ethnography*. Examples of museum research or online communications have not been published often, but it would be good to see them there, alongside the other everyday or exotic cultural sites the journal has documented.

I am currently adapting an ethnographic approach to research about online audiences. For example, I use a workshop method to describe the detailed ways that on-site visitors engage with the contents and spaces of the museum. I then ask museum workers to describe how these kinds of engagements may be happening online. Staff who answer email and phone queries are often expert ethnographers of online visitors without being aware of the significance of their own knowledge. Once some of the audience–content relationships online are made visible, they can be used as a framework for interview or survey fieldwork.

Hopes for visitor empowerment by practitioners of the new museology will need to be resolved by creating new relationships between visitors and the cultural institutions themselves. Recognising that museums do stand in a dominant role, Parker B. Potter (1994, pp. 105–7) has suggested one way to change the power relations: "We who work in museum settings need to recognize our appropriation of culture, and we need to go one step further — we need to appropriate our visitors, too." To Potter, this is done by directly addressing the audience members and revealing "what an exhibition is trying to get him or her to do". Making the interpretation work and making its intentions explicit gives visitors the chance of challenging them.

In the best of worlds, I would like to apply this to visitor research. I would like to see the visitor information that institutions collect and interpret as part of their museum work interpreted and displayed for visitors. I would like visitor research to be the subject of exhibitions, so that visitors see themselves represented there, and may even be able to contest or enrich our conclusions.

The internet environment provides a programmable space where visitor interactions can be collected and displayed easily in real time. The installation of internet screens as part of museum exhibitions raises the possibility of including visitor experience as part of what is "on show" there. Visitors could see the contributions made by others and themselves as they engaged in the space, and might understand that their own presence, and what they take from the experience, is the major reason for the museum continuing its exhibition work. If, in the new museology, visitors provide the focus and rationale for museum work, they should at least be informed that their own engagement is vital to the museum's success.

CHAPTER 8

Gamers as Co-creators: Enlisting the Virtual Audience — A Report from the Net Face

John Banks

Managing audiences is a central dilemma that confronts both media industries and academic researchers. For media industries, it is about delivering audiences to advertisers and creating consumers for product. For academics, it is about knowing an audience — delivering audiences in studies that can be analysed, described and theorised.

Virginia Nightingale (1996, p. 124) sees commercial research into fans as having added another dimension to this audience research — "to the measurable, assessable, and manageable audience as object of commercial research" is added concern for "the personal obsession and commitment to communitas that characterizes the fan". The fan has also become the target of "renewed managerial activity to contain the quixotic preoccupations which become pretexts for the development of new and commercially exploitable fan communities" (Nightingale 1996, p. 124).

Community development has recently become a new employment position and business in the new media industry. Dot.coms and new media industries contract consultants to assist them with developing, implementing and assessing strategies for enlisting the attention and hits of the web audience: clicks hitting sites, users sticking to sites and regularly returning, and participating actively in the website to form potentially new e-commerce markets that can be sold services, information and product.

In the early stages of this interest in building and managing website communities, the aim was often to aggregate numbers around a particular interest area, forming a stable base of regular users who could then be sold to advertisers; those advertisers then paid for banner ads and the right to solicit their products and services to the community. However, the recent dot.com crash and the failure of many of these e-commerce start-ups to generate profits for their venture capitalists have resulted in well-founded scepticism about the applicability of traditional televisual-based understandings of audience as eyes to be delivered to advertisers. The audience — at least as it is understood for traditional media — has escaped the net and resists delivery. Users can ignore banner ads, and click through to fan-produced sites which are administered by other fans rather than marketing departments (and which are often better designed).

Internet technologies and the users forming around them are in the process of constructing a very different "audience", with different practices, expectations, materials, tools and technologies. Some commentators claim that the internet-based communication technologies of email, website forums, chat, and so on are creating an empowered audience/consumer who expects and demands that corporations will not only listen to their views, criticisms and input, but also enter into active dialogue with them. The former paradigm of one-way communication through traditional marketing is giving way to more open-ended exchanges between producer and consumer. Corporations are actively soliciting feedback from consumers and audiences via email and interactive websites. Fan websites, for example, are emerging as important and influential intermediaries, actively managing the relationship between the broader online fan base and the corporation.

Corporations carefully collect and scrutinise data on website traffic and email exchanges to better understand the emerging trends in audience/consumer practices, expectations and demands. How do they manage these relationships? How do they effectively engage in new ways with their potential customers and audiences? In Chapter 7, Patricia Gillard noted that much of the effort to understand and interpret online audiences is restricted to audience measures that detail statistics on numbers of visitors to a website and the location of the server from which the contact has been made. But, as she points out, these statistics "say nothing about the tastes, preferences and purposes of individuals or groups of online visitors". Furthermore, although email responses offer feedback, these exchanges tend to be limited to "comments on technical problems or questions about content". The problem with this approach to feedback, says Gillard, is that it is "based on a range of research approaches, most of which draw on administrative or research traditions that are not well adapted to the dynamic, content-rich and interactive environments" of contemporary websites.

The relationship between audiences/consumers and corporate producers is undergoing significant transformation. Entities such as "audience", "fan", "producer", "corporation" and "consumer" are relational — they emerge from continually transforming networks of relations. It therefore follows that, if the relationships are undergoing potentially significant transformations, then the entities themselves are in the process of being restructured and reorganised. The question this raises is: how do we go about analysing, describing and assessing these emerging trends and transformations?

In this context, the audience needs to be approached as a dynamic process. It is a relation constructed and emerging from a heterogeneous network of materials: subjectivities, practices, technologies, passions, desires and enjoyments; academic methodologies and research agendas; corporate marketing initiatives; venture capital; global media corporate relationships, and so on. Following John Law (1994, p. 2), the central concern is with the "plural processes of socio-technical ordering" — audiences are here implicated in these orderings.

Recent trends in new audience research and practice suggest that audiences and fan communities are elusive and slippery entities (Ang 1991, 1996). They are difficult to pin down, pigeonhole and categorise (Nightingale 1996, pp. 95–100, 126–30). They are objects of desire for both academics and corporate marketing departments. They provoke anxiety in the effort to manage and enlist their passions, commitment, time and dollars.

Which research methodologies can assist us to better describe the activities and practices of audiences? What statistical models and descriptive methodologies can assist us in our efforts to engage with, understand and describe these audience relations? By "us" I mean all of the stakeholders and participants actively involved in the process of building "audience" and, in that process, being *built* ourselves, in often quite unexpected and contradictory ways. Gillard (see Chapter 7) suggests "that a framework of concepts and values has been developed within British cultural studies which could inform new audience research". Virginia Nightingale's (1996) excellent *Studying Audiences* offers a compelling overview and critique of cultural studies work in the field of audience research.

Much of this chapter is informed by the limitations that Nightingale (1996, 1994a, 1994b, 1989) identifies in cultural studies efforts to deploy ethnographic methodology in the study of audience. Grounded in the ethnographic methodology of actor-network theory which seeks "to learn from the actors without imposing on them a priori definition of their world-building capacities" (Latour 1999a, p. 20),[1] my research suggests that the audience is not a something, a pre-existing entity, out there in the social landscape waiting to be enticed, seduced and explained. It is something to be built, dynamically negotiated and coordinated. But this methodology does not stand outside the networks and relations that it is seeking to describe.

What happens when the theory doing the describing is an integral part of the network that is being built? Nightingale (1996, p. 129) comments that "those who produce, license, distribute or manufacture media commodities often deny their dependence on the interpretative communities which generate demand for their work". But what are the uptakes involved when these organisations not only recognise the work of their fans and audiences, but actively work to enrol this activity into their networks? What are the implications when the very approaches that we propose as researchers to describe and analyse these relations are adopted by the organisations as tools for building and managing these networks?

In this chapter, I offer a description of recent initiatives deployed in the computer game industry to engage and interact with online gamers in ways that potentially move beyond the limitations — methodological and theoretical — identified by Gillard. This chapter is very much positioned and written from the very midst, the netface, where these issues are being engaged and grappled with. It is an ethnographic report from a participant-observer at Auran, a computer game development company based in Brisbane, Australia. Like many other computer game developers and publishers, Auran has been actively engaging with online fans who coalesce around game products that are undergoing development and retail release. Auran has been actively thinking through the complex set of issues, problems and opportunities that emerge from managing relationships with online gamer fans.

What follows is not so much a case study as a reflection on a process of engagement. It has emerged from a combination of PhD research and my experience as a company employee from mid-2000. The research commenced back in late 1997 and was focused on the emerging culture of online computer gaming but, as I followed and was guided by the actors involved, it became a study of the relationship among online PC gamers, game development companies and game publishers. In late 1997, I established a research relationship with Auran. I was led to Auran by a growing group of fans forming around *Dark Reign*, a then forthcoming real-time strategy game coproduced by Auran and Activision and published in September 1997 by Activision. The fans were in the process of establishing websites focusing on *Dark Reign*. The sites included game preview content and news such as descriptions of game features, screenshots. A significant feature of *Dark Reign* is support for online multi-player gameplay. Players could join games via the Activision servers and compete online against others, including team games of two against two and four against four.

In 1997, support for online multi-player games was an emerging trend in the PC game industry. Titles such as the first-person shooter *Quake* established their commercial success from their uptakes and extensions as online multi-player experiences. A rich and active online fan culture built up around these titles. These activities included forming teams (clans) for competition against other teams. Clans would have dedicated websites, challenging others and boasting of their victories. This has recently extended to a genre known as MMORPG (massively multi-player online role playing games). Titles such as *Everquest* can only be played online and have been very successful.

A further important feature of the emerging online game culture is fan-created content — extensions and additions to the game software (described as "mods" or "add-ons"). Game development companies release for download from their websites or include with the retail release software package game editing tools to be used by skilled and creative players to produce new material for the game. These tools generally require a relatively high level of computer software and graphic art skill to be used effectively. They are essentially the software tools that the game designers and artists use to produce the retail release title. This content includes skins or textures that change the graphics of elements in the game — for example, the dress and look of the player's character or avatar — and new levels and scenarios; through to complete modifications that verge in some cases on being almost completely new games, or at least a significantly new set of features that add to the player's enjoyment and the possibilities of game play.

This fan-based "producerly" activity could all too easily be read within the tradition of cultural studies as a mundane example of resistant audience practice. Are gamers functioning here as "textual poachers" (Jenkins 1993)? Aren't they taking the products of capital and reworking them according to their own agendas, pleasures and enjoyments? Are our very notions of audience — the texture, landscape and relationality — being transformed by the emergence of these "producerly" practices?

The very way that we pose these questions can predispose us towards particular methodologies and frameworks for producing and constructing responses. Additionally, we should keep in mind that our responses and interpretations do not just stand outside these networks, but play a role in building and making them. Our interpretations are part of the very materials from which these networks are made.

Many of the questions assume something — an entity, object or subject that we can clearly label and define as "gamer", "fan", "audience", "consumer", "producer", "academic" and "corporation". But these are not entities so much as relations: circulating dynamics, processes that define moments or conjunctions in a heterogeneous network of relations that do from time to time coalesce into more or less stable patterns of activity or practice. For example, the "I" of this chapter is not simply an academic researcher. He is also an active game fan and regular consumer of game products and an employee of a game production company in the dual position of online community relations manager and project director. For its part, Auran is not a singular, homogeneous object but is constructed from multiple materials, subjectivities and positions. Defined by a complex set of heterogeneous relations and materials, Auran encompasses a broad range of knowledge practices: programming, digital art creation, marketing, website creation and management, engineering, project management, administration, cultural and new media studies. It is a vehicle for attracting venture capital and is therefore caught up in a network of relations with other corporations (game publishers, etc.). It is partly defined by relations with gamer fans in a range of quite complex ways. However, this relationship with fans is also shaped by a complex series of internal interactions, tensions, negotiations and compromises.

In my position as online community relations manager, I am often positioned within the company as an advocate for and representative of the fans. I seek the release of information and content from development teams. For their part, development teams are often reluctant to release information and material (such as screenshots) too early in the development cycle. Project directors raise the concern that if, for technical and design reasons, significant changes are made subsequent to a public announcement, Auran and the development team will be criticised by fans who perhaps do not always fully understand and appreciate the game development process. They generally prefer detailed game feature information and screenshots to be released when the project is reasonably close to completion. They also have justifiable concerns about meeting feedback requests from the fans, particularly requests for feature additions and modifications while the game is still in development. Developers and project managers worry about "feature-creep" and see it as potentially threatening the stability, quality and deliverability of a software development project.

However, to assume that gamers and the corporation stand in an exterior relationship — on one side the producer and on the other side the consumer or audience — would be a mistake. For a start, many — if not most — of the designers, artists and programmers who work at Auran are also themselves game fans. Many of them participate actively in the fan networks that form around particular game title and genres on the Internet. These gamer-employees bring with them skills, practices and cultures that are very much influenced by their activities as gamers. These practices in turn influence and impact upon Auran at the most basic level of work place practices.

Furthermore, a key expectation of hard-core gamers is that game companies will now actively listen to, engage with and support the fans that form around game titles. This understanding of the game development process both pre- and post-retail release is brought into the industry by game designers, programmers, artists, website development teams, CEOs and marketing departments who, as gamers, are also participants in the online culture of gamer fans. Fans expect that game companies will provide forums in which they can express their views and opinions about games in development and games released. Fans expect to be increasingly involved in the game production process. Fans expect game companies to release editing tools and support the fan community's efforts to create additional content for the game. In short, a hard-core gamer fan expects that game development companies will build a collaborative relationship with them.

Consequently, the focus here will be on the "netface" — the relationships and networks that are in the process of being constructed and managed (by game developers, publishers and fans). I will focus on the efforts that Auran has been making around a product currently in development, *Trainz*, to enlist the passions and commitments of fans in extending the online networks that is to contribute towards the popular (and therefore commercial) success of *Trainz* upon its retail release in late 2001.

Auran began enlisting fans early in its life as a games developer. Members of the real-time strategy community who were participating in my PhD research brought Auran to my attention. The company impressed fans at the time (1997) with its openness to entering into open-ended exchanges regarding the forthcoming game, *Dark Reign*. Auran would promptly enter into email exchanges discussing features of *Dark Reign*. Auran staff (the CEO, Greg Lane, programmers and artists) were also participating in weekly IRC chat sessions organised by a group of fans that administered one of the more popular *Dark Reign* fan websites. The individuals who ran this website (*Dark Reign Chronicles*) were impressed with the level of communication that they enjoyed with Auran.

Over the course of my early visits to Auran, it became clear that the company regarded the ongoing development of relations with gamer fans as an important and integral feature of its business. As the Auran CEO, Greg Lane, described it in one of our early discussions (September 1997):

> We're not sure exactly how important our involvement with the fans will be to eventual sales of *Dark Reign*. But we do believe it is important; it is something that we are very committed to. One of our policies that we have in place [is that] all emails from fans will be answered within 48 hours. I think that the hard-core online gamers do have an influence. They are opinion leaders. They influence the level of presence and credibility that a game title has online. The more fan activity around a game title (creating websites, making additional content) the greater is the title's credibility with gamers who are online. We believe that online gaming activity will only grow in the coming years. So yes, we do believe it is important to listen to the fans. But how important our involvement is for sales is anyone's guess at this stage. But apart from that, it is a lot of fun. The fans obviously enjoy it and the guys here also have fun with it.

Discussions with the company about my research developed into an ongoing dialogue about how to create and manage relationships with online gamer fans. But, as Greg Lane put it to me: "It is one thing to study these things, how about actually being involved in the process of applying these ideas and seeing how they work in practice?" An outcome of my research relationship with Auran in June 2000 was an offer to take up a position as online community relations manager. By then, increasing levels of involvement with online gamer fans had become a noticeable trend in the game industry. My primary role at Auran is to facilitate and manage its relationship with the online fan groups that form around Auran's game titles. A recent example of this increasing collaboration between game development companies and gamers will help to place Auran's endeavours in this area within the context of overall industry developments.

The Sims

Industry insiders and commentators regularly cite *The Sims* (developed by Maxis, published by Activision and released in 2000) as an indicator of the increasing importance of fan-driven activity to the commercial success of game titles. One of the biggest selling PC titles of the past few years, *The Sims*, together with two expansion packs (*Livin' Large* and *House Party*), has sold over three million copies. In *The Sims*, the player creates and runs a virtual household. The game is very much driven by consumer desire, with the player meeting predefined needs (hunger, comfort, energy, fun, social interaction, etc.) through consumer spending — buying bigger houses that can be filled with items such as furniture and entertainment products. In short, *The Sims* is an interior decorating experience with the ability to extend and expand on the homes, reliant on the player's characters climbing the social ladder and obtaining better-paid positions.

But this description of the game only scratches the surface of where the success of this title perhaps lies. In "Learning from *The Sims*", computer game industry commentator J.C. Herz (2001) suggests that the popular phenomenon of *The Sims* is perhaps explained, at least in part, by Maxis's efforts to involve its customers directly in the process of developing and evolving the product. This has reached "the point where customers not only do a large portion of the innovation and marketing but also produce as much intellectual capital as they consume". Fan involvement was integrated into many areas of *The Sims*, including the development process itself and the marketing strategy. The success of *The Sims* very much builds from a sophisticated and user-friendly set of authoring tools that enable fans with no programming skills to create add-ons and modifications for the core game. Fans have used the tools to create custom objects and skins, from household furniture and clothing to naked characters.

Eight months before the retail release, these tools were released online for download. When *The Sims* hit the shelves:

> There were 20 independent tools developers, 50 fan sites, 40 artists hacking up custom content and 50 000 collectors of these user-created objects. When new players arrived having purchased the game, a virtual fan-driven economy was established to provide them with new content. Currently over 200 fans sites supply over 90 per cent of the game's content. (Herz 2001)

Maxis plans to extend and leverage this online community interaction next year, when it releases *The Sims Online*, allowing players to "sell each other SimGoods and SimServices for in-game money" (Herz 2001). Herz concludes that *The Sims* "succeeds tremendously because it allows players with different agendas to interact as consumers, producers, mavens and community leaders and to reap rewards for all of these activities".

The Sims game provides an excellent case study of the computer game industry enlisting and leveraging the online community fans into a commercially successful network. It also instances a trend in online producer–consumer interaction. In the process, the very boundaries and meanings of producer and consumer are undergoing significant and radical transformation. For Will Wright, the designer of *The Sims*, the game production process is heading in the direction "where it's truly a collaborative effort between us, the developers, and the people that buy our products" (in Kim 2000). Pierre Levy (1997; 1998, pp. 80–81), theorist of virtual culture, has captured these trends well with his argument that, in economic terms:

> the production of added value is shifted to the consumer or, rather, the notion of consumption should be replaced by that of the coproduction of merchandise or interactive services ... The virtualization of the market highlights the convergence of consumption and production.

For Levy (1998, p. 78), these trends indicate "the emergence of a qualitatively different transaction space in which the roles of consumer and producer are undergoing profound change".

It is important to note that this type of interaction between producers and consumers is not particularly new. The television and film industries have a tradition, for example, of focus group testing pilots with potential audiences. The recent series, *Big Brother*, is a good example of the TV industry's efforts to explore new modes of interaction with audiences, including the use of websites. The general software industry also has utilised consumers for testing and refining the product development process. In their study, *Competing on Internet Time*, Michael Cusmano and David Yoffie (1998) describe how Netscape leveraged the support and skills of the online programmers to refine the development of the Netscape Navigator Web Browser. In 1998, Netscape published the source code of Communicator 5.0 on the web. Anyone who downloaded the code could modify it; however, Netscape "retained the rights to the Netscape, Navigator, and Communicator brand names and logos, as well as the rights to distribute future products based on the code" (Cusmano and Yoffie 1998, p. 139). Netscape effectively leveraged the Internet for beta testers and extended this to "leverage the thousands of programmers on the Internet to build the world's largest virtual R&D organization" (Cusmano and Yoffie 1998, p. 140). For its part, *The Sims* represents a significant expansion and extension of this trend and promises to transform the relations among internet technologies, software games developers and fan-consumers.

To better ascertain the effects and uptakes of this emerging network of practices upon the "gamer-audience" which is actively using software tools to transform and engage with the game products, it is necessary to examine more closely the nature of gamer fans' relations with the game developer and publisher companies. The following ethnographic description of Auran's relationship with the fans that formed around a game in development, *Trainz*, is a step in this direction.

Auran and *Trainz*

When I first commenced my employment, Auran was in the early stages of developing a new product, *Trainz*. It is a virtual model railroad simulation. Players will be able to collect authentically detailed 3D models of locomotives and rolling stock. It will also allow players to drive the trains through fully 3D train line landscapes from the engineer's cab-view perspective. Finally, on first release, it will include *Surveyor*, an editor that enables players to create layouts. Using

Surveyor, players will be able to manipulate the landscape and place objects such as trees, buildings, track, bridges, tunnels, etc. *Surveyor* will also be modular, meaning that players will be able to join their layouts together. Auran believes that player activity in creating layouts will be very important to the success of *Trainz*. We envisage that player-created layouts will be available for download from *Trainz* fan websites. Furthermore, the modularity of its layouts will encourage the formation of online virtual model rail clubs. Additionally, the open-architecture design of *Trainz* will facilitate the ability for end users to import the 3D models that they create into *Trainz*. (The game does not include the software required to create additional 3D content. Instead, Auran is relying on the extensive diffusion of 3D software-modelling packages such as 3D Studio Max to create the 3D content such as locomotives or buildings.) From the very early stages of the *Trainz* design, it was planned to develop a product that was very open to end user modification and extension.

My brief for *Trainz* was to support and encourage the formation of an active fan community around the product and the Auran *Trainz* website (www.virtualtrainz.com). The decision to establish a website as a vehicle for facilitating dialogue with the online train and rail fans was taken in August 2000, at a very early stage of development. Designed to promote *Trainz*, the website included an overview of the features that it was planned would be supported. The site was also supported with a forum where visitors could post questions and comments about *Trainz*. For example, we started threads asking questions such as: What locomotives would people like to see included with *Trainz*? We also actively engaged in open-ended and extended dialogue with the fan participants about the reasoning behind various design features. The feedback from the forums and email exchanges with train and rail fans would then be regularly discussed in *Trainz* development team meetings. Auran's willingness to design and support a website that actively encouraged and facilitated feedback with our potential customers and fans was also enhanced by the fact that the online services manager, Rachael Nixon, had educational qualifications that included study in the discipline of media and cultural studies. Nixon appreciated and understood the importance and nature of fan culture dynamics and practices. Furthermore, Auran's CEO, Greg Lane, actively supported the importance of online community development for the success of *Trainz*.

Although a promotional and marketing vehicle for the game, the overall aim of the website was to generate feedback from train and rail enthusiasts and enlist them into the process of creating a growing and active online *Trainz* network. Early research indicated that a thriving train and rail fan base already existed on the internet. For example, Vern Moorhouse, a train and rail fan living in a small town in Wales, hosts a website, *Trainsim UK* (www.trainsim.org.uk/index.html) that promotes and encourages railroad simulations. Vern is something of a leader in the online rail sim (for simulation) community. We emailed many of the current hosts of train and rail sim fan sites, including Moorhouse, advising them of the *Trainz* development project and inviting them to participate on the *Trainz* forum. The email also established that we would value input and feedback from the existing rail sim community.

Making contact with existing fan sites was obviously a marketing and promotional exercise. We exchanged links with many of the existing sites and this had the effect of increasing traffic to our site from potential future purchasers of the game. Auran's online department and marketing director analysed website traffic reports weekly to determine the size and trends of traffic, how users were navigating through the site and where the traffic was coming from. For example, we were able to identify which fan sites pushed particularly high traffic through to the website. Fan websites are an important element in the online marketing of games. A network of active and quality fan websites assists with establishing the online presence and awareness of a forthcoming game with gamers. It is common practice in the games industry to release exclusive interviews and game preview content (screenshots, Avis, etc.) to those fan sites that emerge as the leaders in the ramp-up to retail release. For their part, fan site owners regularly approach game developers for exclusive preview content, as their ability to release news about the game development process and publish exclusive preview content assists them with establishing and maintaining their position as the leaders in the online fan community. However, in Auran's case, the relationship with fans was also established to gain feedback on the game's planned features. Establishing the relationship with train and rail fans was not just a marketing exercise aimed at building the hype in the period immediately prior to and after retail release; we regularly posted feature descriptions to the forum in order to obtain fan feedback and response. These dialogues were also often extended to email exchanges.

The feedback obtained from these continuing dialogues with fans has been invaluable in refining the overall game design. It has enabled Auran to clearly understand the expectations that train and rail fans have for a virtual model railroad simulation. However, this closeness has made it difficult at times to manage fan expectations as to what can feasibly be delivered within the time frame and resource constraints of a commercial game development project! Many of the feature requests posted by fans, whilst certainly attractive, would significantly add to the development time and costs. A significant part of our dialogue with fans has therefore involved explaining why many of the features that they would like to see included are unable, at this stage, to be implemented. In short, fans have needed to be educated in the many tradeoffs associated with "games development".

Part of our ongoing relationship with *Trainz* fans has involved weekly previews of 3D locomotive models that the game's development team has created. Fan feedback has assisted the artists to ensure that models are authentic in both specification and livery. In this way, the online train and rail fan community has provided the *Trainz* team with research assistance. Rob Shaw, a knowledgeable train and rail fan employed by Auran as a researcher and 3D artist, has drawn extensively on the community for advice regarding specification details that the *Trainz* artists require when modelling and texturing the locomotive models. Rob regularly posts questions about particular locomotives to the forum, and enters into email dialogues with train and rail fans who may, for example, be enthusiasts of US or British Rail. These enthusiasts will email Rob, describing how some features of a particular model previewed are incorrect. This information is greatly assisting the *Trainz* artists as they review the models in the lead-up to commercial release.

One of the important features of *Trainz* is its inclusion of a broad selection of locomotives and rolling stock from a diverse range of countries and regions. *Trainz* fans from countries such as France, Germany, the United Kingdom, Belgium, Croatia, the United States and Italy provide extremely useful details on locomotives from these nations, enabling us to include and accurately model locomotives from around the world. In fact, Auran receives numerous emails each week from fans requesting that we include their favourite locomotive from their nation and offering assistance in obtaining photos and data. A direct outcome of this enthusiastic virtual research and development effort has been Auran's decision to release regional packs of locomotives and rolling stock after the initial retail release of *Trainz*.

Feedback from the *Trainz* fans has also assisted Auran in clarifying its description of various game features. Initially, our website description of *Trainz* confused the train and rail fans visiting the site. The collectible nature of the *Trainz* models particularly confused fans. Fans posted their concerns and criticisms about this aspect of the game design. Throughout this exchange with fans, we regularly updated the *Trainz* FAQ section that described the collectible feature. We also refined and updated our website description of the game based on the feedback that we were receiving. Internally, this has been a continuing issue of discussion and evaluation throughout the process of the game's development.

Of course, it is often difficult to provide the fans with the full details that impact upon decision-making regarding the business model that supports *Trainz* — much of this information is commercially sensitive and directly involves negotiations with publishers. The level of our responsiveness to fan questions also has led to an expectation that this would be the case on all issues. Questions raised about various features or business issues, and fan demands for the early release of preview content such as screenshots, were on occasion difficult to respond to with the level of detail that the fans expected and demanded, due to commercial constraints like negotiations with potential publishers. The early release of information also had to be carefully balanced with maintaining Auran's position in a competitive market and marketing plans for the ramp-up to release. However, the fan feedback and dialogue through both posts to the *Trainz* forum and private emails have directly contributed to Auran's ongoing review of all aspects of *Trainz*, from design features through to its business model.

An example of fan feedback directly impacting upon game design decisions is the "destructible loco issue". After the first release of *Trainz*, in late 2001, Auran plans to release further modules, including *Trainz Online*, which will support online multi-player game sessions. A concern that *Trainz* fans raised was what would happen if one of our limited, collectible locomotives was damaged or even destroyed in the course of online play. Could they then potentially lose the collectible locomotive that they had purchased? Or, alternatively, would a model damaged or destroyed in an online train crash be returned in its original pristine condition at the end of that play session.

As *Trainz* designers, Auran staff were keen to introduce the ability to track "wear and tear" on locomotives running in online *Trainz*. The locomotives would need to be regularly serviced and repaired if necessary. We were also keen to introduce consequences for online train crashes — for example, in the event that the locomotive was destroyed, players would lose the ability to use that model in online *Trainz*, even if it was a collectible. However, fan feedback to this proposal was heavily against the feature. Players did not want to run the risk of permanently losing their collectible locomotives. Based on this feedback, a decision was made to abandon the idea of destructible locomotives.

The forum and email dialogue with *Trainz* fans provided us with a valuable mechanism for educating the current online train and rail enthusiasts about the game, and enrolling the more active and passionate individuals into the ongoing process of designing it. Based on the early feedback obtained, Auran decided that ongoing involvement with fans and the fan activity around *Trainz* would be important to its commercial success. We believe that a significant number of *Trainz* fans would involve themselves in creating additional content — layouts, new locomotives models, trackside objects and accessories, and new textures or skins so that the locomotive liveries could be changed. Based on this feedback, a decision was made very early in the design process to ensure that the ability to edit *Trainz*, to create new layouts for it using the *Trainz Surveyor* editor, or import new player-created 3D locomotive models into it would need to be relatively end user-friendly. A decision was made to commit considerable development resources to ensuring that *Surveyor* would be relatively user-friendly — that an average gamer would be able to use and enjoy the editing tools to create *Trainz* layouts.

As we anticipated, in the first few months after the launch of the *Trainz* website, Auran was approached by a number of train and rail enthusiasts interested in the possibility of creating third-party content for the game — particularly 3D models of locomotives and trackside accessories such as buildings. The Auran decision to support the ability to import into the game models created in recognised 3D modelling programs, such as 3D Studio Max, enabled individuals to produce models for *Trainz* from an existing software base. This allowed individuals such as 3Drailhound, who hosts a website, *3D Train Stuff* (www.3dtrainstuff.com/) to dedicate their site to producing additional models for both *Trainz* and *Microsoft Train Simulator*. Throughout 2001, as the popularity of both *Microsoft Train Simulator* and *Trainz* increased, individuals and teams interested in producing third-party content for *Trainz* rregularly approached us.

There is an increasing trend for fans to consider commercially releasing their add-on content. For example, the *3D Train Stuff* team proposes to release models for both *Trainz* and *Microsoft Train Simulator* for purchase via its website. Marc J. Nelson, a talented 3D artist, has formed a team of train and Rail Sim fans around the website (http://3dtrains.com), and also plans to commercially release models for download. Auran has developed relationships with these groups and intends to support their efforts by producing additional content for *Trainz*. Throughout the development of the game, Auran has regularly entered into extended dialogues with fans who are interested in pursuing the possibility of creating additional content for the program.

Early in 2001, Auran decided to formalise this arrangement by inviting a group of the most active and passionate fans to participate in a *Trainz* third-party content and beta program. This program, conducted within the terms of a non-disclosure agreement that all participants enter into, will involve releasing the *Trainz Surveyor* editing tools to the participants prior to the retail release of *Trainz*.

The first aim of the program is to provide the development team with feedback from end users. Questions that need to be answered include: Is *Surveyor* as user-friendly as the design aims to be? Is the interface easily understandable? Are changes necessary to make *Surveyor* a more effective tool? How difficult is it to use *Surveyor* to create a layout? Second, the early roll-out program is designed to allow the dedicated fan base that is forming around *Trainz* to start producing layouts that will be downloadable from their websites upon retail release of the game.

Editors like *Surveyor* are used by game development teams, particularly game designers and artists, to implement game designs. Editor tools allow the artists to place art assets within the game, for example. However, depending on the interface, they can require a relatively high level of skill to use effectively. Many of the editors released with game titles are daunting for the average player. Only a very small fraction of "hard-core" dedicated gamers actually use such tools to produce content. However, once produced, that content will then be downloaded and used by the wider fan base of a particular game title. As mentioned earlier, in the very early stages of the *Trainz* development, a decision was made to ensure that the editing tools would be end user-friendly. The *Surveyor* interface is designed in such a way as to assist the player to effectively utilise the tools provided.

The decision to develop end user-friendly tools was partly made in response to feedback from online train and rail enthusiasts to the initial announcement. However, the decision was also influenced by an announcement made by Microsoft in mid-2000 that it would be publishing a train simulator product in 2001. *Microsoft Train Simulator*, developed by the United Kingdom-based Kuju and released in June 2001, is a prototypical train simulator that emphasises the level of authenticity and realism of driving the locomotives provided through the 3D prototypical routes provided with the package. Much like the *Microsoft Flight Simulator* series, it is very much about the level of realism that the simulation attains. After seeing the preview screenshots for *Microsoft Train Simulator*, and taking into account that it would be simulating rail routes hundreds of kilometres in length, the lead designer of *Trainz* held the opinion that any editor released with *Microsoft Train Simulator* would be quite difficult to use and require relatively high skill levels that may well be beyond the average model train enthusiast.

In the promotion of *Microsoft Train Simulator*, Microsoft was stating that the end product would have an open architecture and ship with an editor that allowed players and third parties to create their own routes and import other models (for example, locomotives, rolling stock, buildings, etc.) into *Microsoft Train Simulator* that they had made with a 3D Software package such as 3D Studio Max. In short, much like their flight simulator line product lines, around which a range of third parties and fans produced additional content (aircraft, flight routes, airports, etc), Microsoft hoped that a similar third-party and fan content network would form around *Microsoft Train Simulator*.

Now the *Trainz* designers decided that the locomotive models in *Trainz* should be authentically detailed. This required high polygon count models. A relatively high-end processor and 3D capable video card are required to optimally run a game with high polygon models in a 3D environment. It was not technically feasible to then attempt to place these models within the context of lengthy and detailed prototype rail routes. The decision was therefore made to scale the *Trainz* routes or layouts to be of a size larger than a typical model railroad layout but significantly less than a full-scale prototype route.

The *Trainz* development team also believed that highly detailed smaller scaled layouts would support an end user-friendly editor. The time and resources required to effectively model a prototype route in detail would be considerable and out of the reach of an average train enthusiast with a moderate level of computer skills. Technically, then, the aim of the *Trainz* design is to place in the hands of train and model railroad enthusiasts a collection of highly detailed models, and a set of software editing tools that they can use to create their own layouts.

Throughout late 2000 and early 2001, Auran received a considerable degree of criticism from the passionate train simulator fans that this perceived change in design direction was not what they wanted or expected from a train-rail software game. This criticism was particularly levelled by Vern Moorhouse via posts to the *Trainz* website forum, emails to Auran and commentary posts on his *Trainsim* website. We entered into lengthy exchanges with Vern and other members of the *Trainz* online fan community, seeking to explain and justify the design direction of *Trainz*. From this point, to clarify expectations of what *Trainz* would be, we started to describe *Trainz* as a virtual model railroad and emphasised the ability of players to create layouts with user-friendly tools. From early 2001, Microsoft also commenced its marketing ramp-up to retail release. This involved increasingly enlisting the existing online train and rail fans into its network. For example, Moorhouse was invited to visit Kuju in England for a preview of *Microsoft Train Simulator*. He then posted his favorable views of *Microsoft Train Simulator* on his website. A number of the fans were flown to the United States for "Fanstock", an annual event in which the owners of leading fan sites for forthcoming Microsoft games are invited to exclusive previews of the titles in development.

During this period, the pre-release hype for *Microsoft Train Simulator* was considerable. Microsoft was promising that the simulation's open architecture would support the ability for end users to create their own prototype routes and export models that they had created into the game. They were shipping with the game the very tools that the Kuju development team had used to make *Microsoft Train Simulator*. But the actual tools used by development teams generally require a high degree of skill and so do not include a particularly user-friendly interface. However, these tools would be of use to professional development teams in creating commercial add-on packs for *Microsoft Train Simulator*. Consequently, we at Auran anticipated that gamers would find using the *Microsoft Train Simulator* editor a frustrating and time-consuming process rather than an enjoyable activity — thus providing a market niche for *Trainz* with this section of the market. Throughout the ramp-up to the release of *Microsoft Train Simulator*, Microsoft released very little preview content regarding the editor. Additionally, at this stage it was difficult to counter the speculations of the fans as we were not yet in a position to release previews of *Surveyor* and we wanted to see what the *Microsoft Train Simulator* editor delivered.

In the lead-up to the launch of *Microsoft Train Simulator*, Auran issued a press release that announced we would be supporting

Microsoft Train Simulator by releasing locomotive models that could be imported into and used with the Microsoft simulator. In August 2001, we added a *Microsoft Train Simulator* Add-On Pack area to the *Trainz* website and released a free download of a locomotive model that could be imported into *Microsoft Train Simulator*. It was announced that the *Microsoft Train Simulator* Add-On Packs featuring Auran-produced models would be available for purchase via an online e-commerce system over the next few months.

When *Microsoft Train Simulator* was released in June 2001, the comments and reviews that appeared on train simulator fan websites immediately confirmed the *Trainz* development team's judgment that the editor would not be end user-friendly. Fans were very quickly learning that the editor required a considerable learning curve and was difficult to use. At the time of writing (August 2001), very few fan-produced routes had been released for download on the fan websites. However, a number of talented fan 3D artists had managed to create locomotive models that they had successfully imported into *Microsoft Train Simulator* and made available for download from their websites.

The online fans' response to the difficulties and frustration encountered with using the *Microsoft Train Simulator* editor reinforced Auran's decision to release a user-friendly editor and to support the fans' efforts to create layouts for *Trainz*. By June 2001, *Surveyor* had reached a stage where we could effectively demonstrate its ease of use to fans. It was crucial at this stage to convince the somewhat sceptical fans who were actively participating on the *Trainz* forum that *Surveyor* was user-friendly. A core group of particularly passionate fans were regularly posting their views, opinions, questions and criticisms on the *Trainz* forum and also entering into email dialogues with us. These individuals, emerging as opinion leaders in the *Trainz* online fan community, were largely based overseas, in the United Kingdom, the United States and Canada. However, one of this group, 3801 (the nickname this person uses on the *Trainz* forum), resides in Canberra in Australia. 3801 had established a reputation with the online fans as a knowledgeable train and rail enthusiast, as well as a tentative and constructively critical supporter of the *Trainz* project. We contacted 3801 (we had already been involved in regular email exchanges with him) and invited him to visit the Auran offices in Brisbane for a preview of *Surveyor*. He accepted the offer and was very impressed with the features and user-friendly interface of *Surveyor*. He immediately identified the potential that *Surveyor* offered to the average gamer for creating their own layouts and predicted that, immediately following the release of *Trainz*, many layouts would be available for download from *Trainz* fan websites. He suggested that we may well see virtual model railroad clubs emerge, based on the sharing of layouts.

3801 sought permission to post his impressions of *Surveyor* on both his personal website and on the *Trainz* forum. Auran granted permission with the understanding that certain confidential technical issues could not be publicly commented on, and that he should feel free to express any criticisms that he had of *Surveyor*. His posts about *Surveyor* were very favorable, claiming that it not only met but exceeded Auran's claims for it as a powerful and user-friendly tool. 3801's posts generated considerable interest in and enthusiasm for *Trainz*. Part of his visit to Auran included gaining his input into and participation in Auran's plans to release *Surveyor* and the *Trainz* software generally to a group of the more active and passionate *Trainz* fans for beta testing and feedback purposes. In brief, as described earlier, Auran plans to release the software (at this stage under the terms of a non-disclosure agreement) to a select group of approximately 20 fans who will then use it to create layouts and provide feedback to the *Trainz* development team. We envisage that an outcome of the beta program will also be the creation of layouts that will be made available to purchasers of *Trainz* when it is released.

Subsequent to 3801's visit, we have commenced our ramp-up to the release of *Trainz*. This has included releasing preview in-game screenshots and movies of the game on the website. This includes an episodic series of movies demonstrating how *Surveyor* can be used to create layouts. Combined with the recent release of the free locomotive download for *Microsoft Train Simulator* and the announcement of our plan to release add-on packs for *Microsoft Train Simulator* in the near future, the preview material is attracting rapidly increasing traffic to the *Trainz* website. Forum activity and emails seeking further details about *Trainz* have significantly increased over the past few weeks. One of the challenges confronting Auran is managing and maintaining our level of interaction with a rapidly growing fan community, particularly in the period immediately prior to and just after retail release. We have established an expectation with the community that this interaction will continue. However, we are finding that the core community of active and passionate fans is assisting us by answering many of the questions raised by new visitors to the forum.

At the time of writing (August 2001), we are in the process of finalising the details of our beta test program that we anticipate will provide invaluable feedback to the *Trainz* development team. Auran is also entering into discussions with fan groups who are exploring the possibility of turning their activities into commercial ventures.

In this chapter, I have barely scratched the surface of the complex and heterogeneous materials that constitutes the network of relations that defines *Trainz*. For example, technological objects, processes and sites such as the website, email, chat, the working and design of the software I have simply identified with the noun *Surveyor*. I have not even touched on the story of *Surveyor*, involving as it does the daily work practices of the designers, programmers and artists. The work of the Auran online services team which builds and maintains the technological infrastructure and processes that support the interactions among the fans and between the fans and Auran is also not visible in this account. Added to this is the complex series of commercial transactions and negotiations with software publishers and model railroad companies without which *Trainz* would not emerge into sustainable material existence. I could go on, adding to the series of materials, actors, interactions and relations that constitute and are developing in the process of building *Trainz*. Such technologies and processes do not stand outside the network determining the social relations; they are part of the very materials that constitute the network. Likewise, the gamer as audience and as co-creator does not stand outside this network of relations; they emerge as a moment from them.

The relationship between Auran and the *Trainz* fans also emerges from this network of relations. This dynamic suggests that gamers are increasingly co-creators. As we have seen, they are a vital element in the network that defines *Trainz*. The fate of *Surveyor* and the potential for *Trainz* to grow into a successful online game network, enrolling the attention, passion, energy and dollars of other gamers, very much depends on what the fans will do with *Surveyor* when they have it in their hands. How will they transform it? How will *Surveyor* transform their activities as online gamer fans? Will they take it up and play with it to extend the *Trainz* network? Who is doing the enrolling and who is the enrolled in this process? The answer very much depends on who is doing the asking and what their position in the network is. The gamer as co-creator is a social moment and a potential which emerges from this dynamic and materially heterogeneous network.

Does this emergence of a new gamer audience with potentially more active practices indicate a shift in power between producers and consumers of new media product? Are, for example, the game development companies increasingly sharing control with the end users — the players? Is this shift of control moving into the production process itself? How are the development companies and the fans seeking to manage and exploit these emerging relationships? How are academic researchers positioned by and within these relations? What are the implications and uptakes of these shifts to our understanding of audience in the context of new media such as computer games? Do these trends suggest an even closer engagement and relation between gamers and game development companies? Or is it simply "business as usual", with the activities of consumers being increasingly seduced and incorporated within the networks of corporate capital? It has been beyond the scope of this chapter to answer all these questions, but this report from the netface shows that the provider–audience relation is an increasingly complex and multifaceted one.

Note

1 For an exploration of actor network theory, see also Latour and Woolgar (1986), Latour (1987, 1991, 1993, 1996, 1999b), Law (1994) and Law and Hassard (1999).

CHAPTER 9

Mobilising Readers: Newspapers, Copy-tasters and Readerships

Kerry Green

Newspaper readerships have been in decline over the past three decades. Newspaper editors openly acknowledge their difficulties in reaching a new generation of readers — so much so that sometimes it is claimed that our major dailies have "given up" on attracting young readers. This decline, when coupled with stagnant levels of television viewing, threatens the survival of news as an institution around the world. Over the past decade, newspaper managements have increasingly turned to readership surveys and market research to understand and attempt to arrest this decline. They have also taken a number of steps, turning to lifestyle readership, so-called "soft-news" and targeted lift-outs to reach particular demographic and occupational groupings, as in *The Australian*'s regular media, computing and higher education lift-outs. Yet management attention to such readership development has produced uneven results, failing to turn around declines in readership and to attract new readers to news and newspapers.

In response to declining readership, the Newspaper Association of America (NAA) and the American Society of Newspaper Editors (ASNE) recently co-commissioned two studies: the Newspaper Credibility Project and the Impact Study (NAA/ASNE 2001). The Impact Study surveyed 37 000 readers and non-readers and conducted content analyses on 100 daily newspapers. It concluded that circulation decline was not inevitable and that newspapers could reverse the trend by changing both the culture within newsrooms and the content in their news columns. This research called for nothing less than a thoroughgoing application of readership research to both journalism practice and its organisational culture. There was too little use of readership research and development and there were structural impediments to the effective use of such research where it occurred.

It is sometimes suggested that management attention to readership research and marketing has adversely impacted on news and what counts as news, precipitating declines in the standard of journalism in turn leading to declining readerships. If this is so, we might expect to find readership development a priority within newsrooms and find evidence of the systemic engagement with such readership and marketing research at the level of both journalistic and editorial practice. Drawing on survey research undertaken by the author among Australia's newspaper newsrooms, this chapter reveals a defensive culture resistant to readership and audience research. Contrary to the claim that editorial news issues need to be separated from questions of readership and reaching out to non-readers, this chapter concludes that newsrooms would benefit greatly from a productive engagement with readership surveys and market research. Indeed, this attention is not only useful but necessary if news and newspapers are to remain important and central media in the lives of ordinary men and women.

To date, too much public and industry attention has been paid to the "bad" aspects of the readership development approach. These include: possible interference in editorial independence by marketing and sales; a design for readers that compromises journalistic reporting standards and dumbs down readers; and an orientation to "sales" and "marketing" that encourages advertorials blurring the line between public relations and editorial independence.

By contrast, not nearly enough attention has been paid to the positives of a readership development orientation on the part of journalists and editorial staff. In the face of declining readerships, journalists should be interested in what the market research is telling them about their audience. While journalists pride themselves on their capacity to know and write for their readers/audience, there are few media sectors where such a casual and anecdotal approach to knowing your audience/readership would be judged acceptable. News professionals are paying a high price for their ongoing lack of attention to "knowing their audience". While there is much talk of a market-mindedness penetrating into the production of news, this study shows that there is little evidence of the active use of readership and market research in the formulation and development of news stories. Indeed, the effectiveness of such research is limited by the organisational structure of many newsrooms — and especially Australian daily newspaper newsrooms. This chapter identifies the organisational, professional, cultural and other reasons for not using this research. It argues that journalists and newsroom management need to undergo an organisational change to keep news and newspapers relevant to contemporary circumstances.

As audience engagement with news institutions diminishes, news organisations are forced to ask themselves 'why?' Why are our audiences disappearing? Why are audiences less prepared to engage with us? And what are we doing wrong? Answers to these questions will be meaningless, however, if news institutions and their employees — particularly their journalists — fail to understand the nature of their audiences.

Extensive research on both sides of the Pacific, and to a lesser extent in the United Kingdom, indicates that journalists generally are not well informed about the nature of their audiences. The research shows that journalists have little in common with members of their audiences, are not well informed about them and have difficulty relating to them. Conrad Fink (1988, p. 155), documenting the battle for supremacy between two Dallas newspapers, showed how journalists were "so fundamentally misjudging the public's reading and life-style habits as to raise questions whether they could produce newspapers precisely tuned to their audiences".

It is worth noting that research establishing differences between journalists and their audiences is not new. David Manning White (1957, p. 390) found such differences in his seminal 1949 study. In Australia, John Henningham's (1996) study revealed significant differences on a number of levels between journalists and their audiences, concluding "that journalists and the public in Australia have different ideological values" (1996, p. 95).

Research Implementation

In an attempt to halt circulation and viewer decline, the news industry and institutions within it have engaged in audience research in the hope of making news content more relevant and more palatable to potential audience members. What is this research? Who conducts it? Who uses it?

To answer these questions, I conducted a survey of 324 Australian copy-tasters at 246 Australian newspapers. The survey was not only designed to measure the effect of readership research on the news choices made by copy-tasters, but also to reveal the scope and nature of readership research in the industry. Typically, copy-tasters are the senior journalists responsible for deciding whether a story is at least worthy of being brought to the attention of the daily news conference, or of filling a space left open on a page. They are, consequently, important gatekeepers of news flow.

The survey used a 105-variable questionnaire form delivered to copy-tasters by phone in the period September 1997–March 1998. Newspapers chosen were those listed in *Margaret Gee's Australian Media Guide*, 53rd edition, with circulations of more than 1000. In a number of cases, one person edited more than one title, especially with country and suburban weeklies; in those cases, only one title was included in the survey. Only two of the newspapers approached — *The Gympie Times* and *The Newcastle Herald* — declined to be included. Those interviewed were senior members of their newsrooms, ranging from managing editors to editorial department heads (features departments, sports departments, chief subs). All played gatekeeping roles in their organisations. Respondents represented metropolitan, suburban and provincial (regional daily and weekly) newspapers. The questionnaire was divided into five sections:

1 types of research;
2 research effects on content;
3 gatekeeping;
4 implementation of research; and
5 demographics.

The results show, among other things, that Australian newspapers do readership research according to their size and financial capacity. In this respect, the results reflect Randal Beam's US findings (Beam 1995, p. 29), although Beam reports a higher incidence of readership research in the United States. Of the 324 respondents, 14.5 per cent were metropolitan journalists — 41 working on metropolitan dailies and six on metropolitan Sunday newspapers. Sixty-six (20.4 per cent) worked on regional dailies, 150 (46.3 per cent) on country tri-weeklies, bi-weeklies or weeklies, 54 (16.67 per cent) on suburban newspapers and seven (2.1 per cent) on other types of publications (typically magazines). These figures indicate that the survey was dominated by country journalists. This made it essential to discriminate between metropolitan and country responses in the survey. By controlling for "type of employer" and by performing cross-tabulations in frequency charts, it was possible to discriminate effectively between city and country responses.

Of the 324 respondents, 144 said their papers did not conduct editorial research, but a number of these acknowledged that their papers benefited from research passed on by others — perhaps other papers in their ownership group, or industry representative bodies like the Country Press Association. Perhaps the most reliable indicator was the figure of 111 respondents — more than a third — who said they had no readership research at all to refer to at their organisations.

In general, at one end of the scale the capital city daily and Sunday newspapers conduct continuing research for their editorial departments, while at the other end most country weekly newspapers not only do not conduct any detailed research of their own, but also are largely unaware of research being done by others in the industry. Where research does occur for country weekly newspapers, it is done on behalf of industry groups using national pollsters, or it is done in-house on behalf of advertising departments.

Australia's two major print media organisations, News Ltd and Fairfax, continually conduct research on behalf of the newsrooms of their capital city newspapers. For Fairfax, this concentration on editorial research is the product of recent years, following a long period of relative inactivity. Two more large print media organisations, Australian Provincial Newspapers (APN) and Rural Press, are less active in editorial research. APN gatekeepers reported little editorial research done in recent years, while Rural Press journalists said they had access to "generic" research, which tended to be done for advertising purposes but which was passed on to editorial departments for possible use. Such use was not geographic or title-specific, but rather tended to deal with large markets and did not address specific areas of editorial content. APN had thirteen daily newspapers and dozens of weekly publications grouped in the eastern states when the survey was conducted, while Rural Press publishes weekly and bi-weekly newspapers in country areas throughout the nation.

When asked "who conducts the research for your organisation?", the most frequent response from gatekeepers was "no one", with most of these responses — 75 out of 95 — coming from rural weekly journalists. The next most common response —"Someone at the paper itself" — drew 67 responses, 37 of them from country journalists. The main response from metropolitan journalists — fifteen out of 47 — was: "We hire a commercial survey firm to do it." These responses alone highlight the differences between city and country in terms of editorial research — city journalists enjoy the benefits of professional research firms, while country journalists largely either miss out altogether or rely on an employee whose focus might primarily be on advertising, rather than editorial, outcomes. The industry has also not settled upon a standard time frame for periodic research — respondents reported research occurring from once a year to less than every five years.

Gatekeepers reported the following kinds of readership research conducted for their organisations, with some respondents reporting more than one kind of activity (see Table 9.1)

Table 9. 1: Research Methods

Method	Responses
1. In-paper survey (clip out and mail back)	36
2. Focus group interviews	55
3. Scientifically designed phone surveys	68
4. Scientifically designed in-person surveys	13
5. Other (typically street-corner straw polls)	75
6. None	111

All of the "none" responses were from gatekeepers working on country weeklies, with half of the "clip out and mail back" responses (eighteen out of 36) also coming from country gatekeepers. All of the "in-person survey" responses came from metropolitan journalists. These figures once again illustrate the disparity of resources available to city and country gatekeepers. The results reflect Beam's (1995) findings. Beam noted that the relatively inexpensive "clip out and mail back" surveys, and focus groups, were the two most common forms of readership research in the United States.

Gatekeepers reported the kinds of research conducted by or on behalf of their organisations (again, some respondents reported more than one kind of activity) (see Table 9.2).

Table 9.2: Kinds of Research

1. Demographic (statistical information about readers/non-readers)	115
2. Industry/strategic (penetration, circulation, competitors)	41
3. Content (information about kind of stories readers like)	136
4. Design and layout preferences of readers	19
5. All of the above	1
6. None	107
7. Don't know	10
8. Other (straw polls, informal reader feedback)	19

Significantly, copy-tasters rated their exposure to readership research as very low. They were asked to rate the effect of readership research on their copy-tasting decisions for 22 categories of news, and in only five categories did they acknowledge any strong effect. But even in those five categories, gatekeepers said the effect on the content of their papers was negligible — that is, although the exposure to readership research might have influenced their copy-tasting decisions, very little change actually occurred in the content of the paper. This would indicate that initial copy-tasting decisions were not carried through to publication to any large extent.

The nature of the relationship — or non-relationship — between journalists and audience is partially revealed in section 4 of the survey. When asked to rate the importance of factors affecting news choices, for example, the gatekeepers responded (on a four-point scale) as shown in Table 9.3.

Table 9.3: Importance of Factors Affecting News Choices

(Scale of 1 to 4. 1 = unimportant, 4 = very important)	
Journalism experience	3.44
Feedback from readers	3.28
Peers' opinions	2.70
Readership research	2.60
Feedback from other departments	2.28
What opposition is doing	2.21

But when asked to rate six groups in terms of who knows best what should go on the news agenda, respondents gave the top rating as shown in Table 9.4.

Table 9.4: Who knows best what should go on the news agenda

Journalists	120
Audience	116
Public	55
Audience researchers	15
Government	1
Other authorities	1

In other words, although gatekeepers rated journalism experience higher than readership research (Table 9.3), they rated themselves as the best judges of newsworthiness only 37 per cent of the time (120 out of 324). When the audience (readers) was combined with the public (readers and non-readers), gatekeepers conceded the high ground to their target market by 171 to 120 (53 to 37 per cent of the total). The responses may help to explain gatekeepers' preference for a combined setting/following approach to the news agenda. A figure of just 37 per cent in favour of journalists setting the agenda indicates a lack of confidence on the part of the gatekeepers — something which is reflected in their reluctance to choose between setting the news agenda or following it, and perhaps influenced by the decade-long drop in circulation figures.

Importantly, Tables 9.3 and 9.4 show clearly that journalists rate readership research low on the scale of factors to be considered when making a copy-tasting decision. In Table 9.3, readership research scores a mean of 2.6, above the halfway mark on a scale of one to four, but it ranks only fourth in a list of six factors. In Table 9.4, the government and authority figures (predictably) are dismissed by journalists as having no expertise regarding the news agenda. But audience researchers are barely more highly regarded. Low scores such as these do not necessarily mean that journalists do not value readership research, but they do indicate a low regard for the research these gatekeepers have experienced and the scores may emanate from a lack of knowledge about audience research.

Certainly, other responses to the survey indicate positive attitudes towards good research and indicate poor dissemination of research in newsrooms. In the section of the survey dealing with the implementation of audience research in newsrooms, responses revealed poor implementation, resulting in inadequate knowledge on the part of gatekeepers.

Respondents were asked whether the research philosophy of their paper was understood by the newsroom. On a scale of one to four, where four is a strong positive response, respondents produced a mean response of 2.1 (standard deviation 1.12), indicating a poor to imperfect understanding. They also were asked if the paper's policy about using readership research was clearly enunciated; their mean response of 1.8 (standard deviation of 1.06) indicates that, at the majority of papers, readership research policy is not clearly enunciated. There were no significant differences in the responses of country and city journalists to these questions.

Respondents also were asked to indicate how well their paper's policy on readership research was followed in copy-tasting. Their mean response of 2.3 (standard deviation 1.11) indicates that policies, where they exist, are not well followed at all, although a cross-tabulation showed regional daily journalists were more likely to follow company policy than other journalists.

Gatekeepers largely agreed with their companies' policies about research use (mean 2.7, standard deviation 1.3). While a large proportion of gatekeepers (about a third) did not respond to questions about access to audience data, those who did respond reported that they had reasonable access to data about their own publications (mean 2.9, standard deviation 1.3) and their print competitors (mean 2.0, standard deviation 1.1). Access to data about broadcast competitors was a different matter, however, with the majority (303 of 324 respondents) producing a mean response of just 1.49 (standard deviation 0.91). However, they said readership research was important to them and they would like to have greater exposure to it (mean 3.32, standard deviation 0.93). They saw little danger of market researchers taking over the newsroom (mean 1.9, standard deviation 1.07), or of readership data being abused (mean 2.42, standard deviation 1.09).

Australian journalists therefore have a bifurcated view of readership research. While they feel declining circulation could be arrested by having recourse to readership research results, they also feel journalism experience is more important than research. The inherent dilemma of such a view is apparent in the fact that they rated audience and the general public more suited to setting the news agenda than journalists. The major problem for Australian gatekeepers may lie in their lack of exposure to research and in poor organisational procedures for delivering research findings in an easily understood form. Australian newspapers could well be rewarded with increased circulations if they placed more emphasis on readership research *in their newsrooms*.

That they are ignoring their own research is, however, evident in content analyses carried out at six daily newspapers. Content analyses of six newspapers were conducted in 1999 to test for changes recommended by the newspapers' own readership research. The newspapers were five metropolitan daily or Sunday newspapers and one regional daily newspaper.

Each of the papers had conducted some form of readership research and, as a result, had made recommendations for editorial content change. To test whether change had indeed occurred, a content analysis for each newspaper was conducted in the period six months prior to the recommendations and in the period six months after. In each case, the content categories were constructed around a paper's base content and the recommendations for change. The content analyses showed that in only one of the six could it be said research recommendations had resulted in significant positive change to the paper's content mix. In the other five, the content analyses revealed results ranging from little or no change to change in the direction opposite of that recommended.

Table 9.5 summarises the individual papers' responses to recommendations for content change:

Table 9.5: Summary of Content Changes

Newspaper	No. of categories	+ change (%)	– change (%)	No change (%)
Paper 1	16	2 (12.5)	4 (25)	10 (62.5)
Paper 2	15	5 (33.3)	3 (20)	7 (46.7)
Paper 3	8	1 (12.5)	3 (37.5)	4 (50)
Paper 4	8	1 (12.5)	1 (12.5)	6 (75)
Paper 5	3	0	0	3 (100)
Paper 6	14	8 (57)	1 (7.2)	5 (35.8)
TOTAL	64	17 (26.55)	12 (18.75)	35 (54.7)

Table 9.5 shows that statistically significant positive change occurred in just over a quarter of the categories (26.6 per cent), negative change occurred in almost a fifth of the categories (18.8 per cent) and no change at all occurred in more than half of the categories (54.7 per cent), leading to the conclusion that the newspapers (with the exception of Paper 6) failed to implement their own research recommendations.

Of 64 recommendations for editorial change across six major Australian newspapers, therefore, only seventeen were implemented. Worse, changes directly opposed to twelve other recommendations were actually implemented. Of the 35 other recommendations, the majority registered negative change, although the change did not achieve statistical significance.

On these figures, it is reasonable to assume that readership research has no significant effect on newspaper content at most Australian newspapers. This means that a valuable resource and valuable effort is being wasted. Audience research is a means of not only retaining the readers that newspapers already have, but also reaching out to non-readers, estimated by George Garneau (1994, p. 11) at 13 per cent of the adult population. Turning even a small proportion of that pool into newspaper readers promises substantial circulation and readership gains for newspapers. Garneau (1994, p. 11) quotes McGrath, president of MORI Research, Minneapolis, as saying that "the vast bulk of newspaper content is simply not relevant" to non-readers. McGrath is just one of many experts making such points — audience research is clearly essential if newspapers are to make their content relevant.

If news organisations are to truly mobilise audiences, their newsrooms will need to undergo a culture change that will allow them to see audience research for what it can be — a valuable tool for improving the relationship between journalist and audience members. The Impact Study of Newspaper Readership (NAA/ASNA 2001, p. 16) emphasised the need for a culture change. It found that more than 80 per cent of the 100 US papers it surveyed exhibited defensive rather than constructive cultures. Such defensive cultures were "intent on preserving the status quo and are resistant to change. People are expected to focus on how well they are doing, as opposed to how well the group or the organisation — or the customer — is doing."

Until Australian newsrooms shed their defensive culture and adopt a culture more responsive to outside influences — especially audience influences as represented by readership and market research — the communication process between news organisations and their audiences will continue to be flawed and audience reach, however it is measured, will continue to decline.

Applying Audience Research in Australian Newspapers

The effectiveness of audience research in lifting reader interest at any news organisation will depend on a range of factors, but three will be particularly important: the appropriateness of the research undertaken; the efficiency and skills of the researchers; and the degree to which the research is implemented. Interviews with researchers at News Ltd and Fairfax in Sydney and Melbourne, where the bulk of audience research occurs, reveal a wide range of research topics and methods applied with apparent efficiency by skilled researchers over the past decade. The sheer range and scale of the audience research undertaken — News Ltd conducts hundreds of projects each year — ensures that some of it is high-quality research. Undoubtedly, the first two factors required for effectiveness demonstrably exist at the major metropolitan daily newspapers in Australia. The third factor — effective implementation — is not as guaranteed.

For audience research to be effectively implemented at a newspaper, the research must be: clearly understood by newsroom staff; accepted by newsroom staff as valid and meaningful; and supported by management controls. Interviews with newsroom executives and researchers, and the survey of copy-tasters, indicate that these three conditions rarely coexist in Australian newspaper newsrooms.

Organisational Structure

The conditions rarely coexist in Australian newspaper newsrooms because most Australian news organisations reflect a top-down management approach typical of large organisations. They provide a generally clear line of command, with line managers reporting upwards to their immediate superiors, and they are generally highly departmentalised (see Lacy et al. 1993, pp. 34–36). Ultimate authority generally lies with the owner and is delegated through a publisher to a chief executive officer, and then on to individual line managers.

In a "normal" management structure, such an organisation would have executives in each level of management reporting to the executive in the level above. In the editorial department, then, editorial executives would report to the editor (or editor-in-chief, if one existed). But to whom does the editor report?

In most Australian newspapers, the editor reports to the chief executive officer, as do the other line managers. In many day-to-day bureaucratic issues, such a line of reporting is efficient and sensible. But when the issue of editorial independence is raised, difficulties occur. Editorial independence is enshrined in the Media Entertainment and Arts Alliance Journalists' Code of Ethics, and it holds that reporting of the news must be free from any influence that might "taint" its perceived objectivity. Although not contained in the Code of Ethics, by convention a newspaper's editor is deemed to have total control over the content of the paper, ensuring a church/state type of division between the editorial functions and the commercial functions of the paper. Such a division is necessary because the "public responsibility" role of a news media organisation can sometimes conflict with its commercial aims (Lacy et al. 1993, p. 43; Underwood 1993, pp. 143, 166). But if the editor is the final arbiter on editorial content, that implies seniority over other line managers such as the advertising manager and production manager, whose decisions may be countermanded by the chief executive officer — and a blurring of the chain of command between the editor and those above. This blurring of the chain of command is more evident in some organisations than others and was most evident in the attempted takeover of Fairfax by Packer in 1991, when staff drew up a charter of editorial independence vesting editorial control in the editor, and not the owner (More and Smith 1992, p. 130).

The concept of editorial independence is therefore at odds with an organisational structure which places two or more layers of senior management above the editor and assumes a homogeneity of management issues. The fact that the conflict exists does not necessarily mean that the structure is unworkable — editors in interviews (1996, personal communications) have reported they feel free to go straight to the publisher with concerns, or alternatively that they have the option of resigning if they strongly disagree with management decisions.

While the Australian structure might not be unworkable, it also is not optimal — and where less than optimal conditions exist, implementation of management decisions may be flawed. This is especially true when the decisions concern the character of editorial content and who has control over it.

If the organisational structure of Australian newspapers provides the capacity for conflict upwards, over editorial content between the editor and the editor's superiors, it also provides the capacity for conflict downwards, between the editor and the editor's staff.

If an editor wants to respond to audience research findings by implementing change in the paper's content mix, that change will largely be implemented at the level of the copy-taster. But there can be three and even more organisational layers between the editor and copy-tasters. In small newspapers, the number of layers can be reduced, but even that will not improve the chances of research recommendations being implemented unless other conditions are present. One of those conditions is communication in the newsroom. Communication, according to Robert Giles (1995, p. 79), "is the vital link that influences both individual motivation and group behaviour in the newsroom". To motivate staff to accept change and to achieve change, therefore, an editor must communicate effectively with subordinates, especially including those who perform copy-tasting functions.

Typically, copy-tasters are senior editorial employees — editors and sub-editors — who make decisions about which stories will get into the paper and what prominence will be assigned to them. Copy-tasters are a small subset of the editorial team in any newsroom, but they clearly wield an enormous amount of influence in "constructing reality" for a paper's audience and, just as clearly, a paper relies on their judgment to an enormous extent in addressing its audience.

Continually declining newspaper circulations represent a strong message that the copy-tasters' judgments are faulty. The judgment of the editor, who carries the ultimate responsibility for copy-tasting and who has the power to change the copy-taster, also could be faulty. Major newspaper groups have at least attempted to address the problem with market research to try to define the needs and wants of their audiences.

Organisational Gates

Audience feedback in Australian newspapers tends to be anecdotal rather than empirical. In many organisations, it consists largely of reported fluctuations in circulation figures, filtered phone calls from readers and letters to the editor. Interviews with market research officers of major Australian newspapers show it rarely consists of carefully constructed market research which links the anecdotal evidence to audience needs and wants and/or audience psychological, sociological and demographic characteristics (Balogh 1994; Bunn 1998; Dalrymple 1994; Lithgow 1998; Trodd 1997; Winkler 1998). Even when the feedback is so linked, organisational communication of the information to relevant copy-tasters is distorted in the form of gatekeeping by organisational figures and noise in the form of the psychographic profiles of the copy-tasters and their superiors.

My gatekeepers survey and interviews with the market research departments of major print news organisations have reinforced my experience (34 years in the print news industry) that market research by Australian newspapers overall (as distinct from the major metropolitan newspapers) is patchy, poorly communicated to editorial departments and even more poorly received. And, according to the survey, gatekeepers rate their exposure to market research as low. Henningham (1988, p. 173) reports similar findings in a study of Australian print and broadcast journalists. He quotes Baker as saying that, in a sample of print and broadcast journalists in Melbourne, only two had ever seen audience research data.

Further interviews with copy-tasters and with market research executives suggested the reasons for low exposure are three-fold: the dictum of editorial independence; editorial gates which block the flow of market research information; and the psychographic profile of copy-tasters.

Editorial Independence

The dictum of editorial independence presents a problem upwards (between editors and their superiors), sideways (between departments) and downwards (with journalists' acceptance or otherwise of editorial change). Despite the findings of David Altheide (1976), Philip Schlesinger (1978) and others, news organisations continue to pursue the aim of objectivity in news reporting — of disinterested, unbiased and factual reporting of the news. They purport to do this by a variety of means, but specifically by referring their news choices to a range of "traditional" news values and by maintaining editorial independence from commercial or political influence.

The dictum of editorial independence, as noted earlier, holds that the reporting of news should be free from any influence that might "taint" its perceived objectivity; as a result, it vests the ultimate power to decide what should be published or "spiked" in the editorial department, and specifically in the editor. This dictum often manifests itself in conflict between the advertising and editorial departments of a newspaper, when publication of a negative story (or non-publication of a positive story) is seen to be harmful to an advertiser.

Interviews with market research staff show it also has manifested itself in a reluctance to direct editorial departments to concentrate on specific categories of news or segments of the audience. When market research staff conduct research that is useful to copy-tasters in terms of feedback from their audience, they typically present the research findings to a senior editorial figure (usually the editor in chief) and the relevant editorial department head (features editor, sports editor, finance editor). Implementation of the findings is then left to the department head. In the interviews conducted, market research personnel were extremely reluctant to go further than simply presenting their findings and making general recommendations for change — to do more was seen as intruding upon editorial independence. In no case did a market research department at any newspaper do follow-up research to determine whether the findings had been implemented and whether they had had any effect upon the audience (with the partial exception of one paper). The dictum of editorial independence, while admirable, appears to act as a gate through which editorial market research finds it extremely difficult to pass.

Editorial Hierarchy Gates

If the dictum of editorial independence blocks the flow of useful information between one department and another, the very structure of editorial departments provides further gates. Newsrooms are characterised by their hierarchical structure. At the top, the editor provides a "vision" for the paper, and transmits it to a range of deputy editors, day editors, night editors, associate editors, assistant editors and chiefs of staff, who in turn retransmit that vision to a range of department heads, chief sub-editors, news editors and chief reporters, who then retransmit it to the next layer of journalists below them. The capacity for reinterpretation in this process would in itself seem to be sufficient cause of any failure in the paper's mission to communicate in an interesting and relevant way with its readers — providing the editor's vision was appropriate in the first place.

While market research will help inform and shape the editor's vision, the utility of the research itself will be limited when it is presented to only a small group of editorial executives. In many cases, interviews with market researchers and copy-tasters revealed that research findings were presented to the editor alone. The smaller the group exposed to the research findings, the greater the capacity for reinterpretation as they filter down through the newspaper's hierarchy, and hence the greater the capacity for inefficient copy-tasting. In my survey, three metropolitan department heads said they were never shown research and did not feel they needed to see it, because their editors told them all they needed to know.

Gatekeepers exist in a variety of guises in all organisations, and Thomas Harris (1993) recognises this. In serial communication situations, where information passes through a number of gatekeepers, significant distortion of the original message can occur. Harris (1993, p. 202) refers to a figure from the American Management Association showing that only 20 per cent of the original meaning is received when a communication passes through six sets of gatekeepers.

Harris's description of goal-setting as "leader-centered" is applicable to the use of readership research in newspapers. Where research was actually editorially driven (as distinct from advertising- or circulation-driven), interviews showed department heads in metropolitan daily newspapers were not involved in decisions about the content of the research — or, indeed, in decisions about whether to conduct research at all. Further, when department heads were being interviewed, some volunteered the opinion that it was not their prerogative to participate in such decisions and that they would be told all they needed to know by the editor. Such an attitude suggests a lack of leadership on the part of senior management which could, perhaps, be attributed to a preference for management rather than leadership.

Harris describes the attributes of leaders and managers and says both functionaries have important roles to play in organisations. But he says that "leaders work towards empowerment of subordinates whereas managers concentrate on developing power rather than people" (Harris 1993, p. 373). Harris could be describing here some of the reasons for the lack of clear communication about the application of readership research findings in Australian newsrooms.

Psychographic Gates

The third reason for copy-tasters' low level of exposure to market research lies in journalists' perception of the need for editorial independence and in the attitudes of journalists in general and copy-tasters in particular.

The dictum of editorial independence is related to journalism's perceived role of social responsibility — its mission to inform the public about issues of social consequence, no matter what the commercial or political consequences might be for the news organisation itself. Such a mission could be perceived as being at odds with the mandates of market research, and when journalists believe they perceive such a contradiction, they will feel free to ignore the research findings. Some journalists will take the issue further and decide to ignore all research findings as a matter of principle, an attitude noted by a number of journalism researchers. In particular, John Robinson and Mark Levy (1986, p. 164) noted that, among US television journalists, even a limited demographic knowledge of the audience was not deemed necessary — or even desirable — by a great many journalists. They pointed out that some journalists perceive a dichotomy between giving an audience what it says it wants, and the editorial freedom of the communicator. In other words, even basic demographic research work could impinge on journalistic freedom of expression and is therefore to be regarded at best with suspicion, or preferably ignored altogether.

A dictum which gives journalists the freedom to ignore all or part of the market research produced by their own organisations would be intuitively congenial to many journalists, because it is consonant with their attitude towards society in general. Studies show journalists to be small-l liberal in their political and social attitudes. This liberalism and streak of independence is also remarked upon by Harris (1993, p. 70), who notes the publishing, advertising and television industries are characterised as Macho/Tough guy–gal management cultures. Characteristics of such a culture include a high-risk business environment, with expensive outlays for risk; an environment of quick feedback on the success of decision-making; shared values of youth; intense pressure, fast pace, early rewards; extensive use of rites and rituals, bordering on the superstitious; and an individualistic attitude among employees.

Some of these characteristics are obvious in the newspaper industry. The call for quick feedback, for instance, is satisfied by supplying the daily circulation figures and referring to anecdotal evidence from reader phone calls. It is not, however, likely to be interested in feedback from market research which takes considerably longer to produce. High staff turnover could be a contributing factor to the blank spots identified by survey in copy-tasters' knowledge of readership profiles for their papers. And the individualistic attitude of employees helps explain copy-tasters' disregard for research findings.

Donald White and H. William Vroman (1982, p. 283) contend that group norms give rise to groupthink, which they explain as follows:

> As members become more cohesive, the group can develop a "clubby" atmosphere that emphasizes exclusiveness and superiority. New information brought to the group may be seen as inappropriate or even threatening and therefore may be ignored.

For White and Vroman (1982, p. 283) groupthink is manifest in several recognisable behaviours:

> Members ordinarily have a high *esprit de corps* and may characterize others as "quacks" or "cranks". They feel so secure in their decisions that they nurture an illusion of invulnerability. These groups are quick to rationalize their bad decisions and to cloak that rationalization in an "illusion of morality" (they have only the highest goals in mind ...) Self-censorship minimizes the likelihood that members having contrary views will manifest them, ensuring yet another "illusion of unanimity".

Anyone with more than a passing experience of an Australian newsroom will recognise the characteristics described by White and Vroman — characteristics which ensure that individuality, or at least a perception of it, is enshrined and outside interference is minimised. That such characteristics should exist in Australian newsrooms is hardly surprising — or, indeed, sinister. An *esprit de corps*, involving the development of a collective mindset, arises because newsroom executives work long hours under extreme deadline pressures. Moreover, they tend to work hours not worked by the population at large — night and weekend shifts, afternoon shifts, no public holidays — so their social contact can be limited to contact with each other, or at least to others who work in similar conditions, increasing the chances of the development of a "club" mentality and the rejection of new information.

Not only do these conditions support the rise of a kind of groupthink; they also provide an environment in which journalists are likely to lose touch with the needs and wants of their audiences. Information designed to keep them in touch with their audiences can be produced by the market research divisions of the major newspapers and broadcast organisations — and, indeed, much relevant data is being produced by them now. But until newsrooms can be convinced that it is in their interests to use that information, little hope can be held out for change.

Organisational Culture Change

While an organisation's culture is fundamental to the way it operates, changing it is extremely difficult. But the culture exhibited in many newspapers in Australia is clearly inefficient. A culture in which senior journalists say they are largely unaware of the editorial market research done by their companies, and in which they say their organisations' policies on using editorial research are poorly set out, militates against effective news decision-making. Yet these are just two of the findings from the survey of Australian copy-tasters. Further, a culture in which many copy-tasters listed their own advertising department as the entity most likely to abuse market research, and in which a fear of poorly constructed readership surveys is a recurring theme, is a culture clearly in need of change. Desired changes would include a greater understanding of, and perhaps participation in, the readership research by the copy-tasters themselves — a change likely to be achieved through greater contact between market research employees and copy-tasters.

But the need for change goes beyond a mere rapport between market researchers and copy-tasters. Both structural and newsroom leadership style changes are required. Newspapers serious about overcoming declining circulations must consider adding a review function to market research presentations, to check on and achieve compliance. Herbert Simon (1976), in his classic study of administrative behaviour, lists four functions for review processes of which the first and second, at least, are absent in newsrooms. The first function of review is to determine whether work is being done well or badly at the lower levels of the hierarchy. The second function is to influence subsequent decisions. Clearly, these functions are not occurring with relation to market research use by copy-tasters.

Further, newspapers need to consider their management styles and training, to reduce the number and size of gates through which market research must flow. For greater organisational efficiency to occur in Australian newspaper newsrooms, significant changes would have to occur to newsroom management practices to enable gatekeeping choices to reflect market research findings and contribute to the larger battle to reverse circulation losses.

The organisational structure and culture of Australia's newspaper newsrooms militate against the effective application of readership research recommendations. A lack of communication between and within departments, fear of the loss of editorial independence and the absence of adequate review functions in leadership roles condemn newspapers to continuing failure to implement recommended content changes.

CHAPTER 10

Finding an Audience for a New Service

Mark Balnaves

One of the important functions of audience research is its predictive value. This chapter takes two important case studies in which audience research was used to reformulate strategies for the development of media services. The first and most extensively examined is Telstra's "Gungahlin study", conducted in 1994/95, which examined the factors affecting the likely uptake of new media in the home. The second is the Productivity Commission's 1999–2000 analysis of the likely failure of the government's high-definition digital television model. In both studies, existing strategies for developing the internet and new media services and for developing high-definition television were revealed as flawed, requiring a significant rethink of basic policy.

The Importance of Prediction

Predicting what people will do with media and what society we will end up with as a result is a risky business. Just how risky it can be is revealed in the case of Brian Dermott, who proclaimed in the *Financial Review* in August 1998 (15–16 August, p. 25) that "[T]he concept that we'll see 60 per cent of the population or something like that on the internet will never happen". Apparently internet usage had already peaked in 1998 and it was likely that it would "never rise much above 25 per cent across the whole population". Within months, that particular prediction proved hopelessly wrong. A more considered and long-term prediction, which has become the basis for action of a number of global media corporations and beyond, was that tendered by R. Neuman in his consultancy for Time-Warners: "We are witnessing the evolution of a universal interconnected network of audio, video and electronic text communications that will blur the distinction between interpersonal and mass communication and between public and private communication." (Neuman 1991, p. 12) While Dermott's predictions were clearly wrong by the year 2001, it is not clear that Neuman's predictions, on the societal side, are correct either.

In modern democracies, assumptions about what people actually do with media cannot be, and tend not to be, ignored. Such assumptions are important in decision-making about allocation of resources for development of telecommunications and media infrastructure and content. They are also important in making judgments about data on audiences. It is often assumed that Australians will replicate the behaviour of American households and businesses when it comes to taking up new services. This assumption then becomes the basis not only for Australian prediction, but also for business and government strategy. The successes in the United States of e-commerce and pay TV (and research results which show that success) have variously been used in the Australian context to predict similar successes. This is a simple, but reasonable, example — one that shows how the "should" and "actual" are often combined. It is simple modelling behaviour based on the assumption that American and Australian audiences are similar. Research about audiences for future services has, in the modern setting, become intimately tied to attempts to inform audiences about what they should adopt as new services and how they should act.

Gungahlin, as a case study, is a good example of how collecting data about audiences — what people actually do — involves complex interactions between community, business and government. The case study shows that prediction of adoption of new media in Australia is not simply a market-research–decide cycle but a much more complex political and methodological process. An important characteristic of this process of research development is its hybridity — an hybridity which importantly extends to the methods themselves. Indeed, Gungahlin shows how corporate strategies may change as a result of research, and how a community — initially involved in research as citizens — became a community involved in research as clients. The Productivity Commission's research on digital television is also discussed as an example of how research influences perspectives on policy, audiences and diffusion of new media.

The Gungahlin Study

In 1994, university, community and industry groups, including the Australian Capital Territory (ACT) government, Telstra, ACTEW (Canberra's energy company), *The Canberra Times*, local schools and several other groups combined in an association called InterACT to trial the delivery of internet services to a new residential area in Canberra — Gungahlin. A University of Canberra research team led by the author was chosen to conduct preliminary research, funded by Telstra's social and policy research fund (designed for open public-interest research).

Gungahlin was chosen as an ideal test site because of a report by Cole (1992), commissioned by the ACT government and Telstra, which identified the potential for a high diffusion of computers in the new residential area. Gungahlin is an Aboriginal word, "Goongarline", meaning "little rocky hill" or "white men's house". The suburb is located approximately 10–15 kilometres northeast of Canberra's city centre.

As Markus (1987) has pointed out, having high-interest and high-resource individuals among the early users of an interactive medium is highly favourable to the achievement of universal access in the community. Gungahlin had these characteristics. The aim of InterACT was to conduct public research with Gungahlin residents, to trial new media services, and to use Gungahlin in the media as a model of future services to encourage diffusion (and to explore which services were likely to become universal services). Companies like Telstra also had an interest in the trialling of different methodologies for predicting uptake of new media.

Gungahlin had 1132 households, a population of 3151 consisting of 2175 adults (made up of slightly more women than men — 1117 females to 1058 males) and 976 children. Like other new suburbs, there was a heavy concentration of the adult population in the 18–54 age range — some 93 per cent of the adult population, in fact. Adults in the 25–34 age range made up 41 per cent of the adult population, followed by those in the 35–44 age group at 25 per cent, and then by those aged 18–24 at 15 per cent and those aged 45–54 at 11 per cent; those aged 55 years and over made up only 4 per cent. Given this profile, the child population was unsurprisingly massively concentrated in the under-twelve range, with 80 per cent of all children located there —17 per cent were in the 12–16 years age range and 4 per cent were 17–18 years of age. Two-thirds of all households were couples, either with (41 per cent) or without children (26 per cent); singles living alone made up 13 per cent, groups of adults 8 per cent, sole parents 6 per cent, retirees (couples and singles) 2 per cent and other 3 per cent.

InterACT had a public launch and preliminary research was conducted (and reported in Balnaves and Caputi 1997). Gungahlin residents were then invited to participate in Telstra Multimedia's trial of online services. There were no significant differences by demographic between those who expressed a willingness to participate in the trial of new media and those who did not.[1] Based on ABS household information technology surveys, Gungahlin residents have a higher level of education and a higher level of income compared with other regions of Australia.

The preliminary research confirmed the high diffusion of computers in Gungahlin — over 60 per cent, compared with a national average of 35 per cent. After the preliminary research, Telstra became interested in Gungahlin as client rather than (or as well) as citizen. The Telstra and News Limited partnership, Foxtel, was interested in takeup of its pay TV services and saw Gungahlin primarily as a test site for pay TV, rather than internet and online services. Telstra's offer to provide optical fibre broadband cabling to Gungahlin, as part of the open access InterACT trial, became a contractual trial with service providers for testing on a Telstra Multimedia network.

The University of Canberra research team went from public-interest research with InterACT to contractual research for Telstra Multimedia, with an agreement to release results after a suitable time period.

Telstra Multimedia began cabling Gungahlin, and the research team began a detailed study of the Gungahlin population. However, with the change of federal government in 1996, Telstra Multimedia withdrew from the trial as part of its general drawing back from broadband development. However, ACTEW, Canberra's public energy authority and one of the partners in InterACT, continued research into Canberra as a location for the development of an open-access regional broadband infrastructure. The University of Canberra continued its research with ACTEW's project arm, TransACT. TransACT trialled and piloted a service in Aranda, a suburb in Canberra, and plans to roll out broadband services to the region. ACTEW, like other utilities in the United States, United Kingdom and Canada, saw an opportunity for itself as a provider of broadband telecommunications infrastructure using its existing energy network.

Gungahlin residents never received the services promised by the Telstra Multimedia trial, but the Gungahlin project generated research that changed its strategies and influenced policy. This was especially so with the pay TV strategy. The Gungahlin research demonstrated that internet and online services — and not primarily pay TV — were of major interest to the residents. The internet, at the same time, was diffusing at a rate that would make the Gungahlin trial redundant in many ways. While "narrowband" and "broadband" were buzzwords in the lexicon of telecommunications-literate people, they were not well known in the community. Telstra and other providers were interested in how much "bandwidth" households needed, as well as their expectations of future media. Were their expectations, for example, "narrowband"? Did people even understand the potential of new media? Was pay TV or the internet the "killer application"?

The methodology and the results presented here are an overview of the Gungahlin residential use of media at the early stages of internet growth in 1994–95. Even though a longitudinal study was not conducted in this case, the baseline data from Gungahlin provided sufficient data to identify key influences on adoption (and intended usage) of new media. The Gungahlin study is also good example of an attempt to bring together multiple methodologies to predict what audiences will do.

Methodological Perspectives

As indicated earlier, the mix of methodological approaches was a key feature of this study. Central at the beginning of this study into the diffusion of innovations — in this case, pay TV and new media — was Everett Rogers' (1983) seminal work on innovation diffusion. Rogers proposes a model of the innovation-decision process in five stages: knowledge, persuasion, decision, implementation and confirmation. At the knowledge stage, socioeconomic characteristics, personality traits and communication behaviour can influence awareness and knowledge of a particular innovation. Awareness appears at the knowledge stage. At the persuasion stage, individuals evaluate the characteristics of the innovation according to its relative advantage, compatibility, complexity, trialability and observability. Individuals start assessing the product according to certain criteria (benefits, price, need) and forming favorable or unfavourable attitudes.

Rogers (1983, p. 21) defined adoption as "a decision to make full use of an innovation as the best course of action available". He categorised adopters into five groups according to their level of innovativeness: innovators (2.5 per cent of adopters), early adopters (13.5 per cent), early majority (34 per cent), late majority (34 per cent) and laggards (16 per cent). These categories were subsequently modified in the Gungahlin study. The major problem with Rogers' analysis was that the role of personality in adoption decisions is not well understood (Rogers 1995a, 1995b).

The research methodology for the Gungahlin study built on diffusion methodology and Swiss work on the role of personality and individual factors in adoption. The major independent variables of interest to the study were gender, age, income, education, occupation, computer attitudes and identity styles (personality dispositions that affect media choice). Swiss broadband trials found that traditional demographics did not appear to be good predictors of intentions to adopt new media. There appeared to be specific personality dispositions associated with innovations (Rotach and Keller 1993). Asking questions about 'computers' has been established as a good way to find out about people's attitudes towards new media in general. Eastlick (1993) found, for example, that attitudes towards the characteristics of videotext, particularly its relative advantage and compatibility with needs and experiences, were good predictors of intent to adopt. Cognitive ability has also been linked to computer experience and attitude towards computers, which in turn influences the adoption and usage of computers (Igbaria and Parasuraman 1991).

Work on information-seeking behaviour among adolescents has identified clear decision-making clusters associated with information orientation. Berzonsky (1992) called these clusters "identity styles" and created a set of scales to measure them. Berzonsky's methodology, and the scales, were modified and tested for the Gungahlin study.

The research methodology also used specialised inventories to collect data on time use, the household use of technology, attitudes towards computers, household expenditure and income, social networks and identity styles. Computer attitudes were measured using the standard CATT measure. The CATT measure is a set of questions testing positive and negative views towards computers. Dambrot et al. (1985) note that negative attitudes towards computers usually result in resistance to using new media. The modified CATT allowed investigators to assess the extent to which this relationship holds for other telecommunications technologies and services, and to assess the extent to which attitude towards technology is a predictor of usage.

Another available and highly regarded tool used to measure social density was Hirsch's (1979) Social Density Scale. It too was modified to assess whether individuals have low-density/high-density networks. The more interactions a person has, the more dense the network. Data were collected about the nature of contacts about innovations to identify opinion leaders and directions of influence. These and related indices are well established in the social network literature (Knoke and Kuklinski 1982).

Identity style inventories were used to examine the processes by which personal decisions are made and problems are solved about new media such as the internet. The major identity styles identified in the research literature include:

- *information orientation:* individuals who actively seek out, process and evaluate relevant information before making decisions;

- *normative orientation:* individuals who will be more concerned with conforming to the normative standards and prescriptions held by others such as parental figures; and
- *diffuse orientation:* individuals who tend to delay and procrastinate until situations and rewards dictate a course of action (Berzonsky 1989).

These identity styles look similar to diffusion categories like "innovator", "early adopter", etc., and the role of opinion leaders. The Berzonsky scales, however, are a much more detailed measurement of the relationship between personality and information-seeking. Identity styles are actual decision-making strategies that people use when making decisions about adoption of innovations (new products or new ideas). The "information seeker" (information orientation) actively seeks out information about what he or she wishes to solve. In the case of new media, an information-seeker is one who actively seeks information about new services before purchasing them and, if faced with problems about such services, will seek solutions. The "conformer" (normative orientation) actively seeks out information based on what they think is expected of them. Significant people in their lives are likely to have a great effect on whether or not they will adopt new services. The "procrastinator" (diffuse orientation) will delay purchasing or getting involved with new media services as long as possible. He or she has the motto "let's wait and see". They will only act if the situation and circumstances force it — "my boss has told me to use it so I'd better" or if the services are pleasurable and fun.

Identifying the role and relevance of identity styles (decision-making strategies) in use of media is an important first step in identifying key influences in adoption of new media and intended usage. However, diffusion theory also deals with social networks — the role of groups in influencing the process of diffusion and adoption. The social network data covered both the most important people in each resident's social network and the density of that network. Density is the resident's estimate of how often (at least once a week) people within that network contact each other and by what means (e.g. personal communication, telephone, etc.) The density index has a range of 0 (low density) to 1 (high density).

The research design involved 300 households chosen from the surveyed Gungahlin residents as the experimental group. Fifty households were chosen from outside Gungahlin, in a residential area called Belconnen, as the control group. The results for the experimental group were based on a sample of 618. The mean age of the residents was 31, with 52.5 per cent of the residents male.

Findings

The Gungahlin population is equally divided into "information seekers", "conformers" and "procrastinators". One of the key findings of the Gungahlin study was the role of personality in making decisions on the use of new media. Specific personality types are important predictors of new media uptake. But personality plays no role in predicting adoption of common, existing media. There was no significant difference between the identity styles for telephone communication, personal communication, television, radio and newspapers. Pay TV seemed caught as neither a new medium nor an old medium. In particular, it was perceived to not offer a new set of services relevant to the educational and child-development focus of parents. Rather, it was seen to be offering an enhanced television service — an adjunct to existing services.

The Gungahlin social density results show a significant difference across identity styles for personal communication. "Procrastinators" and "conformers" have higher density social networks than "information-seekers" for personal communication. The number of people in the social network is also correlated to identity style. "Procrastinators" are more likely to have smaller numbers in their social network than do "information-seekers" and "conformers". These social network findings support expectations that those with an "information-seeking" orientation are more likely to take independent action than other identity styles. Making decisions about communications technology — particularly adapting and domesticating the internet in the home — constitutes a variety of such independent decision-making.

As Table 10.1 indicates, "information seekers" had more positive attitudes toward computers than did residents who were "procrastinators". There were significant associations between the decision-making styles and computer attitudes. Post hoc analyses show that "information seekers" had more positive attitudes towards computers than did "procrastinators". "Conformers" shared characteristics of both decision-making styles, but tended to have more positive attitudes towards computers than "procrastinators". Similar trends in the attitudes toward computers were evident for the three decision-making styles in the Belconnen control group.

Unsurprisingly, individuals with higher incomes were more likely to use the then more expensive technologies — such as a mobile phone, a personal computer, a modem, fax and the internet (indirectly expensive because of the need for hardware, etc) — at home. In addition to the use of a fax machine at home, higher attitudes toward computers correlated positively with the use at home of a personal computer, a modem and the internet. The use of a fax machine at home is significantly and positively related to increases in age, higher income and a positive attitude toward computers. But is negatively correlated with female use. These results are not surprising, given that a fax machine is utilised predominantly for business-related purposes and that older males with higher incomes are more likely to require home business equipment. With more women becoming involved in small business, these gender usage patterns may be changing. It remains unclear whether or not positive attitudes were high before these technologies were introduced into the home. Attitudes towards computers had a clear relationship to identity styles and other variables, like age and gender.

Tables 10.1 and 10.2 show how personality — the decision-making strategies — influences media choice. The figures are the residents' rankings of their perceived preference and ease of use of different media. Tables 10.1 and 10.2 show that preference for common media, like the telephone and face-to-face contact, are not affected by personality — the preferences are similar (they are "universal services"). However, email — while preferred by all three decision-making strategies — was not seen as "easy to use" by the procrastinators. Other internet services were preferred and seen as easy to use by the information seekers.

Table 10.1: Perceived Preference by Decision-making Strategies

	Inform. Seeker	No.	Conform.	No.	Procrast.	No.
Telephone	2	179	2	143	2	158
Face-to-face	1	152	1	128	1	133
Email	3	74	3	41	3	30
Television	5	142	5	133	4	148
Radio	6	113	4	98	4	116
Letters, notes memos	4	119	5	85	3	80
Postcards	8	5	4	1	3	4
Magazines	4	64	7	49	5	57
Newspapers	3	115	4	85	5	98
Books	5	57	7	41	6	47
Fax	4	56	3	46	8	33
Video	4	29	3	28	6	27
Internet	2	23	4	16	4	11
Music, stereo, CD	2	12	1	5	2	3
Talking	1	26	1	21	1	33

Values refer to modal rank (1 = most important, most preferred, etc.)

The findings tell us that "information seekers", whether high or low income, male or female, well educated or not, are the people most likely to trial and to adopt new media like the internet. Pay TV was of interest to approximately a third of residents, primarily the "procrastinators", but pay TV was not seen as a new medium. "Procrastinators" had an interest primarily in entertainment media. The "conformers", in Gungahlin, tended to follow the pattern of the "information seekers".

The overall trends from the Gungahlin research suggested that:

1 Older people and not younger people are more likely to be receptive to new media.
2 People who are more receptive to new media are more likely to have lower density social networks.
3 People with a problem-solving orientation (information orientation) are more likely to have positive attitudes towards computers.

Table 10.2: Perceived Ease of Use by Decision-making Strategies

	Inform. Seeker	No.	Conform.	No.	Procrast.	No.
Telephone	2	179	2	143	2	158
Face-to-face	1	151	1	128	1	134
Email	3	73	3	41	6	30
Television	2	140	1	133	3	147
Radio	3	110	4	98	4	114
Letters, notes, memos	3	119	3	85	3	79
Postcards	9	5	4	1	5	4
Magazines	6	63	6	49	4	57
Newspapers	4	113	4	85	3	98
Books	4	55	7	41	6	47
Fax	3	56	5	46	6	32
Video	6	29	3	27	5	27
Internet	3	21	5	16	6	11
Music, stereo, CD	5	12	1	5	15	4
Talking	1	26	1	21	1	32

Values refer to modal rank (1 = most important, most preferred, etc.)

4 Women are more likely to have negative attitudes towards computers, and to use computers marginally less than men, but these negative attitudes do not stop women using computers and do not constitute a barrier to use (this has been confirmed by recent studies in the United States, especially in *The Digital Divide* report).
5 Identity styles directly influence perceived importance, preference and ease of use of advanced media services, but *not* use of common media services.

The findings of the study no doubt reinforced Telstra's interest in maximising narrowband potential and in expanding its plans for internet service provision. Big Pond, Telstra's internet service, followed the Gungahlin study and ACTEW, Canberra's energy and water authority, capitalised on Telstra's departure from the Gungahlin trial, undertaking its own studies into broadband provision within the ACT.

In some ways, the Gungahlin trial shifted the focus from trialling pay TV in a broadband environment to the emergence of the internet as an established medium; there was a shift from 'trials' to providing a service immediately. The expectations of the Gungahlin residents of a broadband trial were, of course, not met.

There are limitations to a study that is dealing with hypothetical services (characteristics like the quality of a service, for example, are not measurable). The presence of the internet in homes in Gungahlin, however, provided an ideal real-life context for assessing preferences and use.

The Governance Cycle

The Gungahlin results are, in some senses, counter-intuitive. The idea that older, not younger, people arc more likely to be receptive to new media seems to contradict the massive digital games surge among young people, for example. But young people's use of games does not contradict the idea that older people with particular identity styles are more likely to be receptive to major new innovations when they arrive. Gungahlin is therefore a good example of using complex audience data to understand the interrelationships of a range of issues.

Gungahlin is also a good example of the governance cycle of media audiences. All the elements of the cycle — the process — are there. Gungahlin is an extension of social cause marketing and the merging of "public" and "private". There is management modality — when the citizens of Gungahlin became the clients of Telstra Multimedia. There is audience and campaign mindedness, with InterACT and Telstra Multimedia intending to use Gungahlin as a model community for other communities to follow. There is a research and evaluation modality, where research was designed to elicit the preference of Gungahlin residents, but where its public nature was also designed to show those residents that their needs were being assessed. There is a citizen mindedness, where — even when the residents of Gungahlin were tied contractually to research and the trial — Telstra Multimedia was accountable for the role of Gungahlin in the public mind as a model of future communication communities.

As already noted in the introduction, the governance cycle the idea that audience behaviour can be regulated and controlled through media campaigns — is particularly effective in English-speaking countries where "co-creation" is well established and where the research technologies are transparent and accountable. Gungahlin was an attempt to influence audience adoption behaviour through modelling of future communication communities.

The Gungahlin research also reinforces the multidimensional character of modern research studies that has already been emphasised in this book. The same research can be used for a variety of policy contexts, many of which were not originally intended. The original purpose of the Gungahlin research was to provide public-interest, publicly accessible research for a consortium called InterACT. The infrastructure provider in that consortium, however, wanted contractual obligations. The contracted research with Telstra Multimedia, however, was still linked to issues of universal service (equitable access for everyone) and still had a public character. When the Gungahlin project stopped, the preliminary research was adopted by other organisations to plan a separate and new service.

The Productivity Commission and Digital Television

The Gungahlin study was an integral part of an attempt to generate demand for new media services — it has a "demand side" orientation (what people *actually* do). Plans to introduce Digital Television (DTV) into Australia, however, have been driven by media companies, manufacturers and regulators wanting to improve the quality of the equipment and services. It is "supply side" in its orientation (what people *should* do). Television networks have made considerable investments in digital media in order to deliver digital television. They have secured from the federal government valuable concessions and guaranteed bandwidth. This development of the technology was not based on demand scenarios but on the perceived benefits of the new media technologies by providers and regulators. Indeed, demand was assumed, as high-definition television was seen to be a service enhancement — not unlike colour television was back in the mid-1970s which took a comparatively short period of time to bed down in Australia (in part because Australia got colour television so late). There was also a concern that, in this new television technology, Australia could be a leader rather than a follower, a standard-setter rather than a standard-taker playing catch-up.

Considerable effort is applied to identifying potential adopters of new media and advertising, through research on variables such as ownership of consumer electronics, age, income and gender. However, the acceptance of new media varies from country to country because people have different needs and values (product cost, product benefit). Americans are known for their love of consumer electronics such as VCRs, personal computers and television sets. The British are known for their concern about price level and social position, rather than love of electronics for their own sake. For Belgians, none of these variables is significant in purchasing decisions (Dupagne and Agostino 1991).

New media have always represented new potential for advertising. Newspapers and magazines offered advertisers the opportunity to intersperse ads with news, front page and back page, and to target specific audiences by readership demographic. Television enabled advertisers to interrupt programming and to advertise to mass audiences, instantly. Print and broadcast have seen technical and service level improvements. Digital TV (DTV) offers the opportunity for enhanced viewing and enhanced access to information. But, unlike print and traditional television broadcasting, DTV is an example of 'technical convergence' — bringing together different media, including internet access.

The Australian federal government chose HDTV — the highest and most expensive standard — in its initial policy formulations, and did so partly to restrict use of digital broadcasting for multichannelling/ datacasting (where non-traditional broadcasters could provide internet-type capability, or de facto broadcasting). Mandating HDTV itself limits the amount of spectrum left to provide additional channels. Free-to air broadcasters, not surprisingly, supported restrictions on datacasting and multichannelling. They wanted the spectrum and the advertising to themselves.

The Australian federal government's assumptions that HDTV would be adopted in Australia were based on the idea that Australians are, generally, rapid adopters of new technology, and that they would like bigger screens (Productivity Commission 1999, p. 126). The federal government and free-to air media providers therefore had a model based on quality standards and assumptions about adoption which left non-traditional broadcasters out of the scene. The federal government's decisions on HDTV are good examples of "supply side" regulation, where plans are made to diffuse new media, regardless of overseas experience and regulatory practice which cautioned against high expectations for audience adoption of HDTV on a large scale.

Industry and community pressure on the federal government led to a review by the Productivity Commission. The Productivity Commission, an independent Commonwealth agency, is the government's principal review and advisory body on microeconomic policy and regulation. It conducts public inquiries and research into a broad range of economic and social issues affecting the welfare of Australians.

The Productivity Commission's draft report *Broadcasting* (1999) worked from what audiences actually *do* with media. The Productivity Commission concluded that:

> High definition television, provided at considerable expense to all, is likely to have a slow uptake. A small number of Australians will enjoy its benefits, but sooner or later all consumers will be required to pay for it, including those least able to do so. They will otherwise be left without television when simulcasting ends. (Productivity Commission 1999, p. 128)

Using Roy Morgan's Single Source database and BDA Planning's analysis of it, the Productivity Commission concluded that only 1.5 per cent of mostly younger people had an interest in all types of media, and especially new media technologies, and another 8 per cent of people from a range of backgrounds also used a wide variety of old and new media. The majority of media users — 55 per cent, according to the Commission's draft report — preferred a single type of media — internet or newspapers, or magazines or radio or television. Those who could afford to buy expensive HDTV were unlikely to buy it and those who could not afford to buy HDTV were most likely to use it. BDA's estimate was that approximately

5 per cent of the population would adopt HDTV (1999, p. 125). The idea that Australians had a preference for "larger screens" was also not warranted.

Central to the Commission's analysis was the identification of high-definition television "as a premium service rather than a medium with general appeal" (1999, p. 247). This was based on an assessment of what it required of consumers: they would need to purchase a large screen and a surround sound system to enjoy its full benefits (1999, p. 247). As a type of "home cinema", it was different "from most household uses of television":

> Whereas home cinemas tend to be set up in rooms dedicated to the purpose, with large screens and expensive audio systems, the ordinary household experience of television is unceremonious and technologically undemanding. (1999, p. 247)

In many ways, the Commission's findings confirmed the results of the Gungahlin study. Like that study, the Commission confirmed the difficulties facing ordinary services (pay TV being one of them) and suggested that the significant opportunities related to the more interactive, online-type services. Media planning agency BDA Planning, which provided analysis for the Commission, enabled it to conclude that:

> Interactive services and multichannelling by commercial broadcasters possess substantially more consumer appeal than high-definition television, especially among those types of media users who watch the most television, the "heavy users" and "filling time" groups. The regulation of these new services has the potential to constrain innovation in new convergent media, reduce consumer demand and slow the conversion process. (Productivity Commission 2000, p. 255)

The Productivity Commission became audience-minded to demonstrate to policy-makers-as-the-audience that the regulatory strategies did not match up with what people actually did with media (or were likely to do). The Commission became campaign-minded by "setting an agenda" for public and policy discussion — namely to liberalise the laws surrounding digital television and to adopt a standard like SDTV that would be less expensive for the consumer.

Conclusion

The Gungahlin and Productivity Commission as case studies demonstrate the role of research in informing policy and strategy. But they are also clear examples of "doing the thinking for them". In the case of Gungahlin, the research was not simply "administrative" or "instrumental". The local Canberra community — from government to schools to neighbourhoods — had an interest in how new media would be used. InterACT, in the first instance, served the role of researcher, trying to reflect the real needs of the Canberra community. Telstra Multimedia provided a trial as the focus. Prediction was relevant both to corporate strategy and to community and government groups interested in adoption of new services. The processes of "co-creation" and of "signalling" are also evident here. Through Gungahlin, Telstra Multimedia was signalling to the broader Australian audience its role in providing advanced services. As a result, the audience data were, in a real sense, "co-created". The fact that Gungahlin failed — as a trial in a physical site — does not limit its significance. The "co-creation" continued after Telstra Multimedia left and resulted in an open-infrastructure plan through Canberra's energy authority, ACTEW.

The Productivity Commission is an example of how an independent government body argued that accountability to the audience has not been undertaken in the planning and legislative process itself. Audience data were not used simply as currency, but as a means of showing that Australians would be disadvantaged by the "supply side" push of the Australian federal government and free-to-air broadcasters.

Note

1 The most significant variation between those not willing to participate in the trial and those willing to participate were among couples without children 29 per cent and 26 per cent respectively. Generally the variations ranged from no variation for groups of adults with children and the "other" category through a 0.4 per cent variation in the case of couples with children to a variation of 2.7 per cent in the case of couples without children.

CHAPTER 11

'Tell Me what You Want and I'll Give You what You Need': Perspectives on Indigenous Media Audience Research

Michael Meadows

Introduction

Knowing an audience has always been a central organising element of effective communication systems — from the information corridors or "Dreaming tracks" which have criss-crossed Australia for millennia to the new digital corridors which continue to expand around the globe. Audience research has been, and remains, a critical part of the marketing process, and much of current media audience research is shaped to meet the needs of the market — including cultural institutions like commercial television and radio stations — delivering audiences to advertisers in manageable units, assuming the existence of a "mass" audience with similar interests (Ang 1991, pp. 63–64).

Fortunately, thinking about audiences has long transcended the narrow commercial conception encompassed by commercial ratings. The explosion of internet use has created new ways in which audiences interact with information. Patricia Gillard (2000, pp. 122–24) argues that, in this new digital environment, we need to think of audiences more broadly than in terms of "passive", "active" or "interactive". She suggests new analytical categories: multiple audiences, defined along "many dimensions"; audiences with specific "purposes" for using media technologies; audiences created in relation to media content; and the relationship between "onsite and online" audiences. The audience — and in particular information about the audience — has never mattered more. Media audience research has emerged as a global industry and, in Australia, organisations like ACNeilsen and Roy Morgan Research exist to provide data-hungry networks with the information they want. But is it the information they need?

Despite the rise of the media audience research industry, sections of the audience remain largely invisible. Minority groups around the world tend to be marginalised because of the dominance of commercial imperatives in media production. Roncagliolo (1991, pp. 206–7) has coined the term "alterative" to describe media which is not bound by dominant ideologies. He suggests that the description "alternative" can be synonymous with poor quality or marginal and so puts forward "alterative" as a substitute. It "gives meaning to the alternative", imbuing it with significant new meaning. Indigenous media might be thought of differently in this way, suggesting that Indigenous audiences, too, may need to be considered within this "alterative" paradigm.

According to the 1996 census, Indigenous people in Australia make up around 2 per cent of the population. This would appear to suggest that, as a group of consumers, they are of little significance. It may also help to explain the dearth of information about Indigenous audiences in Australia for either mainstream or Indigenous media. But if we extend the idea of the audience beyond the constrained notion of the consumer, we can think of audience research in a more circumspect and reflexive way. We should not forget that the information all researchers receive — especially across cultural boundaries — is always "partial". This information is influenced by a range of considerations: attributes like race, class, gender and nationality; a researcher's world view; time constraints; and the ability to create "spaces that foster trust and cooperation" (Mullings 2000, p. 349). It may relate directly to something as simple as telephone access.

Despite a lack of attention paid to urban, regional and remote Indigenous audiences in Australia, there is a growing international research archive of Indigenous audience preferences for locally produced Indigenous programming. The research dealing with Indigenous media audiences in Australia to date has tended to focus on remote areas and has been confined largely to detailing audience demographics rather than program preferences. Australian Broadcasting Tribunal hearings in the 1980s are examples of this (Australian Broadcasting Tribunal 1984, 1985). Indeed, it was not until 2000 that the Indigenous media sector was formally acknowledged as part of a national broadcasting network (Meadows 2000).

Although most Indigenous people live in urban centres, research into urban Indigenous media audiences was virtually ignored until the mid-1990s. And even since then, the number of projects can be counted on one hand. But there has been an increasing realisation by government agencies — and the audience research industry — that they know little about Indigenous people and how or why they use communication technologies. This is a critical element in why much of the communication between Indigenous and non-Indigenous people is ineffective. The 1998 review of the Indigenous media sector, *Digital Dreaming*, found an urgent need for improved interaction between government agencies, service providers and Indigenous people to facilitate strategic planning at the national and international levels (ATSIC 1999, p. 5). A better understanding of how Indigenous audiences are made is a crucial element of this.

In this chapter, I want to touch on some examples of, and some of the issues around, Indigenous audience research. It includes approaches to research which might reveal more useful information about how and why Indigenous people use communication technologies in a variety of settings and in a variety of ways.

The Indigenous Media Environment

> Aboriginal people, both individually and collectively, are turning to film, video and television as the media most likely to carry their messages to one another and into the consciousness of white Australia. (MacDougall 1987, p. 58)

These words by ethnographic filmmaker David MacDougall have proved to be remarkably prophetic. The range of Indigenous media being produced across Australia is impressive — and remains unknown to most of the non-Indigenous population. It offers a huge diversity — from the small, remote communities in central Australia linked by interactive videoconferencing in local languages to the 100 000 people who tune in each week to Radio 4AAA Murri Country in Brisbane. Indigenous voices are being heard across the airwaves in Australia and they're getting louder and louder. The sector not only provides a first level of service to its many communities, but also acts as a bridge between Indigenous and non-Indigenous cultures (Productivity Commission 1999, pp. 100–101).

Gaining access to the airwaves for Indigenous people — or "air rights" — has been as much of a struggle as winning back custodianship of the land. One of the driving forces behind the emergence of the Indigenous media sector is the parlous state of Indigenous languages in Australia. Of the more than 250 languages and 500 dialects spoken here at the time of British invasion in 1788, perhaps fewer than 50 will survive the new millennium (Schmidt 1993). But at the dawn of the new century,. the Indigenous media sector, at least, is extensive:

- more than 100 permanently licensed community radio stations. Eighty-two of these outlets (the Broadcasting for Remote Aboriginal Communities Scheme — BRACS) are the only permanently licensed community television stations in Australia;
- 40 broadcasting groups seeking permanent community radio licences;
- one commercial television station (Imparja, in Alice Springs) and one commercial radio station (Yamitji Media, Carnarvon, in Western Australia);
- more than 50 film, video and multimedia producers; and
- one national newspaper and a large number of regional and local newspapers (NIMAA 1999).

Indigenous media production could well be one of the most dynamic sites in the age of information technology as Indigenous communities manage this important and powerful cultural resource. Indigenous media production is a hybrid process — "a multifaceted and heterogeneous mix of policy issues, practices, and tactics"

(O'Regan and Batty 1993, p. 230; see also Ginsburg 1991, 1993). So the kind of cultural production which emerges — partially as a response to misrepresentation by mainstream media — is diverse. It is about reclaiming identity and the right to participate in identity construction. It is about appropriating technologies and managing them as cultural resources whether they be computers, telephones, video cameras or satellites. The operation of culture as an authorising agency is evident in these many locations.

Evidence exists for the often unproblematic coexistence of two versions of media — local and introduced — side by side in various Indigenous cultural settings. These are two systems of knowledge — two systems of law (Morris 2000). What I am suggesting here is that it is the social relations within Indigenous communities which determine the nature and form of media responses (Marx 1973, p. 495; Kulchyski 1989). Such responses are a strategic management of cultural resources in the Gramscian sense. Michaels (1985a, p. 509) takes a similar view of the Warlpiri's negotiation of broadcast media in central Australia, observing that: "Evidence suggests that here structures of knowledge organise material resources, not the other way around." Culture, in this sense, is part of such processes (Mercer 1989, p. 17). The strategic use of media in Indigenous communities — and Indigenous audiences' relationship to these media — might be thought of in this way. While social, political and historical circumstances have played (and continue to play) a critical role in the emergence of Indigenous communication in Australia and elsewhere, the way in which information technologies are used by many Indigenous communities — and the way in which these media are culturally defined — suggests they have been incorporated into community structures as important cultural resources. The way in which these resources are managed is an indication of this.

The strategic use of media by Indigenous communities presents the opportunity for counter-hegemonic processes to operate, challenging dominant ideas and assumptions about the world. Indigenous media production, by definition, must be authorised in some way by the audience from which it emerges. In this way, as with Inuit cultural production, the audience–producer boundary becomes blurred, even absent (Kulchyski 1989, p. 57). Speaking about Warlpiri cultural production, Michaels (1990, p. 25) describes this as "a Brechtian violation of the producer/audience boundary made possible both by widespread participation and reduced [video] production costs". Despite this difference in remote Indigenous video production, Indigenous media may exist unproblematically alongside mainstream broadcasting, as I have suggested. This is because the mainstream product remains just that — mainstream — and, as such, is removed from the social and political environment which authorises community cultural production. This is clear from the way in which diverse Indigenous communities have negotiated mainstream media in a variety of ways and in a variety of settings — from remote communities in the central Australian desert and the Eastern Arctic to urban and regional production centres in other parts of Australia and the South Pacific (Molnar and Meadows 2000).

Researching Indigenous Media Audiences

Since the early 1980s, research in Central and Northern Australia has looked at ways in which Indigenous people produce their own media, and how they watch introduced television and videotapes. Primarily ethnographic in approach, it has identified strong support and interest by Indigenous audiences in locally produced programming on radio and television (Harris 1980; Thompson 1983; Michaels 1986; Meadows 1988, 1995). This perception amongst Indigenous media workers and audiences in Australia was overwhelmingly expressed to the team of researchers working on the 1998 ATSIC Review of Indigenous Media Policy. This anecdotal evidence was not included in the brief executive summary of the review, *Digital Dreaming* (ATSIC 1999, pp. 69–74).

This approach to Indigenous audience research has some crossover with holistic methods used in communication research in developing countries. Sinha (1989, pp. 436–37) describes an eclectic approach to investigating existing communication patterns in rural communities in India. It includes a wide range of methods, usually associated with anthropological research: participant-observation; informal "chance meeting" interviews; attending "gossip groups"; and observing television viewers. It enables an analysis of the various parts of the communication process and their interrelationships and interactions.

Australian-based researchers have been experimenting with such methods. Examples include Vaughan's (1981) study of how the social structure at Woorabinda influenced community use of mass media; Michaels' (1986) seminal investigation of the Aboriginal invention of television in Central Australia; and Obijiofor's (1988) study of the impact of ABC television on Bamaga and Lockhart River. In working through these ideas, I will draw from two more recent projects: the first urban-based Indigenous radio audience survey in Australia in 1997 (Meadows and van Vuuren 1998) and a 1992 survey of perceptions of television by Torres Strait Islanders (Meadows 1995).

In 1996, Radio 4AAA in Brisbane had amassed some anecdotal evidence of the extent of its coverage and support — from truck and taxi drivers, private car owners, businesses and private dwellings — but had no "marketable data" for seeking sponsorship support. The station requested an audience survey which would provide two clear outcomes: identification of the extent and nature of its audience; and development of audience research methods appropriate for Indigenous media. It included five elements:

- a survey of people attending NAIDOC Week events in 1996;
- a random sample telephone survey of 976 people;
- an employment, training and programming survey of 4AAA;
- face-to-face interviews with representatives from Indigenous community groups; and
- focus group discussions with Indigenous and non-Indigenous listeners (this included male and female prisoner groups).

Quantitative data were collected using a "boosted sample" telephone survey (where a minimum of 50 Indigenous people were included). The survey was conducted by Roy Morgan Research over a seven-day period in early December 1996. Of the 1625 people contacted, 976 completed the survey. Of those, 24 did not listen to radio and were excluded. The questionnaire was completed by 952 respondents. It included 37 questions.

The survey gathered qualitative data through "key people" — key informant — interviews (using a questionnaire) and focus group discussions. The research design drew from several prior studies which had used a variety of approaches to ensure the reliability and validity of the data. Lyons (1981, 1983) and a Roy Morgan Research study (1995) outline in detail the methodological problems facing information-gathering from Indigenous communities, particularly the question of sampling. No lists exist of Indigenous populations from which a random sample might be drawn. Moreover, any attempt to draw up such a list would be viewed with great suspicion by Indigenous people — and with good reason.

During the 4AAA survey design, Roy Morgan Research had no database nor any idea of how to assemble such a database of Indigenous people. It is an indication that minorities and their particular needs have yet to make an impact on the Australian audience research industry. However, it should be acknowledged that Roy Morgan has worked with Indigenous communities and has applied methodologies which seem more appropriate than the commercially driven approaches which tend to dominate the industry. In 1995, the organisation was commissioned to assess the effectiveness of government communication and information strategies in Indigenous communities across the country. It developed a comprehensive methodology which used a sample of urban, rural and remote communities in which it conducted a series of face-to-face interviews (using Indigenous interviewers), "key people" and focus group interviews (Roy Morgan Research 1995, pp. 5–13).

The Roy Morgan study paid each Indigenous respondent $10 to compensate them for the time taken as a result of the interview process (Roy Morgan Research 1995, p. 13). The question of payment was discussed by Lyons in his earlier research with Koori communities in Victoria. In that case, the research team, in consultation with Indigenous community representatives, decided against payment for two reasons: first, because it might induce respondents to "tailor their answers to their view of what was expected by the interviewing team"; and second, because some individuals might "seek out the interview team, wishing to be interviewed so that they would receive payment" (Lyons 1981, p. 260). This is an important issue which needs to be discussed with key Indigenous community representatives early on in negotiations.

Another problem with researching Indigenous issues is the reluctance of interviewees to talk to non-Indigenous interviewers.

One solution is to enlist the knowledge within Indigenous communities to shape the research design. This may include deciding on locations through a series of "key people" interviews, as was the case with Lyons' study of Kooris involved in the court process in Victoria. For Lyons:

> These informal, relatively unstructured interviews were designed to acquaint the people concerned with the general shape of the research that was planned; to seek their views concerning matters that could most usefully be the subject of research; and to seek their cooperation in the research. (Lyons 1981, p. 258)

For the 4AAA research design, the process of designing the questionnaire entailed some compromising, but was an important part of the negotiation process. We settled on straightforward language in a standard greeting, a short list of questions both closed — with "right" or "wrong" responses — and open, with awareness of the sensitivity of information being sought. My approach in the Torres Strait relied more on an open-ended set of questions put to different interviewees. Face-to-face interviews tended to last around 45 minutes to an hour, depending on the interview subject. The "key people" interviews helped to provide a list of possible interviewees, enhanced by being "referred on" to other likely subjects. In the Torres Strait research I undertook in 1992, this was a crucial aspect of the research design because it enabled my arrival at the two selected island communities to be announced. One of the key aspects of the Torres Strait research design was a reliance on "chance meeting" interviews. The two participating island communities — Mer and Boigu — are small, and a stroll along the main street with my local research assistant elicited numerous interviews (Meadows 1995).

To overcome the problem of establishing trust with interviewees, local Indigenous people were involved in the interviewing process in both projects, enabling them to apply the knowledge they possessed. In general, this helped to put Indigenous interviewees at ease, although some of those interviewed, familiar with our researchers, may have influenced the results by being over-zealous in their efforts to tell them what they thought the researchers wanted to hear. This and other pitfalls in cross-cultural research have been well-documented (von Sturmer 1981, pp. 27–30; Brady 1981; Lyons 1981, 1983; Eades 1988; Michaels 1985b, 1986; Roy Morgan Research 1995). This approach has been used many times in seeking information about Native television audiences across the Arctic, where bilingual interviewers (in English and the Dene language of the region) are used (Wilson 1994, pp. 15–16). It underlines again the need to be aware of the subtle nuances of cross-cultural research, particularly if the notion of research is conceived within Western frameworks.

For both the Torres Strait study and the 4AAA audience survey, focus group research — where participants were invited to set the discussion agenda — enabled a broad range of views to be canvassed and compared. For the radio station survey, this proved to be the most difficult element to organise; however, three group discussions were eventually conducted. In the Torres Strait, my research assistant on Mer Island negotiated access to two small community meetings which proved to be invaluable in following up on comments made by individual interviewees. However, this could not happen on Boigu Island, as the death of a senior island man meant that the research had to be curtailed, along with all normal activity on the island. This is an example of another important variable which can be central to the outcome of a research project in a community operating under strict cultural protocols.

The success of cross-cultural research is based on many variables. Perhaps the most important of all is the reason behind the research in the first place. Brady reminds us that the most useful research will be that requested by Indigenous communities — research that will have some relevance for participants. She concludes (1983, p. 282):

> Unless Aboriginal communities feel that they will benefit from the research, or that they have been involved in posing the initial problems, there is always the possibility that phoney information will be given out to researchers. They may give the information which they think the researchers want.

Michaels makes similar observations following his three-year stay with the Warlpiri in Central Australia. He explains that, apart from the rudeness of direct questioning for many Indigenous people, only senior authorities are authorised to speak about specific issues. Even if they agree to speak, he writes, they demonstrate their authority by "maintaining control" of any dialogue (Michaels 1986, p. xviii): "One is taught in sequence, and the sequence is determined by tradition, not by the researcher's desire to fill out a questionnaire or pursue his own research agenda. Mostly what I know is what people chose to teach me."

International Indigenous Research

Indigenous radio and television audience research in Canada, like Australia, has tended to favour the remote northern regions, regardless of the fact that most Native Canadians live below the 60th parallel. Research in the late 1970s examined ways in which Native Canadians across the North responded to mainstream satellite television (Coldevin 1977). Audience surveys in 1993 and 1994 for the Aboriginal television network Television Northern Canada revealed a large Indigenous audience across the North with up to 86 per cent watching "some" of its programs (Wilson 1993a, 1993b, 1994).

In 1998, before Television Northern Canada transformed into the Aboriginal Peoples Television Network, market research in southern Canada by Angus Reid (APTN 1998) in January revealed around four out of five Canadians claiming they would watch the new channel "at some time". Almost half of the sample across Canada said they would tune in "once a week". Another survey by Pollara in June 1998 confirmed findings of strong general audience support for APTN. But this time, an Aboriginal sample was included — 87 per cent of Native people questioned across Canada said they would either "definitely watch" or "probably watch" the Aboriginal television channel (APTN 1998; David 1998). Research techniques adopted in Canada tend towards quantitative methodologies, although much of the data in northern communities were gathered by teams of Indigenous researchers carrying out face-to-face interviews (Wilson 1993a, 1993b, 1994).

Maori, like their Indigenous counterparts in Australia and Canada, are highly urbanised. Around 71 per cent of Maori live in eighteen population centres across New Zealand (Joint Maori/Crown Working

Group 1996). Telephone surveys in 1998 by ACNielsen and Brauoda Research revealed significant Maori audiences for Maori radio across New Zealand with 35 to 69 per cent listenership at various times of the day (Berwick 1999) confirming earlier research (Te Mangai Paho 1996, p. 13). Research into viewing audiences for a 1996 pilot broadcast for the new national Maori television channel revealed around half the Maori population of Auckland were viewers (Te Mangai Paho 1996, p. 21). This strong audience response confirmed the importance and popularity of Maori television and was significant in encouraging the development and launch of the national Maori television service late in 1999. The studies cited here show that Maori audiences for Maori broadcasting are significant, particularly in urban areas.

Most of the data available on Maori media audiences tend to come from standard survey approaches by organisations like ACNeilsen and a "multi-pronged method" used by Brauoda Research, described as "user friendly for Maori" (Berwick 1999, p. 3). Berwick refers to the "key person interview" as a "potentially interesting system" which sets up a research tree, or "whakapapa" — and provides a possible alternative methodology for investigating the nature of Maori media audiences. She observes that research into Maori media habits suggests that television is used "both as a background medium and as a primary medium of attention". Berwick writes (1999, p. 3): "Ethnographic research indicates that the way people use radio and television is not necessarily the way assumed by panel systems." She concludes that it is an indication that the process of audience research is extremely complicated.

Conclusion

Gillard (2000, p. 125) has underlined the importance and potency of "careful fieldwork which incorporates the perspectives of those studied", giving rise to research findings which can be used as a basis for "professional intervention and political action". Equally, she acknowledges the importance of ethnographic and qualitative methods — observation, interviews and focus groups — in producing "detailed accounts" of how audience groups "construct their own meaning and cultural activity within a particular site". She concludes that only with a clear picture of audience activity is it possible to identify the "gaps" from both the audience side and in content or services. While speaking primarily about new approaches to online audiences, she suggests an eclectic approach which seems to resonate with successful cross-cultural research experiences.

But while a holistic approach seems the most useful in charting Indigenous media audience activities, we should be careful in how we analyse the data. We should not lose sight of the significant differences *between* Indigenous communities.

Indigenous media are seen by their Indigenous audiences as part of a process of "putting the record straight" on Indigenous issues, widely perceived to be misrepresented in the mainstream media. But they also provide communities with a first level of service. The research from Australia, Canada and New Zealand suggests that Indigenous media, built on a strong local or regional social base, are attracting — and will continue to attract — significant local audiences. A range of appropriate research methodologies need to be carefully applied to enable this information to contribute to the policy process. Despite an accumulation of information about Indigenous audiences in Australia, we must continue to acknowledge its "partial" nature — and the "partial" ways in which it has impacted so far on the Australian mediascape. Much more needs to be done in following up on the trends visible from these various approaches to enable a clearer picture of Indigenous audiences to emerge. The next question — and it is a big one — is how this information can be incorporated usefully into the communication policy process.

CHAPTER 12

Theorising the Diasporic Audience

Stuart Cunningham

Introduction

The dynamics of "diasporic" video, television, cinema, music and Internet use — where peoples displaced from homelands by migration, refugee status, or business and economic imperative employ media to negotiate new cultural identities — offer challenges for how public media and public culture generally are thought about in our times. Drawing on research published in *Floating Lives: The Media and Asian Diasporas* (Cunningham and Sinclair 2000), on dynamics which are industrial (the pathways by which these media travel to their multifarious destinations), textual and audience-related (types of diasporic style and practice where popular culture debates and moral panics are played out in culturally divergent circumstances amongst communities marked by internal difference and external "othering"), this chapter will interrogate further the nature of the public "sphericules" formed around diasporic media.

The research team that authored *Floating Lives: The Media and Asian Diasporas* mapped the mediascapes of Asian diasporic communities against the background of the theoretical and policy territory of understanding media use in contemporary, culturally plural societies. In this chapter, I will expand upon the nature of the public spheres activated around diasporic media as a specific form of public communication, by engaging with public sphere debates and assessing the contribution that the research conducted for *Floating Lives* might make to those debates.

The public sphere, in its classic sense advanced in the work of Jürgen Habermas (1989, 1962), is a space of open debate standing over and against the state as a special subset of civil society in which the logic of "democratic equivalence" is cultivated. The concept has regularly been used in the fields of media, cultural and communications studies to theorise the media's articulation between the state and civil society. Indeed, Nicholas Garnham (1995) claimed in the mid-1990s that the public sphere had replaced the concept of hegemony as the central motivating idea in media and cultural studies. This is certainly an overstatement, but it is equally certain that, almost 40 years since Jürgen Habermas first published his public sphere argument, and almost 30 years since it was first published in outline form in English (Habermas 1974), the debate over how progressive elements of civil societies are constructed and how media support, inhibit, or indeed are coterminous with, such self-determining public communication continues strongly.

The debate is marked out by those, on the one hand, for whom the contemporary Western public sphere has been tarnished or even fatally compromised by the encroachment of commercial media and communications (e.g. Schiller 1989), and by those for whom the media have become the main, if not the only, vehicle for whatever can be held to exist of the public sphere in such societies. Such "media-centric" theorists within these fields can hold that the media actually *envelop* the public sphere. For John Hartley (1999a, pp. 217–18):

> The "mediasphere" is the whole universe of media ... in all languages in all countries. It therefore completely encloses and contains as a differentiated part of itself the (Habermasian) public sphere (or the many pubic spheres), and it is itself contained by the much larger semiosphere ... which is the whole universe of sense-making by whatever means, including speech. ... [It] is clear that television is a crucial site of the mediasphere and a crucial mediator between general cultural sense-making systems (the semiosphere) and specialist components of social sense-making like the public sphere. Hence the public sphere can be rethought not as a category binarily contrasted with its implied opposite, the private sphere, but as a "Russian doll" enclosed within a larger mediasphere, itself enclosed within the semiosphere. And within "the" public sphere, there may equally be found, Russian-doll style, further counter-cultural, oppositional or minoritarian public spheres.

Hartley's topography has the virtue of clarity, scope and heuristic utility, even while it remains provocatively media-centric. This is mostly due to Hartley's commitment to the strictly textual provenance of public communication, and to his interest in Lotman's notion of the semiosphere, more so than Habermas's modernist understanding of the public sphere standing outside of and even over and against its "mediatisation".

I will complicate this topography by suggesting that minoritarian public spheres of the type constituted by diasporic communities are rarely sub-sets of classic nationally bound public spheres, but are nonetheless vibrant, globalised but very specific spaces of self- and community-making and identity (see, for example, Husband 1998, p. 47). I agree with Hartley, however, in his iconoclastic insistence that the commercial realm must be factored into the debate more centrally and positively than it has been to date. There is typically no or very marginal involvement of the public sector courted for diasporic media, in part because the intellectual property and copyright status of much of it is dubious.

I will also stress another neglected aspect of the public sphere debate developed by Jim McGuigan (1998, p. 92): the "affective" as much as "effective" dimension of public communication, which allows for an adequate grasp of entertainment in a debate dominated by ratiocinative and informational activity. McGuigan (1998, p. 98) speaks of a "rather softer" conception of the public sphere than is found in the work of Habermas and others, and develops these ideas around the significance of affective popular politics expressed through media mobilisation of Western responses to poverty and aid campaigns. Underdeveloped, though — and tantalisingly so — is the role played by the entertainment content of the media in the formation and reproduction of public communication (McGuigan 1998, p. 98, quoting Garnham 1992, p. 274). This is the domain on which such strongly opposed writers as McGuigan and Hartley might begin to at least share an object of study.

Todd Gitlin (1998) has posed the question of whether we can continue to speak of the ideal of *the* public sphere/culture as an increasingly complex, polyethnic, communications-saturated series of societies develop around the world. Rather, what might be emerging are numerous public "sphericules". Gitlin (1998, p. 173) asks: "Does it not look as though the public sphere, in falling, has shattered into a scatter of globules, like mercury?" Gitlin's answer is the deeply pessimistic one of seeing the future as the irretrievable loss of elements of a modernist public commonality.

The spatial metaphor of fragmentation, dissolution and of the centre not holding assumes there is a singular nation state to anchor it. Thinking of public sphericules as constituted beyond the singular nation state, as "global narrowcasting of polity and culture", assists in restoring these sphericules to a place of undeniable importance for contemporary, culturally plural societies and any media, cultural and communication studies claiming similar contemporaneity. This place is not necessarily counter-hegemonic, but it is certainly culturally plural and dynamically contending with Western forms for recognition.

There are now several claims for such public sphericules. One can speak of a feminist public sphere and international public sphericules constituted around environmental or human rights issues. They may take the form of "subaltern counterpublics", as Nancy Fraser (1992) calls them, or they may be termed taste cultures, such as those formed around gay style (which does not, of course, exclude them from acting as "counterpublics"). As John Hartley and Alan McKee put it in *The Indigenous Public Sphere* (2000, p. 3), these are possibly peculiar examples of public spheres, since they are not predicated on any nation that a public sphere normally expresses. Rather, they are the "civil societies" of nations without borders, without state institutions and without citizens.

These authors go on to suggest that such public spheres might stand as a model for developments in late modern culture generally, with do-it-yourself citizenship based on culture, identity and voluntary belonging rather than on rights derived from, and obligations to, a state. My present argument is in part a contribution to the elaboration of such a project. However, there are still undeniably relations of dominance, and "mainstreams" and "peripheries". The metaphor is not simply a series of sphericules, overlapping to a greater or lesser extent. While this latter explanatory model goes some distance towards explaining the complexity of overlapping taste cultures, identity formations, social commitments and specialist understandings which constitute the horizon of many — if not most — citizen-consumers in post-industrial societies, there are broad consensus and agenda-setting capabilities which cannot be gainsaid in enthusiasm for embracing *tout court* a "capillary" model of power. The key, as Hartley and McKee themselves identify (2000, pp. 3, 7), is the degree of control over the meanings created about and within the sphericule, and by whom this control is exercised.

In contrast to Gitlin, then, I argue that ethno-specific global mediatised communities display in microcosm elements we would expect to find in "the" public sphere. Such activities may constitute valid and indeed dynamic counter examples to a discourse of decline and fragmentation, while taking full account of contemporary vectors of communication in a globalising, commercialising and pluralising world.

Ongoing public sphere debates in the field, then, continue to be structured around dualisms which are arguably less aids than inhibitors of analysis: dualisms like public–private, information–entertainment, cognition–affect or emotion, public versus commercial culture and — the "master" dualism — public sphere in the singular or plural. What follows makes no pretence at catching up these dualisms in a grand synthesis, but rather offers a contribution to a more positive account of the operations of media-based public communication — in this case, ethno-specific diasporic sphericules — which place a different slant on highly generalised debates about globalisation, commercialisation and the fate of public communication in these contexts.

The Ethno-specific Mediatised Sphericule

First, they are "sphericules" — social fragments that do not have critical mass. Nevertheless, they share many of the characteristics of the classically conceived public sphere. They provide a central site for public communication within globally dispersed communities, stage communal difference and discord productively, and work to articulate insider ethno-specific identities — which are, by definition, "multi-national", even global — to the wider "host" environments.

The audience research for *Floating Lives* was conducted in communities in Australia. While Australia is, in proportional terms, the world's second largest immigrant nation next to Israel, the relatively low numbers of any individual group (at present, over 150 ethnic groups speaking over 100 different languages) has meant that a critical mass of a few dominant non-English speaking background (NESB) groupings has not made the impact that Hispanic peoples, for example, have made in the United States. No one non-Anglo Celt ethnic group has reached "critical mass" in terms of being able to operate significantly as a self-contained community within the nation. For this reason, Australia offers a useful laboratory for testing notions of diasporic communities which need to be "de-essentialised": adapted to conditions where ethnicities and sub-ethnicities jostle in ways that would have been unlikely or impossible in their respective homeland settings or where long and sustained patterns of immigration have produced a critical mass of singular ethnicities.

Sinclair et al.'s (2000) study of the Chinese in *Floating Lives* posits that the sources, socio-economic backgrounds and circumstances of Chinese immigrant arrivals in Australia have been much more diverse than those of Chinese communities in the other great contemporary immigrant-receiving countries such as the United States, Canada, Britain and New Zealand, or earlier immigrant-receiving countries in Southeast Asia, South America, Europe and Africa. To make sense of "the" Chinese community is to break it down into a series of complex and often interrelated sub-groupings based on geographical origin — mainland (PRC); Southeast Asia (Indonesia, Malaysia and Singapore); Taiwan; Indochina (Vietnam, Laos, Cambodia); Hong Kong — together with overlapping language and dialect use.

Similarly, Cunningham and Nguyen's (2000) Vietnamese study demonstrates that there are significant differences amongst a quite small population along axes of generation, ethnicity, region of the home country, education and class, recency of arrival and conditions under which arrival took place. And, for the Fiji Indians in Manas Ray's (2000) work, if it was legislated racial discrimination that compelled them to leave Fiji, in Australia they find themselves "othered" by, and othering, the mainland Indian groupings who contest the authenticity of Fiji Indian claims to rootedness in Indian popular culture.

The formats for diasporic popular media owe much to their inscription within such "narrowcast" cultural spaces and share many significant attributes: karaoke, with its performative, communal and de-aestheticised performative and communal space (Wong 1994); the Vietnamese variety music video and "Paris/Sydney/Toronto by Night" live show formats (Cunningham and Nguyen 2000); and the typical "modular" Bollywood film and accompanying live and playback music culture (Ray 2000).

Against the locus of examination of the "diasporic imagination" as one of aesthetically transgressive hybridity produced out of a presumed "ontological condition" occupied by the migrant subject, these are not necessarily aesthetically transgressive or politically progressive texts. Their politics cannot be read off their textual forms, but must be grasped in the use to which they are put within the communities. In *Floating Lives*, we see these uses as centring on popular culture debates — where communities contend around the politics, identity formations and tensions of hybrid popular forms emerging to serve the diasporas.

Much diasporic cultural expression is a struggle for survival, identity and assertion, and it can be a struggle which is as much enforced by the necessities of coming to terms with the dominant culture as it is freely assumed. The results may not be pretty. The instability of cultural maintenance and negotiation can lead, at one extreme, to being locked into a time warp with the fetishised homeland — as it once might have been but no longer is or can be — and, at the other, to assimilation to the dominant host culture and a loss of place within one's originary culture. It can involve insistent reactionary politics. Due to the necessity to fund expensive forms of media for a narrowcast audience, it can lead to extreme over-commercialisation. Naficy (1993, p. 71) cites a situation in 1987 when Iranian television in Los Angeles was scheduling over 40 minutes of advertising per hour. And it can also lead to textual material of excoriating tragedy — such as the (fictional) self-immolation and (actual) atrocity scenarios played out in some, respectively, Iranian and Croatian video — as recounted by Naficy (1993) and Kolar-Panov (1997).

Second, there is explanatory payoff in pursuing the specificity of the ethno-specific public sphericule in comparison to other emergent public spheres. Like the classic Habermasian bourgeois public sphere of the café society of eighteenth and nineteenth century France and Britain, they are constituted as elements of civil society. However, our understanding of civil society is formulated out of its dualistic relationship to formal apparatuses of political and juridical power. Ethno-specific sphericules constitute themselves as potentially global civil societies which intersect with state apparatuses at various points (immigration law, multicultural public policy and, for the irredentist and the exilic, against the regimes which control homeland societies). It follows that ethno-specific public sphericules are not congruent with international taste cultures borne by a homogenising global media culture. For diasporic groupings *were* parts of states, nations and polities, and much of the diasporic polity is about the process of remembering, positioning and, by no means least, constructing business opportunities around these pre-diasporic states and/or nations.

It is out of these realities that the assumption grows that ethnic minoritarian publics contribute to the further fragmentation of the majoritarian public sphere, breaking the "social compact" subsuming nation and ethnicity in state which has been foundational for the modern nation state. Irredentist politics and "long-distance" nationalism, where the prime allegiance continues to be to an often defunct state or regime, are deemed non-progressive by most commentators. However, a focus on the popular culture of diasporas and its place in the construction of public sphericules complicates these assumptions, as it shows that a variety of voices contend for recognition and influence within the micro-polity, and great generational renewal can arise from the vibrancy of such popular culture.

Sophisticated cosmopolitanism and successful international business dealing sit alongside long-distance nationalism — the diasporic subject is typically a citizen of a Western country, is not stateless and is not seeking the recognition of a separate national status within their "new" country, like the prototypal instances in the European context such as the Basques, the Scots or the Welsh. These sphericules are definitively transnational — even global — in their constitution, but are not the same as emerging transnational polities and cultures of global corporate culture, world-spanning NGOs and international bodies of governments.

Perhaps the most consistent relation, or non-relation, that diasporic media have with the various states into which they are introduced is around issues of piracy. This gives another layer to the notion of civil cultures standing over against the state. Indeed, given that significant amounts of the cultural production exist in a para-legal penumbra of copyright breach and piracy, there is a strong desire on the part of the entrepreneurs who disseminate such product to keep their distance from organs of the state. It is apparent that routinised piracy makes a "shadow system" of much diasporic media, as Kolar-Panov (1997, p. 31) dubs ethnic minority video circuits as they are perceived from outside, operating in parallel to the majoritarian system, with few industry linkages.

Third, they reconfigure essentialist notions of community and reflex anti-commercialism. These sphericules are communities in a sense which goes beyond the bland homogeneous arcadia that the term "community" usually connotes. On the one hand, the ethno-specific community assumes an importance greater by far than the term usually means in mainstream parlance, as the community *constitutes* the markets and audiences for the media services — there is almost no cross-over or recognition outside the specific community in most cases of diasporic cultural production. The "community" therefore becomes an economic calculus, not just a multicultural demographic instance. The community is to an important extent constituted *through* media (cf. Hartley 2000, p. 84), insofar as media performance is one of the main reasons to meet together, and there is very little else available as a mediator of information and entertainment. These media and their entrepreneurs and audiences work within a de-essentialised community and its differences as a condition of their practice and engagement.

Diasporic media are largely commercially driven media, but are not fully fledged markets. They are largely constituted in and through a commercial culture, but this is not the globalising, homogenising commercialism that has been posed by neo-Marxist political economists as threatening cultural pluralism, authenticity and agency at the local level. With notable exceptions like global Chinese popular cultural forms such as cantopop and Hong Kong cinema, which have experienced significant cross-over into both dominant and other emerging contemporary cultural formations, and the Indian popular Bhangra music and Bollywood cinema which are still more singularly based in Indian homeland and diasporic audiences, this is small-business commercialism which deals with the practical specificities of cultural difference at the local level as an absolute precondition of business viability.

Fourth, the spaces for ethno-specific public communication are media-centric, and this affords new configurations of the information-entertainment dualism. Given the at times extreme marginalisation of many diasporic groupings in public space and their lack of representation within leaderships of influence and persuasion in the dominant forums of the host country, ethno-specific media become, by default, the main organs of communication outside certain circumscribed and defined social spaces, such as the Chinatowns, Koreatowns, the little Saigons, the churches and temples, or the local video, spice and herb parlours.

It is a media-centric space but, unlike the way that media-centricity can give rise to functionalist thinking (media are the cement that forms and gives identity to the community), it should be thought of as rather "staging" difference and dissension in ways that the community *itself* can manage. There are severe constraints on public political discourse amongst, for example, refugee-based communities like the Vietnamese. The "compulsive memoralisation" (Thomas 1999, p. 149) of the pre-communist past of Vietnam and the compulsory anti-communism of the leadership of the Vietnamese community is internalised as unsavoury to mainstream society. As part of the pressure to be the perfect citizen in the host society (Hage 1998, p. 10), there is considerable self-censorship in the public critical opinion expression. This filtering of political partisanship for external consumption is also turned back on itself in the community, with attempts by members of the community to have the rigorous anti-communist refugee stance softened (by the mid-1990s, only 30 per cent of the Vietnamese community in Australia were originally refugees) met with harsh rebuke. In this situation, Vietnamese entertainment formats (discussed below) operate to create a space where political and cultural identities can be processed in a self-determining way, where voices other than the official, but constitutive of community sentiment, can speak.

Media-centricity also means, in this context, a constant blurring of the information–entertainment distinction, giving rise to a positive sense of a "tabloidised" sphericule wherein McGuigan's (1998) *affective* as well as *effective* communication takes on another meaning. The information–entertainment distinction — usually maintained in the abundance of available media in dominant cultures — is blurred in the diasporic setting. As there is typically such a small diet of ethno-specific media available to these communities, they are mined deeply for social (including fashion, language use, and so on) cues, personal gossip and public information as well as the entertainment of singing along to the song or following the fictional narrative. Within this concentrated and contracted informational and libidinal economy, "contemporary popular media as guides to choice, or guides to the attitudes that inform choices" (Hartley 1999a, p. 143) take on a thoroughly continuous and central role in information and entertainment for creating a negotiated *habitus*.

The Vietnamese

The Vietnamese are by far the largest refugee community in Australia. For most, "home" is a denigrated category while "the regime" continues in power, so media networks — especially music video — operate to connect the dispersed exilic Vietnamese communities. As Cunningham and Nguyen (2000) argue in *Floating Lives*, there are obviously other media in play (community newspapers, Hong Kong film and video product), but music video carries special significance and allows a focus on the affective dimension of public communication. Small business entrepreneurs produce low-budget music video, mostly out of southern California (but also Paris), which are taken up within the fan circuits of America, Australia, Canada, France and elsewhere. The internal cultural conflicts within the communities centre on the felt need to maintain pre-revolutionary Vietnamese heritage and traditions; to find a negotiated place within a more mainstreamed culture; or to engage in the formation of distinct hybrid identities around the appropriation of dominant Western popular cultural forms. These three cultural positions or stances are dynamic and mutable, but the main debates are constructed around them, and are played out principally within variety music video formats.

Whilst by no means exhausting the media diet of the Vietnamese diaspora, live variety shows and music video are undeniably unique to it, as audio-visual media made specifically by and for the diaspora. These media forms bear many similarities to the commercial and variety-based cultural production of Iranian television in Los Angeles studied by Naficy (1993) in his benchmark *The Making of Exile Cultures*, not least because Vietnamese variety show and music video production is also centred on the Los Angeles conurbation. The Vietnamese grouped there are not as numerous or rich as Naficy's Iranians, so have not developed the extent of the business infrastructure to support the range and depth of media activity recounted by Naficy. The business infrastructure of Vietnamese audiovisual production is structured around a small number of small businesses operating on very low margins.

To be exilic means not — or at least not "officially" — being able to draw on the contemporary cultural production of the home country. Indeed, it means actively denying its existence in a dialectical process of mutual disauthentification (Carruthers 2001). The Vietnam government proposes that the Viet Kieu (the appellation for Vietnamese overseas which carries a pejorative connotation) are fatally Westernised. Ironically, the diasporic population makes a similar counter-charge against the regime, proposing that the homeland population has lost its moral integrity through the wholesale compulsory adoption of an alien Western ideology — Marxism-Leninism.

Together, the dispersed geography and the demography of a small series of communities frame the conditions for "global narrowcasting" — that is, ethnically specific cultural production for widely dispersed population fragments centripetally organised around their disavowed state of origin. This makes the media, and the media use, of the Vietnamese diaspora fundamentally different from that of the Indian or Chinese diasporas. The latter revolve around massive cinema and television production centres in the "home" countries that enjoy international cachet. By contrast, the fact that the media uses of the

Vietnamese diaspora are globally oriented but commercially marginal ensures that they flourish outside the purview of state and major commercial vectors of subvention and trade.

These conditions also determine the small business character of the production companies. These small enterprises run at low margins and are constantly undercut by piracy and copying of their video product. They have clustered around the only Vietnamese population base that offers critical mass and is geographically adjacent to the much larger entertainment–communications–information complex in Southern California. There is evidence of internal migration within the diaspora from the rest of the United States, Canada and France to Southern California to take advantage of the largest overseas Vietnamese population concentration and the world's major entertainment–communications–information complex.

Over the course of the 20 and more years since the fall of Saigon and the establishing of the diaspora through flight and migration, a substantial amount of music video material has been produced. Thuy Nga Productions, by far the largest and most successful company, organises major live shows in the United States and franchises appearance schedules for its high-profile performers at shows around the global diaspora. It has produced over 60 two- to three-hour videotapes since the early 1980s, as well as a constant flow of CDs, audio-cassettes and karaoke discs in addition to documentary specials and re-releases of classic Vietnamese movies. The other companies, between them, have also produced hundreds of hours of variety music video.

Virtually every overseas Vietnamese household views this music video material, most regularly attend the live variety performances on which the video material is based, and a significant proportion have developed comprehensive home libraries. The popularity of this material is exemplary, cutting across the several axes of difference in the community: ethnicity, age, gender, recentness of arrival, educational level, refugee or immigrant status, and home region. It is also widely available in pirated form in Vietnam itself, as the economic and cultural "thaw" that has proceeded since Doi Moi policies of greater openness has resulted in extensive penetration of the homeland by this most international of Vietnamese forms of expression.

As the only popular culture produced by and specifically for the Vietnamese diaspora, these texts attract an emotive investment within the overseas communities which is as deep as it is varied. The social text that surrounds — indeed engulfs — these productions is intense and multi-layered, and makes its address across differences of generation, gender, ethnicity, class and education levels, and recentness of arrival.

The key point linking attention to the textual dynamics of the music videos and media use within the communities is that each style cannot exist without the others, because of the marginal size of the audience base. From the point of view of *business* logic, each style cannot exist without the others. Thus, at the level both of the individual show/video and company outputs as a whole, the organisational structure of the shows and the videos reflects the heterogeneity required to maximise audience within a strictly narrowcast range. This is a programming philosophy congruent with "broadcasting" to a globally spread, narrowcast demographic: "The variety show form has been a mainstay of overseas Vietnamese anti-communist culture from the mid seventies onwards." (Carruthers 2001)

In any given live show or video production, the musical styles might range from pre-colonial traditionalism to French colonial era high modernist classicism, to crooners adapting Vietnamese folk songs to the Sinatra era and to bilingual cover versions of *Grease* or Madonna. Stringing this concatenation of taste cultures together are comperes, typically well-known political and cultural figures in their own right, who perform a rhetorical unifying function: "Audience members are constantly recouped via the show's diegesis, and the anchoring role of the comperes and their commentaries, into an overarching conception of shared overseas Vietnamese identity." This is centred on the appeal to "core cultural values, common tradition, linguistic unity and an anti-communist homeland politics" (Carruthers 2001).

Within this overall political trajectory, however, there are major differences to be managed. The stances evidenced in the video and live material range on a continuum from "pure" heritage maintenance and ideological monitoring to mainstream cultural negotiation, through to assertive hybridity. Most performers and productions seek to situate themselves within the mainstream of cultural negotiation between Vietnamese and Western traditions. However, at one end of the continuum, there are strong attempts both to keep the original folkloric music traditions alive and to keep the integrity of the originary anti-communist stance foundational to the diaspora, through very public criticism of any lapse from that stance. At the other end, Vietnamese-American youth culture is exploring the limits of hybrid identities through the radical intermixing of musical styles.

The Fiji Indians

In a remarkably short time — essentially since the coups of the late 1980s which pushed thousands of Fiji Indians out of Fiji and into diasporas around the Pacific Rim in cities like Vancouver, Auckland and Sydney — the community in Sydney has fashioned a vibrant popular culture based on consumption and celebration of Hindi filmdom and its associated music, dance and fashion cultures. It is an especial irony that a people "extracted" from mainland Indian polity and culture a century or more ago — for whom the relationship with the world of Hindi film is a purely imaginary one — should embrace and appropriate such a culture with far greater strength than those enjoying a much more recent connection to the "homeland".

Manas Ray's (2000) analysis of the Fiji Indian public sphericule in *Floating Lives* is structured around a comparison with the expatriate Bengalis. The two groups are contrasted on a caste, class and cultural consumption basis, and Ray stresses that, given that there is no critical mass of sub-ethnicities within the Indian diaspora in Australia, cultural difference is definitional. The Bengalis are seen as locked into their history as bearers of the Indian project of modernity which they assumed centrally under the British Raj. The once unassailed centrality which the educated Hindu Bengali gentry, the *bradralok*, enjoyed in the political and civic institutions of India has been challenged in the decades since independence by the subaltern classes:

> It is from this Bengal that the *bradralok* flees, either to relatively prosperous parts of India or, if possible, abroad — to the affluent West, taking with them the dream of a nation that they were once so passionate about and the cultural baggage which had expressed that dream". (Ray 2000, p. 142)

The Bengali diaspora, argues Ray (2000, pp. 14–43), frames its cultural life around the high culture of the past, which has become a "fossilised" taste culture.

In startling contrast to the Fiji Indian community (which is by far the highest consumer of Hindi films) for the Indian Bengalis, Indian-sourced film and video is of little interest and is even the subject of active disparagement. The literature and other high cultural forms, which once had "organic links to the independence movement and to early post-independence hardship and hope", have fossilised into a predictable and ageing taste culture remarkably similar whether the Bengali community is in Philadelphia, Boston, London, Düsseldorf, Dubai or Sydney (Ray 2000, p. 143). The issues of inter-generational deficit as the young turn to Western youth culture are evident.

The politics of popular culture are fought out across the communal fractions and across the generations. The inter-communal discord between mainland Indians and Fiji-Indians, which are neither new nor restricted only to Australia — where many mainland Indians continue to exhibit deeply entrenched casteist attitudes and Fiji-Indians often characterise mainland Indians with the same kind of negativity they were wont to use for ethnic Fijians — are often played out around media and film culture. There are elements of a fully blown popular culture debate being played out. At the time of a particularly vitriolic controversy in 1997, the editor of the mainland *Indian Post* argued that, while the Fiji-Indians are "good Hindus" and "they are the people who spend", their "Westernised ways" and "excessive attachment to filmy culture" bring disrepute to the Indian community as a whole (Dello 1997). The resolution to these kinds of issues is often found in the commercial realities that Fiji Indians are the main consumers of the products and services advertised in mainland Indian shops!

Despite virtual slavery in the extraction period and uprootedness in the contemporary period, the affective dimension of the Fiji Indian public sphericule is deeply rooted in Hindu belief and folklore. The *Ramayan* thus was used to heal the wounds of indenture and provide a cultural and moral texture in the new settlement. A strong emotional identification to the *Ramayan* and other expressions of the Bhakti movement — a constrained cultural environment, continued degradation at the hands of the racist white regime, a disdain for the culture of the ethnic Fijians, a less hard-pressed post-indenture life and, finally, a deep-rooted need for a dynamic, discursive site for the imaginative reconstruction of motherland — were all factors which, together, ensured the popularity of Hindi films once they started reaching the shores of Fiji. This was because Hindi film deployed the *Ramayan* extensively, providing the right pragmatics for the "continual mythification" of home (Ray 2000, p. 156).

As a result, second-generation Fiji-Indians in their twice-displaced settings of Sydney, Auckland or Vancouver have developed a cultural platform that, though not counter-hegemonic, is markedly different from their Western host cultures. In contrast, "the emphasis of the first generation Indian Bengali diaspora on aestheticised cultural forms of the past offers to second generation very little in terms of a home country popular youth culture with which they can identify" (Ray 2000, p. 145).

CHAPTER 13

After *South Park*: The SBS Audience

Chris Lawe Davies

Introduction

SBS television began broadcasting in October 1980 as Australia's second national network, nearly 25 years after ABC-TV's debut in 1956, and some 30 years after the first waves of migrants began arriving in Australia, mainly from Europe, after World War II. At first, SBS-TV was simply another service for migrants. But as it has grown, it has had to survive under a more complex set of demands than either the ABC or the commercial channels. The greatest challenge came in 1991, when it gained the right to run advertising. While the network was still largely government funded, the demands of part-commercialisation placed the network in a dilemma. How was it to satisfy its public charter to appeal to a broad range of language and interest groups, and at the same time meet the needs of advertisers?

SBS-TV addressed this dilemma by capitalising on its strengths as a public broadcaster. Rather than trying to be like a commercial network and meet the expectations of the advertising industry to build high average audiences, SBS patiently worked on "turning around" the expectations of the advertising industry to accept a high-quality viewing environment, with smaller average audiences. As a result, its advertising revenue is growing.

SBS-TV has gone through four phases in its audience development to reach its current position. The first phase (1980–82) saw the establishment of the network as part of a range of "post arrival migrant services" — broadcasting, English language teaching, special housing, health and community services — in belated recognition of their needs. The second phase (1983–90) saw the Hawke Labor government grapple with the economics of what had been established and promote the "mainstreaming" of a range of government services including the SBS. The SBS might have found itself merged with the ABC but for strong ethnic community opposition to the merger.

Drastic changes began to occur with SBS's incorporation in 1991. The years 1991–94 mark the third phase, and a turbulent reassessment of the relationship between the foreign language network and the rest of English-speaking Australia. Advertising was introduced and, with it, a need to broaden the audience base. SBS-TV abandoned its old positioning strategy, encapsulated in the slogan "Bringing the World Back Home", and repositioned itself in terms of a more cosmopolitan mode of address through the high-profile slogan "The World is an Amazing Place". To some, this new positioning was a denial of first principles.

The fourth phase (1995–2000) has seen much of the heat disappear from debates about SBS-TV's role and performance. No longer simply known as "the ethnic channel", talk around SBS is more likely to focus on particular programs. One such program is *South Park*, designed to broaden audience appeal to young people, but also to broaden social debates, using satire to focus on the prejudices of the dominant social groups towards minorities — a change from programs looking largely at minorities. This shift has only been possible in an audience market less focused on charters and first principles, and an advertising market which is not only subject to massive increases in technical and service diversity, but is also less dominated by the homogenising effect of only three other TV networks. In these circumstances, SBS's steady accumulation of audiences through quality viewing is increasingly seen as a workable and interesting alternative to the other commercial channels.

Introducing the Service, 1980–82

SBS first went to air in 1975 as radio when the Whitlam Labor government launched the stations 2EA and 3EA in Sydney and Melbourne respectively. The motivation was to supply information on government services, particularly the newly introduced Medicare, to immigrant communities whose grasp of English was not yet strong. SBS-TV came five years later when, partly for the same reasons and partly because "multiculturalism had become good politics", Liberal Prime Minister Malcolm Fraser moved towards its establishment. There were two three-month test transmissions over the ABC in late 1979 and early 1980 before the full launch on United Nations Day, 28 October (Patterson 1988, p. 367).

Initially, the relationship between SBS-TV and its audience was straightforward and highly instrumental — literally an extension of government policy on migration. SBS had been a recommendation of the Galbally Inquiry into migrant services in 1978. The early slogan, "Bringing the World Back Home", articulated the first phase of the network–audience relationship as one of post-arrival migrant servicing. Its genesis and early years were blatant expressions of social policy. After all, little had been done for migrant Australians since the push to increase Australia's population began in the late 1940s. SBS was part of the rush of migrant services of the 1970s and 1980s which, besides broadcasting, included language teaching, housing, welfare and the formation of ethnic lobby groups and government advisory bodies.

Mainstreaming, 1983–90

In the second and third phases of SBS-TV audience development, broader social and policy initiatives began to shape SBS's future. The second phase began in 1983 when the early blush of social reform was fading, and SBS was becoming larger and more expensive. Between 1983 and 1986, SBS television transmission time increased from 41 hours to 67 hours a week. Daytime transmission began in February 1985, and the following January the logo changed from "Network 0/28" to "SBS-TV", when the network also ceased operating on VHF (channel 0) and became UHF only in all markets (SBS 1994a).

When Fraser lost power to Labor's Bob Hawke in 1983, the Labor government immediately set up the Connor Inquiry into ethnic broadcasting. It was the first major inquiry dedicated to the topic. And, while the government was keen to maintain the ideal of migrant servicing through the SBS, the scope and size of the audience needed to be enlarged. Idealism was giving way to pragmatism. Means had to be found to pay for it. This thinking essentially provided Hawke and his cabinet with two options: cushion production and administration costs by merging the SBS with another broadcaster (the ABC); or introduce other means of financing the SBS, namely through non-government funding.

As noted earlier, attempts to merge the SBS with the ABC failed. What saved the SBS and kept its independence in the early mainstreaming phase was the strength of the ethnic lobby, which brought massive pressure to maintain the SBS in its first principles. Interestingly, those same ethnic lobby and advisory groups had been formed during the 1970s as part of the same policy agenda. The SBS was "their own" network. Maintaining the SBS meant retaining the same policy agenda of post-arrival migrant servicing which had given many non-English speaking Australians their belated recognition in the policy process.

If merger did not seem practicable, part-commercialisation seemed the next best thing. But if the SBS to was to be partly commercial, this meant changing its relationship with its audience. This did not just mean increasing the size of the audience to make it attractive to advertisers, but also broadening its appeal away from an almost exclusive focus on "ethnic" Australia to include "mainstream" Australia. *Increasing* and *broadening* the audience amounted to the same thing, because the rapid growth curve for the ethnic audience — many of whom watched more commercial television than accept — had reached a plateau. The only means of maintaining growth was to broaden the target audiences away from ethnicity towards the general audience.

The political philosophy of "mainstreaming" had dominated much of the Hawke–Keating governments' agenda during the 1980s. It was a form of pragmatism which seemed in stark contrast to the "idealism" of Whitlam and even Fraser, whose governments had spawned ethnic broadcasting along with a range of other social reform initiatives. However, this pragmatism in turn produced disappointment, and even cynicism, among the people whose dream was to remain the proud custodians of a unique multilingual network. By the late

1980s and early 1990s, their resistance to mainstream Australia wanting to change "their" network was waning. Veteran broadcaster and lobbyist George Zangalis was one who voiced the growing cynicism and suggested: "If merger was proposed now people wouldn't be shedding a tear." (Zangalis 1994)

The SBS was incorporated under its own legislation in 1991. Part of this incorporation was the requirement that the SBS partly finance itself through advertising. In fact, sponsorship — or non-product, corporate-image advertising — was first introduced to the SBS in June 1989 to help pay for the World Cup soccer series (SBS 1994). Sponsorship led to advertising — five minutes each hour between programs as part of the 1991 incorporation. In one stroke, the SBS had partially been freed of government control, but at the same time it had also to survive in the commercial marketplace. The 1994 corporate slogan change, "The World is an Amazing Place", marked the shift from an exclusive focus on "bringing home" the many heritages which make up Australian society to a greater interest in the world "out there" as a phenomenon not necessarily linked with Australia's social and public policy.

By the 1990s, the language incorporating the SBS used the term multicultural in addition to multilingual. By now it meant the audience of the SBS was non-English speaking communities, as well as those whose first language was English: the SBS's role was to service the former with their heritage languages, and educate the latter by broadening their sense of what constituted culture, outside the narrow confines of English-only language programming. In this sense, the SBS was still socially reformative, but it was also broader and potentially more economical, and finally more exposed to the vicissitudes of the market.

Turning to the Market, 1991–98

The period 1991–98 was characterised by a general "turn" to the market. Incorporation and the remit to advertise in 1991 were the obvious motivations. In 1994, the SBS channelled its promotion budget into a massive campaign to "reposition" the network. The new slogan ("The World is an Amazing Place"), new logo, promotions and set of approaches were all designed to broaden the SBS audience to include in a more overt way English-speaking Australians, particularly those in the higher socio-economic bracket, who would help fund the network's expansion. At the same time, the rationale for this "broadening" was that it constituted better social policy, as it included the culturally dominant Anglo groups and not just ghettoised minorities, in a more complex and inclusive picture of social heterogeneity.

The June 1994 campaign was the culmination of nine months of planning, using input from at least ten consultancies in the fields of advertising, marketing, media and design. Essentially the campaign was to promote SBS-TV to advertisers as well as audiences. There had been other campaigns in the past, promoting individual programs (product campaigns), but never a corporate image campaign for the SBS. Something different had to be done, because the SBS seemed unable to build its average audience much above 3.5 per cent — even though individual programs had scored much higher than that.

Programs which the SBS still boasts about — *The Civil War* (1991), *7th World Youth Championship Soccer* (1992), *World Cup Soccer, 'Argentina–Australia'* (1993) — were all heavily promoted and gained the channel's highest ever ratings to date: 14.6 per cent, 17 per cent and 27 per cent respectively (SBS annual reports, 1991–92, p. 44; 1992–93, p. 102; 1993–94, p. 50). But their success had done little to increase the overall audience share for the SBS. The lack of an audience flow-on effect from these high-rating programs to the rest of the schedule was of major concern (Woodward 1995). As an SBS-TV publication of the time (SBS 1994b) noted, the SBS had been around for fourteen years, it had been broadcasting corporate sponsorship for five years, and it had been legally allowed to run commercials for eighteen months. Levels of interest from advertisers and audiences were still too low, especially at such a mature stage in its "life-cycle". So drastic was the perceived need to do something about it that the SBS cancelled all other program advertising to concentrate on the (corporate image) "Amazing Place" 1994–1995 campaign (Woodward 1995). It was the biggest ever advertising campaign undertaken by the SBS and was directed both at the advertising industry ("the trade") and the public.

The 1994 annual accounts record advertising and sponsorship contributed around 10 per cent to gross revenue — $10.7 million

(SBS Annual Report 1993–94, p. 90). At the same time, the ABC, which did not carry advertising, was receiving around 14 per cent of its total revenue from its own endeavours (ABC Annual Report 1993–94, p. 91).

During the 1990s, the SBS bought daily ratings from ACNielsen for five capital cities, and also commissioned Newspoll surveys twice a year, which ran tracking studies — asking the same questions each time to chart changes in viewing patterns (Woodward 1995). The basis of measurement for the SBS became households rather than individuals; as the channel was achieving only just over one viewer each household (SBS Annual Report 1993–94, p. 135), this measure expressed the "size" of the SBS audience in the best possible light. (Commercial stations, by contrast, looked better on a "people" rather than "homes" basis, as they were achieving two or three viewers for each household (Woodward 1995).)

Measured by the standard industry Target Audience Rating Points (TARPs) system, the early story at the SBS was not inviting for advertisers. TARPs give the percentage audience share of the SBS in relation to all other broadcasters, not in terms of the number of households reached by the broadcaster, but in terms of how many households on average are watching each quarter hour (Sievers 1995). This figure is never good for a public broadcaster, which — because of its obligation to provide programming of broad appeal — finds people making brief visits to the channel but not necessarily staying for longer than a single program. That is, the number of households watching on average each quarter hour (standard counting period) is never high at the SBS, but the number reached over a day's or a week's viewing is high. In the SBS's case, the weekly CUME (accumulated reach) figure was up to 45 per cent of the population (Sievers 1995), yet its "share" of audience (at any one time), which is the average proportion of people watching, was around one-fifteenth of that. (The obverse situation applies to commercial broadcasters, which have a high average audience figure, but a relatively low reach. The same people, fairly much, watch night after night. There is little churn, with programming aimed at gaining audience share early in the evening — usually with the news — then holding it for the rest of the night.)

SBS-TV cannot, of course, use purely audience-maximising motives to organise its programming. It has a broader "social", not commercial, brief. This left the advertising agency the SBS contracted, BAM/SSB, with a problem of using an almost static schedule to increase audience figures. The 1993 advertising research for the "Amazing Place" campaign argued that "SBS diversity is both a strength and a potential weakness" (BAM/SSB 1993b). Clearly the strength lay in its public service broadcasting role; its potential weakness revealed doubts about the SBS's ability to perform commercially. In advertising terms, "diversity can diffuse SBS's image and encourage viewers to 'cherrypick'" (BAM/SSB 1993b).

Cherrypicking (the habit of audiences paying brief visits to channels) prevents TARPs from building but, for reasons given above, is probably inevitable on a public service broadcasting station. Aiming to change the habit, but at the same time recognising the necessity of having to live with cherrypicking at least in the short term, the SBS was left with little option but to make a virtue of that necessity. It attempted to construct a positive TARP story by dropping advertising rates to the point where the "cost per TARP" (CPT) for the SBS was lower than for any other channel. The SBS listed itself as having a CPT on peak viewing for a specific market segment of $1090. It claimed "comparable commercial" networks were listed as having CPTs of $1480 (BAM/SSB 1993a).

Again, CPTs are a standard industry measure but, if referring to a limited but strong audience segment, can disguise the low overall TARP figure. Of course, price cutting diminishes the appeal of a TV channel; however, when placed within an environment of quality viewing and high socio-economic audience, the low CPT figure becomes a pleasant bonus for advertisers who might expect the high-TARP commercial TV stations to have scale economy advantage.

While virtue could be made of a small, quality audience, the strategy documents nonetheless endorsed the conventional wisdom of the advertising industry that TARPs count. They indicate a need on the SBS's part to straddle the apparently contradictory positions of having to convince advertisers of the benefits of a small audience watching quality programming, while at the same time trying to build TARPs. There are two ways of building TARPs. The first is to add more viewers to the audience schedule — that is, to increase "reach". The second is to increase the number of hours the audience watches the SBS — that is, to increase "frequency". In the simplest possible terms, TARPs = Reach x Frequency. Increase reach or frequency, or increase both, and the TARP figure increases. The first TARP-building strategy accepts cherry-picking; the second tries to "reform" it.

Within this scenario, public-service obligations and commercial necessity find themselves on a potential collision course. Inevitably, though, the agency advising on the campaign had little choice but to recommend a narrowly targeted audience sector which would enable TARPs to build through frequency, but at the same time (hopefully) not by diminishing "reach" (Woodward 1995). That is, the agency wanted to boost "frequency" by getting the same people to watch more often. The agency set a quantitative benchmark to increase audience share from 3 per cent in June 1994 to 6 per cent in June 1995 (Woodward 1995; BAM/SSB 1993b). That mark was never achieved, although a gradual increase in share was evident. SBS audience consultant Ken Sievers claimed the average audience share in June 1995 was 3.4 per cent (Sievers 1995). At the same time, the SBS said it had attracted an extra million viewers during the period of the campaign. That is, the slight increase in share (3 to 3.4) probably came as a result of increased reach rather than frequency. It is unlikely, therefore, that the cherry-picking habit was reformed. If that bigger pool of viewers came from a narrower socio-economic segment, the public service broadcasting obligation (of broad appeal) was in danger of being compromised.

The two preliminary aims of the campaign, of "broadening" the audience and "binding" together diverse segments, become somewhat problematic in the face of the need to also build TARPs. Inevitably, the job of combining the three activities — broadening, binding and building — proved only possible if some of the less marketable groups were left out of the marketing equation. One of the potential losers was the ordinary blue-collar ethnic community member who found sub-titles too demanding, only watched their own language material and preferred commercial television anyway (Keig and Co. 1994). But this would mean bisecting the ethnic audience, with one part deemed to have specific linguistically based needs (foreign) with little potential for audience growth, while the other would be sheared off and included in the general (English-speaking) population of broad-interest, demanding viewers. That is, the potential for growth of the SBS was defined now in terms of viewing behaviour, not ethnicity. The binaries suggested by this scenario are:

specific country	omni-cultural;
narrow interests	broad interests;
"foreign"	Australian;
no growth	potential growth;
public obligation	commercial reality.

Arguably, the revised thinking about the SBS which initially came out of the "Amazing Place" campaign was shifting the broadcaster from the left-hand column to the right-hand one.

The SBS Audience of the Mid-1990s

According to the SBS audience data, in the mid-1990s, very few young people and children watched the SBS (13.3 per cent of the audience); the audience was predominantly males aged over eighteen (48.4 per cent), with viewing increasing with age. In terms of a more specific age breakdown, the three biggest audience categories were men over 40 (27 per cent); women over 40 (23 per cent) and men aged 18–39 (22 per cent). Relative to their proportions in the general population, the three groups were over-represented on the SBS. Younger women were not big watchers (SBS Annual Report 1993–94).

In terms of place of birth, by far the biggest audience category on the SBS was the Australian born (62.6 per cent), but this was below its social proportion (75.9 per cent). All other categories in this case of overseas (OS) born viewers were over-represented on the SBS: English speaking (ES) countries are 14.3 per cent of the audience (10.6 per cent in the general population); non-English speaking (NES) 12.3 per cent (6.3 per cent); Asia Pacific 5.4 per cent (4.3); and Europe 5.4 per cent (2.9 per cent). Table 13.1 shows the audience composition for the whole SBS audience and breaks it down further into movies and news — providing further instances of the relative importance to NES audiences of these programming genres as compared with the Australian born.

Table 13.1: Proportion of SBS Audience Percentages, 1994

Country of birth	All people	All SBS viewers	SBS movies	SBS news
Australia	76	63	57	55
OS, ES	11	14	17	18
OS, NES	6	12	13	18
Asia/Pacific	4	5	5	7
Europe	3	5	7	10

Source: Lawe Davies (1998, Apps 4.2.1, 4.2.2)

These figures suggest that the SBS penetrated communities of overseas-born Australian residents far more effectively than it did the Australian born; it was just that the numbers of overseas born were fewer. In terms of the "social utility" of the SBS, therefore, its core audience appeared to be people born overseas; while in commercial terms, its majority audience was Australian born. It is important to emphasise that these figures, especially those for Australian born, have no linguistic or heritage significance. However, they focus the SBS dilemma in which the commercial imperative (building TARPs through appeal to English-speaking predominantly Anglo-Celtic audiences) is set against the public service obligation (servicing minority interests).

The SBS used three socio-economic categories in its demographic tables of the time. These were: (1) AB — senior managers, professionals; (2) C1 — clerks, teachers, salespersons, service industry workers; and (3) C2/D/E — tradespeople, machine operators, drivers, police, labourers and related workers. Their audience proportions were 27.4 per cent, 41.6 per cent and 31 per cent respectively. The white-collar category (C1) was not only also the biggest category in the community (38.1 per cent), according to SBS figures, but was also over-represented on the SBS. The blue-collar group (C2/D/E) was also marginally over- represented on the SBS. Surprisingly, there were proportionately fewer AB group viewers in the SBS audience than in the community as a whole. Nevertheless, despite its low numbers, this group was considered the core demographic in the SBS audience (BAM/SSB 1994a). This suggests that numbers alone do not govern commercial decisions.

The final demographic variable was density of viewing. Heavy viewers were the biggest viewers of the SBS (43.2 per cent) in the mid-1990s; medium viewers were next (35.7 per cent); and light were about half the number of heavy viewers (21.1 per cent). Heavy and medium viewers were over represented on the SBS, as each constituted about one-third of the community.

In summary, in the mid-1990s, the majority audience on the SBS was older males, born in Australia, in white-collar occupations who were heavy viewers, and who tended to "cherry pick". Presumably, therefore, one aspect of the campaign, which sought to increase TARPs through increased frequency, was targeted at getting this majority audience to watch more often. However, as was suggested above, there is little or nothing in the demographic data to justify major policy decisions, such as moving away from ethnic viewers, who presumably percolate through all categories but with a preponderance in the blue-collar segment. Faced with the seemingly endless task of chasing variables in the demographic data, the temptation was to simplify complexity by reducing it into binary sets. Woodward (1995) again:

> We've found through Newspoll and AIS Media we have two distinct audiences: one is an ethnic audience; one is the educated AB demographic. Basically it's soccer versus documentaries. Movies cater for both.

Consolidating the New ('Commercial') Culture, 1998–2000

The third phase bedded in a whole "new culture" at SBS-TV — that of accommodating commercial and charter demands. By 2000, the SBS annual report (1999–2000, p. 99) showed the organisation as a whole running a net operating surplus of $10.1 million, with the contribution from advertising ($22.8 million) having doubled over the third and fourth phases, with a further $3.1 million added by production services: sub-titles and pay TV. There had also been a moderate increase in government appropriations from $85.5 million in 1993–94 (1993–94 annual report, p. 90) to $107.5 million in 1999–2000. The net contribution from commercial activity in 1999–2000 was $34.5 million, compared with $16.1 million in 1993–94. One of the consequences of thc SBS raising money in the marketplace was a slowed increase in government funding, with the ratio of advertising to government appropriations having reduced from 1:8 in 1993–94 to 1:5 in 1999–2000. This would suggest a clear trend for the network to be increasingly funded through commercial activity. The 1998–99 annual report suggested the increased growth in advertising revenue was a result of signal splitting, allowing commercials into a fragmented market. And, of course, the driving logic behind increased advertising was increasingly popular programming (SBS annual report 1998–99, p. 66).

With the new economy thus established, the fourth phase saw the consolidation of new audience strategies, with specific aspects of the audience profile being addressed — namely young people, who had always been a problem for the SBS. In earlier schedules, people identifying as migrants — and therefore being in need of migrant services such as special broadcasting, language teaching, health, housing, and so on — tended to be concentrated in the communities which first started coming to Australia in the late 1940s and 1950s — mainly from Europe (Lawe Davies 1998, Ch. 4). The early SBS program schedule tended to reflect these interests in terms of movies and documentaries, with fare of largely adult appeal. Only sport and the occasional soap opera series seemed to attract younger people. An added difficulty was that the children of those migrants, and subsequent generations, did not automatically identify with migrancy. Generally their English language skills were more developed because as children they had had broad exposure. Their language abilities and cultural orientation lay beyond what many of them saw as old-world "heritage" programming. In short, the SBS audience was "ageing". And, like any network, if the SBS was to invest in the future of an expanding and increasingly competitive audience market, it had to find ways of getting young people into the schedule. It was no coincidence that the repositioning of "The World is an Amazing Place" campaign in the mid-1990s provided the opportunity for the network to "think laterally" about ways of getting young people included.

The 1996 SBS Annual Report spoke of "the SBS's lack of a youth audience". This was partly a question of generational change and migration and partly a scheduling problem — SBS programming, it seems, wasn't hip. Solutions to the problem began to emerge soon afterwards. *South Park*, an irreverent satire about prejudice, seemed outrageously to fit the bill. By the year 2000, the annual report was able to claim:

> SBS Television has gained a considerably higher profile among audiences in the 13–17 years and the 18–24 ... [with] average weekly reach in Australia's five major cities ... increased from 628 000 in 1997 to 880 000 in 1998 — a 40 per cent jump. (SBS 1999–2000 annual report, pp. 26, 27)

The jump in 1998 coincided with the introduction of *South Park* on 3 January as a weekly half-hour series. After an initial eleven-week season with significant audience reach — 3.5 per cent average weekly and 15.8 per cent over the series — it was run a second time, as a full hour over seven weeks. It was during the second series that the reach figures started to build and indicate that the SBS was really on to something. It gained 15.8 per cent average weekly reach, and 34.8 per cent over the seven-week second season. In all, that year, it ran four seasons of one-hour instalments (32 weeks in total), with a peak average weekly reach of 16.9 per cent in September–October. The fourth series ran over the summer — November 1998 to March 1999 — and achieved an impressive 50.5 per cent reach over the seventeen weeks, with the average weekly reach slightly lower at 14.8 per cent. This, of course, demonstrates one of the characteristics of "reach" — that it is agglomerative: the longer you run a series, the more people you'll pick up. Following this conventional wisdom, the SBS ran another long series of fourteen weeks in 1999, achieving 12.9 per cent weekly and 40.3 per cent over the season. Another successful long season of 20 weeks saw demand easing somewhat. There was only one more series, with interest continuing to soften. The general audience figures are summarised in Table 13.2.

The series reach figures for both households and individual viewers peaked in the seventeen-week summer holiday season 1998–99. However, the highest weekly reach and peak ratings over all capital city markets occurred earlier, in the July–August 1998 season, with the highest average ratings in September–October of the same

Table 13.2: *South Park* Gross Audience

Telecast periods	Day and time	Average weekly reach* %	Average weekly reach* 000s	Series reach* %	Series reach* 000s
11 weeks 3 Jan–28 March 1998	Saturday 8.30–9.00 p.m.	3.5 1.8	157 230	15.8 10.3	710 1283
7 weeks 20 July–31 Aug 1998	Monday 8.00–9.00 p.m.	15.8 10.0	708 1250	34.8 26.6	1561 3315
8 weeks 7 Sept–26 Oct 1998	Monday 9.30–10.30 p.m.	16.9 9.3	760 1154	38.4 26.8	1722 3339
17 weeks 23 Nov–15 March 1999	Monday 9.30–10.30 p.m.	14.8 8.5	672 1076	50.5 37.2	2291 4722
14 weeks 20 Sept–27 Dec 1999	Monday 8.30–9.30 p.m.	12.9 7.2	587 916	40.3 28.4	1828 3611
20 weeks 3 Jan–17 April 2000 24 April–15 May 2000	Monday 8.30–9.00 p.m.	8.4 4.8	385 620	35.9 25.3	1646 3251
12 weeks 9 Oct–25 Dec 2000	Monday 8.30–9.00 p.m.	11.4 6.6	523 847	38.4 27.3	1758 3510

*The top line is households while the second line is total people.
Source: Nielsen via SBS Audience Research, 2001.

year. Brisbane was the only city where *South Park* was consistently less popular than in other cities (SBS/Nielsen 2001). This highlights the fact that there is not necessarily a relationship between ratings and reach. The longer the season, the more reach builds. The shorter the reporting period, the closer the relationship between ratings and reach.

While *South Park* was clearly a significant audience builder for the SBS, the figures in Table 13.2 do not indicate how well the strategy of "youth appeal" was working for the network. In addition, there were other aspects of the audience besides youth which also had to be kept in mind. Besides "age", the SBS had other colorations it wanted to emphasise — gender, for instance, to address its reputation as an older male channel; and social stratification, in terms of its needing to keep the A1 appeal for advertisers.

Age/gender as a Proportion of the Demographic

Table 13.3 suggests that, over the period January 1998–December 2000, males aged 18–24 were proportionately the biggest fans of *South Park*, but women in that age range were not far behind, with an early season reach of 21.5 per cent and 15.65 per cent of their total demographic respectively. Teens aged 13–17 (gender not specified) were also strong at 17.6 per cent. Men and women in the slightly older demographic, 25–39 years, were also significant at around 12 per cent season reach. However, appeal to men and women over 40 years fell quite sharply. This pattern appears to immediately address the earlier audience profile, where older males dominated.

By the second season, teens (13–17 years) had become the dominant audience group as a proportion of the demographic (60.9 per cent) and more middle-aged men and women were tuning in. However, young children (aged 5–12) were also becoming a significant group at 30.1 per cent. The audience appeal seemed to be spreading out in both directions from the late teen and young adult demographic. More young women were watching, and older people of both sexes were also hearing about the show.

In the third season, teenagers still led the reach figures (55.7 per cent over males aged 18–24 at 51.7 per cent); children were showing less interest; but young and middle-aged women were holding their interest. Older men were also holding their interest. The fourth season saw young men (18–24) regain their lead (68.6 per cent), closely followed by teens, and the pattern held fairly consistently.

Age/gender as Raw Figures

One of the important issues to remember when looking at audience figures is the size of the group within the total population or sample can vary from group to group, thus skewing the percentage figures. From Table 13.4, it can be seen that the age group 25–39 in men and women (the back end of the "baby boomers") is a bigger population group than 18–24. This has the effect of artificially reducing the percentage figures. What the percentage figures become, therefore, are "penetration" figures — or the proportion of that demographic which is switched on to a particular program. As such, they still have meaning. But if we look purely at raw figures — the number of people/households — we get a quite different picture. Table 13.3 summarises the seven seasons in terms of percentage figure reach; Table 13.4 does so in terms of raw figure reach. This table suggests that *South Park* appeals most to men and women in their late twenties and thirties — up to middle age — with teens coming third. Both percentage and raw figures are important to the SBS: the first shows the significance of the program *within* the demographic category; the second shows the proportion of the total audience. While raw figures are of most interest to advertisers in terms of the general bulk of the audience, the percentage figures indicate accuracy of

Table 13.3: Reach for *South Park*, Ranking by Proportion of Demographic

	Child	Teen	M 18-24	M 25-39	M 40-55	F 18-24	F 25-39	F 40-55
1		2nd	1st	4th		3rd	5th	
2	5th	1st	2nd	4th		3rd		
3		1st	2nd	4th		4th	5th	
4		2nd	1st	3rd		4th	5th	
5		2nd	1st	3rd		4th	5th	
6		2nd	1st	3rd		4th	5th	
7		2nd	1st	3rd	5th		4th	

Source: SBS/ACNielsen (2001)

Table 13.4: Reach for *South Park*, Ranking by Total Number of Viewers

	Child†	Teen	M 18-24	M 25-39	M 40-55	F 18-24†	F 25-39	F 40-55
1	3rd	4th	5th	1st			2nd	
2	4th	1st	5th	2nd			3rd	
3		2nd	5th	1st	4th		3rd	
4		3rd	5th	1st	4th		2nd	
5	5th	3rd		1st	4th		2nd	
6		4th	5th	1st	3rd		2nd	
7		4th		1st	3rd		2nd	5th

Source: SBS/ACNielsen 2001

targeting a particular group, and for the SBS indicate its charter significance — what proportion of a social group finds SBS-TV important and useful.

Table 13.4 suggests a fairly consistent picture for the two biggest audience groups for the SBS — men and women in their late twenties and thirties — up to middle age. They are helped in this by constituting a larger proportion of the population generally.

Australian Born ... Who Are They?

The next aspect of the audience is country of birth. Considering the SBS has a range of audiences in its multicultural brief, what did the heritage composition of the audience actually look like? Table 13.5 shows again the useful distinction between "penetration" (percentage) of a community by a form of programming and raw bulk audience figures.

Table 13.5: Series Reach, by Country of Birth

Series	Australia		O/S-ES		O/S-NES	
	%	000s	%	000s	%	000s
1	10	954	11.9	160	10.7	169
2	29.8	2,847	21.1	283	11.8	185
3	25.9	2,474	22.8	305	35.6	560
4	38.8	3,733	32.5	458	31.8	531
5	28.1	2,702	31.7	448	27.6	461
6	25.1	2,418	26.8	365	25	468
7	29.7	2,862	27.5	374	14.6	274

If Table 13.5 is read across, the comparison of the rows suggests that, while penetration of the social groups organised around country of birth seems to peak for all around the fourth series, the numerical representation of Australian born is far greater than the other two categories. Again, this is largely explained by the size of the Australian-born group. Being substantially bigger than either of the other social groups, then, penetration of 38 per cent is very high. And, while 32.5 per cent for overseas-born English speaking is almost comparable penetration, the raw numbers are about one-eighth. The same applies to the 31.8 per cent for overseas-born non-English speaking. Their numerical representation is not high, but the significance of the program to the social group is roughly comparable with the rest of the population. If the SBS charter — "to appeal to all Australians" — is kept in mind, the program would appear to be on target, especially when it is remembered that *South Park* is a satire, dealing with the prejudices held by mainly "WASP" social participants. Arguably, the program is highly effective on these grounds, with significant appeal to Australian born. As a bigger numerical group, lower penetration figures would normally be expected. The fact that penetration is roughly equal across the three groups inflates the significance of Australian born for this particular program.

But it would be a mistake to assume that the category "Australian born" constituted only a "WASP" constituency in Australia — or even in America, where the program is produced. SBS head of TV, Peter Cavanagh, suggests that that category in Australia is also culturally diverse. The first wave of migrants started arriving in Australia in the late 1940s. Their children probably now themselves have grandchildren. That is, we are now talking about the category Australian born as also including up to third- or fourth-generation children of Italian, Greek and other central European nations, not to mention people of long-standing Chinese, Lebanese, German and Italian heritage, to name only a few, who came to Australia earlier in the twentieth or even nineteenth century. The extent to which these people constitute "multicultural" Australia is a moot point. Without wanting to chase down precise definitions about what is and is not multicultural — probably an endless and therefore finally pointless pursuit — people at the SBS are increasingly using the term "diversity" to refer to the range of heritages and needs of their audiences (more on this below). Peter Cavanagh again: "Diversity is no longer a fringe thing … it's mainstream." (Cavanagh 2001) *Pizza* is a locally produced program introduced in 2000 which appeals precisely to this group. Figures 13.1 and 13.2 provide a clearer picture of the patterns of heritage viewing.

There is no need to produce tables for the last social grouping — socio-economic status — as again the categories AB (Upper) C1 (Middle) and C2 (Working) roughly pan out as very similar

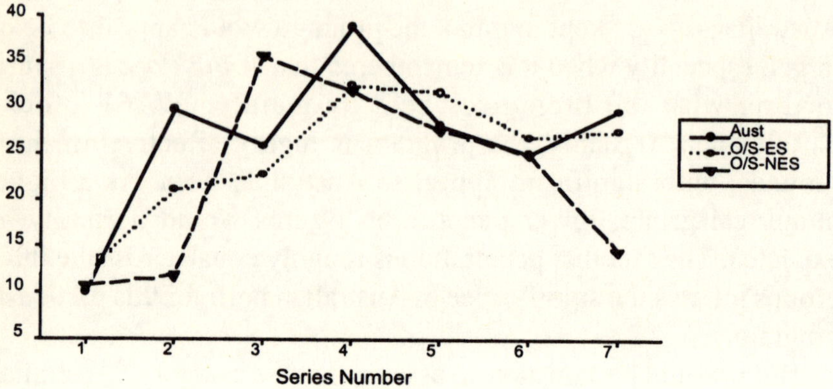

Figure 13.1: Series Reach, Per Cent of Country of Birth

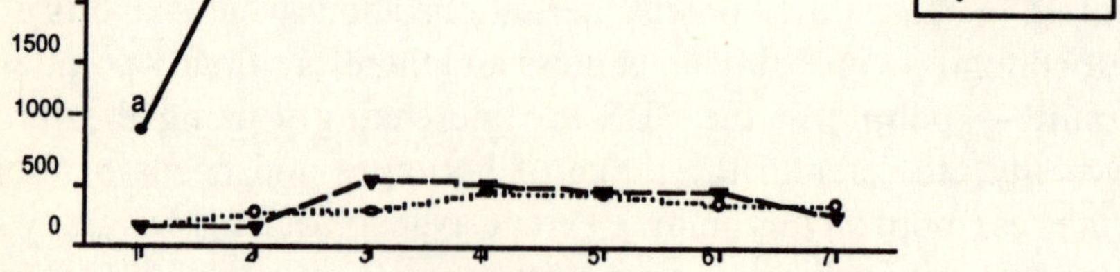

Figure 13.2: Series Reach, Total People — Country of Birth

percentages for each category. Some weeks there are significant differences, other weeks they are very similar. However, it is worth noting that this equal representation across the three social strata categories reflects one of the aims of the "World is an Amazing Place" campaign — to increase the viewing of the social ABs, who were previously the smallest group of viewers. Clearly they like satire.

But the SBS has more than one string to its youth audience bow. Besides *Pizza*, other programs introduced in 2000 were, *Neon Genesis, Evangelion, Strangers with Candy* and *Dr Katz* (from the makers of *South Park*). Other mainly youth appeal programs were *Alchemy, Classic Albums, Rock Family Trees* and a 'number of stand-alone documentaries on artists such as Blur, Iggy Pop, Bob Marley, and Jimi Hendrix' (SBS annual report 1999–2000, p. 27). However, arguably it is *South Park* which has been highly significant in terms of "positioning" the network within a dynamic and charter-specific audience frame.

The Charter

As the SBS management sees it, the charter sets out three duties for the SBS: to service LOTE communities; to reflect multiculturalism to all Australians; and thereby to add diversity and innovation to the broadcasting industry (Long 1995). Only the first of these carries a LOTE obligation; the second acts as a rationale for high levels of spoken-English programming (in addition to subtitled-English) and the third, arguably, is what provides much of the excitement and energy within SBS-TV.

However, the third requirement — "being different" (from the rest of the industry) — is a governing culture within the SBS management, from news to movies and arts programs. It is not only used by the SBS management as a means of meeting the charter, but was the central plank in the "marketing strategy" of the "World is an Amazing Place" campaign (BAM/SSB, 1993a). However, the question remains as to what extent is "being different", colourful, exciting and "amazing" satisfying a more extensive reading of the charter requirements, beyond the three functions delimited by SBS management?

Under the enabling legislation, the SBS is required in section 6(1) to:

> provide multilingual and multicultural radio and television services which inform, educate and entertain all Australians, and in doing so, reflect Australia's multicultural society.

There are five other paragraphs which detail the kind of contribution the SBS should make specifically to the development of an Australian multiculturalism. But multiculturalism is also an obligation carried in the enabling legislation of all Australian television broadcasters. Section 6(1)(a)(i) of the ABC legislation requires:

> broadcasting programs and television programs that contribute to a sense of national identity and inform and entertain, and reflect the cultural diversity of the Australian community (ABC, 1983).

Under its charter, the ABC also has an obligation to 'take account of ... the multicultural character of the Australian community' (section 6(2)(a)(iv)). Both public broadcasters are to "have regard to the services" provided by each other. Under the *Broadcasting Services Act* 1992, commercial and community broadcasters are also required to "develop and reflect a sense of Australian identity, character and cultural diversity" (section (3)(e)).

While the proportion of the SBS legislation given to elaborating the multicultural charter is far greater than for the other broadcast sectors (six out of nine paragraphs), in all three pieces of legislation, all three sectors probably fall short in certain ways. At the same time, all broadcast media and the journalists' union have developed codes for dealing with issues of indigeneity and gender and, in the cases of ABC and the SBS, other aspects of cultural diversity as well (see FACTS 1994; FARB 1994; ABC 1993; SBS 1994b; MEAA 1993).

Cultural Diversity

When *South Park* returned to SBS-TV on Monday, 9 October 2000, the network claimed it was "bigger, better and funnier than ever" (SBS October Program Guide 2000). Making the usual references to the program's social role of "smashing prejudice", the network's

What's On magazine referred to the introduction of the character Timmy, a new student at South Park Elementary, in the following terms:

> About the only thing Timmy can do is say his name in a deep and wicked voice and flail his arms at the same time. Ignorant of the fact that Timmy is intellectually challenged, Mr Mackey and the staff believe Timmy has Attention Deficit Disorder (ADD), which relieves him of the responsibility to do any homework. (SBS 2000)

In a nutshell, it is a neat argument for how some kids get left out and fail. The problem of ADD as a misdiagnosis of behaviour caused by other social or physiological factors is widespread in Australia as well. But this comment perhaps raises more fundamental issues about the breadth of the SBS brief, and of seeing how the SBS audience is not a simple binary between ethnic and non-ethnic Australia. Arguably, *South Park* is one of the new programs which addresses a contemporary global cultural diversity. Indeed, this aspect of SBS programming has not only been fundamental to the network from its beginning, but was overtly reinforced during the third and fourth phases through the "World is an Amazing Place" campaign when it replaced "Bringing the World Back Home". That is, we are talking here about a fundamental difference between multiculturalism and cultural diversity.

Arguably, a wider sense of "culture" has been deployed by the organisation over a range of other "minoritarianisms" (O'Regan 1993). And since it is now no longer constrained by an apparent obligation only to service migrant communities, the term "multiculturalism" has to some extent been abandoned by the organisation in practice (Robinson 1995), although it is still the public rationale for the SBS. In its place, programmers and marketers alike speak of "cultural diversity", which moves the focus to the "cultural fractions" of Australian society. If multiculturalism (cultural diversity) is by definition the recognition and legitimation of that which was previously ignored — the inclusion and enfranchisement of all Australians (Office of Multicultural Affairs 1990, p. vii), by recognising the marginality of some of them — inevitably ethnicity sits alongside other hitherto ignored cultural fractions such as sexual preference, gender, disability, indigeneity, the arts, intellectualism, minority sports, arcane music, and so on. Cultural diversity, then, is a diversity of fractions beyond ethnicity (Robinson 1995). The "World is an Amazing Place" advertising slogan of 1994 was an attempt to tie these diverse interests into a programming schedule and finally into a corporate image for the SBS. This milieu of minoritarian interests was thereby marketed to the "AB" social demographic, within which resides, presumably, sufficient liberalism to cope with the scope and size of the contradictions. "Amazement" was not only appropriate, but also convenient.

Conclusion

The 1994 campaign marked a significant turning point in SBS-TV after fourteen years of operation. The year 2000 saw a consolidation of the SBS-TV brand across not only a culturally diverse marketplace, but its growing significance in the commercial marketplace as well. Clearly, though, the demands of its charter are forcing the SBS to fragment its market to the point where it is difficult to build a bulk audience profile. This is the SBS legacy, given by governments who were unable or unwilling to entirely fund the network. The price of its relative autonomy in the form of incorporation was that it also had to face the vicissitudes of the commercial marketplace. There has been at least one other success story of a "chartered" network also performing strongly as a commercial broadcaster — Britain's Channel 4, which began about the same time as the SBS and which currently maintains an audience share of over 15 per cent, and is financially self-sufficient — indeed, profitable. The SBS, on the other hand, is reaching an audience share of about 4 per cent (Sievers 2001) and is still 80 per cent government funded. However, the remits of the two broadcasters are different. Channel 4 is like the SBS in that it caters to a liberal, arthouse, socially progressive audience, but it is a single-language network, able to consolidate and build on the same target group night after night. The SBS, on the other hand, has a range of markets, and while English language programs constitute half the programming, and English subtitles translate the rest, there is still a sense in which the 60-odd language groups regularly catered for by the SBS constitute a profound fragmentation of the commercial television audience potential. Head of television at the SBS, Peter Cavanagh, points out that Channel 4 is becoming increasingly commercial in its programming, whereas the SBS is "holding the line" on delivering charter programming as its first priority (Cavanagh 2001).

Even in its heyday, *South Park* only ever peaked at ratings of 19 per cent in one market (Melbourne) and in Brisbane never went much above 14 per cent (SBS/ACNielsen 2001). Peak ratings on one show are certainly of interest to advertisers. But the real commercial challenge for the SBS is to sustain those audiences across a number of programs, night after night. The charter still locks the SBS into the public service domain where reach rather than TARPS is the major building block. The challenge is to convince advertisers that a quality, smaller loyal audience with broad programming remit, and which builds over extended seasons, is a sustainable, quality environment in which to promote their products, at the same time as it promotes a better society. Head of marketing at the SBS, Pat Quirk-Parry, says the SBS is a "discretionary medium". She suggests "advertisers need [networks] Seven, Nine and Ten to survive … [but] the SBS talks to audiences in a quite different atmosphere" (Quirk-Parry 2001). Some evidence of this is the qualitative research carried out by Quadrant for the network, which asks people what they like about SBS advertising. Inevitably people respond that they think the commercials are better quality. In fact, the commercials are the same ones that appear on the other commercial networks. The program context is what is different.

The SBS is slowly but surely meeting what were once considered contradictory demands of charter versus commercial, but in a media marketplace which is becoming increasingly complex and competitive. Not only is the SBS facing increased competition from the "single-language" broadcast market — particularly with new players from the pay TV sector — but specialist language television services available through satellite and on the internet are going to the very heart of the SBS market. So far, pay TV, internet and direct satellite services are not competing for the advertising dollar, but they are still taking potential audience attention.

CHAPTER 14
Voter Communication

John Penhallurick

It is commonplace to describe voters as increasingly resembling audiences in presidential-style campaigns driven by opinion polls. Political parties do not have it easy when it comes to persuading voters to vote for them. Just as marketers tell us that brand loyalty has declined with consumer products, so political scientists inform us that party loyalty has also witnessed a steep decline.[1] Certainly politicians and political parties — like marketers of all persuasions — are increasingly recognising differences within the population. These are not differences based on the various ways in which social policy has organised the population, such as through gender, race, ethnicity, region or urban versus rural population, but on geodemographic calculations which slice through these populations. This chapter will examine both current and two newer research strategies for handling cultural and social diversity — geodemographic and cognitive mapping research strategies — in the context of electoral campaigning.

Political parties face a common problem. Ever since Paul Lazarsfeld's (1944) seminal study of voting intentions over the course of the 1940 US presidential election, *People's Choice*, it has been clear that the mass media have little influence in changing people's minds and at best have a reinforcement effect. And marketers arc well aware that the proliferation of media sources, and increasing pressures on the time available for media use, have combined to make audiences much harder to reach via mass media. A few years ago, the combined reach of the US free-to-air television networks dropped below 50 per cent, down from 90 per cent in 1980. Even those who can be reached by mass media are significantly less attentive to messages through those media.[2] If, in an era of mediated politics, voters are audiences who need persuading, then political parties must persuade in a context where persuasion is not an easy task. Political parties are therefore interested not only in targeting their campaigns to those who can be persuaded — swinging voters — but also in developing campaigns which serve to reinforce rather than challenge people's attitudes. Their strategy is to secure small rather than large changes, and their weapon to do so is the very concerns of those likely to be swinging voters. These considerations have led to the development and utilisation of sophisticated research techniques such as geodemographics and cognitive mapping.

Computer technology now offers political parties new tools for identifying persuadable voters and for persuading them to give, if not their primary vote, at least a higher preference to their party than to their main competitor. In several elections over the last fifteen years, and most recently in 1998, a party has formed government in the House of Representatives even though it won a minority of the two-party preferred vote in the elections for the lower house. In 1998, the ALP received 50.98 per cent of the national vote and lost the federal election, while the Liberal/National Party Coalition received 49.02 per cent and won (Australian Electoral Commission 1999). In this case, the Liberal Party successfully targeted marginal seats with the result that Labor's large majorities in safe seats were not of much help in the event of uneven swings.

Mapping software, such as Mapinfo™, helps parties to target specific areas and plan their submissions to the Australian Electoral Commission on the redistribution of electoral boundaries. Using information on the returns from each voting booth, and by making assumptions about the areas from which each booth draws voters, parties make inferences about which areas are more or less favourable to them. In previous elections, such data have played a major part in Liberal and Labor Party election strategy. Suppose a voting booth showed 70 per cent two-party preferred going to the Liberal Party: the party could decide that it did not need to spend a lot trying to reach the already converted. Likewise, a booth with only 30 per cent as the two-party preferred vote going to the Liberal Party could lead the party to decide that it was a waste of money trying to convert the opposition's voters. A third group of voting booths might fall within the 55–45 per cent two-party preferred going to the Liberal Party: the party might then conclude that these booths contained swinging voters who would repay the maximum concentration of persuasive efforts.

The problem is that this middle result could itself reflect a number of quite different situations. The neighbourhood feeding the voting booth might consist of an overwhelming number of swinging voters; it might consist of half strongly pro-Liberal voters and half strongly pro-Labor voters; it might have one-third strongly pro-Liberal voters, one-third strongly pro-Labor voters and one-third genuine swinging voters. Taking into account data on the level of the Liberal primary vote versus Liberal votes on the basis of second or lower preferences, the possible combination starts to become extremely complicated. It is simply not possible to resolve these differences with voting booth data alone. Parties need to look elsewhere for help.

Small-area census data software packages such as CData™ provide one possible solution. These allow parties to analyse small areas in terms of variables such as household and individual income, occupation, home ownership and so forth — all factors which might predict party sympathies. For some $10 000, anyone can buy CData™, which will make available on a desktop unprecedented amounts of information about every collection district in Australia. The collection district (CD) is the smallest unit about which the Bureau of Statistics will make available aggregate data, and in urban areas each CD contains about 150 to 200 households. Parties already use CData™ to target particular small areas in relation to local issues such as the building of freeways or the disposal of parkland.

Since parties have the returns from every voting booth from previous elections, they can relate these on a probability basis to the CDs from which people voting at that booth came. Through combining data sets in this way, the parties could then say that, for example, approximately 15 per cent of the people who voted at booth A were managers or professionals, while only 6 per cent of the people who voted at booth B were. And the party researchers might try by various ways, including the use of demographic information while conducting polls, to link voting intentions to demographically defined groups. But here again it is difficult to infer voting intention from a small number of individual demographic characteristics — all males aged 30–34 do not think, act and vote the same way.

Furthermore, if you have 34 500 CDs (as was the case in the 1996 census), a huge amount of guesswork is required at the level of individual booths. There is also a well-known problem with trying to gather demographic data from a public opinion poll, in that in trying to analyse demographic data from the sample in an opinion poll, it is almost impossible to combine more than two variables before you become lost in statistical noise.[3]

But remedies are at hand. Newer computer-based technologies allow parties to predict votes, identify persuadables and devise optimal message strategies with still greater sophistication and accuracy. Prominent among these tools are geodemographics and cognitive mapping.

Geodemographics

Geodemographics has been used in political campaigns for some time in the United States. My first acquaintance with geodemographics came from an article in the US journal, *Campaigns & Elections* by Jonathon Robbin (1980). Robbin realised that a better approach to analysing demographics could be obtained from the insight that, when it comes to where people live, "Birds of a feather flock together". He stated:

> Humans group into natural areas [where] the resources — physical, economic and social — are compatible with their needs. They create or *choose* established neighbourhoods which conform to their lifestyle of the moment. The neighbourhood or community can be viewed as the smallest unit of homogeneous population where adjacent households, and the individuals dwelling in them, make up a distinct social group which shares demographic and economic characteristics. (1980, p. 28)

He also commented on the mobility of people in seeking compatible neighbourhoods as their life circumstances change:

> As people's lives change, they may move on to more accommodating surroundings ... At each stage in their life cycles, individuals join their peers in appropriate communities. In their twenties, they typically marry and choose relatively transient rental housing. In their thirties, they buy

> homes suitable for raising small children. In their forties, they are launching teenagers into society, and in their fifties are settling down to increased community participation as their family responsibilities wane … During their sixties and beyond, they seek out domiciles suited to leisure and retirement. (1980, p. 28)

The Australian evidence points to similar mobility on the part of Australians. The Australian Electoral Office claims that approximately 20 per cent of registered voters change their address in any one year; and we know from the 1996 census that only 54.66 per cent of persons were living in the same dwelling as they were five years earlier. With the decline in the notion of lifelong employment, the likelihood is that mobility will increase still further.

The procedure with geodemographics is to construct a typology of the basic units of the census. With a large data set (the 1996 census CD data set contained over 5000 cells over information for each of some 34 500 CDs), this is not a trivial matter. In principle, the data set needs to be reduced to eliminate redundancy in the variables; then ideally the reduced set of variables should be factor-analysed to determine which variables are most important in discriminating between CDs; and finally both agglomerative and hierarchical cluster analysis should be used to arrive at the optimal set of clusters.

Robbin identified 40 clusters. Given an address, it is possible to allocate any individual to a cluster. Parties can then analyse information obtained from polling in terms of the geodemographic clusters to which informants belong. Robbin comments:

> The result is a set of robust relationships of neighborhood type to political attitudes which identify the "right" kind of *neighborhoods* for selective targeting … small areas with the same Cluster classifications can be selected for repeated contact by phone, mail or canvas. Knowing the Cluster composition of mass media audiences, Claritas can evaluate these on an index of "right" to "wrong". (1980, p. 32)

Robbin also points out that geodemographics can be used to generalise the results of limited polling to a much wider area — making it possible to project "average behaviour in each Cluster as observed in a sample to all clustered areas throughout the country".[4]

Robbin gives an example of the use of geodemographics in relation to a right-to-work initiative in Missouri in 1978. Early polls showed the initiative, which was opposed by organised labour, passing by 60 per cent to 40 per cent. Matt Reese and Associates combined Robbin's cluster data with poll information to identify favourable and persuadable clusters, "and to determine which issues and attitudes were to be dealt with in the messages delivered to voters inhabiting each cluster group" (1980, p. 33). On this basis, specific message strategies were devised for favourable clusters, and delivered via phone calls, direct mail and selected mass media channels that were known to disproportionately reach favourable clusters. In addition, predictions were made for each county on the basis of the cluster profile of each county. The results bore out the efficacy of geodemographic targeting (Robbin 1980, p. 34) with a "hit rate of 72 per cent correct estimates". As a result of organised labour's efforts using Reese and Robbin's Claritas clusters, the actual vote reversed the proportions shown in the July polls. The amendment was defeated by 59 per cent voting "no" to 41 per cent voting "yes" (see also Mockus 1980).

All Australian electorates, both federal and state, can be similarly analysed. To illustrate this, Figure 14.1[5] shows the Australian federal electorate of Brand, held in 2001 by the Leader of the Opposition, Kim Beazley. The different overlay patterns in this map illustrate different Geotarget™ clusters. The frequency of each cluster is indicated in brackets in the legend, and the number assigned to each cluster reflects its ranking in terms of an "Index of Advantage". Urban clusters run from 1 to 23, and rural clusters are ranked quite separately and range from 41 to 53.[6] From the legend, it is obvious that the bulk of urban clusters in Brand fall into the lower half of the cluster range, with 54 CDs in Cluster 21, 43 in Cluster 11, 16 in Cluster 19, 12 in Cluster 14, 11 in Cluster 17 and 10 in Cluster 22.

Figure 14.2 shows the federal electorate of Bennelong, held at the time by the Prime Minister, John Howard. As might be expected of a safe Liberal seat, in this electorate there is a strong skewing towards more advantaged clusters, the most frequent being Cluster 3, with 69 CDs. There are 105 CDs in the most advantaged clusters 1 to 5, versus only 39 CDs in the less advantaged clusters from 12 to 23.

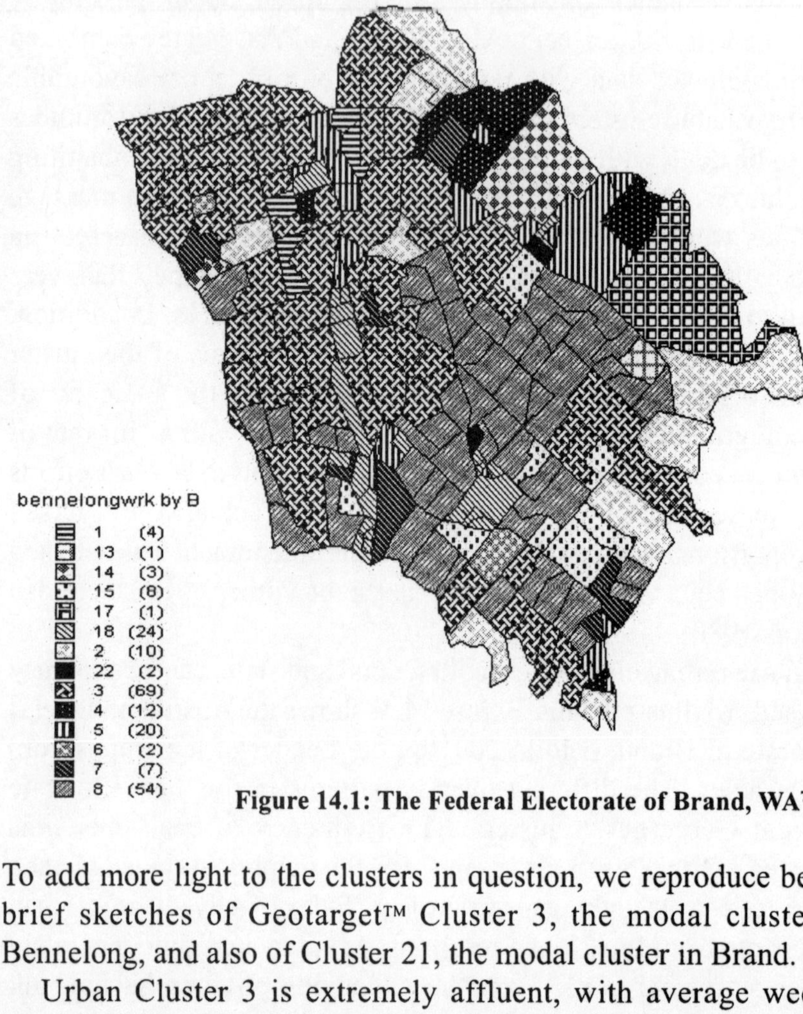

Figure 14.1: The Federal Electorate of Brand, WA[7]

To add more light to the clusters in question, we reproduce below brief sketches of Geotarget™ Cluster 3, the modal cluster in Bennelong, and also of Cluster 21, the modal cluster in Brand.

Urban Cluster 3 is extremely affluent, with average weekly household income of $1118. Australia-wide, it includes 1118 CDs (≈239 500 households). Like Cluster 2, it includes mature families, living in separate houses with high levels of ownership, and very high stability. It also has many male and female professionals but differs from Cluster 2 in having fewer managers, a higher proportion of non-Anglo background ethnics, and in being more outer suburban (99.11 per cent major urban). Weekly individual income has high skewings for males above $800, and for females above $500. This cluster might be characterised as "rich, with more ethnic families". High concentrations of this group are in suburbs such as

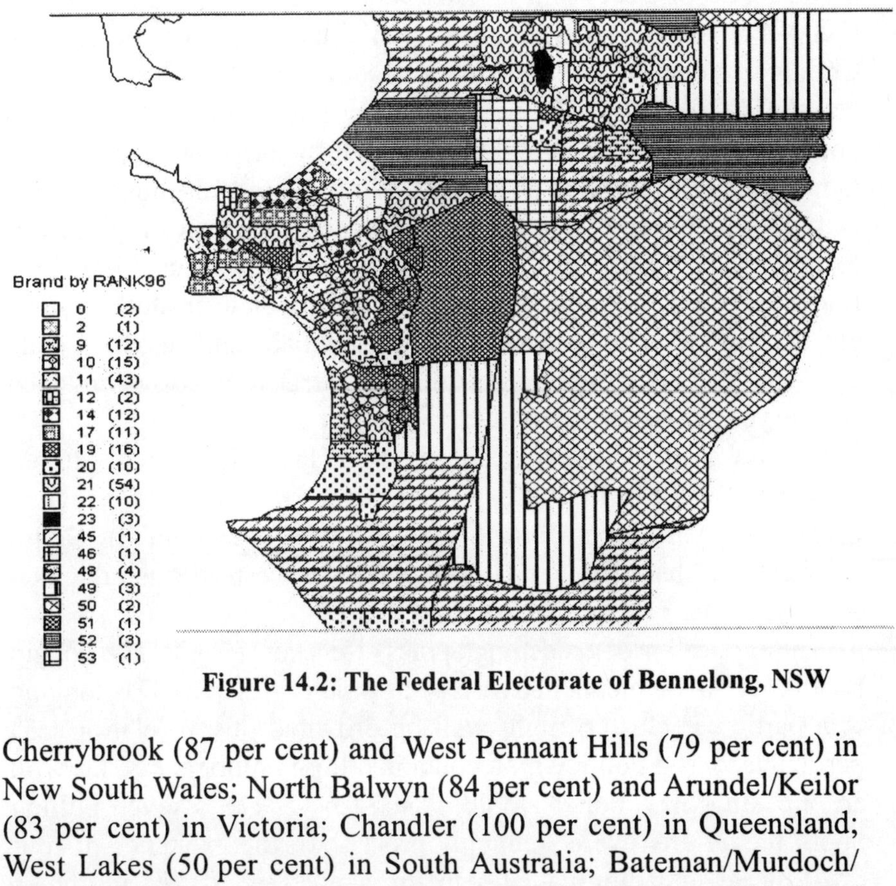

Figure 14.2: The Federal Electorate of Bennelong, NSW

Cherrybrook (87 per cent) and West Pennant Hills (79 per cent) in New South Wales; North Balwyn (84 per cent) and Arundel/Keilor (83 per cent) in Victoria; Chandler (100 per cent) in Queensland; West Lakes (50 per cent) in South Australia; Bateman/Murdoch/Winthrop (100 per cent) in Western Australia; and Bruce/Giralang/Kaleen (36 per cent) in the ACT.

Urban Cluster 21 consists of 1316 CDs (≈281 300 households), and is somewhat more other urban (56.99 per cent) than it is major urban (43.01 per cent). It is slightly less stable than average, and has average weekly household income of $585. It has high skewings for unemployed male and female, and in terms of individual income, males are more than 20 per cent above national means only in the range $400–$599, with significant lows above $800, and females only at $300–$399, with lows above $600. Under the category of age, we find a very unusual pattern for both sexes: high scores for 0–4, then significantly low for 5–29,35–44 and 50–64, then very high again above 65. At least the high scores for 0–4 can be related to high scores for males and females Married 20–29. In other words, this is a cluster of young families and elderly couples and singles. Children attend government schools, and the cluster has very low non-Anglo ethnicity. The typical family is a couple with children under 15 (12 per cent above the national mean) or a single-parent family (very significant high scores), living in a separate house, which is being purchased on a mortgage or rented (with very high scores for rented from State Housing Authority). Under "occupation", we find high scores for tradesperson male, intermediate production male and female, elementary clerical and sales female, and labourers male and female. This cluster might be characterised as "disadvantaged Aussie young families and elderly".

Cluster 21 is relatively diffused: Blue Haven/Budgewoi (46 per cent) in New South Wales; Deception Bay (61 per cent) in Queensland; Elizabeth North and West (37 per cent) in South Australia; Kallista/Kwinana (71 per cent) in Western Australia; and Burnie (34 per cent) in Tasmania.[8]

The application of geodemographics offers new insights into polling booth data. As we mentioned earlier, the proclivities of a CD belonging to a particular cluster might well be drowned out in relation to a particular voting booth which contained high numbers of CDs with an opposing bias. For example, if sixteen CDs in a given polling booth feeder area were staunchly pro-Labor, the existence of four pro-Liberal or swinging CDs in the same feeder area might be undetectable. However, given that every CD can be assigned to a Geotarget™ cluster, a frequency count of CDs by cluster statewide, in terms of their participation in voting booths displaying different voting patterns, can counteract the skewings in individual voting booths and display their overall political alignment.

The data in Table 14.1 display the overall voting tendencies of the clusters identified above for Queensland in the 1998 federal election. While 64.37 per cent of CDs belonging to Cluster 3 (56 out of 87) occurred in booths in the Liberal Party two-party preferred greater than 55 per cent category, only 2.30 per cent (two out of 87) fell into booths with Liberal Party two-party preferred less than 45 per cent. The high incidence of Cluster 3 in John Howard's electorate helps to explain why it has a Liberal member. Conversely, in relation to Cluster 21, the fact that 55.29 per cent of CDs belonging to that cluster fell into booths registering Liberal Part two-party preferred less than 45 per cent helps to explain why Brand currently has a Labor member.

Another area where geodemographics can be of decisive assistance is in relation to polling. By keying one's polling to the cluster of informants, the results can be generalised to the whole state, and since every electorate can be analysed in terms of constituent clusters, accurate polling will allow one to predict the outcome in every electorate. Alternatively, one could focus one's polling on just the swinging clusters whose behaviour is likely to determine the outcome in marginal seats. For example, in the Aston by-election in July 2001, analysis of the electorate revealed that, of 53 CDs in the electorate that belonged to clusters defined as swinging for the state, 35 (or 66 per cent) belonged to a single cluster, Cluster 10. Obviously the voting preferences of voters from this cluster was of decisive importance in the outcome of this by-election.

Computer technology also helps in the matter of "poll information to identify favourable and persuadable clusters, and to determine which issues and attitudes were to be dealt with in the messages delivered to voters inhabiting each cluster group", to use Robbin's words quoted above. As a prelude to explaining how, we need first to clarify some preliminary matters. First, in terms of persuading and influencing people, audiences are not empty vessels into which sources are free to pour whatever ideas they wish, without resistance. The clear implication of the Human Information Processing (HIP) paradigm, the dominant theory in cognitive psychology for many years, is first that HIP is complex, multistaged and involves massive filtration and distortion of incoming information; and second that, unless incoming information is consistent with the information already stored in the mind of the receiver, it has little chance of being perceived, attended to, processed, stored or recalled. If it is attended to and processed despite these handicaps, it is likely to be distorted in the direction of the information already stored in the mind of the receiver. To make things still more difficult for those seeking to persuade, it is

Table 14.1 Queensland Voting Tendencies in the 1998 Federal Election

Cluster	Sec-state	Total CDs	LP2pp >=55%	% Cluster	Mean LP2pp	LP2pp 45–55%	% Cluster	Mean LP2pp	LP2pp <=45.0%	% Cluster	Mean LP2pp
3	Maj urb	87	56	64.37	62.50	29	33.33	48.74	2	2.30	42.43
21	Maj urb	170	18	10.59	57.95	58	34.12	49.38	94	55.29	38.55

Maj urb = Major Urban; LP2pp=Liberal Party two-party preferred vote; Sec-state=Section of state.

known that dramatic conversions like St Paul's about-face on the road to Damascus rarely occur outside the pages of the New Testament. Under normal circumstances, it is unrealistic to hope to move people more than a small distance in the direction desired.

It follows that the key to successful persuasion in a political context is to be able to identify those who can be persuaded — that is, people where a small shift in cognitions will lead to a change in the way votes and preferences are allocated. Second, it is important to find out as accurately as possible how they think about the topic about which we wish to communicate. Finally, one would like to have some quantitative evidence of what the best message strategy is to move a given group of people in the direction desired.

Such desiderata can be supplied by Cognitive Mapping™, based on the Galileo™ system, which offers the opportunity of mapping a cognitive domain with an open-ended ratio-level scale. Many studies have supported the reliability and validity of the Galileo™ system (cf. Serota et al. (1977); Gilham & Woelfel (1977); Craig (1977); and Woelfel & Fink (1980). Both Cognitive Mapping™ and Galileo™ are simultaneously methods, particular uses of statistical techniques and computer programs. In essence, both provide sophisticated ways of taking people's constructs and establishing how far apart they are from each other. While they have a complex statistical base, their aim is to represent relationships multidimensionally.

The first step is to conduct a depth interview, the most qualitative of all methodologies, with a sufficient sample drawn from your target audience. Once sufficient depth interviews have been conducted, they can be content-analysed to identify the key concepts that are mentioned most often by most members of the group interviewed. It is now possible to do this via a computer-based text analysis program. Once a set of key concepts has been identified, those concepts can be plugged into a standard questionnaire.

That questionnaire asks informants to estimate the distance, or relatedness, between each possible pairing of the concepts, using a standard stipulated distance as a criterion pair. In the case of voting behaviour, distances between an ideal concept and competing parties or candidates have repeatedly been demonstrated to form a reliable guide to voting behaviour. The best form of ideal concept is one involving the self-concept in a form of behaviour, as in "The Party I Would Vote For" or, more specifically, "The Party I would Vote for in the House of Representatives".

These ideas can be best represented through a concrete example. In June 2000, students from the University of Canberra conducted a study of the ACT electorate that combined the use of Cognitive Mapping™ with the Galileo™ program with geodemographics, and specifically Geotarget™. The plan was to conduct two distinct studies: one relating to voting intentions, the other to perceptions of issues in relation to the major parties.

Although the first step in a Cognitive Mapping study is usually in-depth interviews with the target group or groups to identify the key filter categories in terms of which they think about the concept, we had neither the time nor the resources to do this. In any event, the concepts to include in any study of voting intentions were fairly self-evident. These were:

1. Party I would choose in the House of Representatives
2. Liberal Party
3. Labor Party
4. National Party
5. Australian Democrats
6. One Nation
7. Green Party
8. Party I would choose in the Senate

In the case of the issues study, we took the issues that were being ranked in importance by conventional polls such as Newspoll™. We then modified them slightly to be appropriate for a Galileo™ questionnaire. For example, in terms of simply ranking issues, it is sufficient to specify "Unemployment". But to measure the relationships between this and other issues, we need to make it more specific — a benefit which informants would be likely to relate differentially to different parties, such as "reducing unemployment". Thus the concepts to be used in the issues study were:

1. Party I Would Vote For
2. Strong Leadership
3. Good Economic Management
4. Tax Reform
5. Welfare Reform
6. Care for the Environment
7. Better Health System
8. Help for Families
9. Reducing Unemployment
10. Better Education System
11. Labor Party
12. Liberal Party

Each student was provided with a set of potential phone numbers, all from the same geodemographic cluster, and asked to complete two each of the two questionnaires by ringing those phone numbers. The result was that 67 of the completed questionnaires for each of the two studies were received — not enough to do a full geodemographically based analysis but, given the geodemographic clusters from which the completed questionnaires were drawn, enough to do an overall Galileo™ study and provide a reasonably representative sample of the ACT electorate.[9]

The Issues Study

Of particular importance in the issues study were the relative distances between the concepts "Party I Would Vote For", "Liberal Party" and "Labor Party" on the one hand, and the other "issues" concepts listed above on the other. A criterion of "Good" and "Bad" as being 100 units apart was used — a lower score would mean a close match between the issue and the Party concerned while a higher score would mean the opposite.

Perhaps the first point to make is that the distances from the ideal "Party I Would Vote For" and the issues are quite large. They range from 35.1 for "Reducing Unemployment" to 46.8 for "Better Education System". This indicates that voters have a healthy scepticism about the ability of parties (and governments) to solve major and complex problems. If the electorate were made up of idealists, we might expect to see distances like 10 between "Party I Would Vote For" and "Care for the Environment".

The issues break into three distinct groups. Closest to "Party I would Vote For" is "Reducing Unemployment" (35.1), closely followed by "Good Economic Management" (35.7), and "Strong Leadership" (36.4). These might be called the core issues. Then a little further off, we find "Tax Reform" (38.4) and "Better Health System" (38.7). Somewhat further away is a third group: the closest of these is "Welfare Reform" (44.6); then we have "Care for the Environment" (44.7), "Help for Families" (45.6) and "Better Education System" (46.8).

Using calculations based on experience with Galileo™, the two-party preferred vote was 46.3 per cent Liberal compared with

53.7 per cent Labor at the time. (This favouring of Labor might be expected from a study of ACT informants, given the role of the public service in Canberra, and the general perception that the Labor Party means bigger government and hence more public service jobs.)

However, this overall Labor lead needs to be tempered by a consideration of scores on issues. (Indeed, issues become very much the focus during election campaigns.) Here a more complex picture emerges which, if anything, sees the Liberal Party in the advantageous position. With "issues", the crucial measure is the distance between, on the one hand, the party in question and the issue and, on the other hand, the distance between the ideal — "The Party I Would Vote For" — and the issue. The more that the position of a political party approximates this ideal distance, the more votes they would obtain. For "Reducing Unemployment", Labor is closer but by only 0.7 (Liberal Party 46.1, Labor Party 45.4) — both are about ten units further away than "The Party I Would Vote For" (35.1). In relation to "Good Economic Management", Labor is ahead but only marginally by 0.9 (Liberal Party 45.8, Labor Party 44.9) — both parties are about ten units beyond the ideal position (35.7). On the third issue, "Strong Leadership", it is interesting that, in this Labor-favouring sample, the Liberal Party (43.1) is well ahead of the Labor Party (46.4), and less than seven units from the ideal position.

In the second group of concepts, the Liberal Party (41.8) had a strong lead over the Labor Party (48.5) in relation to "Tax Reform", and the Liberal Party was only 3.4 units from the ideal position. However, Labor (44.0) had a strong lead over the Liberal Party (53.4) in relation to "Better Health System", with Labor only 5.3 from the ideal point.

Turning to the third, and most distant, group of concepts, we find that Labor is often closer to the concept, but sometimes closer to the concept than is the ideal point. For example, Labor (39.9) is much closer to "Welfare Reform" than is the Liberal Party (49.3), but the ideal distance (44.6) is greater than the Labor Party distance, and the two parties are actually exactly the same distance (4.7) from the ideal distance. As a result, "Welfare Reform" would not appear to be a plus for the Labor Party. "Care for the Environment" is clearly to Labor's advantage: 46.3 to 56.4 for the Liberals, with Labor very close (1.6 units) to the ideal position (44.7). The last two concepts, "Help for Families" and "Better Education System", pattern like "Welfare Reform" — that is, the Labor Party is much closer (39.4 and 41.6 respectively) than Liberal Party (53.5 and 54.2) to the concepts, but the ideal position is in both cases further from the concepts than is the Labor Party. There is also little difference between Labor's difference from the ideal concept (6.21 units) and Liberal'sdifference (7.9) in relation to "Help for Families". Similarly, the Labor Party is only marginally closer to the ideal position (5.2 units) with "Better Education System" than is the Liberal Party (7.4). In other words, the fact that Labor Party is identified much more with these concepts is not in itself a significant vote-winning fact, because these informants feel somewhat ambivalent about these issues and rate them as significantly less important than the core and second ranked groups.

Table 14.2: Distances from "Party I Would Vote for", "Liberal Party" and "Labor Party"

	Party I Would Vote For	Liberal Party	Labor Party
1. Party I would vote for	0	55.9	48.8
2. Strong leadership	36.4	43.1	46.4
3. Good economic management	35.7	45.8	44.9
4. Tax reform	38.4	41.8	48.5
5. Welfare reform	44.6	49.3	39.9
6. Care for environment	44.7	56.4	46.3
7. Better health system	38.7	53.4	44.0
8. Help for families	45.6	53.5	39.4
9. Reducing unemployment	35.1	46.1	45.4
10. Better education system	46.8	54.2	41.6
11. Labor Party	48.8	58.8	0
12. Liberal Party	55.9	0	58.8

From the input means matrix, the coordinates for the Metric Multidimensional Space were generated. The space generated with Cognitive Mapping is a fully metric space, such that the distances between points in the map corresponds precisely with the distances in the input matrix. There are two main uses for the Metric Multidimensional Space. One is to compute the overall degree of distance between either the cognitive spaces of two groups; the other — more useful in the context of a political campaign — is to compute the degree of change between the same group at an earlier time (such as before the start of a persuasive campaign) and a later time (such as at the end of the persuasive campaign). In this way, one can measure accurately what effects the persuasive campaign has had on people's schemas.

The other main use is to determine the effectiveness of different message strategies. Empirical research on the effects of messages on cognitive maps is to show that, when two concepts A and B are linked in a message, the distance between A and B diminishes. If we link A with both B and C, then A tends to move in the direction of the geometric mean of B and C. Since we also know that, in the choice between competing parties, informants will vote for the party that is closest to their ideal concept (in this study, represented by "The Party I Would Vote For"), we can then ask: mathematically, with what concepts should we link the concept to be promoted (here, "Liberal Party") in order to move it maximally towards the ideal concept? The program can list the best single concept, the best pair of concepts, the best three concepts and the best four concepts. Each is associated with an angle and the best message strategy is the one with the smallest angle. We stress that this calculation is based on the structure of the metric multidimensional space, and does not necessarily relate to the ranking of issues in the means matrix. Note that the figures quoted in the next paragraphs represent degrees between vectors in the space, not distances between concepts. It also might be noted that the optimal two or three concepts generated using geometric means may be quite different from the optimal single concept (as we shall see below).

The results in the issues study was that, in order to move the "Liberal Party" closer to "The Party I Would Vote For", the best single concept was number four, "Tax Reform" (48.4 degrees); the best two concepts were number two, "Strong Leadership" and "Tax Reform" (40.4 degrees); and the best three concepts were "Strong Leadership", "Tax Reform" and number nine, "Reducing Unemployment" (38.5 degrees); while the best four concepts were "Strong Leadership", "Tax Reform", "Reducing Unemployment" and number six, "Care for the Environment" (37.4 degrees)

Thus the optimal message strategy for moving "Liberal Party" closer to "The Party I Would Vote For" for this group (i.e. ACT voters in general) would be the four-concept strategy: "Vote Liberal, because the Liberal Party provides strong leadership. The Liberal Party has successfully managed Australia's biggest ever tax reform. The Liberal Party has demonstrated effective care for the environment through its Natural Heritage Fund. And the Liberal Party has reduced Unemployment from XX per cent when it took office to YY per cent. Vote Liberal."

We re-ran the issues data, this time asking for the optimal message strategies to move the Labor Party closer to "The Party I Would Vote For". Not surprisingly, the combinations of concepts were very different from those that were optimal for the Liberal Party. The best single concept was number eight, "Help for Families" (49.2 degrees); the best two concepts were number five, "Welfare Reform", and number six, "Care for the Environment" (41.9 degrees — note how in this instance the best single concept is not among the best two concepts!); the best three concepts were "Welfare Reform", "Care for the Environment" and number ten, "Better Education System" (38.6 degrees); and the best four concepts were "Welfare Reform", "Care for the Environment", "Help for Families" and "Better Education System" (39.1 degrees).

Thus, mathematically, the optimal message strategy for the Labor Party to move closer to "The Party I Would Vote For" for this sample would be the three-concept combination. Thus, at a conceptual level, Labor should put out the message: "A Labor government will reform the welfare system, provide better care for the environment and improve Australia's education system."

The Voting Study

The data sets in the issues study make it possible to pick out persuadable voters. Voting behaviour can be predicted in terms of the relative distances between an ideal point (such as "The Party I Would Vote For") and the concepts of competing parties, and in terms of changes in those key distances over time. With cognitive mapping, the persuadables are those people where the differences between the distances "Labor Party" — "Party I Would Vote for" and "Liberal Party" — "Party I Would Vote For" are small. For example, if an informant put the Liberal Party 35 units from the "Party I Would Vote For" and the Labor Party 32 units from the "Party I Would Vote For", we can say that, at present, this person would vote for Labor. But an improvement of only four units in the position of the Liberal Party — something which is achievable — or, equally, a demotion of four units in the position of the Labor Party would switch this person to voting Liberal.

The value of such data emerges from being able to trace patterns of preferences in the voting patterns of individual informants not only in relation to first preferences, but also critically in relation to lower preferences. It might be that there is little that can be done to persuade a particular voter, or group of voters, not to give their first preference, say, to the Australian Democrats. But in House of Representative elections, such a vote is likely to be distributed, and it becomes crucial whether the Liberal Party receives a higher preference than the Labor Party, at whatever level those preferences are distributed.

With a large sample, it is possible to pick out such persuadable voters, and to identify them not only in terms of their geodemographic cluster, but also in terms of demographic groups within clusters. And it is possible to select all records belonging to such individuals, and from this to calculate the optimal message strategy to persuade them to give their final preference to one party above the other. It is also possible to collect information on what their favourite TV programs are, and what newspapers or magazines they read.

We thought it might be a useful illustration to extract from individual records key data on individual distances that allow us to predict that individual's voting pattern in the House of Representatives and the Senate. We abbreviate "Party I Would Choose in the House of Representatives" as "Party HR" and "Party I Would Choose in the Senate" as "Party Sen".

Informant 1: **Cluster 1, Male, Age 18-25, HH Income $40 000–$40,999, Always votes Liberal, Voted Liberal last HR election**

Party HR & Liberals	0	Party Sen & Liberals	0
Party HR & Labor	100	Party Sen & Labor	100
Party HR & Nationals	72	Party Sen & Nationals	40
Party HR & Democrats	80	Party Sen & Democrats	80
Party HR & One Nation	150	Party Sen & One Nation	230
Party HR & Greens	60	Party Sen & Greens	10

This voter will certainly give the Liberals his first preference in the HR and in the Senate, though note the improvement in the rating of the Greens in the Senate!

Informant 8: **Cluster 2, Female, Age 45–54, HH Income $30 000–$39 999, Usually votes Democrat, Voted Democrats last HR election**

Party HR & Liberals	60	Party Sen & Liberals	70
Party HR & Labor	30	Party Sen & Labor	40
Party HR & Nationals	60	Party Sen & Nationals	60
Party HR & Democrats	50	Party Sen & Democrats	30
Party HR & One Nation	70	Party Sen & One Nation	70
Party HR & Greens	70	Party Sen & Greens	70

This informant would give first preference to Labor, and does not appear persuadable. She would vote Democrat in the Senate and give her first preference to Labor.

Informant 19: **Cluster 3, Female, Age 26–34, HH Income $5000–$5999, Usually votes Liberal, Voted Liberal in last HR election**

Party HR & Liberals	50	Party Sen & Liberals	70
Party HR & Labor	40	Party Sen & Labor	30
Party HR & Nationals	60	Party Sen & Nationals	40
Party HR & Democrats	60	Party Sen & Democrats	60
Party HR & One Nation	70	Party Sen & One Nation	40
Party HR & Greens	80	Party Sen & Greens	50

Despite her voting history, this informant would vote Labor in both the House of Representatives and the Senate. However, given her history, and given the difference between Party HR & Liberals and Party HR & Labor, she would qualify as persuadable.

***Informant 31:* Cluster 7 Female, Age 26–34, HH, Income $30 000–$39 999, Usually votes Labor, Voted Labor in the last HR election**

Party HR & Liberals	25	Party Sen & Liberals	25
Party HR & Labor	25	Party Sen & Labor	25
Party HR & Nationals	70	Party Sen & Nationals	50
Party HR & Democrats	20	Party Sen & Democrats	60
Party HR & One Nation	70	Party Sen & One Nation	50
Party HR & Greens	20	Party Sen & Greens	30

Despite her voting history, this informant is a classic persuadable. On these figures, she would vote either Democrat or Green in the House of Representatives, but Liberal and Labor would tie for her third preference. In the Senate, Liberal and Labor tie for her vote.

***Informant 37:* Cluster 14 Female, Age 18–25, HH Income below $5000, Swinging Voter, voted for "Other" in last HR election**

Party HR & Liberals	80	Party Sen & Liberals	80
Party HR & Labor	80	Party Sen & Labor	90
Party HR & Nationals	50	Party Sen & Nationals	70
Party HR & Democrats	40	Party Sen & Democrats	50
Party HR & One Nation	40	Party Sen & One Nation	70
Party HR & Greens	50	Party Sen & Greens	70

This young female voter appears to be alienated from both the major parties, and would probably vote Democrat in the House of Representatives and Senate. But Liberal and Labor are tied for final (and effective) preferences in the House of Representatives. Liberal would get her Senate preference ahead of Labor, but the two parties are very close. A preference persuadable.

Although the individual data above was extracted "manually", it should be stressed that, with a large data-set, as during a real election campaign, records of large numbers of voters could be analysed by writing a computer program in SAS.[10]

Conclusion

The studies reported here demonstrate the power of Cognitive Mapping in a political context. Cognitive Mapping was used by the Liberal Party in its campaign for the mid-2001 by-election for the federal seat of Aston. All Cluster 10 households were targeted with personalised direct mail implementing the optimal message strategy to move the Liberal Party towards The Party I Would Vote for, as determined for this group by Cognitive Mapping. Since several voting booths were pure Cluster 10, it was possible to determine that this strategy increased the two-party preferred vote for the Liberal Party in this cluster by between 8 and 12 per cent — thereby enabling the Liberal Party to win this seat. Computer-based technologies such as geodemographics and Cognitive Mapping™ clearly offer parties significant advantages when it comes to communicating with voters.

While the "discourse of geodemographics" is comparatively new to the Australian political landscape, the need to discover voter intentions in greater detail and to influence those intentions in small increments is well established. Traditional polling and survey methodologies, however, are at a limit if greater information is required on people's "cognitive maps". The two studies reported on here show how Cognitive Mapping works in a political context and how fine-tuned the idea of the "swinging voter" has become.

Notes

1 Aitkin (1983, p. 16) gives figures: Always voted Labor 33 per cent; Always voted Liberal/Country Party 27 per cent; Voted for different parties 39 per cent; Don't know 1 per cent.

2 The increase in the flow of information into the home, and the decline in the amount of attention paid to mass media, are well chronicled by Neuman and de Sola Pool (1986); Anderson's (1985) study also provides powerful evidence that, much of the time, television is little more than a background medium.

3 To understand this, let us assume that you try to gather information on six variables and that you use the same number of categories for each variable as the census does. So let's assume you have two values for gender; 21 for age (five-yearly intervals); 31 for ethnicity (30 specific and one "Other"); fifteen for individual income; eighteen for industry worked in; and nine for occupation. The usual way to combine information from multiple variables is cross-tabulation. This involves cross-multiplying the number of categories in each variable. For the six variables we have just specified, this would yield 3 163 860 cells. Since the largest commercially drawn sample is 2400, the bankruptcy of this approach should be self-evident.

4 I believe that in speaking of generalising results right across the country in relation to politics, Robbin is overstating the matter. In an Australian context, I would recommend only generalising results within each state.

5 For technical reasons, rural CDs must be analysed separately from urban CDs. Note that the urban and rural rankings are separate. That is, the fact the top

rural cluster is 41 does not mean that it ranks below urban cluster at 23.

6 Brand includes a small number of rural CDs. However, the larger area covered by these rural CDs makes the full map of the electorate long and narrow, and if we made the scale of the map sufficient to include all CDs in the electorate, it would be difficult to see the more numerous and more closely packed urban CDs clearly.

7 Although we have cited postcodes that display these clusters in unusually high concentrations, such postcodes are actually atypical. The typical postcode contains CDs from at least six different clusters, and often far more. (This reveals the fallacy of postcode marketing, and the flaw in that assumption that by targeting a particuarly postcode, you are targeting a relatively homogeneous group.)

8 The distribution of completed questionnaires by cluster for each of the studies was: Cluster 1, 7; Cluster 2, 11; Cluster 3, 2; Cluster 4, 8; Cluster 6, 22; Cluster 7, 2; Cluster 9, 3; Cluster 14, 3; Cluster 19, 8; Cluster 20, 8; Cluster 22, 8; Cluster 23, 4. Given that the numbers of the clusters represent a ranking by an Index of Advantage, it was certainly not the case that the measurements were obtained only for the most affluent and educated clusters.

9 This is in contrast to most multidimensional scaling algorithms available in statistics packages, which are non-metric. In these cases, it is assumed without any further evidence that the non-Euclidean characteristics of the species generated by fully metric programs are due to measurement error, and a smoothing factor, usually involving dropping the input matrix to its ordinal level, is arbitrarily applied to force the data into Euclidean space. On the superiority of fully metric MDS, the profound unreliability of non-metric MDS, see Woelfel & Barnett (1982). A striking fact in the issues space is that the warp factor, a figure that represents the ratio of the sum of positive eigenvalues to the sum of all eigenvalues, is 1.000, which means that the data are completely consistent. This is surprising, in that usually in the cognitive map of a group, there is some inconsistency in the data set. Note that this does not reflect measurement error, but real inconsistencies in the minds of informants. That people are sometimes inconsistent in their cognitions should not come as a surprise. In fact, there are whole schools of theory in social psychology, notably cognitive dissonance theory, that argue that the existence of inconsistent beliefs or attitudes is the main engine for attitude change.

10 It should be remembered that these questionnaires in the ACT studies were administered not by professional interviewers, but by second-year university students.

References

Aboriginal and Torres Strait Islander Commission (ATSIC). 1999. *Digital Dreaming: A National Review of Indigenous Media and Communications, Executive Summary*. Canberra: ATSIC.

Aboriginal Peoples Television Network. 1998. Licence Application. Ottawa, 5 June.

ACNielsen 1999. *TV Trends*. Sydney: ACNielsen.

—— 2001a. *Media Advisor*. www.acnielsen.com.au/product.asp?productID=14 Accessed 5 August.

—— 2001b. *Panorama*. www.acnielsen.com.au/product.asp?productID=18# Accessed 5 August.

Aitkin, D. 1983. The changing Australian electorate. In *Australia at the Polls*, ed. H.R. Penniman, pp. 11–34. Sydney: Allen & Unwin.

Alasuutari, Pertti. 1999. Introduction: three phases of reception studies. In *Rethinking the Media Audience*, ed. P. Alasuutari. London: Sage, pp. 1–21.

Altheide, David L. 1976. *Creating Reality: How TV News Distorts Events*. Beverly Hills: Sage.

American Demographics 1996. 1 November, p. 60.

Anderson, D.R. 1985. Online cognitive processing of television. In *Psychological Processes and Advertising Effects*, eds L.F. Alwitt and A.A. Mitchell. Hillsdale, NJ: Erlbaum.

Ang, Ien. 1991. *Desperately Seeking the Audience*. London: Routledge.

—— 1996. *Living Room Wars: Rethinking Media Audiences for a Postmodern World*. London and New York: Routledge.

Arbitron 2001. Arbitron TV, Cable and Radio Audience Meter Passes Important U.S. test Milestone. Press Release, 31 July. www.arbitron.com/newsroom/archive/article1.htm. Accessed 1 August 2001.

Arendt, Hannah. 1986. Communicative power. In *Power*, ed. S. Lukes. Oxford: Basil Blackwell.

Atkin, D.J. 1993. Adoption of cable amidst a multimedia environment. *Telematics and Informatics* vol. 10, no. 1, pp. 51–58.

Australia Council. 1997. Audience development and advocacy. Web page accessed 19 April 1997. www.ozco.gov.au. Excerpted from BIZTRAC and Donovan Research. *Marketing and the Arts: A Study of Marketing and Audience Development by Australian Arts Organisations.* Sydney: Australia Council.

—— 2000. *Directions 1999–2001.* 2nd edn. Sydney: Australia Council.

Australian Broadcasting Authority 2000. *Children's Views About Media Harm: A Collaborative Project Between the University of Western Sydney and the Australian Broadcasting Authority*, Monograph 10, Sydney.

Australian Broadcasting Corporation. 1993. *ABC Editorial Policies.* Sydney: ABC.

Australian Broadcasting Tribunal. 1984. *Satellite Program Services Inquiry.* vols 1 and 2, July, Canberra: AGPS.

—— 1985. *Remote Commercial Television Services: First Report.* Canberra: AGPS.

Australian Bureau of Statistics. 1991, 1995, 1999. *Attendance at Selected Cultural Venues.* Canberra: Australian Bureau of Statistics.

—— 1994. *How Australians Use Their Time.* Canberra: ABS.

—— 1998a. *Household Use of Information Technology.* Canberra: ABS.

—— 1998b. *Public Attitudes to the Arts 1997.* Canberra: ABS.

Australian Council of Social Services (ACOSS). 1997. *Young People, Gambling and the Internet.* Sydney: ACOSS.

Australian Electoral Commission. 1999. *Electoral Pocketbook.* Canberra: AEC.

Australian Museums On Line (AMOL). 1998. *Visitors Centre Stage: Action for the Future* website. http: amol.phm.gov.au/AMOL/evrsig/evrsig.html

Australian Pensioners and Superannuants Federation. 1995. *Older Australians and the Arts.* Sydney: APSF.

Bagnall, Diana 1999. The Y factor, *The Bulletin*, 16 March, pp. 14–19.

—— 2001. "Mums and dudes", *The Bulletin*, 23 January, pp. 18–23.

Balnaves, M. 1993. The sociology of information. *Australia and New Zealand Journal of Sociology* vol. 29, no. 1, pp. 93–111.

Balnaves, M. and Caputi, P. 1993. Corporate actors and corporate constructs: To what extent are personal constructs personal? *International Journal of Personal Construct Psychology* vol. 6, no. 2, pp. 119–38.

—— 1997. Technological wealth and the evaluation of information poverty. *Media International Australia* no. 83, pp. 92–102.

Balnaves, M., Caputi, P. and Williamson, K. 1991. The development of a methodology for assessing telecommunications needs: preliminary steps towards an index of information and communication poverty. *Australian Journal of Communication* vol. 18, no. 3, pp. 99–118.

Balogh, M. 1994. Personal interview, Sydney, 24 January.

BAM/SSB. 1993a. Positioning and Research Needs, unpublished report [SBS].

BAM/SSB. 1993b. *Building the SBS Brand: A Presentation to SBS*, 10 September.

Barbieri, Thimoty and Paolini, Paolo. 2000. Cooperative visits for museum www sites a year later: evaluating the effect. *Museums and the Web 2000*, www.archimuse.com/mw2000/index.html.

Barker, Martin ed. 1984. *The Video Nasties: Freedom and Censorship in the Media*. London: Pluto Press.

Barnathan, Julius. 1964. The business of research. In *Television Station Management: The Business of Broadcasting*, ed. Yale Roe. New York: Hastings House, pp. 171–80.

Barnett, G.A., Danowski, J.A and Richards, W.D. 1993. Communication networks and network analysis: A current assessment. *Progress in Communications Sciences* no. 12, pp. 1–19.

Barwise, Patrick and Ehrenberg, Andrew. 1988. *Television and Its Audience*. London: Sage.

Batt, Daniel. 1994. A brief history of Generation X. *On Being*, October, p. 22.

Baudrillard, Jean. 1988. *Selected Writings*. Cambridge: Polity Press.

Bauer, R.A. 1971. The obstinate audience: the influence process from the point of view of social communication. In *The Process and Effects of Mass Communication*. eds W. Schramm and D.F. Roberts, pp. 326–46. Urbana: University of Illinois Press.

BDA Marketing and Planning. 1999. *Report on Project 2*. Report for the Productivity Commission, 24 September.

Beachy, Stephen. 1994. AIDS and the apocalyptic imagination. In *Next: Young American Writers on the New Generation,* ed. Eric Liu,. New York: W.W. Norton, pp. 17–37.

Beam, Randal A. 1995. How newspapers use readership research. *Newspaper Research Journal* vol. 16, no. 2, pp. 28–38.

Bennett, Tony. 1995. *The Birth of the Museum: History, Theory, Politics*. London: Routledge.

Bennett, Tony, Emmison, Mike and Frow, John. 1999. *Accounting for Tastes: Australian Everyday Cultures*. Melbourne: Cambridge University Press.

Bennett, Tony, Miller, Toby, Swanson, Gillian and Tait, Gordon. 1990/91. Youth cultures and arts policies. *Culture and Policy* vol. 2, no. 2, pp. 135–56.

Berg, Bruce. 1989. *Qualitative Research Methods for the Social Sciences*. Boston: Allyn & Bacon.

Bernstein, Jonathan. 1994. The generation game. *The Face*, July, pp. 40–49.

Berwick, Patricia. 1999. *Audience Issues and Maori Broadcasting: Report to the Board of Te Mangai Paho*. Wellington, April.

Berzonsky, M.D. 1989. Identity style: conceptualization and measurement. *Journal of Adolescent Research* vol. 4, no. 3, pp. 268–82.

Bishop, J.E. 1995. AMA urges FDA regulation of tobacco. *The Washington Post*, 22 June, p. F3.

Boëthius, Ulf. 1995. Youth, the media and moral panics. In *Youth Culture in Late Modernity*, eds Johan Fornäs and Göran Bolin. London: Sage, pp. 39–57.

Bowen, Jonathan P. and Bowen, Jane S.M. 2000. The website of the UK Museum of the Year, River and Rowing Museum, www.rrm.co.uk/', *Museums and the Web 2000*, www.archimuse.com/mw2000/index.html.

Bowles, D. 1995. Telephone penetration: industrial countries vs LDCs. In *Beyond Competition: The Future of Telecommunications*, ed. Don M. Lamberton. Amsterdam: Elsevier.

Brady, Maggie. 1981. Some problems of method and theory in Aboriginal research. In *Research and the Delivery of Legal Services*, ed. P. Cashman. Sydney: Law Foundation of New South Wales, pp. 281–85.

Braverman, Harry. 1974. *Labour and Monopoly Capital*. New York: Monthly Review Press.

Brown, Les. 1971. *Television: the Business Behind the Box*. New York: Harvest, Harcourt Brace Jovanovich.

Buckingham, David, Davies, Hannah, Jones, Ken and Kelley, Peter. 1999. Public service goes to market: British children's television in transition. *Media International Australia incorporating Culture and Policy* no. 93, pp. 65–76.

Bulbeck, Pip. 1998. Turner releases first major kids' consumer survey. *Australian Pay-TV News*, 30 July.

Bunn, Andrew. 1998. Personal communication, 5 January 1998.

Bureau of Transport and Communication Economics. 1995. *Communication Futures Project.* Final Report. Canberra: Commonwealth of Australia.

Burton, Lee. 1993. *Children's Programs: The Child's View*. Prix Jeunesse Foundation and Bavarian Broadcasting, Munich.

Bye, Clarissa. 1997. Kids' TV snared by the web. *Sun-Herald*, 2 November, p. 16.

Carruthers, Ashley. 2001. National identity, disaporic anxiety and music video culture in Vietnam. In *House of Glass: Culture, Modernity and the State in Southeast Asia,* ed. Y. Souchou. Singapore: Institute of Southeas Asian Studies (ISEAS).

Cavanagh P. 2001. Interview, Head of Television, SBS, Peter Cavanagh, January.

Charity Times. 1999. UK debating social marketing. 14 May p. 45

Chatman, E.A. 1996. The impoverished life-world of outsiders. *Journal of the American Society for Information Science* vol. 47, no. 3, pp. 193–206.

Chesterfield, Ken. 2000. Interview with Mark Balnaves, Gold Coast, 1 August.

Cleary, Yvonne. 2000. An examination of the impact of subjective cultural issues on the usability of a localized website —The Louvre Museum Website. *Museums and the Web 2000*, www.archimuse.com/mw2000/index.html

Close, Helen and Donovan, Robert. 1998. *Who's My Market? A Guide to Researching Audiences and Visitors in the Arts*. Sydney: Australia Council. Available at www.ozco.gov.au/resources/publications/marketing/whosmymarket/index.htm

Coldevin, Gary O. 1977. Anik I and isolation: television in the lives of Canadian Eskimos. *Journal of Communication* Autumn, pp. 145–53.

Cole, P. 1992. *A Proposed Televillage in Gungahlin, ACT.* Consultant's Report to the ACT Government and AOTC.

Coleman, Peter. 1969. The coming war in advertising. *The Observer*, no. 31, pp. 677–80.

Costantoura, Paul 2000. *Australians and the Arts*. Sydney: Australia Council.

Coombs, H.C. 1981. *A Trial Balance*. Melbourne: Macmillan.

Coupland, Douglas. 1995. Generation X'd. *Details*. June, p. 72.

Courier-Mail. 1994. Teens dumping TV for mags, 17 September, p. 3.

Craig, R.T. 1977. Limiting the scope of the spacial model of communication effects. *Human Communication Research* no. 3, pp. 309–25.

Craik, Jennifer. 1996. The potential and limits of cultural policy strategies. *Culture and Policy* vol. 7, no. 1, pp. 177–204.

Crain, R. 1994. USA: social marketing misses the mark — Benetton, Body Shop. *Advertising Age* 26 September, p. 22.

Cranny-Francis, Anne and Gillard, Patricia. 1990. Soap opera as gender training: TV and teenage girls. In *Feminine/Masculine and Representation*, eds Terry Threadgold and Anne Cranny-Francis. Sydney: Allen & Unwin.

Crawford, Ben and Perkins, Zara. 1994. The Xorcist, *Black & White* no. 8, pp. 36–39, 113.

Creative Industries Task Force. 1998. *Creative Industries Mapping Document*. London: Department of Culture, Media and Sport. Available on www.culture.gov.uk/creative/creative_industries.html

Cullingford, Cedric. 1984. *Children and Television*. Aldershot: Gower.

Cumberbatch, Guy and Howitt, Dennis. 1989. *A Measure of Uncertainty: The Effects of the Mass Media*. London: J. Libbey.

Cunningham, Stuart and Sinclair, John eds. 2000. *Floating Lives: The Media and Asian Diasporas*. Brisbane: University of Queensland Press.

Cunningham, Stuart and Nguyen, Tina. 2000. Popular media of the Vietnamese diaspora. In *Floating Lives: The Media and Asian Diasporas*, eds S. Cunningham and J. Sinclair. Brisbane: University of Queensland Press, pp. 91–135.

Cupitt, Margaret, Jenkinson, Daniel, Ungerer, Judy and Waters, Brent. 1998. *Infants and Television*. Sydney: Australian Broadcasting Authority.

Cupitt, Margaret and Stockbridge, Sally 1996. *Families and Electronic Entertainment*. Sydney: Australian Broadcasting Authority.

Cusumano, Michael and Yoffie, David B. 1998. *Competing on Internet Time: Lessons from Netscape and its Battle with Microsoft*. New York: The Free Press.

Cyberkids: Children's Social Networks. 9/7/1999. www.hull.ac.uk/children5to16programme/details/valentine.htm

Dale, David. 2001. What did you finish watching last night? *The Age*, 28 April.

Dalrymple, Karen. 1994. Personal communication, 11 July.

Dambrot, F.H., Watkins-Malek, M.A., Silling, S.M., Marshall, R.S. and Garver, J. 1985. Correlates of sex differences in attitudes toward and involving computers. *Journal of Vocational Behavior* no. 27, pp. 71–86.

David, Jennifer. 1998. Seeing ourselves, being ourselves: broadcasting Aboriginal television in Canada. *Cultural Survival Quarterly* Summer, p. 39.

Davis, Mark. 1999. *Gangland: Cultural Elites and the New Generationalism*, 2nd edn, Sydney: Allen & Unwin.

Dean, Katherine. 1994. Noise pollution. *Juice*, February, p. 7.

Dean, Mitchell and Hindess, Barry. 1999. Introduction: government, liberalism, society. In *Governing Australia: Studies in Contemporary Rationalities of Government*, eds M. Dean and B. Hindess. Melbourne: Cambridge University Press, pp. 1–19.

Deane, Joel. 1994. The branding of a generation. *On Being* October, pp. 22–27.

Dello, S. 1997. Interview with Manas Ray, Sydney.

Department of Communications and the Arts (DOCA) 1994, *Creative Nation: Commonwealth Cultural Policy*, Canberra: AGPS.

Department of Communications, Information Technology and the Arts. 1999. *Securing the Future: The Final Report of the Major Performing Arts Inquiry* (Nugent Report). Canberra: DoCITA 44/99.

DiMaggio, Paul. 1987. Classification in Art. *American Sociological Review* no. 52 (August), pp. 440–55.

—— 1996. Are art-museum visitors different from other people? The relationship between attendance and social and political attitudes in the United States. *Poetics* no. 24, pp. 161–80.

—— 2000. Social structure, institutions, and cultural goods: the case of the United States. In *The Politics of Culture: Policy Perspectives for Individuals, Institutions, and Communities*, eds G. Bradford, M. Gary and G. Wallach, with preface by James Allen Smith. New York: The New Press and The Center for Arts and Culture.

DiMaggio, Paul and Pettit, Becky. 1999. Surveys of public attitudes toward the arts: what surveys tell us about the arts' political trials — and how they might tell us even more. *Arts Education Policy Review*. vol. 100, no. 4, pp. 32–37.

Director of White House Drug Control Policy, Atlanta. 1998. FDA Children and Tobacco. *PR Newswire*.

Downs, G.W., and Mohr, L.B. 1976. Conceptual issues in the study of innovation. *Administrative Science Quarterly* 21, pp. 700–714.

Drucker, Peter. 1996. *The Executive in Action: 3 Classsic Works on Management*. New York: HarperBusiness.

Drumwright, M.E. 1996. Company advertising with a social dimension: the role of noneconomic criteria. *Journal of Marketing* vol. 60, no. 4, pp. 71–87.

Dunn, Gwen. 1977. *The Box in the Corner: Television and the Under-fives*. London: Macmillan.

Dupagne, M. and Agostino, D.E. 1991. High definition television: a survey of potential adopters in Belgium. *Telematics and Informatics* vols 1/2, pp. 9–30.

Durkin, Kevin. 1995. *Computer Games and their Effects on Young People: A Review*. Sydney: Office of Film and Literature Classification.

Durkin, Kevin and Aisbett, Kate. 1999. *Computer Games and Australians Today*. Sydney: Office of Film and Literature Classification.

Dutton, W.H., Rogers, E.M. and Suk-Ho Jun. 1987. Diffusion and social impacts of personal computers. *Communication Research* vol. 14, no. 2, pp. 219–50.

Eades, Diane. 1988. They don't speak an Aboriginal language, or do they? In *Being Black: Aboriginal Cultures in "Settled" Australia*, ed. I. Keen. Canberra: Aboriginal Studies Press, pp. 97–115.

Eastlick, M.A. 1993. Predictors of videotex adoption. *Journal of Direct Marketing* vol. 7, no. 3, pp. 66–74.

Edgar, Patricia. 1977. *Children and Screen Violence*. Brisbane: University of Queensland Press.

Elebash, Camille. 1984. The Americanization of British political communications. *Journal of Advertising* vol. 13, no. 3, pp. 50–58.

Ericson, Richard, Baranek, Patricia and Chan, Janet. 1987. *Visualizing Deviance: A Study of News Organization*. Toronto: University of Toronto Press.

Ettema, James S. and Whitney, D. Charles. 1994. The money arrow: an introduction to audiencemaking. In *Audiencemaking: How the Media Create the Audience*, eds J. Ettema and D.C. Whitney, Thousand Oaks: Sage, pp. 1–18.

Evans, Jacob E. 1954. *Selling and Promoting Radio and Television*. New York: Printers' Ink Publishing.

Eveland, J.D. 1987. Diffusion, technology transfer, and implementation: thinking and talking about change. *Knowledge* no. 8, pp. 303–24.

Federation of Australian Commercial Television Stations (FACTS). 1994. *Commercial Television Industry Code of Practice (including Advisory Notes on Aboriginal and Torres Straits Island People, Cultural Diversity and Women and Men)*. Sydney: FACTS.

Federation of Australian Radio Broadcasters (FARB). 1994. *Guidelines on the Portrayal of Indigenous Australians (Aboriginal and Torrest Strait Islander Peoples) on Australian Commercial Radio*. Sydney: FARB.

Fink, Conrad C. 1988. *Strategic Newspaper Management*. New York: Random House.

Fitzgerald, N. 1997. Florida has $70 million in tobacco spoils for agency to snuff teen smoking. *Adweek* vol. 18, no. 49, p. 3.

Foster, Des. 2000. Interview with Mark Balnaves, Sydney, 30 June.

France, Kim. 1994. Douglas Coupland: Interview in *Elle* Magazine. In *The GenX Reader*, ed. Douglas Rushkoff. New York: Ballentine Books, pp. 11–16.

Fraser, Nancy. 1992. Rethinking the public sphere: a contribution to the critique of actually existing democracy. In *Habermas and the Public Sphere*, ed. C. Calhoun. Cambridge, MA: MIT Press, pp. 109–42.

Fussell, Paul. 1984. *Class: A Guide Through the American Status System*. New York: Touchstone Books, illustrated by Martim De Avillez.

Garneau, George. 1994. Reaching Potential Readers. *Editor & Publisher*, 7 May, pp. 11–12.

Garnham, Nicholas. 1992. The media and the public sphere. In *Habermas and the Public Sphere*, ed. C. Calhoun, pp. 359–76. Cambridge, MA: MIT Press.

—— 1995. The media and narratives of the intellectual. *Media, Culture and Society* vol. 17, no. 3, pp. 359–84.

Ghilardi, Lia. 2001. Cultural planning and cultural diversity. In *Differing Diversities: Transversal Study on the Theme of Cultural Policy and Cultural Diversity Followed by Seven Research Position Papers*, ed. T. Bennett. Geneva: Cultural Policy and Action Department, Council of Europe, January, pp. 116–27.

Giddens, Anthony. 1991. *Modernity and Self-identity: Self and Society in the Late Modern Age*. Cambridge: Cambridge University Press.

Giles, Robert H. 1995. *Newsroom Management: A Guide to Theory and Practice*. Detroit: Media Management Books.

Gillard, Patricia. 1989. *An Ethnography of Children's Viewing in the Family Context*. Sydney: University of New South Wales.

—— 1994. Insight from the inside: a new perspective on family influences over children's television viewing and its implications for teachers of English. In *Global Voices: Culture and Identity in the Teaching of English*, eds J. Milner and C. Pope. Washington: National Council of Teachers of English, pp. 106–19.

—— 1997. Customer focus and audience development in cultural institutions. Invited paper at the Cultural Organisations and Multimedia Conference, "Customer Focus in a Digital World", State Library of Victoria, 31 October.

—— 1998. Audience development strategies in new media environments. Paper presented at the "Convergence" Conference, Brisbane, 20 November, www.gu.edu.au/cmp/Cpapers.html

—— 2000. Shaping audiences online: principles of audience development for cultural institutions. *Media International Australia incorporating Culture and Policy* no. 94, pp. 117–30.

Gillham, J. and Woelfel, J. 1977. The Galileo system of measurement: preliminary evidence for precision, stability and equivalence to traditional measures. *Human Communication Research* no. 3, pp. 222–34.

Ginsburg, Faye. 1991. Indigenous media: Faustian contract or global village? *Cultural Anthropology* vol. 6, no. 1, pp. 92–112.

—— 1993. Aboriginal media and the Australian imaginary. *Public Culture* no. 5, pp. 557–78.

Gitlin, Todd. 1998. Public sphere or public sphericules? In *Media, Ritual and Identity*, eds T. Liebes and J. Curran. London and New York: Routledge, pp. 175–202.

Goldman, Debra. 1994, The X factor. In *The GenX Reader*, ed. Douglas Rushkoff. New York: Ballentine Books, pp. 287–89.

Gordon, T. 1976. Subject abilities to use MDS: effects of varying the criterion pair. Unpublished research paper, Temple University, Philadelphia, PA.

Gordon, T. and Deleo, H.C. 1976. Structural variation in "Galileo" space: Effects of varying the criterion pair in multidimensional scaling. Paper presented at the Annual Meeting of the International Communication Association, Portland, Oregon.

Gray, Ann. 1999. "Audience and reception research in retrospect: the trouble with audiences". In *Rethinking the Media Audience: The New Agenda*, ed. P. Alasuutari. London: Sage, pp. 22–36.

Greenberg, David. 1994. In the shadow of the sixties. In *Next: Young American Writers on the New Generation*, ed. Eric Liu. New York: W.W. Norton, pp. 69–80.

Grocer 1995. UK: mass marketing with a social conscience. 22 April, p. 14.

Grossberg, Lawrence. 1992. *We Gotta Get Out of this Place: Popular Conservatism and Postmodern Culture*. New York: Routledge.

—— 1994. The deconstruction of youth. In *Cultural Theory and Popular Culture: A Reader*, ed. John Storey. Hemel Hempstead: Harvester Wheatsheaf, pp. 183–90.

Guccione, Bob Jr. 1995. Foreword. In *Marketing to Generation X*, ed. Karen Ritchie. New York: Lexington Books, pp. vii–xi.

Guldberg, Hans. 2000. *The Arts Economy 1968–1998: Three Decades of Growth in Australia*. Sydney: Australia Council.

Habermas, Jurgen. 1974. The public sphere. *New German Critique* vol. 1, no. 3, pp. 49–55.

—— 1989. *The Structural Transformation of the Public Sphere: An Inquiry into a Category of Bourgeois Society*. Cambridge: Polity Press.

Hage, Ghassan. 1998. *White Nation: Fantasies of White Supremacy in a Multicultural Society.* Sydney: Pluto Press.

Hall, Stuart. 1982. The rediscovery of "ideology": the return of the repressed in media studies. In *Culture, Society and the Media*, eds Michael Gurevitch, Tony Bennett, James Curran and Janet Woolacott. London: Methuen, pp. 56–90.

Hall, Stuart, Clarke, John, Jefferson, Tony and Roberts, Brian. 1976. Subcultures, culture and class: a theoretical overview. In *Resistance Through Rituals: Youth Subcultures in Post-war Britain*, eds Stuart Hall and Tony Jefferson. London: Hutchinson, pp. 9–74.

Hall, Stuart, Critcher, Chas, Jefferson, Tony, Clarke, John and Roberts, Brian. 1978. *Policing the Crisis: Mugging, the State, and Law and Order*. London and Basingstoke: Macmillan.

Hall, Stuart and Whannel, Paddy. 1994. The young audience. In *Cultural Theory and Popular Culture*, ed. John Storey. Hemel Hempstead: Harvester Wheatsheaf, pp. 69–75.

Hamblett, Charles and Deverson, Jane. 1964. *Generation X*, London: Library, p. 33.

Harms, Ilse and Schweibenz, Werner. 2001. Evaluating the usability of a museum website. *Museums and the Web 2001*. Selected Papers from an International Conference, pp. 43–52

Harris, Stephen. 1980. *Culture and Learning: Tradition and Education in Northeast Arnhem Land.* Darwin: Professional Services Branch, Northern Territory Department of Education.

Harris, Thomas E. 1993. *Applied Organizational Communication: Perspectives, Principles, and Pragmatics*. Hillsdale, NJ: Lawrence Erlbaum Associates.

Hartley, John. 1983. Encouraging signs: television and the power of dirt, speech and scandalous categories. *Australian Journal of Cultural Studies* vol. 1, no. 2, pp. 62–82.

—— 1992a. *The Politics of Pictures: The Creation of the Public in the Age of Popular Media*. London: Routledge.

—— 1992b. *Tele-ology: Studies in Television*. London: Routledge.

—— 1999a. *Uses of Television*. London and New York: Routledge.

—— 1999b. What is journalism? The view from under a stubbie cap. *Media International Australia incorporating Culture and Policy*, no. 90, pp. 15–33.

Hartley, John and McKee, Alan 2000. *The Indigenous Public Sphere*. Oxford: Oxford University Press.

Harvey, David. 1989. *The Condition of Postmodernity*. London: Blackwell.

Hebdige, Dick. 1979. *Subculture: The Meaning of Style*, London: Methuen.

—— 1988. *Hiding in the Light: On Images and Things*, London: Routledge.

Henderson, R., Deane, F., Barrelle, K. and Mahar, D. 1995. Computer anxiety: correlates, norms and problem definition in health care and banking employees using the Computer Attitude Scale. *Interacting with Computers* vol. 7, no. 2, pp. 1002–13.

Henningham, John. 1988. *Looking at Television News*. Sydney: Longman Cheshire.

—— 1996. Australian Journalists' Professional and Ethical Values. *Journalism and Mass Communication Quarterly* vol. 73, no. 1, pp. 206–18.

—— 1997. The journalist's personality: an exploratory study. *Journalism and Mass Communication Quarterly* vol. 74, no. 3, pp. 615–24.

Herman, Edward S. and McChesney, Robert W. 1997. *Global Media: The New Missionaries of Corporate Capitalism*. London: Cassell.

Herz, John. C. 2001. Learning from *The Sims*. www.thestandard.com/article/display/0,1151,22848,00.html 19 March.

Heuristics for Web Communication. 2000. Special Issue of *the Journal of Technical Communication*, vol. 47, no. 3.

Hicks, Carolyn. 1996. "The only things that aren't fake are you, me and Sprite": ironies and realities in Generation X advertising. *Metro* no. 106, pp. 71–82.

Hill, David B. 1984. Political campaigns and Madison Avenue: a wavering partnership. *Journal of Advertising* vol. 13, no. 3, pp. 21–26, 58.

Hindess, Barry. 1988. *Choice, Rationality and Social Theory*. London: Unwin Hyman.

Hirsch, G.J. 1979. Psychological dimensions of social networks: A multi-method analysis. *American Journal of Community Psychology* no. 8, pp. 159–72.

Hodge, Bob and Tripp, David. 1986. *Children and Televison: A Semiotic Approach*. Cambridge: Polity Press.

Hoffman, E. and Roman, P.M. 1984. Information diffusion in the implementation of innovation process. *Communication Research* vol. 11, no. 1, pp. 117–40.

Hooper, R. 1994. Multimedia — mad or momentous? *IIC Communications Topics* no. 10, pp. 2–22.

Howe, Neil and Strauss, William. 1993. *13th Gen: Abort, Retry, Ignore, Fail?* New York: Vintage.

—— 1994. The new generation gap. In *The GenX Reader*, ed. Douglas Rushkoff. New York: Ballentine Books, pp. 290–96.

Huberman, Anthony. 2001. Unseen Discussions: artist@hotmail.com Museums and the Web 2001, www.archimuse.com/mw2001/abstracts/prg_95000340.html

Hulktrans, Andrew. 1994. The slacker factor. In *The GenX Reader*, ed. Douglas Rushkoff. New York: Ballentine Books, pp. 297–303.

Hunter, Ian. 1994. *Rethinking the School.* Sydney: Allen & Unwin.

Husband, Charles. 1998. Differentiated citizenship and the multi-ethnic public sphere. *The Journal of International Communication* vol. 5, nos 1 and 2, pp. 134–48.

Igbaria, M. and Parasuraman, S. 1991. Attitudes towards microcomputers: development and construct validation of a measure. *International Journal of Man–Machine Studies*, no. 35, pp. 553–73.

Jacka, Elizabeth. 1994. Researching audiences: a dialogue between cultural studies and social science. *Media Information Australia* no. 73, pp. 45–51.

Jameson, Frederic. 1984. Postmodernism, or the cultural logic of late capitalism. *New Left Review* no. 146, July/August, pp. 53–92.

—— 1991. *Postmodernism, or the Cultural Logic of Late Capitalism.* London: Verso.

Jenkins, Henry. 1993. *Textual Poachers: Television Fans and Participatory Culture.* London: Methuen.

Joint Maori/Crown Working Group on Maori Broadcasting Policy. 1996. *Second Report.* Wellington, November.

Jones, Megan. 1993. Libs blame ads for loss. *B&T*, 2 April, pp. 5, 37.

Kaid, Lynda L., Nimmo, Dan and Sanders, Keith R. eds. 1986. *New Perspectives on Political Advertising.* Carbondale Ill: Southern Illinois University Press.

Katz, Stanley N. 1999. A Conversation with Stanley N. Katz. *National Arts Stabilization Journal* vol. 2, no. 3. Available from the Center for Arts and Cultural Policy Studies website. www.princeton.edu/~artspol/nasjartl.html. Accessed 6/9/2000.

Katz, Stanley and DiMaggio, Paul. 1998. *Cultural Policy: A Perspective.* Princeton: Princeton University Center for Arts and Cultural Policy Studies, www.princeton.edu/~artspol/cultpol.html.

Kawashima, Nobuko. 1998. Knowing the public. A review of museum marketing literature and research. *Museum Management and Curatorship* vol. 17, no. 1, pp. 26–35.

Keevle, B. 2000. Measuring the Usability Index of Your Website. www3.sympatico.ca/bkeevil/sigdoc98/index.html.

Keig and Co. 1994. SBS positioning and advertising strategy development. Unpublished report, February.

Keller, P. 1994. *Telematics and Growth.* IATAFI Conference, Bergen.

Kellett, John. 1994. *Zoom! A Close Up on Teenage Australia*. Sydney: Boom.

Kelly, Lynda. 1999. Developing access to collections through assessing user needs. Paper presented at Museums Australia Conference, Albury, May 1999.

Keys, Wendy. 1999. Children's television: a barometer of the Australian media policy climate. *Media International Australia incorporating Culture and Policy* no. 93, pp. 9–25.

Kim, Amy Jo. 2000. Interview with Will Wright. *Great Places: The Newsletter for Savvy Community Builders* vol. 1, no. 2, 5 September.

Klein, Hans-Joachim. 1993. Tracking visitor circulation in museum settings. *Environment and Behavior* vol. 25, no. 6, pp. 782–800.

Knoke, D. and Kuklinski, J.H. 1982. *Network Analysis*. Beverly Hills: Sage.

Koeppel, D. 1990. Trench warfare over tobacco. *Adweek's Marketing Week*, 17 December, p. 29.

Kolar-Panov, Dona. 1997. *Video, War and the Diasporic Imagination*. London and New York: Routledge.

Kulchyski, Peter. 1989. The postmodern and the paleolithic: notes on technology and native community in the far north. *Canadian Journal of Political and Social Theory* vol. XIII, no. 3, pp. 49–62.

Kurzeme, Indra and Herman, Catherine. 1999. Our virtual clients: changing to meet the challenge, www.librariesvictoria.vicnet.net.au/gulliver

Lacy, Stephen, Sohn, Ardyth B. and Wicks, Jan LeBlanc. 1993. *Media Management: A Casebook Approach*. Hillsdale, NJ: Lawrence Erlbaum Associates.

Lambert, W. 1995. FDAs move to regulate tobacco seen aiding suits against industry. *Wall Street Journal*, 14 July, p. 12.

Landler, Mark. 1992. They want their MTV. They don't want ABC, NBC, CBS … *Business Week*, 14 December, p. 40.

Latour, Bruno. 1987. *Science in Action: How to Follow Scientists and Engineers Through Society*. Cambridge, MA: Harvard University Press.

Latour, Bruno. 1988. *The Pasteurization of France*. Trans. Alan Sheridan and John Law. Cambridge, MA: Harvard University Press.

—— 1991. Technology is society made durable. *A Sociology of Monsters: Essays on Power, Technology and Domination*, ed. John Law. London: Routledge, pp. 103–31.

—— 1993. *We Have Never Been Modern*. Trans. Catherine Porter. Cambridge, MA: Harvard University Press.

—— 1996. *Aramis or the Love of Technology*. Trans. Catherine Porter. Cambridge, MA: Harvard University Press.

—— 1999a. On recalling ANT. In *Actor Network Theory and After*, eds John Law and John Hassard. Oxford: Blackwell.

—— 1999b. *Pandora's Hope: Essays on the Reality of Science Studies*. Cambridge, MA: Harvard University Press.

Latour, Bruno and Woolgar, Steve. 1986. *Laboratory Life: The Construction of Scientific Facts*. 2nd edn. Princeton: Princeton University Press.

Law, John. 1991. Introduction: monsters, machines and sociotechnical relations. In *A Sociology of Monsters: Essays on Power, Technology and Domination*, eds John Law and John Hassard. London: Routledge, pp. 1–23.

—— 1994. *Organizing Modernity*. Oxford: Blackwell.

Law, John and Hassard, John eds. 1999. *Actor Network Theory and After*. Oxford: Blackwell.

Lawe Davies, C.R. 1998. Multicultural broadcasting in Australia: policies, institutions and programming, 1975–1995, PhD thesis, University of Queensland.

Lawson, Annie. 2001. New ratings to help Seven's revenue, *The Age*, 8 May.

Lawson, Valerie 1993. GST: The hydra that ate its own ad campaign. *Australian Financial Review* 6 April, p. 22.

Lazarsfeld, Paul. 1968. *People's Choice*. 3rd edn. New York: Columbia University Press.

Lealand, Geoff. 1998. Where do snails watch television? Preschool television and New Zealand children. In *Wired Up: Young People and the Electronic Media*, ed. S. Howard. London: UCL Press.

Lesch, W. and Middenhorf-Brand, M. 1997. Cigarettes and health: historical controversies and constraints. *Health Marketing Quarterly* vol. 14, no. 3, pp. 698–90.

Levy, Pierre. 1997. *Collective Intelligence: Mankind's Emerging World in Cyberspace*. Trans. Robert Bononno. New York: Plenum Trade.

—— 1998. *Becoming Virtual: Reality in the Digital Age*. Trans. Robert Bononno. New York: Plenum Trade.

Lewis, Jon. 1992. *The Road to Romance and Ruin: Teen Films and Youth Culture*. New York: Routledge.

Lindlof, T. 1988. Media audiences as interpretive communities. In *Communication Yearbook 11*, ed. J. Anderson. Newbury Park: Sage.

Lipman, J. 1992. Joe Camel's bad press could be a boosting brand. *Wall Street Journal*, 14 May.

Lithgow, Juliette. 1998. Personal communication, 7 January 1998.

Liu, Eric ed. 1994. *Next: Young American Writers on the New Generation*. New York: W.W. Norton.

Livingstone, Sonia and Bovill, Moira 1999. *Young People, New Media*. Report of the research project, "Children, Young People and the Changing Media Environment". London: London School of Economics and Political Science.

Logan, R.A. and Longon, D.R. 1999. Rethinking anti-smoking media campaigns: two generations of research and issues for the next. *Journal of Health Care Finance* vol. 25, no. 4, pp. 77–99.

Long M. 1995. Interview, Managing Director, SBS, Artarmon, 28 June.

Lukes, Steven ed. 1986. *Power*. Oxford: Basil Blackwell.

Lyons, Gregory. 1981. Surveying Aboriginal opinion concerning the law: some methodological considerations. In *Research and the Delivery of Legal Services*, ed. Peter Cashman. Sydney: Law Foundation of New South Wales, pp. 45–59.

——. 1983. Aboriginal perceptions of courts and the police: a Victorian study. *Australian Aboriginal Studies* no. 2, pp. 45–59.

MacDougall, David. 1987. Media friend or media foe? *Visual Anthropology* vol. 1, no. 1, pp. 54–58.

Mackay, Hugh. 1993. *The Middle Years*. Lindfield: Mackay Research.

—— 1995. Personal interview, 26 July.

—— 1997. *Generations: Baby boomers, their parents and their children*. Sydney: Pan Macmillan.

Maclean, Hunter. 1999. How teens got the power: Gen Y has the cash, the cool — and a burgeoning consumer culture. *Maclean's*, 22 March, p. 42.

Mannheim, Karl. 1927. The problem of generations. *Essays on the Sociology of Knowledge*. London: Routledge and Kegan Paul, pp. 276–321.

Manolis, Chris, Levin, Aron and Dahlstrom, Robert. 1997. A Generation X scale: creation and validations. *Educational and Psychological Measurement* vol. 57, no. 4, pp. 666–84.

Markus, M.L. 1987. Towards a "critical mass" theory of interactive media: universal access, interdependency, and diffusion. *Communication Research* no. 14, pp. 491–511.

Marshall, Fiona. 2001. Making good use of user input: incorporation of public evaluation into the system development process. *Museums and the Web 2001*, www.archimuse.com/mw2001/papers/marshal/marshall.html

Martin, A. 1987. Media and social change — with special reference to television. *Pacific Islands Communication Journal* vol. 15, no. 1, pp. 3–21.

Martin, David. 1994. The whiny generation. In *The GenX Reader*, ed. Douglas Rushkoff. New York: Ballentine Books, pp. 235–37.

Marx, Karl (trans. Nicolaus Martin). 1973. *Grundrisse*. Harmondsworth: Penguin.

Massing, M. 1996. How to win the tobacco war. *The New York Review of Books* vol. 43, no. 12, pp. 32.

McCaughan, Dave. 1994. Generation 2000. *McCann Monitor*. Sydney, McCann-Erickson, March.

—— 1995. Personal interview, 26 July.

McGuigan, Jim. 1998. What price the public sphere? *In Electronic Empires: Global Media and Local Resistance*, ed. D. K. Thussu. London, Arnold, pp. 91–107.

McMahon, Siobhan. 1996. Exposing the myth of the generation gap. *Reader's Digest*. July, pp. 19–25.

McNair, Ian. 2000. Interview with Mark Balnaves, Sydney, 29 June.

McQuail, Denis. 1997. *Audience Analysis*. London: Sage.

McRobbie, Angela. 1994. *Postmodernism and Popular Culture*. London: Routledge.

Meadows, Michael. 1988. The jewel in the crown: the coming of television to the Torres Strait could be as significant as the impact of religion there, 117 years ago. *Australian Journalism Review* vol. 10, nos 1 and 2, pp. 162–69.

—— 1995. 'Voice blo mipla all ilan man': Torres Strait Islanders' struggle for television access. In *Public Voices, Private Interests: Australia's Media*, eds J. Craik, J. James Bailey and A. Moran. Sydney: Allen & Unwin, pp. 179–98.

—— 2000. Silent talking: Indigenous media policy and the Productivity Commission. *Media International Australia incorporating Culture and Policy* no. 95, pp. 29–48.

Meadows, Michael and van Vuuren, Kitty. 1998. Seeking an audience: Indigenous people, the media and cultural resource management. *Southern Review* vol. 31, no. 1, pp. 96–107.

Media Entertainment and Arts Alliance. 1993. *Policy Paper on Aboriginal Affairs*. Sydney: MEAA.

Meehan, Eileen R. 1990. Why we don't count: the commodity audience. In *The Logics of Television: Essays in Cultural Criticism*, ed. Patricia Mellancamp. London and Bloomington: Indiana University Press/BFI, pp. 117–37.

Mercer, Colin.1989. *Antonio Gramsci: E-Laborare, or the Work and Government of Culture*. Paper delivered at TASA '89, La Trobe University, Melbourne, December.

Merchants of Cool. 2001. Dir. Barak Goodman, Frontline/10/20 Productions, LLC, screened on SBS TV, 17 July 2001.

Meyrowitz, Joshua. 1985. *No Sense of Place: The Impact of Electronic Media on Social Behaviour*. New York: Oxford University Press.

Michaels, Eric. 1985a. Constraints on knowledge in an economy of oral information. *Current Anthropology* vol. 26, no. 4, pp. 505–10.

—— 1985b. Ask a foolish question: on the methodologies of cross-cultural research. *Australian Journal of Cultural Studies* vol. 3, no. 2, pp. 49–59.

—— 1986. *Aboriginal Invention of Television Central Australia 1982–1985*. Canberra: Australian Institute of Aboriginal Studies.

—— 1990. A model of teleported texts (with reference to Aboriginal television). *Continuum* vol. 3, no. 2, pp. 8–31.

Migliorini, Pino. 1998. *The World is Your Audience: Case Studies in Audience Development and Cultural Diversity*. Sydney: Australia Council.

Miller, Jane. 1995. *Vox-pop: The New Generation X Speaks*. London: Virgin.

Miller, Peter V. 1994. Made-to-order and standarized audiences: forms of reality in audience measurement. In *Audiencemaking*, eds J. Ettema and D.C. Whitney. Thousand Oaks: Sage, pp. 57–74

Mills, Stephen and Wallace, Christine. 1993. Manna from Canada. *Australian Financial Review*, 19 March, Weekend, pp. 1, 3.

Mitterauer, Michael. 1992. *A History of Youth*. Oxford: Blackwell.

Mockus, J. 1980. Geodemographics II: targeting your turnout. *Campaigns & Elections* vol. 1, no. 2, pp. 55–63.

Molnar, Helen and Meadows, Michael. 2000. *Songlines to Satellites: Indigenous Communication in Australia, the South Pacific and Canada*. Sydney: Pluto Press.

More, Elizabeth and Smith, Keith eds. 1992. *Case Studies in Australian Media Management.* Sydney: Macquarie University Graduate School of Management and AFTRS.

Morgan, Gary. 2000. Interview with Mark Balnaves, Melbourne, 28 June.

Morley, David. 1986. *Family Television: Cultural Power and Domestic Leisure.* London: Comedia.

Morris, Christine. 2000. Constitutional dreaming. In *Beyond the Republic: Meeting the Global Challenges to Constitutionalism*, eds C. Samford and T. Round. Sydney: Federation Press, pp. 290–99.

Muir, Ian. 1992. Understanding and managing audience demand: the tyranny of television ratings. In Case Studies in Australian Media Management, eds Elizabeth More and Keith Smith. Sydney: Australian Film Television and Radio School and Macquarie University.

Mullings, Barbara. 2000. Insider or outsider, both or neither: some dilemmas of interviewing in a cross-cultural setting. *Geoforum* no. 30, pp. 337–50.

Mungham, Geoff and Pearson, Geoff. 1976. Introduction: troubled youth, troubling world. In *Working Class Youth Culture*, eds Geoff Mungham and Geoff Pearson. London: Routledge and Kegan Paul, pp. 1–9.

Murdock, Graham and McCron, Robin. 1976. Youth and class: a career of confusion. In *Working Class Youth Culture*, eds Geoff Mungham and Geoff Pearson. London: Routledge and Kegan Paul, pp. 10–26.

Museums Australia. 2001. EVR SIG, www.museumsaustralia.org.au/members.htm

Naficy, Hamid. 1993. *The Making of Exile Cultures: Iranian Television in Los Angeles.* Minneapolis: University of Minnesota Press.

National Indigenous Media Association of Australia (NIMAA). 1999. *The Indigenous Communications Sector: An Essential Service Provider.* Submission to the Productivity Commission inquiry into broadcasting, May.

National Institute of Labour Studies in conjunction with the Australian Bureau of Statistics. 1994. *Employment and Employment Growth in the Australian Culture–Leisure Industries: An Examination of Existing Data and Future Requirements.* Report prepared for the Department of Communications and the Arts. Canberra: Department of Communications and the Arts.

National Post 1995. Canada: lines blur between philanthropy and social marketing. 29 November, p. 25

Neely, Don. 2000. Interview with Mark Balnaves, Sydney, 2 August.

Neely, Mark. 2000. Interview with Mark Balnaves, Sydney, 2 August.

—— 2001. Phone interview with Mark Balnaves and Tom O'Regan, Brisbane–Sydney, 5 August.

Nelson, Gwen. 2000. Interview with Mark Balnaves, Sydney, 29 June.

Neuman, R. 1991. *The Future of the Mass Audience.* New York: Cambridge University Press.

Neuman, W. Russell and de Sola Pool, Ithiel. 1986. The flow of communications into the home. In *Media, Audience and Social Structure*, eds Sandra J. Ball-Rokeach and Muriel G. Cantor. Newbury Park: Sage.

Newman, Bruce I., and Sheth, Jagdish N. eds. 1985a. *Political Marketing: Readings and Annotated Bibliography.* Chicago: American Marketing Association.

Newspaper Association of America and American Society of Newspaper Editors 2001. *The Power to Grow Readership: Research from the Impact Study of Newspaper Readership*. Readership Institute, Northwestern University.

Nightingale, Virginia. 1994a. Improvising Elvis, Marilyn and Mickey Mouse. *Australian Journal of Communication* vol. 21, no. 1, pp. 1–20.

—— 1994b. Shifty characters and shady relations. *Media Information Australia* no. 73, pp. 40–44.

—— 1989. What's "ethnographic" about ethnographic audience research? *Australian Journal of Communication* vol. 16, pp. 50–63.

—— 1996. *Studying Audiences. The Shock of the Real.* New York: Routlege.

Nixon, Mary. 1981. *TV is Funny, Boring, Exciting but I Love It.* Melbourne: Monash University.

Noble, Grant. 1975. *Children in Front of the Small Screen.* London: Constable.

Objiofor, Levi. 1988. ABC Television and Remote Aborigine Communities: An Exploratory Study, unpublished Master of Business (Communication) Research Project, Queensland University of Technology, March.

Office of Multicultural Affairs. 1990. *National Agenda for a Multicultural Australia: The Year in Review*. Canberra: AGPS.

O'Neil, Helen and Mills, Stephen. 1986. Political advertising in Australia: a dynamic force meets a resilient object. In *New Perspectives on Political Advertising,* eds L.L. Kaid, Dan Nimmo and Keith R. Sanders, Carbondale IL: Southern Illinois University Press.

O'Neill, R. 1997. Close but no cigar: a comparative analysis of the FDA's attempt to regulate tobacco use. *The George Washington Journal of International Law and Economics* vol. 30, nos 2/3, pp. 481–507.

O'Regan T. 1993. *Australian Television Culture*. Sydney: Allen & Unwin.

—— 1998. Thinking about policy utility: some aspects of Australian cultural policy development in a South African context. *Critical Arts* vol. 12, nos 1 and 2, pp. 1–23.

O'Regan, Tom and Batty, Philip. 1993. An Aboriginal television culture: issues, strategies, politics. In *Australian Television Culture,* ed. T. O'Regan. Sydney: Allen & Unwin, pp. 169–92.

Osborne, Dale, Wheeler, Juliet and Elliott, David. 1999. *Selling the Performing Arts: Identifying and Expanding Audiences for Music, Dance and Theatre.* Sydney: Australia Council.

OzTAM 2001a. "Terms and Definitions". OzTAM website, www.oztam.com.au/discoveryguide/termsanddefinitions.html Accessed 5 August.

OzTAM 2001b. "The Rating Process". www.oztam.com.au/discoveryguide/ratingprocess.html Accessed 5 August.

Palmer, Patricia (now Gillard). 1986a. *Girls and Television.* Sydney: Social Policy Unit, New South Wales Ministry of Education.

—— 1986b. *The Lively Audience: A Study of Children Around the TV Set*. Sydney: Allen & Unwin.

Patterson, R. 1988. The Special Broadcasting Service and the construction of ethnic radio and multicultural television, PhD thesis, Griffith University.

Peters, Tom. 1987. *Thriving on Chaos: Handbook for a Management Revolution*. London: Pan Books.

Planet. 1994. What's all this about Generation X?, Spring, pp. 32–40.

Plomarit, Katherine. 1994. Generation X: market segment or market myth? Unpublished essay submitted for the subject CMKB35: Marketing Horizons, University of Western Sydney, Hawkesbury Campus.

Poole, M.S. and Van de Ven, A.H. 1988. Methods for studying innovation processes. In *Research on the Management of Innovation,* eds A.H. Van de Ven, H. Angle and M.S. Poole. Cambridge, MA: Ballinger.

Postman, Neil. 1983. *The Disappearance of Childhood: How TV is Changing Children's Lives*. London: W.H. Allen.

Potter, David. 1967. The historical perspective. In *The Meaning of Commercial Television,* ed. Stanley Donner. Austin: University of Texas Press, pp. 51–68.

Potter, Parker B. 1994. Appropriating the visitor by addressing the second person. In *Museums and the Appropriation of Culture*, ed. Susan Pearce. London: Athlone Press, pp 103–28.

Productivity Commission 1999. *Broadcasting, Draft Report*. Canberra: Ausinfo.

—— 2000. *Broadcasting*, Report no. 11. Canberra: Ausinfo.

Quadrant Research Services. 1997. *To Sell Art, Know Your Market*. Sydney: Australia Council.

Quirk-Parry P. 2001. Interview, Head of Marketing, SBS, January 2001.

Rath, A. 1999. India: marketing goes social. *Business World* 6 February.

Ray, Manas. 2000. Bollywood down under: Fiji Indian cultural history and popular assertion.In *Floating Lives: The Media and Asian Diasporas*, eds S. Cunningham and J. Sinclair, pp. 136–84. Brisbane: University of Queensland Press.

Renaud, J.L. 1994. Superhighway, super demand? *ATM: Advanced Television Markets* no. 4, pp. 4–11.

Ricketson, Matthew. 1993. *20Twenty: A Clearer View of Today's Twenty Year Olds*. Melbourne: Clemenger.

Ritchie, Karen. 1995. *Marketing to Generation X*. New York: Lexington Books.

Robbin, J. 1980. Geodemographics: The new magic. *Campaigns & Elections* vol. 1, no. 1, pp. 25–45.

Robinson D. 1995. Interview, Head of Marketing, SBS, Sydney, 27 June.

Robinson, John P. and Levy, Mark R. 1986. *The Main Source*, Beverly Hills: Sage.

Rogers, E.M. 1962. *Diffusion of Innovations*. New York: Free Press.

—— 1992. Prospects for a cooperative extension system in education. *Knowledge: Creation, Diffusion, Utilization* vol. 13, no. 3, p. 248.

—— 1995a. Interactive communication technology in business organisations. *Journal of Business Communication* vol. 32, no. 2, p. 175.

—— 1995b. Lessons for guidelines from the diffusion of innovations. *The Joint Commission Journal on Quality Improvement* vol. 21, no. 7, p. 324.

Rogers, E.M. and Kincaid, D. 1981. *Communication Networks: Toward a New Paradigm for Research*. New York: Free Press.

Rogers, E.M. and Shoemaker, F. 1973. *Communication of Innovations*. Glencoe: Free Press.

Roncagliolo, Rafael. 1991. Notes on "the alternative". In *Video the Changing World*, eds N. Thede and A. Ambrosi. Montreal: Black Rose Books, pp. 206–8.

Rotach, M.C. and Keller, P. 1993. *Telematik und Qualitatives Wachstum*. Institut fur Verkehrsplanung, Transporttechnik, Strassen-und Eisenbahnbau (VT). Zurich: Verlag der Fachvereine.

Roy Morgan Research. 1995. *Aboriginal and Torres Strait Islander Needs Study*. Final Report, for Departments of Social Security, and Human Services and Health, August.

Royal Melbourne Institute of Technology (RMIT). 1992. *Basic Telecommunications Needs: A Study of Domestic Users*. Melbourne: RMIT.

Ruddy, Bruce. 1994. The techno kids. *Sunday Mail*, 13 February, pp. 71–7, 106.

Rushkoff, Douglas. 1994a. Introduction: us, by us. In *The GenX Reader*, ed. Douglas Rushkoff. New York: Ballentine Books, pp. 3–8.

—— 1994b. Here we are. In *The GenX Reader*, ed. Douglas Rushkoff. New York: Ballentine Books, p. 10.

—— 1994c. *The GenX Reader*, New York: Ballentine Books.

Sabato, Larry J. 1981. *The Rise of Political Consultants: New Ways of Winning Elections*. New York: Basic Books.

Safe, Mike and Whittaker, Mark. 1994. The baby boomers of 1994. *Australian Magazine*, 26–27 February, pp. 10–18.

Schiller, Herbert. 1989. *Culture Inc: The Corporate Takeover of Public Expression*. New York: Oxford University Press.

Schlesinger, Philip. 1978. *Putting "Reality" Together: BBC News*. Beverly Hills: Sage.

Schmidt, Annette. 1993. *The Loss of Australia's Aboriginal Language Heritage*. Canberra: Aboriginal Studies Press.

Schröder, Kim Christian. 1999. The best of both worlds? Media audience research between rival paradigms. In *Rethinking the Media Audience: The New Agenda*, ed. P. Alasuutari. London: Sage, pp. 38–68.

Schuler, D. 1994. Community networks: building a new participatory medium. *Communications of the Age* vol. 37, no. 1, pp. 39–51.

Schulze, Jane. 2001a. "Row over Ratings Continues". *The Age*, 20 February.

—— 2001b. Rocky outlook for Nine. *The Australian*, 20 June.

Screven, C. 1993. Visitor studies: an introduction. *Museum International*, no. 178, pp. 4–5.

Sefton-Green, Julian ed. 1998. *Digital Diversions: Youth Culture in the Age of Multimedia*. London: UCL Press.

Semper, Rob, Wanner, Noel, Jackson, Roland and Bazley, Martin. 2000. Who's out there? A pilot user study of educational web fesources by the Science Learning Network (SLN) (www.sln.org). *Museums and the Web 2000*, www.archimuse.com/mw2000/index.html.

Senate Select Committee on Community Standards Relevant to the Supply of Services Utilising Electronic Technologies. 1995. *Report on R-Rated Material on Pay TV.* Canberra: Commonwealth of Australia.

Serota, K.B., Cody, M.J., Barnett, G.A. and Taylor, J.A. 1977. Precise procedures for optimizing campaign communication. *Communication Yearbook 1*, ed. B.D. Ruben. New Brunswick, NJ: Transaction Books, pp. 475–91.

Sheldon, Linda and Loncar, Milica. 1996. *Kids Talk TV: "Super Wickid" or "Dum".* Sydney: Australian Broadcasting Authority.

Sheldon, Linda, Ramsay, Gillian and Loncar, Milica. 1994. *"Cool" or "Gross": Children's Attitudes to Kissing and Swearing on Television.* Monograph 4. Sydney: Australian Broadcasting Authority.

Shoebridge, Neil. 1999. A new campaign produces the desired result: a nation of quitters. *Business Review Weekly*, 15 February, pp. 66–67.

Sievers, K. 1995. Interview, Senior Audience Consultant, SBS, Artarmon 27 June.

—— 2000. Interview with Mark Balnaves, Sydney, 30 June.

—— 2001. Interview, Senior Audience Consultant, SBS, January.

Simon, Herbert A. 1976. *Administrative Behavior: A Study of Decision-making Processes in Administrative Organizations.* 3rd edn. New York: Macmillan.

Simpson, M. and Madden, G. 1994. *Residential Demand for Broadband Service Subscription: Demand Estimation and Social Impact.* Perth: Curtin University of Technology, Institute for Research into International Competitiveness.

Sinclair, John, Yue, Audrey, Hawkins, Gay, Pookong, Kee and Fox, Josephine. 2000. Chinese cosmopolitanism and media use. In *Floating Lives: The Media and Asian Diasporas*. eds S. Cunningham and J. Sinclair. Brisbane: University of Queensland Press, pp. 35–90.

Sinha, Arbind. 1989. A holistic approach to communication research: an alternative methodology. *Media, Culture and Society* no. 11, pp. 435–42.

SBS Annual Reports. 1991–92; 1992–93; 1993–94; 1998–99; 1999–2000. Sydney: SBS.

Special Broadcasting Service. 1994a. *Going National*, promotional pamphlet, Sydney: SBS.

—— 1994b. *Brief History of the SBS*. SBS mimeo. Sydney: SBS.

—— 1994c. *Codes of Practice*. Sydney: SBS.

SBS/ACNeilsen. 2001. *South Park* Audience Performances, unpublished data supplied by SBS Audience consultant Ken Sievers.

Spradley, J.P. and McCurdy, D.W. 1972. *The Cultural Experience. Ethnography in a Complex Society*. Chicago: SRA.

Stone, G.C. 1987. *Examining Newspapers*. Beverly Hills: Sage.

Strauss, William and Howe, Neil (1991), *Generations: The History of America's Future, 1584–2069,* New York: William Morrow and Company.

Streeter, Thomas. 1996. *Selling the Air: A Critique of the Policy of Commercial Broadcasting in the United States*. Chicago: University of Chicago Press.

Strickland, Katrina. 1994. Magazines the loaded medium for teenagers. *The Australian*, 8 September, p. 26.

Sunday Mail. 1994. Tweens, Ys up to old ad tricks, 17 July, p. 29.

Sunday Mail Magazine. 1996. The last innocents: the boomers, 14 April, pp. 3–4.

—— 1998. *Growing Up Digital: The Rise of the Net Generation*. London and New York: McGraw Hill.

Tapscott, Don. 1998. *Growing Up Digital: The Rise of the New Generation*. New York: McGraw Hill.

Te Mangai Paho.1996. *Post Election Brief*. December.

Thomas, Mandy. 1999. *Dreams in the Shadows: Vietnamese-Australian Lives in Transition*. Sydney: Allen & Unwin.

Thompson, Douglas. 1983. Claims of stardom. *Education News* vol. 18, no. 5, pp. 10–12.

Throsby, David. 2001. *Economics and Culture*, Cambridge and Melbourne: Cambridge University Press.

Tindall, Kevin, David Reid and Neville Gordon. 1975. *Television: 20th Century Cyclops*. Sydney: Sydney Teachers' College.

Tolhurst, Kenneth. 1980. *Australians' Attitudes to the Arts*. Sydney: Australia Council.

Trodd, S. 1997. Personal interview, Sydney, 7 December.

Trotter, Robin. 1998. The changing face and function of museums. *Media International Australia incorporating Culture and Policy* no. 89, pp. 47–61.

Tulich, Katherine. 1994. Kids with cash. *The Bulletin*, 12 July, pp. 23–26.

Turow, Joseph. 1997. *Breaking up America: Advertisers and the New Media World*, Chicago: University of Chicago Press.

Underwood, Doug. 1993. *When MBAs Rule the Newsroom*. New York: Columbia University Press.

USA National Youth Anti-Drug Media Campaign. 1998. *PR Newswire*.

Valdes, Lesley. 2000. The age of the audience. In *The Politics of Culture: Policy Perspectives for Individuals, Institutions, and Communities*, eds G. Bradford, M. Gary and G. Wallach, with preface by James Allen Smith. New York: The New Press and The Center for Arts and Culture, pp. 170–77.

Valente, T.M. and Rogers, E.M. 1995. The origins and development of the diffusion of innovations paradigm. *Science Communication* vol. 16, no. 3, pp. 242–73.

Vaughan R.A. 1981. *A "Uses and Gratifications" Study of Mass Communication and Information Communication of the Aboriginal Population at Woorabinda*. Research Project, School of Humanities and Social Sciences, Capricornia Institute of Advanced Education, 30 November.

von Sturmer, John. 1981. Talking with Aborigines. *Australian Institute of Aboriginal Studies Newsletter* no. 15, pp. 13–30.

Walker, J. 1998. Australia: global marketing hindered by social traditions. *Adnews*, 3 July, p. 20.

Wark, McKenzie. 1993. Planet of noise: so who are Generation X and why are they saying all these terrible things about us? *Juice*, December, pp. 74–78.

Warneford, P. 1993. Election ads helped Libs lose. *Ad News*, 26 March, pp. 15–16.

Warneke, Ross. 2001a. Numbers crunch. *The Age*, 22 February.

—— 2001b. Why Seven's numbers are on the up and up. *The Age*, 24 June.

Webster, J.G. 1998. The audience. *Journal of Broadcasting and Electronic Media* vol. 42, no. 2, pp. 190–207.

White, David Manning. 1957. Mass culture in America: Another point of view. In *Mass Culture: The Popular Arts in America*, eds Bernard Rosenberg and David Manning White. New York: Collier-Macmillan, pp. 13–21.

White, Donald D. and Vroman, H. William. 1982. *Action in Organizations*. 2nd edn. Boston: Allyn and Bacon Inc.

Wice, Nathaniel. 1994. Generalization X. In *The GenX Reader*, ed. Douglas Rushkoff. New York: Ballentine Books, pp. 279–86.

Williams, Angie, Coupland, Justine, Folwell, Annette and Sparks, Lisa. 1997. Talking about Generation X: defining them as they define themselves. *Journal of Language and Social Psychology* vol. 16, no. 3, pp. 251–77.

Williamson, K., Balnaves, M. and Caputi, P. 1992. Information, communication and telecommunications: a pilot study of the behaviour of citizens. *Prometheus* vol. 10, no. 2, pp. 311–22.

Wilmoth, Peter. 2001. Move on TV ratings. *The Age*, 21 April.

Wilson, Thomas C. 1993a. Satellite television in the Canadian Arctic 1974–1992: cultural replacement and regeneration. Paper presented at the Post Colonial Formations Conference, Griffith University, Brisbane, 14–17 July.

—— 1993b. Some demographic characteristics of the population of northern Canada. Paper prepared for Television Northern Canada, 31 August.

—— 1994. *The Native Communications Society of the Western Northwest Territories: A Report on the 1994 Audience Survey*, Ottawa.

Wimmer, Roger D. and Dominick, Joseph R. 1997. *Mass Media Research: An Introduction.* Belmont: Wadsworth Publishing Company.

Winkler, Robert. 1998. Personal communication, 6 February.

Winn, Marie. 1977. *The Plug-in Drug*. New York: Viking.

Woelfel, J. and Barnett, G.A. 1982. Multi-dimensional scaling in Riemann space. *Quality and Quantity* no. 16, pp. 469–91.

Woelfel, J. and Fink, E.L. 1980. *The Measurement of Communication Processes: Galileo Theory and Method*. New York, Academic Press.

Wong, D. 1994. "I want the microphone": Mass mediation and agency in Asian-American popular music. *TDR (The Drama Review)* vol. 38, no. 3, pp. 152–67.

Woodward J. 1995. Interview, Promotions Manager, SBS, Sydney, 26 June.

Wright, Philip. 1989. The quality of visitors' experiences in art museums. In *The New Museology*, ed. Peter Vergo. London: Reaction Books, pp. 119–48.

Wyatt-Spratt, Neridah, Wyatt-Spratt, Pam, Haley, Jane and McKoy, Lisa 1997.

Access All Areas: Guidelines for Marketing the Arts to People with Disabilities. Sydney: Australia Council.

Young People, New Media. 3/7/1999. http://lito.lse.ac.uk/yound_people/summary.html

Zaldivar, R.A. 1998. US: kids of Baby Boomers a savvy generational force. Australian Associated Press wire service, 6 March.

Zangalis, George. 1994. Interview, Community Broadcasting Association of Australia annual conference, Australian National University, Canberra, 3 December.

Zimmerman, H.D. 1994. The design of future telematic systems for private customers. *Electronic Markets* vol. 12, pp. 11–12.

Zinn, Laura, Power, Christopher, Yang Jones, Dori, Cuneo, Alice Z. and Ross, David. 1992. Move over boomers: the busters are here — and they're angry. *Business Week*, 14 December, pp. 34–40.

Index